Renewing Tradition

Princeton Theological Monograph Series

Series Editor, K. C. Hanson

Recent volumes in the series:

Philip Harrold
*A Place Somewhat Apart: The Private Worlds of
a Late Nineteenth-Century Public University*

Anette Ejsing
Theology of Anticipation

Caryn Riswold
Coram Deo: Human Life in the Vision of God

Paul O. Ingram, editor
Constructing a Relational Cosmology

Richard Valantasis et al., editors
The Subjective Eye: Essays in Honor of Margaret Miles

Stephen Finlan and Vladimir Kharlamov, editors
Theosis: Deification in Christian Theology

John A. Vissers
The Neo-Orthodox Theology of W. W. Bryden

Byron C. Bangert
Consenting to God and Nature

Sam Hamstra, editor
The Reformed Pastor by John Williamson Nevin

David A. Ackerman
Lo, I Tell You a Mystery

Renewing Tradition

*Studies in Texts and Contexts
in Honor of James W. Thompson*

edited by
Mark W. Hamilton
Thomas H. Olbricht
Jeffrey Peterson

Pickwick *Publications*
An imprint of *Wipf and Stock Publishers*
199 West 8th Avenue • Eugene OR 97401

RENEWING TRADITION
Studies in Texts and Contexts in Honor of James W. Thompson
Princeton Theological Monograph Series 65

Copyright © 2007 Mark Hamilton. All rights reserved. Except for brief quotations in critical publications or reviews, no part of this book may be reproduced in any manner without prior written permission from the publisher. Write: Permissions, Wipf & Stock, 199 W. 8th Ave., Eugene, OR 97401.

ISBN 10: 1-59752-828-5
ISBN 13: 978-1-59752-828-3

Cataloging-in-Publication data:

Renewing tradition : studies in texts and contexts in honor of James W.
     Thompson / edited by Mark W. Hamilton, Thomas H. Olbricht,
     and Jeffrey Peterson.

Eugene, Ore.: Pickwick Publications, 2007
Princeton Theological Monograph Series 65

xvi + 318 p.; 23 cm.

ISBN 10: 1-59752-828-5
ISBN 13: 978-1-59752-828-3

1. Bible—Criticism, interpretation, etc. 2. Church history—Reformation. 3. Preaching. I. Thompson, James, 1942-. II. Hamilton, Mark W. III. Olbricht, Thomas H. IV. Peterson, Jeffrey. V. Series.

BR166 R65 2007

Manufactured in the U.S.A.

Contents

List of Contributers / vii
List of Abbreviations / ix
Preface / xiii

✤ Traditions in Context

1. Praising God with "One Mouth"/ "One Voice" / 3
   —*Everett Ferguson*
2. Early Christian Missionary Practice and Pagan Reaction: 1 Peter and Domestic Violence against Slaves and Wives / 24
   —*John T. Fitzgerald*
3. The *Virtus Feminarum* in 1 Timothy 2:9–15 / 45
   —*Abraham J. Malherbe*
4. Mark and the Inclusion of the Gentiles / 66
   —*Allan J. McNicol*

✤ Traditions in Texts

5. The Rhetoric of Adventure:
   Deuteronomy 1:19–46 and Gilgamesh III / 83
   —*Mark W. Hamilton*
6. Hebrew Poetics and Biblical Interpretation:
   Insights from Psalm 120 / 104
   —*Rick R. Marrs*
7. The Faith (Faithfulness) of Jesus in Hebrews / 116
   —*Thomas H. Olbricht*
8. Christ our Pasch: Shaping Christian Identity in Corinth / 133
   —*Jeffrey Peterson*
9. The First Theologian: The Originality of Philo of Alexandria / 145
   —*Gregory E. Sterling*
10. Rhetorical Strategy in Isaiah 1–5 / 163
    —*John T. Willis*
11. Seeing the Faith as Paul Sees It / 181
    —*Wendell Willis*

❄ Renewing Contexts

12 Hebrews and Philosophy: A Question of Intersection / 195
    —Frederick D. Aquino

13 A Reluctant Bride:
    Finding a Life for Damaris of Athens (Acts 17:34) / 207
    —J. W. Childers

14 Looking Through the Fish-Eye Lens: Panoramic Exegesis for Preaching / 236
    —Thomas G. Long

15 Language and the Reshaping of Life:
    Speech-Act Theory and the Use of the Bible as Scripture / 249
    —Roy F. Melugin

16 The Reformation and Believer's Baptism:
    Erasmus and the Anabaptists on the Great Commission / 264
    —Darren T. Williamson

Publications of James W. Thompson / 283
Scripture Index / 289
Index of Other Ancient Literature / 299
Modern Author Index / 311

Contributors

Everett Ferguson (Ph.D. Harvard University)
  Professor of Church History Emeritus
  Abilene Christian University

John T. Fitzgerald (Ph.D. Yale University)
  Associate Professor of Religious Studies
  University of Miami

Abraham J. Malherbe (Th.D. Harvard University)
  Buckingham Professor of Divinity Emeritus
  Yale University

Allan J. McNicol (Ph.D. Vanderbilt University)
  Cox Professor of New Testament
  Austin Graduate School of Theology

Mark W. Hamilton (Ph.D. Harvard University)
  Associate Professor of Hebrew Bible
  Abilene Christian University

Rick R. Marrs (Ph.D. The Johns Hopkins University)
  Associate Dean and Professor of Old Testament
  Pepperdine University

Thomas H. Olbricht (Ph.D. University of Iowa)
  Distinguished Professor Emeritus of Religion
  Pepperdine University

Jeffrey Peterson (Ph.D. Yale University)
  Wright Associate Professor of New Testament
  Austin Graduate School of Theology

Contributors

Gregory E. Sterling (Ph.D. Graduate Theological Union)
Senior Associate Dean and Professor of New Testament and Christian Origins, University of Notre Dame

John T. Willis (Ph.D. Vanderbilt University)
Coffman Professor of Old Testament
Abilene Christian University

Wendell Willis (Ph.D. Southern Methodist University)
Associate Professor of New Testament
Abilene Christian University

Frederick D. Aquino (Ph.D. Southern Methodist University)
Associate Professor of Theology
Abilene Christian University

J. W. Childers (D.Phil. Oxford University)
Carmichael-Walling Associate Professor of Early Christianity
Abilene Christian University

Thomas G. Long (Ph.D. Princeton Theological Seminary)
Bandy Professor of Preaching
Candler School of Theology, Emory University

Roy F. Melugin (Ph.D. Yale University)
Research Professor of Old Testament
Brite Divinity School, Texas Christian University

Darren T. Williamson (Ph.D. Simon Fraser University)
Assistant Professor of History
Cascade College

Abbreviations

AB	Anchor Bible
ABD	*Anchor Bible Dictionary*
ABR	Australian Biblical Review
ABRL	Anchor Bible Reference Library
ALGHJ	Arbeiten zur Literatur und Geschichte des hellenistischen Judentums
ANF	*Ante-Nicene Fathers*
ANRW	*Aufstieg und Niedergang der römischen Welt*
BDAG	*Greek-English Leixcon of the New Testament and Other Early Christian Literature*, ed. W. F. Bauer, F. W. Danker, W. F. Arndt, and F. W. Gingrich, 3d edition
BETL	Bibliotheca ephemeridium theologicarum lovaniensium
BHK	Biblia Hebraica Kittel
BHS	Biblia Hebraica Stuttgartensia
BHO	*Bibliotheca hagiographica orientalis*
Bib	*Biblica*
BKAT	Biblischer Kommentar, Altes Testament
BR	*Biblical Research*
BTS	*Bible et terre sainte*
BZ	*Biblische Zeitschrift*
BZNW	Beihefte zur Zeitschrift für die alttestamentliche Wissenschaft
CBQ	*Catholic Biblical Quarterly*
CBQMS	Catholic Biblical Quarterly Monograph Series
CC	Continental Commentaries
CHE	*Christian Higher Education*
ConBOT	Coniectanea biblica: Old Testament Series
CRINT	Compendia rerum iudaicarum ad Novum Testamentum
CSCO	Corpus scriptorium christianorum orientalium
CSR	*Christian Scholar's Review*
CWS	Classics of Western Spirituality

Abbreviations

DBI	*Dictionary of Biblical Interpretation*, ed. John H. Hayes
EB	Echter Bibel
ECC	Eerdmans Critical Commentary
EKK	Evangelisch-katholischer Kommentar
EKKNT	Evangelisch-katholischer Kommentar zum Neuen Testament
EPRO	Etudes preliminaires aux religions orientales dans l'empire romain
ExpTim	*Expository Times*
GBS	Guides to Biblical Scholarship
GKC	*Gesenius' Hebrew Grammar*, ed. E. Kautzsch, trans. A. E. Cowley
GNO	Gregorii Nysseni Opera
GRBS	Greek, Roman, and Byzantine Studies
HALOT	*The Hebrew and Aramaic Lexicon of the Old Testament*, ed. L. Koehler, W. Baumgartner, and J. J. Stamm
HKNT	Handkommentar zum Neuen Testament
HTKNT	Herders theologischer Kommentar zum Neuen Testament
HTR	*Harvard Theological Review*
HTS	Harvard Theological Studies
HUCA	*Hebrew Union College Annual*
HUT	Hermeneutische Untersuchungen zur Theologie
IDB	Interpreters' Dictionary of the Bible, 4 vols., ed. G. W. Buttrick
Int	*Interpretation*
JBL	*Journal of Biblical Literature*
JRS	*Journal of Roman Studies*
JSJSup	Journal for the Study of Judaism Supplements
JSNTSup	Journal for the Study of the New Testament Supplement Series
JSOT	*Journal for the Study of the Old Testament*
JSOTSup	Journal for the Study of the Old Testament Supplement Series
JTS	*Journal of Theological Studies*
KAT	Kommentar zum Alten Testament
LCL	Loeb Classical Library
LHBOTS	Library of Hebrew Bible/Old Testament Studies
LQ	*Lutheran Quarterly*
LS	*Louvain Studies*

LSJ	*A Greek-English Lexicon*, ed. H. Liddell, R. Scott, and H. Jones, 9th edition
NAC	New American Commentary
NCBC	New Century Bible Commentary
NewDocs	*New Documents Illustrating Early Christianity*
NHC	Nag Hammadi Codices
NIB	*The New Interpreter's Bible*
NICNT	New International Commentary on the New Testament
NIDOTTE	*New International Dictionary of Old Testament Theology and Exegesis*
NIGTC	New International Greek Testament Commentary
NovT	*Novum Testamentum*
NovTSup	Novum Testamentum Supplements
NPNF	*Nicene and Post-Nicene Fathers*
NTD	Neue Testament Deutsch
NTL	New Testament Library
OBT	Overtures to Biblical Theology
OGIS	*Orientis graeci inscriptions selectae*, ed. W. Dittenberger
OrChr	*Oriens Christianus*
OTL	Old Testament Library
OTP	*Old Testament Pseudepigrapha*, ed. James H. Charlesworth
PAC	Philo of Alexandria Commentary Series
PG	Patrologia graeca
PL	Patrologia latina
ResQ	*Restoration Quarterly*
SBLDS	Society of Biblical Literature Dissertation Series
SBLSBS	Society of Biblical Literature Sources for Biblical Study
SBLSymS	Society of Biblical Literature Symposium Series
SBLTT	Society of Biblical Literature Texts and Translations
SC	Sources chrétiennes
SEG	Supplementum epigraphicum graecum
SHR	Studies in the History of Religions
SJT	*Scottish Journal of Theology*
SNTSMS	Society for New Testament Studies Monograph Series
SNTSMS	Society for New Testament Studies Monograph Series
SPhA	*Studia Philonica Annual*
StPatr	*Studia patristica*
StSN	Studia Semitica Neerlandica
TDNT	*Theological Dictionary of the New Testament*

Abbreviations

TDOT	*Theological Dictionary of the Old Testament*
THKNT	Theologischer Handkommentar zum Neuen Testament
TLZ	*Theologische Literaturzeitung*
TU	Texte und Untersuchungen
UF	*Ugarit Forschungen*
VT	*Vetus Testamentum*
VTS	Supplements to Vetus Testamentum
WMANT	Wissenschaftliche Monographien zum Alten und Neuen Testament
WUNT	Wissenschaftliche Untersuchungen zum Neuen Testament
ZAH	*Zeitschrift für Althebraistik*
ZDMG	*Zeitschrift der deutschen morgenländischen Gesellschaft*

Preface

Religious traditions renew themselves by reexamining their past and by seeking from it meaningful orientations toward the future. When that past includes a sacred text that itself arose in the process of tradition-making, the possibilities for renewal abound, particularly when the texts' readers engage deeply the competing or complementary ideas that coexist within and beyond those of the tradition itself. Never is this truer than with the Bible and with those traditions that attend to its perpetual ability to open doors to God and the things of God.

The contributors to this volume explore some of the numerous ways in which biblical texts and their interpreters have sought to renew their communities of readers by critical engagement with social structures, philosophical currents, and the community's uses of authoritative texts, traditions, and practices. The editors have imposed no agenda upon their fellow authors but have grouped their essays into three broad categories: traditions in context, traditions in texts, and renewing contexts. These rubrics reflect the fact that the Bible arose out of a critical interaction with ancient intellectual currents broadly conceived and has continued to function in a long (and far from finished) series of contexts around the world. While these essays make contributions to a range of particular discussions about Israelite and early Christian texts and their later uses down to the present, we can merely collect snapshots of the extraordinary work of art that is the now three thousand year-old tradition of biblical interpretation.

Traditions, because of their deep rootedness in the currents of human history, must address the basic structures of society, including their potential for adding or subtracting from human well-being. Thus our authors consider issues of music in communal formation (Ferguson), domestic violence against slaves and wives (Fitzgerald), roles of women (Malherbe), and the Gentile mission in early Christian reflection (McNicol).

Since the biblical tradition centers upon the use of authoritative texts, we must seriously consider the ways in which texts work. Thus our authors consider the rhetorical dimensions of Deuteronomy and Gilgamesh

Preface

(Hamilton) and of Isaiah 1–5 (J. Willis), the stylistic and aesthetic aspects of Psalm 120 (Marrs), the intersection of christology and to some extent philosophy (Olbricht), the use of philosophy in the making of theology (Sterling), and Paul's efforts at community formation (Peterson, W. Willis).

Moreover, the use of these texts continues in ever more robust ways. This ever-generative feature of the biblical tradition creates several issues that need addressing, such as the intersection of the Bible with philosophy (Aquino), the function of preaching (Long), and the nature of reading (Melugin). Of the many examples of biblical interpretation that deserve careful examination, two appear here: the traditions around Damaris from Acts 17 (Childers) and the nature of baptism in the Reformation (Williamson). We respectfully offer this collection to our colleagues in biblical studies and beyond.

More pertinently, we offer this collection as a token of our affection and admiration of our friend and colleague James Weldon Thompson. The human propensity to honoring persons of achievement, especially when they are friends, is one of the more endearing traits of our species. Those of us who have experienced James's steadfast friendship, his unaffected style of interaction, and his impatience with pretense and self-promotion think of him as a true credit to biblical studies and the Church.

James's work as a scholar speaks for itself. His studies of the letter to the Hebrews and of Paul in their intellectual contexts (especially Middle Platonism) have contributed significantly to the ongoing quest for placing the New Testament in its socio-intellectual setting. Although his publications in this area date back more than thirty years, his best work is occurring now, and we may anticipate path-breaking contributions ahead. His more recent work on preaching and pastoral care in Paul both situate the Apostle in his own world, and just as importantly, offer correctives of some contemporary ministerial practices and invitations for improvements. Since 1993 James has served as the editor of *Restoration Quarterly*, a significant venue for research in biblical studies, church history (especially of the Stone-Campbell Restoration Movement), and contemporary theology. His more popular works make available to a lay audience thoughtful, well-informed, and spiritually rewarding interpretations of much of the New Testament.

His achievements, however, do not end at the printing press. For more than thirty years, he has taught ministers and others at the Institute for Christian Studies (now Austin Graduate School of Theology) and Abilene Christian University. Students of the past and the present speak of him as a prepared, stimulating, and creative teacher unafraid of experimentation for a new generation of learners. At both institutions he also served as an administrator, first as President of ICS and then as Associate Dean of ACU's Graduate School of Theology. His colleagues respect his ability to enlist them for work as needed and otherwise to get out of their way, certainly a too rare set of skills in university administrators!

James has also been an engaged citizen of the varied communities to which he belongs. He has served on innumerable committees in the University. His friends know his devotion to his ecclesial tradition, Churches of Christ, to which he has made significant contributions for more than forty years. Currently he serves as Secretary of the Southwest Region of the Society of Biblical Literature, a challenging task that benefits others far more than the holder of the office.

Perhaps most of all, it is James the man who inspires the sort of loyalty and respect that would lead friends and colleagues to write a volume such as this one. His devotion to his wife Carolyn, and hers to him, serve as a model for others. Although it is conventional in a Festschrift to utter a few obligatory niceties about the honoree's spouse, in this case we must do more and note that James and Carolyn enjoy a close partnership. They complement each other to such an extent that each deserves considerable credit for the other's successes. Carolyn's work as copyeditor of *Restoration Quarterly*, as an encourager of many of James's younger colleagues, as an amateur (but astute) biblical scholar, and as a professor of German in her own right warrant the fullest praise we can give.

A book like this requires the work of many hands. The editors thank their families and their fellow authors for making this volume possible. Special thanks go to Kelly Shearon and David Skelton, Mark Hamilton's assistants, for their work in preparing the manuscript for publication. We also are grateful to the College of Biblical Studies at Abilene Christian University and its dean, Jack Reese, for financial support of this project.

Dag Hammarskjöld once mused that "Except in faith, nobody is humble . . . . And, except in faith, nobody is proud . . . . To be, in faith, both humble and proud: that is, to *live*, to know that in God I am nothing, but that God is in me."[1] On behalf of a person of faith who is both humble and proud, and thus truly alive, we express our prayers for many years of success ahead.

Mark W. Hamilton
Thomas H. Olbricht
Jeffrey Peterson

---

[1] Dag Hammarskjöld, *Markings* (trans. Leif Sjöberg and W. H. Auden; New York: Knopf, 1968), 86 (emphasis in the original).

Traditions in Context

1

Praising God with "One Mouth" / "One Voice"

Everett Ferguson

THE Greek phrases "one mouth" (ἐν στόμα) and "one voice" (μία φωνή) had multiple idiomatic uses, an important one of which had to do with music, especially vocal music.¹ The principal study that sparked interest in the phrase "one voice" was by Johannes Quasten, who found in the phrase support for the idea that early Christians favored monophonic singing.² My wider examination of occurrences of the phrase shows the emphasis on unity and harmony, which Quasten also noted, but not an indication of monophony itself.³ Indeed there was a recognition by

---

¹ I made a preliminary exploration of these usages in "Toward a Patristic Theology of Music," *StPatr* 24 (1993): 266–83, esp. 280–83). With the aid of the *Thesaurus Linguae Graecae*, I now offer a more thorough examination.

² His treatment of *Una voce dicentes* is now available in English: Johannes Quasten, *Music and Worship in Pagan and Christian Antiquity* (Washington, D.C: National Association of Pastoral Musicians, 1983), 66–72.

³ Robert A. Skeris, Χρῶμα Θεοῦ: *On the Origins and Theological Interpretation of the Musical Imagery Used by the Ecclesiastical Writers of the First Three Centuries, With Special Reference to the Image of Orpheus* (Altötting: Copperath, 1976), 122, states that "one voice" refers to the spiritual unity and enthusiastic zeal of common worship, uniting worshipers with one another, God, and the heavenly liturgy (as Quasten said) but that Quasten over-interprets when he sees "one voice" as a technical musical term for unison singing, since joint acclamations were the actual background of the musical image. See also his notes on 176–77 and 202, n. 256. This study will provide more detailed documentation in support of Skeris's observations. For early Christian singing see now Edward Foley, *Foundations of Christian Music: The Music of pre-Constantinian Christianity* (Collegeville: Liturgical,

Christian authors of differences in human voices. The main idea in "one mouth" and "one voice" was the particpation by all of a given group in a unified expression.

"One Mouth"

The Greek Bible represents some of the principal usages in Greek literature as a whole. Romans 15:6 provides my title and the starting point for this study.

> May the God of steadfastness and encouragement grant you to be of the same mind [τὸ αὐτὸ φρονεῖν] in accordance with Christ Jesus, so that together with one mouth [ἐν ἑνὶ στόματι] you may glorify the God and Father of our Lord Jesus Christ. (Rom 15:5–6)

This prayer is part of Paul's instructions on unity among Christians in Rome and how to coexist with their differences in customs. He wanted them to live together in harmony, and this unity would find expression in praising God with one accord (ὁμοθυμαδόν) as if from one mouth.

Origen provides the earliest surviving commentary on the verse: "For 'one mouth' is uttered where one and the same understanding and speech proceeds through the mouths of diverse people."[4] This seems to be a fair and accurate summary of the import of the phrase from a Christian scholar learned in secular and biblical literature. To the uses of "one mouth" in that other literature we turn.

Second Chronicles 18:12 records what a messenger of kings Jehoshaphat and Ahab said to the prophet Micaiah: "Look, the prophets spoke with one mouth [ἐν στόματι ἑνί][5] good things concerning the king; let your words be as one of them." These court prophets delivered a common message, words with the same import.

Particularly important for our study, both for what it says and for its use later, is the introduction to "The Song of the Three Youths": "Then

---

1996), especially ch. 5, and on monophony the quotation, "'Unison,' in the primitive Christian community, could well have been more like heterophony, or 'the simultaneous statement . . . of two or more different versions of what is essentially the same melody'" (110 n. 81).

[4] *Commentary on Romans* 10.7.6; translation by Thomas P. Scheck, *Origen Commentary on the Epistle to the Romans Books 6–10* (Washington, D.C.: Catholic University of America Press, 2002), 271.

[5] NRSV, "with one accord." Henceforth I will normally render the phrase literally without repeating the Greek.

the three in the furnace as from one mouth [ὡς ἐξ ἑνὸς στόματος] hymned, glorified, and blessed God."[6] The qualification "as" or "as if" was frequently used with the idiom to signal its nonliteral use. The youths' words in their hymn of praise were the same so that it was as if they spoke with only one mouth.[7]

The idiom "one mouth" had long been present in classical Greek. One usage was for a group voicing their viewpoint by acclamation. The playwright Aristophanes has a line, "All the council cried out with one mouth" (*Knights* 670).[8] Plato emphasized common agreement by use of the phrase when he spoke of "the universal voice [literally 'one mouth'] of mankind" (*Republic* 2, 364a). He united the two phrases that are the subject of this study in making his point about unified agreement: "With one voice and from one mouth they must all agree that the laws are all good" (*Laws* 1.634e).[9]

Turning to Christian usage, we find that the earliest noncanonical Christian use of the phrase "one mouth" was with reference to prayer: "When we with harmony in conscience have gathered together in the same place, let us cry to God fervently as from one mouth" (*1 Clem.* 34.7). The emphasis on harmony in the context adds to the sense of united prayer.

Irenaeus piles up the expressions of oneness in speaking of the church believing and teaching the same faith:

> The church, although scattered throughout the world, carefully preserves [this faith], as living in one house. She likewise believes these things, as having one soul and the same heart, and harmoniously preaches, teaches, and delivers them, as possessing one mouth. (*Against Heresies* 1.10.2)

The church everywhere (we allow Irenaeus some exaggeration) adhered to and taught the same message, as if speaking with one mouth.

The *Hortatory Address to the Greeks*, falsely ascribed to Justin Martyr and probably from the third century, speaks of the harmony of the pro-

---

[6] Daniel 3:51 LXX (Sg Three 28 in English translations of the Apocrypha). I translate the text of Theodotion instead of the Septuagint, for Theodotion was preferred for Daniel by the church fathers. "From one mouth" was the form of the phrase more common than "with one mouth."

[7] Cyprian, *On the Lord's Prayer* 8 quotes the verse as an example to the church for its prayers. The youths spoke the same words, "although Christ had not yet taught them how to pray."

[8] For classical works I largely follow the translations in the Loeb Classical Library, but I have often introduced modifications.

[9] The whole passage is quoted by Eusebius, *Preparation for the Gospel* 12.1.2 (573c).

phets in revealing the things of God because of their inspiration by the divine Spirit. They gave divine instruction "as if with one mouth and one tongue" (8).

Gregory Thaumaturgus's *Paraphrase of Ecclesiastes* 12:11 says that "some people will pass on those wise lessons" they have received, "as if everyone from one mouth described in unison and in greater detail what was entrusted to them."[10]

Returning to the motif of praising God, we find several fourth-century references. The *Apostolic Constitutions* in a chapter that refers to both praying and hymning unites heavenly and human beings in glorifying God:

> As all the heavenly natures of the incorporeal powers glorify God harmoniously, so also all human beings on earth with one mouth and one attitude glorify the one true and only God. (7.56.1)[11]

The agreement in words of the mouth reflects the inner harmony of disposition. This work is now thought to reflect the hand of a Neo-Arian, specifically Eunomian, compiler, but the same thought is expressed by a champion of the Neo-Nicene cause, Basil the Great. In describing a vigil by his congregation in Caesarea of Cappadocia, he says: "All in common as from one mouth and one heart, offer up to the Lord the psalm of confession, each making the words of repentance their own" (*Letter* 207.3). The description speaks of reciting the same words without indicating sameness of tone.

Basil's friend, Gregory of Nazianzus, juxtaposes the "one voice" of the tower of Babel (Genesis 11) and Christians with allusion to Romans 15:6:

> We have become one lip, one voice [language] in contrast to those who built the former tower. They were in agreement for evil, but for us the things of harmony are for all the best in order that together we might with one mouth glorify Father, Son, and Holy Spirit. (*Oration* 23 ["On Peace"].3).

---

[10] John Jarick, *Gregory Thaumaturgos' Paraphrase of Ecclesiastes* (SBLSCS 29; Atlanta: Scholars, 1990), 303. I have followed with modifications his text and translation.

[11] Similar words are found in a near contemporary text but without the phrase "one mouth": "All of us in the congregation sing in a loud voice, as if we were all singing that which the invisible natures sing: 'Holy, holy, holy is the Lord of Sabaoth'" (Theodore of Mopsuestia, *On Eucharist and Liturgy* 6; translated by A. Mingana, *Woodbrooke Studies* 6 (1933): 100.

Once more, the emphasis is on the "togetherness" of the group in its vocal praise rather than on the musical manner.

A later Latin contemporary, Paulinus of Nola, evoked The "Song of the Three" to describe Christian song: "So let the holy lyre of our combined voices resound as though three tongues were singing with one mouth" (*Songs* 21.275). This statement more nearly evokes the practice of monophony, but even so the context, where an instrument of discordant notes brought into harmony serves as an illustration of vocal harmony, stresses agreement and unity.[12]

John Chrysostom did not preach on Rom 15:6 in his *Homilies on Romans*, but he did recall its phraseology. He describes monks rising and "having made one choir, with their conscience bright, all as if from one mouth sing hymns harmoniously to the God of all" (*Homilies on Matthew* 68[69].3). He continues in the next section to contrast the songs of monks with the music of the theater: "Here the grace of the Spirit sounds forth, employing instead of aulos, kithara, or syrinx, the mouths of the saints" (68[69].4).

He combines the phrases "one mouth" and "one voice" in discussing 1 Cor 14:33, but "one voice" is used literally and only "one mouth" is used metaphorically. Rebuking his congregation for talking on other matters in church, he pleads for their silence so that the one leading an activity was the only person speaking.

> There ought to be always but one voice in the church, just as there is one body. The one reading speaks alone, and even the bishop sits and maintains silence. The chanter chants alone; although all give the response, the voice is borne as from one mouth. The one who preaches, preaches alone. (*Homilies in 1 Corinthians* 36.9)

Chrysostom maintains his point about a single voice at a time by describing the congregational responses to the singing of the Psalms by the chanter as the many voices of the congregation so united as to come from one mouth.

The unifying theme in these varied uses of "one mouth" is that of different persons being in agreement, an agreement expressed principally in the same spoken words. This agreement might take the form of acclama-

---

[12] See my "Patristic Theology of Music," 279 n. 64, 281 n. 72. The use of instruments as analogies for harmony in the human body and soul was common in patristic authors; it was an illustration drawn from contemporary culture and did not reflect the use of instruments in church. See my article, "The Active and Contemplative Lives: The Patristic Interpretation of Some Musical Terms," *StPatr* 16 (1985): 15–23; idem, *A Cappella Music in the Public Worship of the Church* (3d ed.; Fort Worth: Star, 1999).

tions, voicing a common opinion or judgment, teaching the same thing, prayer, or especially praising God in song.

"One Voice"

"One voice" is a parallel phrase to "one mouth," but it is much more frequent and thus offers more variety in usage. Many of these uses are the same as "one mouth," and the underlying idea again is agreement or harmony. The phrase sometimes has the literal sense in the forefront, yet some of the metaphorical uses lose a connection with vocal expression. Once more, I begin with texts from the Greek Bible.

Genesis 11:1 describes all the people of the earth at one time as having "one lip and one voice [φωνὴ μία]," meaning one language.[13] In Exod 24:3 "all the people with one voice" gave their acceptance to the words of the Lord delivered to them by Moses. A musical use occurs in 2 Chron 5:13, which states that "There was one voice [sound, i.e., harmony] in the trumpeting and singing and proclaiming with one voice of acknowledgement and praise to the Lord." The thought of the Greek translators here could hardly have been of monophonic or strictly unison sound, since trumpeters and singers were both involved, so the emphasis was upon the notes of the instruments and singers being in harmony. In 4 Macc 8:29, when the tyrant tried to persuade the seven brothers to eat defiling food, "they all with one voice together, as if from the same soul," refused. Thus was described their united response. These four texts exemplify the meanings for "one voice" of a common language, united expressions of acceptance (the words of God) or refusal (commands of a pagan ruler), and harmony of musical sounds.

The New Testament adds specific content to these usages. Acts 24:21 quotes Paul as referring to "this one statement [voice]" he made concerning the resurrection of the dead.[14] Acclamations or shouting in unison is represented by Acts 19:34, where the mob at Ephesus "became one voice, all crying out for about two hours, 'Great is Artemis of the Ephesians!'" This unison shouting involved all saying the same words together without any necessary implication of the same tone. There is a literal use of the

---

[13] Isa 28:11 has "lips and tongues" as equivalent; it is quoted in 1 Cor 14:21. Once more, I will not repeat the Greek but by the words "voice" or "sound" indicate the presence of the phrase.

[14] Quoted by John Chrysostom in his *Homilies on Acts* 50 on Acts 23:19–21 (PG 60.346).

phrase "one voice" in Rev 9:13, "I heard one [a single] voice from the four horns of the altar."

Classical usage of "one voice" is even more varied and more extensive. It was noted above that Plato uses "one voice" with "one mouth" (*Laws* 1.634e). The same work witnesses to the classical usage of φωνή or language: "many slaves who speak the same language [voice]" (*Laws* 6.777c). The literal meaning is found in the statement that "sound which passes through the mouth whether of all or of an individual is one yet infinite" (*Philebus* 17b). Plato gives an explicit statement to monody, but in the metaphorical language of the "harmony of the spheres." In speaking of the seven planets and the Siren, he has the phrase, "hymning a single tone [or note, i.e., sound]" with "the eight forming one harmony" (*Republic* 10, 617b).

Aristotle shows a literal use of "one voice."

> Why does a human being show great variety of voice, but other animals have only one, unless they are of different species? Or, has the human being only one voice, though many varieties of speech [or many languages]. (*Problems* 10.38, 895a)

Another literal use appears in an illustration from music. "The two [notes] played against one voice [or, sound] make the other note imperceptible" (*Problems* 19.16, 918b). A nonliteral grammatical use of φωνή occurs in the phrase, "affirm a single predicate [meaning, significance]" (*Interpretation* 11, 20b).

Diodore of Sicily was fond of the phrase and often used it for unison acclamations. "They united in acclaiming him [Gelon of Syracuse] with one voice benefactor, savior, and king" (*Library* 11.26.6). Describing agreement on a course of action, he wrote, "with one voice they asked their commander to lead them" (ibid. 11.19.3). In keeping with the Greek custom of choosing their generals, the multitude cried out in an election "as if from one voice" (ibid., 16.10.3). (The qualification "as if" is frequent.) "When [Demetrius] had called together an assembly under arms . . ., the crowd shouted with a single [one] voice" (ibid. 19.81.2). Always implicit or explicit was the idea that a large number were involved.[15]

Dionysius of Halicarnassus employs the expressions, "The Romans cried out with one voice" (*Roman Antiquities* 4.67.2), and "one mind and

---

[15] Other passages include these: "The people cried out as if with one voice" (*Library* 11.92.4); "all as if with one voice were clamoring" (ibid. 16.79.3); "as 500,000 men shouted with one voice" (ibid. 17.33.4); "there came forth from all one voice" (ibid. 19.81.2).

voice" (ibid. 6.87.1). Dio Chrysostom expresses harmonious agreement with the phrase, "speaking the same language [voice]" (*Oration* 39.3).

Plutarch uses "one voice" with some frequency in his extensive works. Sometimes this is literal, "In the theater [at Delphi] one voice reaches all" (*The Obsolescence of Oracles* 8; *Moralia* 414c). Or again, "They give the name 'Seven-voiced' to the Stoa at Olympia, which reverberates many times from a single utterance [voice]" (*Talkativeness* 1; *Moralia* 502d). Or, "one voice" could be used for a phrase, "Then expressing this one word [voice]," followed by a short quotation (*Pompey* 72.2). Similarly, "So great influence had a flatterer's one word [voice]" (*Demetrius* 18.7).

A nonliteral use by Plutarch is indicated by an incident where many were probably not shouting the same words but words that had the same meaning: the soldiers and horsemen were "crying out loudly with one voice," ordering the private citizens out of their way (*Galba* 26.3). The phrase often is used for acclamations, whether spontaneous or organized. "One cry [voice] came from all, recognizing Galba as emperor" (ibid. 14.5). When Timoleon arrived at the theater, "the people would greet him and call him by name with one voice" (*Timoleon* 38.3). "The people of Utica assembled together, calling Cato with one voice their benefactor, savior, the only one free and only one unconquered" (*Cato the Younger* 71.1). As a general expression of unity and harmony Plutarch gives this description: "a lover of harmony among nations, community of cities, unanimity [one voice] of council and assembly [theater]" (*Aratus* 10.2).

Plutarch has one usage in a description of musical practice at Greek banquets that closely approximates Christian language: some say "that first the guests would sing the god's song together [κοινῶς, 'in common'], all raising their hymn with one voice" (*Table-Talk* 1.1, *Moralia* 615b). Then each person who wanted to do so sang individually in turn to the accompaniment of a lyre. These solo performances thus contrasted with the group or unison singing that was characterized as "with one voice."

A work of the first or second century CE ascribed to Apollodorus contains the riddle of the sphinx that uses the word "voice" with the meaning "name": "What has one voice [name] and yet becomes four-footed and two-footed and three-footed?" (*Library* 3.5.8).[16] The answer is a human being, for a person begins by crawling on "all fours," learns to walk on two legs, and in old age requires the assistance of a walking stick.

---

[16] The riddle is also included in the *Greek Anthology* 14.64.1, with the phrase "whose name [voice] is one."

Lucian of Samosata describes a crowd in a theater displeased with an actor in this way: "They all cried out in a single [one] voice" (*On Dance* 76). In another place he speaks of a crowd shouting, "All cried out with one voice as if by prearrangement" (*Nigrinus* 14).

Athenaeus uses "one voice" to refer to the "same language" (*Learned Banquet* 1.6.87 and 2.1) or to making "one sound" (ibid.1.10.83). Chariton (second century CE?) employs the phrase to introduce a statement, "sending forth one voice" followed by a quotation (*Chaerea and Callirhoe* 8.1). The grammarian and rhetor Aelius Herodianus (second century CE) represents the literal meaning, "one sound among many languages," and the grammatical sense, "they seek two [grammatical] cases in one sound." Cassius Dio contains a literal use of "one voice" but qualified by "if indeed": "[M]ention the things which the whole people would have celebrated with one tongue, if indeed they could speak with one voice" (*Roman History* 44.36.2).

The Neoplatonist Plotinus describes complete unity with the phrase "It is as if one voice and one word" (*Enneads* 6.4.14). Toward the close of pagan Greek literature the rhetor Libanius has the phrase, "everywhere the same word [voice]" (*Letters* 1350.3).

Thus we find over the long span of classical Greek literature a variety of uses of "one voice," not always as a set idiom: the literal meaning of one sound, standing for a word or a statement, the same spoken language, agreement in attitudes or policies, most frequently in unison acclamations whether staged or spontaneous, and the heavenly bodies "singing" the same tone or a group singing the same words together.

Jewish authors picked up the Greek classical and biblical uses of the idiom "one voice." Philo quotes Gen 11:1 and then gives an allegorical interpretation of the "one lip" and "one voice" as the agreement in evil deeds (*Confusion of Tongues* 1.1; 5.15). He describes an occasion in Alexandria where the crowd called for the death penalty against Isidorus: "They all cried out together [ὁμοθυμαδὸν][17] with one voice" (*Flaccus* 17.144). In contrast to this shouting out a negative condemnation, there is a positive affirmation recorded by Josephus of the greeting the Jews gave to Alexander the Great: "All the Jews together greeted Alexander with one voice" (*Antiquities* 11.8.5, 332).

"The Book of the Similitudes," the latest component of *1 Enoch*, often speaks of praying and glorifying "with one voice." Thus, "[T]he holy ones who dwell in the heavens above will unite with one voice, and sup-

---

[17] This word for "one accord" is often used in connection with "one voice."

plicate, and pray, and praise, and give thanks, and bless in the name of the Lord of Spirits" (47.2).[18]

> And all those in the heavens above received a command, and power and one voice and one light . . . [T]hey will all speak with one voice, and bless, and praise, and exalt, and glorify the name of the Lord of Spirits. . . . [A]nd they will raise one voice, and will bless, and praise, and glorify, and exalt (him) . . . and they will all say with one voice: "Blessed is he, and blessed be the name of the Lord of Spirits for ever and ever." (61.6, 9, 11)[19]

Although I have limited this study primarily to Greek literature without thorough examination of Latin and Hebrew texts, I note that the late rabbinic *Midrash Rabbah on Song of Solomon* gives as one interpretation of Song of Solomon 8:13, "When Israel go into their synagogues and recite the *shema'* with devotion, with one voice and with one mind and thought." This kind of recitation is contrasted with reciting "inattentively, one before the other," and without fixing "their minds on the words" (8.13.2).[20] An interpretation of 8:14 is, "When Israel recite the *shema'* with one mouth, one voice, one chant" (8.14.1).[21]

The Christian edition of the *Ascension of Isaiah* also has the motif of the angels in heaven praising God with one voice, stated three times. The angels on the right (who had the greater glory) and on the left of the throne in the fifth heaven "all sang praises with one voice" (7.15).[22] In the sixth heaven all the angels were equal, and Isaiah joined in their praise: "And there they all named the primal Father and his Beloved, Christ, and the Holy Spirit, all with one voice" (8.18). In the seventh heaven there was one "whose glory surpassed that of all," and all the righteous from Adam forward and all the angels "worshiped him, and they all praised him with one voice, and I also was singing praises with them" (9.28). It is difficult to draw conclusions from these statements about the nature of the singing, but since a human joined with the angels ("my praise was like theirs"; 8.18

---

[18] Translation by Michael A. Knibb, *The Ethiopic Book of Enoch* (Oxford: Clarendon, 1978), 2:133.

[19] Ibid., 2:149–50.

[20] Translation by Maurice Simon, *Midrash Rabbah, Song of Songs* (London: Soncino, 1939), 324.

[21] Ibid., 325.

[22] Translations are by M. A. Knibb in OTP 2:166; subsequent quotations on 2:169, 171; cf. the similar translation of C. Detlef G. Müller in Wilhelm Schneemelcher, ed., *New Testament Apocrypha* (Louisville: Westminster John Knox, 1992), 2:612, 614, 616.

and 9.28), the "one voice" would seem to refer to the content of the united praise and not to the tonal likeness of the sound.

This Jewish Christian theme of the righteous joining the angels in praising God with one voice occurs also in the *Apocalypse of Peter* 19. The righteous were in a place of bliss where angels were present, and "All who dwell there had an equal glory, and with one voice they praised God the Lord, rejoicing in that place."[23]

This heavenly praise was a model for the earthly church. Ignatius of Antioch uses a comparison from instrumental music to express the unity desired in the congregation but then describes Christian practice as vocal music.

> For your justly famous presbytery, worthy of God, is attuned to the bishop, as strings to a kithara. On account of this by your unanimity and harmonious love, Jesus Christ is being sung. Now each of you together become a choir so that being harmoniously in unanimity and receiving the keynote from God in unity, you may sing with one voice through Jesus Christ to the Father. (*Ephesians* 4.1–2)

The emphasis in the passage is clearly on unity and harmony. The unison singing might have been monodic, but what Ignatius seems to have had in mind was the whole congregation participating in a harmony that found expression in singing the same thing. Unison tonality would not seem to be required by "one voice" any more than by other words in the description; if it was practiced, that would have to be established by other information about vocal music practices of the time.

---

[23] Translation by Müller in *New Testament Apocrypha*, 2:635. The passage occurs in the Greek fragment from Akhmim but not the Ethiopic translation of the work. Note the quotation above under "One Mouth" from *1 Clem.* 34.7 about prayer, which immediately follows a quotation of the angels' declaring "Holy, holy, holy" from Isa 6:3. For later expressions of the motif note the vision of Saturus in the *Martyrdom of Perpetua and Felicitas* 12 (202 CE), in which the martyrs were carried to the throne of God where they heard "a united voice [*uocem unitam*] saying 'Holy, holy, holy'." The Greek version has φωνὴ ἡνωμένη. Epiphanius in the fourth century emphasized that the Cherubim and Seraphim spoke the doxology "Holy" three times, not twice, once only, or four times, "but three sounds [φωνάς] exhibiting unity [ἑνικάς]" (*Ancoratus* 10.3); and again the angels "say the 'holy' with one voice and one word and one perfection, glorifying the Trinity together in Unity and the Unity in Trinity" (ibid. 26.3–4). For the Jewish idea of the union of the heavenly and earthly liturgy and the practice of all with one voice praising the Lord, see Karl Erich Grözinger, *Musik und Gesang in der Theologie der frühen jüdischen Literatur: Talmud Midrasch Mystik* (Tübingen: Mohr Siebeck, 1982), 312–13, 333.

14 Renewing Tradition

A papyrus of the *Acts of Paul* contains the statement, "The lion said with one voice" (Papyrus Hamburg 5, 4), followed by a long quotation, but this is conjectured to be a corruption for "a divine voice."[24] The *Acts of Peter* records the whole mass of brothers and sisters in Rome, wishing to rescue Peter from his arrest, "crying out with one voice, 'What harm has Peter done . . . ?'" (36[7]).

Besides speaking of "one mouth," Irenaeus offers two problematic references to "one voice." He describes Marcus the Gnostic as teaching that

> The restitution of the universe will occur when all things will return to one letter and make one and the same sound [ἐκφώνησιν]. He proposes that the "Amen" that we say together is an image of this sound. (*Against Heresies* 1.14.1)

Although using a different form of the word φωνή, Irenaeus's statement indicates that the unison congregational "Amen" at the conclusion of prayers could be expressed as spoken with "one voice." A textual problem attaches to a passage where the surviving Greek breaks off in the middle of a difficult Latin reading. I offer this translation, following a conjectural reading:

> All the Scripture given to us by God will be found by us to be harmonious, and the parables will agree with the things said plainly. The things said [in Scripture] clearly will explain the parables, and through the many varied expressions one harmonious melody will be sung by us while we praise God in hymns. (*Against Heresies* 2.28.3)[25]

I take it that something may have dropped out of the text in transmission that would clarify that Irenaeus was making a comparison between the varied voices of Scripture teaching a harmonious message and the varied voices of the congregation united in the praise of God.

A text of uncertain date, but probably later than Irenaeus, comes from one of those groups whom Irenaeus so strenuously opposed as Gnostic. The *Holy Book of the Great Invisible Spirit*, better known as *The Gospel of the Egyptians*, is preserved in Coptic in the Nag Hammadi codices. It con-

---

[24] Wilhelm Schneemelcher in idem, *New Testament Apocrypha*, 2:253 and 267 n. 17.

[25] The Greek of the latter part reads: διὰ τῆς τῶν λέξεων πολυφωνίας ἓν σύμφωνον μέλος ἐν ἡμῖν αἰσθήσεται [which could be read as ᾀσθήσεται, according to my translation] . . . ; the Latin reads: *per dictionum multas voces unam consonantem melodiam in nobis sentiet, laudantem hymnis Deum.* See the notes in W. W. Harvey, *Sancti Irenaei Libros quinque adversus haereses* (Cambridge: Typis academicis, 1857), 352, and *ANF*, 1:400.

tains a passage about singing similar to expressions in orthodox writers, except for its description of the objects of the praise:

> [T]he spiritual church increased in the four lights of the great, living Autogenes, the god of truth, praising, singing, (and) giving glory with one voice, with one accord, with a mouth that does not rest, to the Father, and the Mother, and the Son, and their whole pleroma. (NHC 3: 2, 55, 5–11 = 4:2, 66, 14–23)[26]

Here praising, singing, and glorifying combine as being done in accord or unanimity by the church with the one voice of the mouth. Despite the uncertain date and certainly unorthodox character of the document, it well expresses the worship practices in song by the mainstream of the church.

Clement of Alexandria has a metaphorical use, "employing the only one voice of writing," that is, the one medium of writing instead of speaking (*Miscellanies* 1.1.14.4). Drawing on the language of sacrifice from the ancient world, he interpreted the altar as "the congregation of those devoted to prayer, as if having one common voice and one mind" (ibid. 7.6.31.8). The same imagery applies to song as to prayer.

> The union of many in one, a unity that out of many varied sounds receives a divine harmony, becomes one symphony [συμφωνία], following the one choir director and teacher, the Word, resting in the same truth and saying 'Abba, Father' [Rom. 8:15]. (*Exhortation* 9.88)

Particularly important for our purposes is a passage that apparently quotes in part from Plutarch, *Moralia* 615b above:

> Among the ancient Greeks at their drinking parties and after-dinner cups they were accustomed to sing a song called the skolion in the manner of the Hebrew Psalms, for "all raise the paean in common with one voice." Sometimes they passed around in turn the toasts of the ode. (*Instructor* 2.4.44.3)

As in Plutarch, Clement uses "one voice" for the group singing together in contrast to the individual singing. For purposes of understanding Jewish and Christian musical practice, he gives the important testimony that the Hebrew Psalms were sung corporately.

---

[26] Translation by Alexander Böhlig and Frederik Wisse in James M. Robinson, ed., *The Nag Hammadi Library in English* (San Francisco: Harper & Row, 1988), 213–14; cf. the similar translation by Bentley Layton, *The Gnostic Scriptures* (Garden City: Doubleday, 1987), 112.

Origen picked up the reference in Gen 11:1 to one voice for one language.[27] He also used the phrase for the unity of Scripture: "The prophecies are not divided but were spoken and written as by one Spirit truly working harmoniously and by one voice in one soul" (*Commentary on Matthew* 14.1 on Matt 18:19). Origen furthermore applied "one voice" to prayer and song.

> [Whether Greeks or Romans] each in his own language prays to God and praises him as one is able. And the Lord of every language hears those praying in every language as, if I may speak thus, one voice according to the meaning expressed in different languages. (*Against Celsus* 8.37)

Origen qualifies his statement, his philological training seeming to indicate to him there was an accommodative sense in the phrase while he recognized it as a common usage.

Eusebius of Caesarea uses "one voice" in the sense of "identical utterance" for the message of two revelatory visions (*Church History* 6.11.2). "This one voice [=statement]" refers to a quotation from Psalm 29 (*Questions of the Gospel to Stephen*; PG 22.912); "with one word and one voice" introduces a quotation of Matt 28:19 (*Proof of the Gospel* 3.6; 132a). The most frequent metaphorical use in Eusebius, however, is to express agreement. Thus there is the combination "one mind and one voice" (*Preparation for the Gospel* 14.3; 719d). The agreement among the prophets was possible because "they all spoke with one voice by the divine Spirit" (*Proof of the Gospel* 5 int. 25; 208d). The two phrases of our study are combined in Eusebius's exaggerated rhetoric about Constantine: "All the nations . . . with one voice and one mouth confessed that Constantine by God's grace made the common good to shine upon human beings" (*Life of Constantine* 1.41.2).[28] Eusebius often expresses the unity and harmony of Christian singing but without the use of the phrases in our study.[29]

Athanasius uses the phrase "one voice" to describe a congregational acclamation, "O Christ, send help to [emperor] Constantius" (*Apology to Constantius* 10), and the congregational "Amen" at the conclusion of

---

[27] *Selections in Genesis*; *Philocalia* (compiled by Basil and Gregory Nazianzus) 22.7.

[28] Other statements are "all these things from one voice" (*Ecclesiastical Theology* 2.9.12); "summoning them by one voice" (*Theophany* frg. 1.6).

[29] "Unison voices . . . united in soul and attitude, with one mind and in agreement of faith and piety, we send up a unison melody in the words of the Psalms" (*Commentary on Psalms* 91 [English 92].2–3; PG 23.1172D–1173A); "one symphony and harmony" (twice) (ibid. 70 [71]. 222–24; PG 23.786C-D).

prayer—it is better to assemble in one place so as to speak "as with one and the same voice in perfect harmony" so that "such a great assembly of people might become one voice when they say the 'Amen' to God" (ibid. 16).

Basil the Great of Caesarea in Cappadocia represents the usages already established. The literal meaning of one sound occurs with reference to a mother sheep who recognizes her lamb, although all "have the same sound, color, and smell" (*Hexaemeron* 9.4.32).[30] Basil picks up the meaning "one language" from Gen 11:1 (*Homily on Pentecost* 3; PG 52.811).[31] "One voice" can stand for "one word" in the sense of a saying or statement, Basil's most common use of the phrase.[32] Similar to this is the metaphorical use for the collective voice of people. For a group saying the same thing, he writes, "There is only one voice [or cry] in all, who recount their pitiable and sad condition" (*Letters* 243.2).[33] One person can speak for others: "Your whole fatherland addresses these words to you through our one voice" (*Letters* 96.1).[34] In a musical context for congregational singing Basil emphasizes its unifying quality:

> Who can consider as an enemy one with whom he has sung to God with one voice? Hence singing of the psalms in unity . . . harmoniously draws the people to a symphony of one choir. (*Commentary on Psalms* 1.2; PG 29.212)

---

[30] Cf. Pseudo-Basil, *Commentary on Isaiah* 1.31 on Isa 1:13–14 (PG 30.180B) for many feast days referred to by the same voice, i.e., word or name.

[31] The reverse of the story of the confounding of languages in Genesis 11 in the story of Pentecost in Acts 2 is developed in terms of the unity of the faith in the pseudo-Basil, *Commentary on Isaiah* 13.259 on Isa 13:4—"[The verse refers to] sending forth the one voice of the faith. . . . The voice is one and it is like many sounds of the nations. On one hand, one according to the agreement of faith, but like many sounds on account of the division of tongues [languages] of fire by the Holy Spirit upon each of the apostles who were about to spread the gospel to the nations of the earth [Acts 2]" (PG 30.573B).

[32] *Homily on the Festival* (PG 28.1073) referring to 2 Cor 5:17; *Homily on the Assumption of the Lord* (PG 28.1105) referring to Matt 16:16; *Homily on Envy* (PG 31.613) referring to 1 Sam 18:7; *Against Eunomius* (PG 29.553) referring to a pronouncement by Eunomius; *Homily on "I pull down my barns"* (PG 28.1073)—"You know one voice [one saying], 'I have not'; I will not give; for I am poor'"; *Letters* 237.2—"He handed over to the senate all the clergy of the church in Caesarea by one voice [decree or pronouncement]"; *Against Sabellius and Arius* (PG 31.613)—"from this one word [voice]"; *On the Faith* prol. 8 (PG 31.692)—"one word [voice] is sufficient."

[33] For another example: "There is only the one sound of demanding creditors and hounded debtors" (*Letters* 74.3). Cf. Pseudo-Basil, *Commentary on Isaiah* quoted in n. 31.

[34] Similar, but more literal, is the statement, "All these things are described by the one voice of Paul" (*Against Eunomius*; PG 29.580).

"One voice" once more represents the communal singing, which here creates unity as well as expressing it.

The same pattern of usage recurs in Gregory Nazianzus. In a letter to Basil he could describe the latter's voice as "one [unique] among all things" (*Letters* 46.4). "One voice" stands for "a single expression" or phrase (*Oration* 43 ["Panegyric on Basil"].68), or to one statement from Isaiah (*Oration* 4 ["Against Julian"].15).[35]

We noted above on "one mouth" Nazianzen's allusion to Gen 11; he uses the meaning of language also in reference to the Pentecost miracle: "Did they each hear in their own language so that, permit me to say so, one sound was spoken but many sounds were heard?" (*Oration* 41 ["On Pentecost"].15). (He preferred to punctuate Acts 2:6 so that the miracle was in the speaking of other languages rather than in the hearing.) There is an analogy from vocal music, with reference to Exodus 15, that fits what other Christian authors said: "Taking up one voice, harmonized by the one Spirit, let us sing that victory ode which Israel then sang over the Egyptians" (*Oration* 4 ["Against Julian"].12).

Gregory of Nyssa has a literal use of the phrase in reference to speech: [One] "cannot utter the names of three persons with one sound [voice] at the same time" (*Against Eunomius* 1.203 [16]; GNO 1,86,3; PG 45). His extensive use of "one voice" for the most part seems to be equivalent to "one word" or "one saying." Often the reference is to a text of Scripture,[36] but other statements could be capsuled in the phrase.[37] Among the notable applications of the usage is to the uniform message of Scripture: "You heard all [law, prophets, Gospels] calling out together with one voice 'love' and saying 'philanthropy'" (*Usury* 9; GNO 9, 204, 11). With allusion to

---

[35] Similarly, "one voice" for "a single word" or argument; *Oration* 31 ("On the Holy Spirit"), 17.

[36] "One cry [voice] to God," quoting Ps 106:6–7 (*Inscriptions of the Psalms* 1.8.82; GNO 5, 55, 13); "one word [or cry, voice]," referring to Ps 106:13 (ibid., 1.8.87; GNO 5, 56, 26); "this one expression [or word, voice]" on Ps 54:24 (ibid., 2.13.202; GNO 5, 144, 5); "the one utterance [voice] of Paul" (*Refutation of the Confession of Eunomius* 169 [2.13]; GNO 2, 383, 17 [PG 45.544]); "whatever is encompassed in the one word [voice], 'He made' [Gen 1:1]" (*On the Creation of Humanity* [likely spurious]; GNO Supplement, 66, 6); "this one word [voice] is an antidote," Matt 5:9 (*Beatitudes* 7; GNO 7.2, 154, 12).

[37] "This one single expression [voice]" (*Against Eunomius* 1.210 [17]; GNO 1, 88, 6); "since the title [voice] is one and the same" (*Refutation of the Confession of Eunomius* 79 [2.8]; GNO 2, 345, 4–5; PG 45.501); "in order that we might learn by the one word [voice]" (*On Canticles* hom. 10 on Cant 5:1; GNO 6, 310, 14–15); "it is possible to encompass all their nonsense in one word [voice]" (*On the Deity of the Son and Holy Spirit*; GNO 10.2, 126, 16; PG 46.561). Eunomius himself is quoted as saying, "one and the same name" (*Against Eunomius* 3 [7].5 .18; GNO 2, 166, 14; PG 45.745)

Gen 11:1 is the statement, "Whenever all the church in agreement with the good becomes one lip and one voice" (*Canticles* hom. 7 on Cant 4:3; GNO 6, 228, 14).[38] Gregory gives a similar metaphorical application:

> Just as there was "one lip and one voice" before the confusion of tongues, so also now all the nations and the whole world and all human beings become one hearing and one heart when the one Word resounds in them all. (*Inscriptions of the Psalms* 2.12.171)[39]

Literal speaking is involved in a confession of faith: "One word [voice] was heard to all these things, Christ being confessed in the mouths of the saints" (*The Forty Martyrs* 1b; GNO 10.1, 149, 25; PG 46.764).

The *Confessions of Cyprian* (of Antioch—apparently an invented person) mention the unison Amen as a response to songs:

> Thereupon we went into the church, and [one could there] see the choir, which was like a choir of heavenly men of God or a choir of angels taking up a song of praise to God. To every verse they added a Hebrew word [as] with one voice, so that one might believe that there were not [a number of] men but rather one rational being comprehending a unity, which gave off a wonderful sound. (17)[40]

The huge corpus of John Chrysostom will serve to complete our survey of "one voice" in Greek patristic literature. He too frequently uses "one voice" for "one phrase" or "one saying." Thus in preaching on Acts 17:24 Chrysostom says that "one phrase [voice]" of Paul overthrew the ideas of philosophers (*Homilies on Acts* 38; PG 60.270).[41] "By one expression [voice]," Luke 23:43, Jesus introduced the thief on the cross into paradise

---

[38] With reference to Gen 11:1, "All humanity lived together with one language" (*Against Eunomius* 2.253; GNO 1, 300, 7; PG 45.996).

[39] "All humanity lived together with one language [voice]" (*Against Eunomius* 2.253; PG 45.996).

[40] Translation in Johannes Quasten, *Music and Worship*, 70; Greek text 104 n. 53.

[41] Similarly, "concerning this one statement [Acts 23:19–21] which I [Paul] cried out" (*Homilies on Acts* 50; PG 60.346). Also, Abraham "obeyed the one voice of God who called" (*On Stephen*; PG 59.506); "from one word [voice]" (*On the Beheading of John*; PG 59.489); "having heard only one word [or phrase, voice] of the one pursuing" (*On the Change of Names*; PG 51.142); "the one word [voice] of the Gospel" (*Encomium on John the Evangelist*; not in PG; for publication information see M. Geerard, *Clavis Patrum Graecorum*, vol. 2 [Turnhout: Brepols, 1974], #4750). This usage is common in the spuria attributed to Chrysostom—"uttered one word [voice]" (*On One Born Blind*; PG 59.552); "how he set in order the whole world by one word [voice]" (*On John the Theologian*; PG 59.613); "the word [voice] is one, distributed according to the obligation of each one" (*On Forgiveness*; PG 60.759).

(*On the Ascension*, hom. 4; PG 52.799).⁴² There are several references to the "one lip, one voice" of Gen 11:1.⁴³ "One mouth" and "one voice" occur with reference to a secular acclamation: "In the theater as from one mouth they cry out all with one voice, they all in harmony call him protector and ruler of the city" (*On Vainglory and Education of the Young* 4).⁴⁴

With reference to verbal petition, Chrysostom speaks of the people of Antioch "calling upon God with one and the same voice with much earnestness" (*To the People of Antioch* 15.3). Prayer in the liturgical assembly is described in the following words:

> You are able to pray in private, but the prayer does not have such power as when done with all the members of the household, as when the whole body of the church together sends up petition with one voice, the priests being present and lifting up the prayers of the community. (*On the Obscurity of the Prophets*; PG 56.182)

This is a striking statement of the power of congregational prayer when prayed in unity. With that power in mind, Chrysostom exhorts, "Let us all join in prayer, and let us lift up one voice in their behalf" (*Homilies on Romans* 7 on Rom 3:31).

A particularly interesting passage pertains to the singing of psalms in church. Chrysostom has referred to young and old, rich and poor, women and men. His description of their equality in church includes this description of their participation (including women) in psalmody:

> Behold, when the Psalm is introduced it blends the different voices, provides one harmonious ode to be offered up, and joins the dead and the living. The blessed prophet (David) sings with us; he speaks and all answer with the responses.

---

⁴² Another sermon has literally "one word": "So simply by one word [voice], 'Yes,' you lead him into paradise" (*On the Four Days of Lazarus*; PG 48.782). A possibly spurious sermon says that "The thief is saved because of one word [voice] of faith" (*On the Cross and the Thief* 6.3). A related statement from another spurious sermon says, "to raise all with one word [voice] as he had done with Lazarus" (*On the Dance of Herodias*; PG 59.552).

⁴³ Frequently in *On the Devil*, e.g., "because there was in all people one language [voice] as if also one nature" (1.2; also three times in 1.4—PG 49.246); several times in *On the Obscurity of the Prophets* (PG 56.179 [three times], 180, 182, 186 [twice], 187 [twice]); *Homilies on Genesis* 30, several times (PG 53.273), but once instead of "one lip" he has "one tongue" with "one voice" (PG 53.277); *Homilies on 1 Corinthians* 24 on 1 Cor 13.

⁴⁴ Later in the work there is reference to "what pagans spend in return for a single shout [voice] of applause" (12).

> There is not here slave or free, rich and poor, ruler and private person. All have been welded together into one chorus out of all. Heaven and earth are combined. Neither does man have freedom of speech nor is woman silent and stands speechless; but all enjoy equal honor, and we offer up a common sacrifice, a common offering. This one does not have more than another, and that one more than this, but all in the same honor, one voice out of different tongues, offer to the Creator of the world. The difference is not in slave and free, not in rich and poor, not in female and male, but in attitude, in diligence, in readiness, in evil and in virtue. (*De studio praesentium* 5.1; PG 63.487)

Without using the exact phrase "one voice," as the preceding quotation does, Chrysostom elsewhere expresses the same thought:

> Our tongues are the strings of our kithara, putting forth a different sound yet a godly harmony. For indeed women and men, old and young, have different voices but they do not differ in the word of hymnody for the Spirit blends the voice of each and effects one melody in all. (*On Psalms* 145 [English 146].2; PG 55.521.)[45]

These passages demonstrate that the emphasis for Chrysostom was on agreement and unity in the words sung, not on identity of sound. The one melody was the work of the Spirit not of the unison voices of the congregation.

Although the burden of this paper has been on the Greek writers, the study may be rounded out by quoting two Latin authors contemporary with Chrysostom on the one voice of Christian music. Ambrose, bishop of Milan, borrowing in part from a passage in Basil quoted above, wrote:

> A psalm . . . produces one song from various and sundry voices in the manner of a cithara. . . . The apostle admonishes women to be silent in church, yet they do well to join in a psalm; this is gratifying for all ages and fitting for both sexes. . . . With what great effort is silence maintained during the [scriptural] readings! If one person recites, the entire congregation makes noise; but when a psalm is read, it is itself the guarantor of silence because when all speak [in response] no one makes noise. . . . A psalm joins those with differences, unites those at odds and reconciles those who have been

---

[45] For other references to the different voices of men and women, of old and young, see my "Patristic Theology of Music," 280 n. 65. Note Basil, *Hexaemeron* 4.7 (PG 29.93C), for "the mingled voices of men, children, and women" arising to God in an assembly of the church.

offended, for who will not concede to him with whom one sings to God in one voice? (*Explanation of the Psalms* 1.9)[46]

Singing together, by actively engaging the whole congregation, kept order in the assembly and had a unifying effect.

Niceta of Remesiana, in the Balkans where Latin and Greek met, wrote the first known treatise of hymn singing:

> [After quoting "The Song of the Three Youths," he says,] You see that it was for our instruction that we are told that the three boys humbly and holily praised God with one voice. Therefore, let us sing all together, as with one voice, and let all of us modulate our voices in the same way. If one cannot sing in tune with the others, it is better to sing in a low voice rather than drown the others. In this way he will take his part in the service without interfering with the community singing . . . . When we sing, all should sing; when we pray, all should pray. So when the lesson is read, all should remain silent, that all may equally hear. (*On the Utility of Hymn Singing* 13)[47]

Niceta clearly envisions not everyone singing "on key," although that was desirable. His "one voice" is the joint participation by all.

Christian writers used the phrase "one voice" in a variety of ways: predominately to refer to a single saying or statement, "one word," to mean "one language" (in comments on or allusions to Gen 11:1), or for acclamations. In the context of worship the phrase was used for united prayer, the ratification "Amen," or for congregational psalmody (whether the whole song or more often the responses to the text sung by a cantor). The phrase emphasized corporate agreement.

Conclusions

It may seem obvious, but should be stated, that this study deals with vocal sounds. This is explicit in the phrase "one mouth," but it applies also to "one voice." Although the word φωνή could mean "sound" as well as "voice," in the phrase "one voice" it most often means vocal sound and its

---

[46] Translation by James McKinnon, *Music in Early Christian Literature* (Cambridge: Cambridge University Press, 1987), 126–27. The first brackets are my addition; the second is McKinnon's correct interpretation.

[47] Translation by Gerald Walsh, *The Writings of Niceta of Remesiana* (Fathers of the Church 17; New York: Fathers of the Church, 1949), 75. This important document is little studied, but see Calogero Riggi, "Pregare all'unisono secondo Niceta di Remesiana," *StPatr* 23 (1989): 162–70.

idiomatic uses are derived from that meaning. Thus in musical contexts the phrases have to do almost exclusively with vocal music.

In keeping with the general metaphorical use of the phrases "one mouth" and "one voice," the emphasis in worship contexts also is on agreement and unity. The use of these phrases in reference to prayer parallel those in reference to song. Hence, "one voice" did not mean "unison" in the modern sense of monophony but "unison" in the sense of joint, unified participation by all. The singing may actually have been monophonic, but these phrases do not, as Quasten contended, establish this usage. The translation "unison" for "one voice" is not justified if by unison one means monophonic singing, but it is appropriate if by it one means congregational participation.

2

Early Christian Missionary Practice and Pagan Reaction

1 Peter and Domestic Violence against Slaves and Wives

John T. Fitzgerald

IN the contemporary United States of America, "Christianity" is often understood as the defender of family values and of traditional forms of social life.[1] Such an understanding is not only perpetuated by the media but also articulated by countless Christians themselves. Although this depiction of Christianity as the champion of traditional values and social structures is unquestionably grounded in reality, it also skews that reality. Not all Christians are social and theological conservatives, and certainly not on every important issue. Other Christians, embracing biblical values, feel themselves compelled to criticize and challenge various aspects of conventional morality and time-honored forms of social life. The activities of such individuals are a salutary reminder that Christianity, even or

---

[1] This paper is a tribute to James W. Thompson, whose numerous contributions have enriched the theological life of both the academy and the church. Research on this paper was completed during my time as a Visiting Research Scholar at the School of Biblical Studies and Bible Languages, North-West University, Potchefstroom, South Africa. I am grateful to participants in the School's "New Testament and Greek Colloquium" for their sage comments and questions about an earlier version of this paper. For helpful stylistic and other suggestions, I am indebted to Stephen Sapp of the University of Miami and to the editors of this volume.

especially in the United States, has often taken a socially and politically revolutionary form. For instance, Christian faith played a vital role in the abolitionist movement of the nineteenth century as well as the civil rights movement of the twentieth century, two momentous endeavors that dramatically changed the shape of American culture.

Religion has the power both to subvert and to sustain society, and Christianity is a prime example of religion's capacity to manifest itself in both revolutionary and reactionary ways. The reality is that religions usually exercise these diverse powers simultaneously, supporting some aspects of a given culture and transforming others. Yet religion's multiple social functions are rarely recognized, or at least emphasized, by either participants or critics. Usually, only one social function of a particular religion is highlighted, and depending on the specific function being exercised, that religion will be viewed as radical, moderate, or conservative.

This one-dimensional, reductionistic social analysis was typical of many pagans in regard to earliest Christianity. For the vast majority of pagans, Christianity was a domestic troublemaker. Instead of being viewed as defenders of family values (as in modern America), the first Christians were accused of undermining them and thereby destroying the unity and concord of domestic life. This perception of Christianity as inimical to the family and as a dangerous social threat was in large part a response to the missionary activity of the early church.

Early Christian Missionary Practice and the Reaction by Pagans

In their evangelistic efforts, the first Christians endeavored to convert all members of a household. When they succeeded, they naturally rejoiced and gave emphasis to this kind of conversion. The author of Acts, for example, is keen to point out instances where this occurred, such as with the households of Cornelius (10:24, 44–48; 11:14), Lydia (16:15), and the Philippian jailer (16:31–34). It is easy to understand why Acts celebrates conversions of entire households. Such conversions brought more people into the church at a time when it was small and socially insignificant. Much more importantly, however, such conversions functioned to unify the members of the converted household. The converted shared a common religious experience and commitment, and they were able to support one another as they endeavored to lead Christian lives and endured abuse from nonmembers of their household who frowned upon their membership in this strange new religious cult.[2]

Whereas such household conversions were religiously and socially the ideal, they were few and far between. It was rare when a *paterfamilias* or head of the household, such as Stephanas (1 Cor 1:16; 16:15, 17), became a Christian and led his whole household into the church's fellowship.[3] Faced with an unresponsive *paterfamilias*, the first Christians did not refrain from seeking to persuade other members of that household. That is, the early Christians were content to convert individuals within households and did not insist upon the conversion of the entire family. The consequences of this pragmatically necessary but audacious strategy were enormous, not simply for the manner in which the church grew but also for the way in which non-Christians viewed the new religion.

When individuals within a household became Christians but the *paterfamilias* or other powerful members of the household did not, the situation was quite different for all concerned. This was particularly the case if the *paterfamilias* was scandalized by the Christian message and viewed it as moronic (1 Cor 1:23). From his perspective, Christians were domestic troublemakers who were willing to disturb families and to destabilize whole households for the sake of their religion. In their eagerness to save the world, Christians did not shy away from shattering the unity and sanctity of the family, the basic unit of society and thus of the state (Aristotle, *Pol.* 1.2; Cicero, *Off.* 1.54). For such a pagan *paterfamilias*, Christianity was not an innocuous religious phenomenon that could be derisively ignored but what Tacitus (*Ann.* 15.44) called a "pernicious superstition" (*exitiabilis superstitio*) that threatened not simply "the family" but his own family. Tacitus elsewhere uses the adjective *exitiabilis* (*Ann.* 16.5) of a "deadly disease" (*morbo*), and Suetonius (*Claudius* 25.3) uses it of "destructive disagreements" (*discordias*) that necessitate external intervention before they prove fatal. Tacitus's application of the word to Christianity reflects the view that this new cult is not simply "atrocious" (*atrocia*) and "shameful" (*pudenda*) but a dangerous and "misanthropic" (*odio humani*) "evil" (*mali*)

---

[2] For the problems and challenges faced by new converts, see Abraham J. Malherbe, *Paul and the Thessalonians: The Philosophic Tradition of Pastoral Care* (Philadelphia: Fortress, 1987), esp. 34–60.

[3] The conversion of the *paterfamilias* to the Christian faith did not necessarily mean that all members of the household followed his example. Onesimus, for instance, was originally a pagan slave in Philemon's household and only became a Christian at a later time. For pagan slaves in Christian households from later periods of church history, see Robert M. Grant, *Early Christianity and Society: Seven Studies* (San Francisco: Harper & Row, 1977), 91–92.

that is ignored at one's own peril. Therefore, it is no wonder that he uses *exitiabilis* ("pernicious") of the Christian religion in the context of Nero's famous persecution of the church in Rome (*Ann.* 15.44).

Given this view of Christianity as a social menace, members of the household who dared to "join this new cult" risked ridicule and reprisals from an unsympathetic *paterfamilias*. Their situation was thus quite different from that of the converts whose *paterfamilias* shared their faith in Christ. Instead of experiencing familial concord and receiving strong encouragement from the *paterfamilias* and other sympathetic members of the household, these new Christians frequently encountered scorn and hostility. This was particularly the case with those who were culturally perceived as the weaker and inferior members of the household, such as women and slaves. In point of fact, these individuals had shown incredible courage and spiritual strength in being willing to embrace a religion that the head of the household despised or dismissed. The pagan *paterfamilias*, for his part, was convinced that the Christians had targeted precisely such people because they were the most likely to accept their message.

Given on the one hand the emphasis in early Christianity on absolute fidelity to Jesus and on the other the ancient Mediterranean insistence on familial loyalty as a core cultural value, it was inevitable that faith in Christ would be socially divisive, tearing families apart. The words of Jesus left little room for compromise. "Whoever comes to me and does not hate father and mother, wife and children, brothers and sisters, yes, and even life itself, cannot be my disciple. Whoever does not carry the cross and follow me cannot be my disciple" (Luke 14:26–27).[4] "Whoever does not hate father and mother cannot be my disciple, and whoever does not hate brothers and sisters, and carry the cross as I do, will not be worthy of me" (*Gos. Thom.* 55:1–2).[5] "Whoever loves father or mother more than me is not worthy of me; and whoever loves son or daughter more than me is not worthy of me; and whoever does not take up the cross and follow me is not worthy of me" (Matt 10:37–38). In the *Gospel of Thomas*, this principle is embodied by Jesus even in regard to his own parents: "Whoever does not hate [father] and mother *as I do* cannot be my [disciple], and whoever does [not] love [father and] mother *as I do* cannot be my [disciple]. For my mother [. . .], but my true [mother] gave me life" (101:1–3).[6] For those who placed faith above family, conflict was inevitable.

---

[4] Unless otherwise indicated, all citations of the Bible are from the NRSV.

[5] Translations of the *Gospel of Thomas* are taken from the Scholars Version (SV).

[6] Emphasis mine. Whereas unbelieving natural parents are to be hated, believing spiritual

The New Testament contains various reflections of this conflict and of households divided by the Christian faith. Two basic statements addressing this situation are attributed to Jesus. The first saying, which draws on Mic 7:6 and its depiction of a total collapse in familial social relations,[7] occurs in various forms in three Christian gospels. Luke's version is as follows:

> Do you think that I have come to bring peace to the earth? No, I tell you, but rather division! From now on five in one household will be divided, three against two and two against three; they will be divided: father against son and son against father, mother against daughter and daughter against mother, mother-in-law against her daughter-in-law and daughter-in-law against mother-in-law (12:51–53).

Similar but characteristically different is the *Gospel of Thomas*, which reads,

> Jesus said: People probably think that I have come to cast peace upon the world. They do not recognize that I have come to cast conflicts upon the earth: fire, sword, war. For there will be five in a house: there will be three against two and two against three, father against son and son against father, and they will stand alone (16:1–4).[8]

The third version is that of Matthew:

> Do not think that I have come to bring peace to the earth: I have not come to bring peace, but a sword. For I have come to set a man against his father, and a daughter against her mother, and a daughter-in-law against her mother-in-law; and one's foes will be members of one's own household (10:34–36).

The second saying attributed to Jesus also occurs in three gospels, each in a context dealing with persecution. In Mark, Jesus warns his disciples, "Brother will betray brother to death, and a father his child, and

---

parents, who are the disciple's true parents and impart life, are to be loved. *Gos. Thom.* 101:3 is unfortunately fragmentary, but it is clear from the context that it provided the basis for Jesus' alleged hatred toward his mother. For Mary as someone who does not understand Jesus, see Mark 3:21, 31–35.

[7] On Mic 7:1–7, see esp. Hans Walter Wolff, *Micah: A Commentary* (trans. Gary Stansell; CC; Minneapolis: Augsburg, 1990), 200–10, and Marvin A. Sweeney, *The Twelve Prophets* (2 vols.; Berit Olam; Collegeville: Liturgical, 2000), 2:405–8.

[8] For purposes of enhanced clarity, I have slightly modified the SV translation. Those who stand "alone" are the true disciples; see *Gos. Thom.* 49; 75.

children will rise against parents and have them put to death; and you will be hated by all because of my name" (13:12–13a). Similarly, the Lukan Jesus warns, "You will be betrayed even by parents and brothers, by relatives and friends; and they will put some of you to death. You will be hated by all because of my name" (21:16–17). Again, the Matthean Jesus warns, "Brother will betray brother to death, and a father his child, and children will rise against parents and have them put to death; and you will be hated by all because of my name" (10:21–22a).

Other texts could also be mentioned,[9] but these are sufficient to indicate the domestic divisiveness of early Christianity and its consequences for Christian members of divided households. It is my thesis that heads of pagan households responded to the Christianization of their families by using a traditional form of household management, viz., threats, intimidation, and physical violence, in order to dissuade the new converts from continuing to proclaim and practice their faith. That is precisely how Homer in the *Iliad* depicts Zeus as managing his divine household, and many of his earthly counterparts followed his brutal example.[10] If domestic violence was already a component of how a *paterfamilias* sought to control members of his household, there is every reason to believe that he would have used it unhesitatingly against those who embraced the Christian faith.

One of the major differences between the ancient and modern worlds has to do with the composition of households. As is well known, ancient households were more comprehensive than modern nuclear families. The key difference for the purposes of this essay is that household slaves (οἰκέται) were viewed as members of the household, were often the victims of domestic violence, and occasionally were themselves guilty of such conduct. Indeed, violence toward slaves appears to have been the most prevalent form of domestic violence in the ancient world,[11] though that assessment is necessarily restricted to households that were sufficiently affluent to include slaves. In households that did not have slaves, wives and children were the main victims when the *paterfamilias* was the aggressor.[12] In this essay, I shall focus on domestic violence against slaves and

---

[9] Conflict between relatives, friends, and neighbors appears as a stock motif in various prophetic and apocalyptic texts; see, for example, Isa 19:2; 4 Ezra 5:9; 6:24; *1 Enoch* 56:7; 100:1–2.

[10] See especially Katerina Synodinou, "The Threats of Physical Abuse of Hera by Zeus in the Iliad," *Wiener Studien* 100 (1987): 13–22.

[11] In addition to what follows, see Plutarch, *Cohib. ira* 459d; 459f–460a; 460c; 462e.

[12] Hellenistic moralists were well aware that all family members were a prime target for

forego discussing in any detail the abuse suffered by wives and children.[13] I shall mention violence against wives, however, where consideration of this problem is useful in elucidating the plight of slaves.[14]

1 Peter and Domestic Violence

Of the texts and circumstances found in the New Testament, the situation depicted in 1 Peter is most germane to my discussion. Although I shall not offer an exegesis of the relevant passages (esp. 1 Pet 2:18–3:6), I shall illustrate the kinds of violence to which household slaves were subjected (1 Pet 2:18–25), especially by masters who were harsh (σκολιοῖς) and needed little provocation to inflict pain (λύπας) and suffering (πάσχοντες) on the slaves who irritated them (1 Pet 2:18–20). Given the extraordinary attention that the author of 1 Peter devotes to Christian slaves in regard to their masters and the way in which he adduces Christ as a paradigm for how and why slaves are to suffer (1 Pet 2:21–25), it is crystal clear that domestic violence against slaves was a major form of the persecution reflected in 1 Peter.[15]

Others in the household, especially Christian wives, were also victims of domestic violence and had to be encouraged to maintain the courage that they had shown in embracing the Christian faith without the blessing of their husbands. They were not to give in to fear and intimidation (μὴ φοβούμεναι μηδεμίαν πτόησιν), no matter what harm they might suffer from their husbands (1 Pet 3:1–6) or anyone else (3:14). Although both slaves and wives were told to be submissive (2:18; 3:1), their situations were fundamentally different. Whereas the author of 1 Peter hopes that the behavior of the wife, including her deferential obedience (3:6),

---

anger and abuse. Plutarch, for instance, in his *On the Control of Anger*, mentions parents (455c), wives (455f, 457a, 460f, 462a, 464a), children (455c, 457a), sons (464a), and daughters (455f) as potential victims.

[13] Friends, who were frequently de facto members of the family, were also among those who suffered violence. See, for example, Plutarch, *Cohib. ira* 460f: "Thinking ourselves despised, we . . . treat harshly wife and slaves and friends." See also 461a, c. Translations of pagan authors are those in the Loeb Classical Library, where available. Slight modifications are not usually indicated.

[14] I have treated violence against wives more fully in "Domestic Violence in the Ancient World: Preliminary Considerations and the Problem of Wife-Beating," which is scheduled to appear in a volume tentatively titled *Animosity, the Bible, and Us* (ed. H. F. van Rooy, F. J. van Rensburg, and J. T. Fitzgerald).

[15] On the general topic of slavery and the New Testament, see now J. Albert Harrill, *Slaves in the New Testament: Literary, Social, and Moral Dimensions* (Minneapolis: Fortress, 2006).

will lead to the conversion of the pagan husband (3:1–2), he entertains no such hopes in regard to the slaves' conduct. He simply wants to ensure that the slaves' behavior provides no basis for the suffering to which they will almost inevitably be subjected. His goal for them is God's approval, not their master's conversion (2:20). Consequently, whereas he offers wives a strategy for avoiding domestic violence, he provides slaves a rationale for enduring it.

From a pagan's perspective, the conversion of wives, slaves, and other members of the household undermined the unity and concord of the family, and inasmuch as the family was the basic unit of society, this destabilization of the household threatened the state. This is the perception that the author of 1 Peter wishes to combat, and he does so by encouraging Christians to honor the emperor and his representatives, and to do what is right (1 Pet 2:13–17). In short, he asserts that the Christianization of individuals within the household does not threaten either the family or the state, and the good conduct of Christians should demonstrate this truth and thereby put to rest the foolish apprehensions of the non-Christian world (1 Pet 2:15). The following discussion will demonstrate that the author's assessment of the situation was grounded in a firm knowledge of the abuse, both actual and potential, that occurred in many ancient households.

Domestic Violence: The Different Situations of Slaves and Wives

Ancient households varied considerably in the number of οἰκέται or domestic slaves they contained. Some had only one or two slaves, whereas others had considerably more domestics. Horace, for example, had three household slaves at Rome and eight slaves who worked on his country farm. That number pales in comparison to the 400 domestics who served in the town house of L. Pedanius Secundus, a Roman senator at the time of Nero.[16] Whether few or many, all household slaves were potentially subject to corporal punishment, especially if they did or said something to displease their masters. The orator Demosthenes was only reflecting social reality when he noted that a slave "had to answer for all his offenses with his body" (*Andr.* [= *Or.* 22].55). For Demosthenes, this corporal accountability was the crucial distinction between a slave and a free person, who could protect his person and account for his offenses by paying a fine.

---

[16] S. Scott Bartchy, "Slavery, New Testament," in *ABD* 6 (1992): 65–73, esp. 69.

Evidence from various kinds of ancient materials indicates that slaves were not only the members of the household most often beaten and assaulted but also the group with the highest mortality rate among victims. Legally, they were the master's property and could be dealt with essentially at the master's pleasure. Apart from some severe penalties for the premeditated murder of a slave, the checks against masters killing their own slaves in a fit of anger were essentially financial and moral, and the slaves' families posed no real obstacle to domestic violence. Wives, by contrast, had birth families from which they had come, and a strong check on a husband's capacity to batter his wife was her family, to which the husband would have to answer. And the more geographically proximate the wife's family, the greater the deterrence her family would likely have posed.[17]

For this reason, spousal abuse was probably a sporadic rather than a regular occurrence in archaic and classical Greece.[18] During that period, arranged marriage was an instrument of family alliance, with Greek women retaining extremely close ties to their birth families even after marriage. Having a father-in-law and/or brothers-in-law living practically next door was not a setting that was conducive to spousal abuse, especially if the in-laws happened to be bigger, stronger, and more numerous than the husband.[19] Furthermore, dowries likely functioned not only as a deterrent to divorce but also to domestic violence. Dowries needed to be returned to the wife's father at the time of divorce, and if the full dowry could not be returned, the Athenian ex-husband had to pay interest on the unreturned portion, doing so at the quite hefty rate of 18% per year. Consequently, "a threat from the woman's family to initiate a divorce and take back the dowry might be enough to prevent a man from ill-treating his wife."[20]

---

[17] My treatment of wives in archaic and classical Greece has been strongly influenced by Professor Thomas K. Hubbard of the Classics Department, University of Texas at Austin. Of course, I alone bear responsibility for any errors in the analysis provided here.

[18] Domestic violence against wives certainly occurred in classical Athens; see, for example, Aristophanes, *Lys.* 519–20.

[19] On arranged marriage as the general rule in classical Athens and marriage as a means of family alliance, see Sue Blundell, *Women in Classical Athens* (Classical World Series; London: Bristol Classical Press, 1998), 29, 33, 48. Of course, marriage was not restricted to residents of the same town, for marriages also united families living in different villages. As Blundell, *Women in Classical Athens*, 29, correctly notes, "For some of the women living in the rural communities of Athens, marriage also meant a move to another village or town, which might be some distance from her parents' home." Yet even then, most wives still lived in the same general geographical area as their birth families.

[20] Blundell, *Women in Classical Athens*, 41.

But that situation began to change in the Hellenistic and Roman periods. Although still the norm, arranged marriage was less universally practiced in the context of large urban centers,[21] and, more important, physical mobility was greatly enhanced.[22] The result was that many wives now lived far apart from their birth families and the protection from domestic violence that those birth families provided. Consequently, it is highly likely that incidences of domestic violence increased dramatically during the Greco-Roman period because greater physical mobility resulted in many wives living far away from the places where they were born and reared, and far apart from their birth families and circle of close friends. Without the social sanctions of a small, close-knit community to prevent spousal abuse, occurrences almost certainly became far more prevalent.[23]

The recognition that geographical separation from the wife's birth family may occasion maltreatment by her husband appears as early as Gen 31 when Jacob takes his wives Leah and Rachel and leaves the house of

---

[21] On the history of Greek marriage from the archaic period to the time of Augustus, see now Anne-Marie Vérilhac and Claude Vial, *Le mariage grec du VIe siècle av. J.C. à l'époque d'Auguste* (Bulletin de correspondance héllénique, Supplément 32; Athens: Ecole Française d'Athènes; Paris: Dépositaire, de Boccard Edition, 1998); for Greek marriage and the married woman in the Hellenistic period, see Claude Vatin, *Recherches sur le mariage et la condition de la femme mariée à l'époque hellénistique* (Bibliothèque des Écoles françaises d'Athènes et de Rome 216; Paris: E. de Boccard, 1970). On Roman marriage, see esp. Susan Treggiari, *Roman Marriage: iusti coniuges from the Time of Cicero to the Time of Ulpian* (Oxford: Clarendon, 1991).

[22] On the greatly enhanced physical mobility of people by the time of the early Roman Empire, see Abraham J. Malherbe, "The Cultural Context of the New Testament: The Greco-Roman World," in *NIB* 8:12–26, esp. 12–13. Of the various factors that contributed to this greater physical mobility, two may be mentioned. The first was the emergence of Koine Greek as the lingua franca of the Greco-Roman world, which facilitated communication between those who spoke different native languages. The second was the network of roads built by the Romans and by local municipal benefactors. This capillary net of roads, along with wayside inns and taverns, as well as the practice of hospitality, made travel much easier. On travel in antiquity, see Lionel Casson, *Travel in the Ancient World* (Toronto: Hakkert, 1974); and on Roman roads, see Raymond Chevallier, *Roman Roads* (Berkeley: University of California Press, 1976). For students of early Christianity, the discussion by William M. Ramsay ("Roads and Travel in the New Testament," in *A Dictionary of the Bible* [ed. James Hastings; 5 vols.; New York: Scribner, 1898–1904], 5:375–402) is still valuable. On the different kinds of hospitality in the ancient world, including that extended to travelers, see John T. Fitzgerald, "Hospitality," in *Dictionary of New Testament Background* (ed. C. Evans and S. Porter; Downers Grove: InterVarsity, 2000), 522–25.

[23] See esp. Augustine, *Conf.* 9.9.19, who depicts wife-beating as a common phenomenon in Thagaste. If spousal abuse was a routine occurrence in Thagaste, a small municipality in Numidia, it would certainly have been more widespread in the large urban centers of the Mediterranean world.

Laban, his father-in-law, to return home. When Laban overtakes Jacob, he stresses that Leah and Rachel are his daughters (31:43) and accuses his son-in-law of treating them like prisoners of war (31:26). Given the fact that Laban is unable to prevent Jacob's departure, the question arises as to what he can do to protect his daughters from their "abusive" husband when he is no longer physically present to do so (31:43).[24] Before jumping immediately to Jacob's defense, one should recall that Jacob clearly did not regard Leah and Rachel with equal affection, and he treated the latter as the "loved" wife and the former as the "hated" or "disliked" one (29:30, 31–35; 30:16–20; see also Deut 21:15–17). From Laban's perspective, therefore, what reason was there to think Jacob might not soon take other wives and begin to treat Rachel with less regard or even mistreat her and Leah?[25] His solution is a covenant between them (Gen 31:24) in which Jacob agrees under oath (31:53) that he will not abuse Leah and Rachel.[26] Invoking Yahweh as witness, Laban tells Jacob, "If you *ill-treat* my daughters, or if you take wives in addition to my daughters, though no one else is with us,[27] remember that God is witness between you and me" (31:50). Consequently, once the covenant is formalized by sacrifice (31:54), Yahweh becomes the official adjudicator between Laban and Jacob (31:53), the guardian of their oath-sacrifice (*Eidopfer*), and thereby the protector of Laban's daughters against spousal abuse.[28]

---

[24] As Gerhard von Rad, *Genesis: A Commentary* (3rd rev. ed.; OTL; London: SCM, 1972), 309, notes, "In a strange land [Laban's] daughters had no legal protection."

[25] I am presenting the story from the perspective of Laban, who views Jacob's unannounced departure as morally reprehensible and accuses him of various offenses, including the plunder of his household (31:26–30). Readers of the Jacob-Laban cycle of stories know, however, that it is Laban who has consistently wronged Jacob. Moreover, Leah and Rachel accuse Laban of being an abusive father who regards them as foreigners (31:14–16). That Leah as Jacob's "disliked wife" prefers her husband to her father is particularly telling as to the true situation.

[26] My treatment of this passage is restricted to the intrafamilial conflict between Jacob and Laban and ignores other important features of the pact between the two men.

[27] N. H. Snaith, "Genesis XXXI 50," *VT* 14 (1964) 373, captures the thrust of the clause when he translates "when no man of our (father's) kin is watching." See also Claus Westermann, *Genesis 12–36* (trans. John J. Scullion; CC; Minneapolis: Augsburg, 1985), 488: "when no one is there to see."

[28] To break an oath in the ancient world is to commit perjury, which is fundamentally a religious offense against the deity in whose name one swears (Exod 20:7). For oaths and perjury in the ancient world, see John T. Fitzgerald, "The Problem of Perjury in Greek Context: Prolegomena to an Exegesis of Matthew 5:33; 1 Timothy 1:10; and *Didache* 2.3," in *The Social World of the First Christians: Essays in Honor of Wayne A. Meeks* (ed. L. M. White and O. L. Yarbrough; Minneapolis: Fortress, 1995), 156–77, and "Eid: IV.

The Hebrew word translated above as "ill-treat" is the *piel* of ענה, one of several Hebrew terms for abuse and maltreatment. The meaning of the term in the Hebrew Bible is quite broad, ranging from physical oppression to mental anguish, and it can even indicate rape (Gen 34:2; Judg 20:5; 2 Sam 13:12, 14, 32).[29] In all likelihood, its use in Gen 31:50 is intentionally broad, designed formally to cover abuse of any kind, whether physical, mental, or sexual.[30] Yet the appearance of the same term in Gen 16:6 is suggestive, for there it describes the way in which Sarai oppressed her slave-girl Hagar, treating her so severely that she fled (16:6, 8) to escape her affliction (16:11). Similarly, the same word is used to describe the physical pain that Joseph endured as an imprisoned slave when his feet were placed in fetters and an iron collar was put around his neck (Ps 105:18), and it likewise describes the physical oppression of the Hebrews as the slaves of the Egyptians (Gen 15:3; Exod 1:11–12; Deut 26:6). Against this backdrop, the implication is that to ill-treat a wife is to treat her like a slave,[31] and not with the dignity and affection that any wife deserves.[32] And what prompts Laban's concern for his children and their rights is the physical separation from his daughters that will ensue from Jacob's departure.

Neues Testament," in *Religion in Geschichte und Gegenwart: Handwörterbuch für Theologie und Religionswissenschaft* (ed. H. D. Betz et al; 4th ed.; 8 vols.; Tübingen: Mohr Siebeck, 1998–2005), 2:1125–26. The oath-sacrifice was also a part of Greek society, attested as early as Homer. See now Margo Kitts, *Sanctified Violence in Homeric Society: Oath-making Rituals and Narratives in the Iliad* (Cambridge: Cambridge University Press, 2005); and John T. Fitzgerald, "Perjury in Ancient Religion and Modern Law: A Comparative Analysis of Perjury in Homer and United States Law," *The New Testament and Early Christian Literature in Greco-Roman Context: Studies in Honor of David E. Aune* (ed. J. Fotopoulos; NovTSup 141; Leiden: Brill, 2006), 183–202.

[29] *HALOT* 2:852–54. For discussions of the term, see Paul Wegner, "ענה," in *NIDOTTE* 3:449–52, and Erhard Gerstenberger, "ענה II," in *TDOT* 11:230–52, who, however, errs by suggesting that the verb in Gen 31:50 simply means "to slight" (237). Much more is involved than that minimalizing interpretation of the term suggests.

[30] Sexual abuse is not only coerced intercourse but also the withholding of conjugal rights. For the latter, see *b. Yoma* 77b, von Rad, *Genesis*, 312, and Rashi (according to Kenneth A. Mathews, *Genesis 11:27–50:26* (NAC 1B; Nashville: Broadman & Holman, 2005), 534 n. 387.

[31] Compare Laban's earlier complaint that Jacob was treating his wives like prisoners of war (Gen 31:26), and the claim that Shechem, in raping Dinah, had treated her like a whore (Gen 34:31).

[32] For a different interpretation—that Jacob is not to deprive Rachel and Leah of their livelihood—see J. Paradise, "What Did Laban Demand of Jacob? A New Reading of Genesis 31:50 and Exodus 21:10," in *Tehillah le-Moshe: Biblical and Judaic Studies in Honor of Moshe Greenberg* (ed. M. Cogan, B. L. Eichler, and J. H. Tigay; Winona Lake: Eisenbrauns, 1997), 91–98.

Whether the abuse of wives was a sporadic or regular feature of domestic life prior to the Greco-Roman period, it is certain that violence against slaves was well-nigh universal in the ancient world and not limited to particular regions or time periods. Of course, this does not mean that all slaves in all households were abused—far from it. Many slaves were loved and treated with extraordinary kindness by their masters.[33] But it does mean that violence against slaves was a recurring feature of domestic life through antiquity, and it is to a description of that violence that we now turn, drawing particularly upon the evidence provided by moralists and philosophers of the Greco-Roman world. The latter were well aware of the ways in which various masters mistreated their slaves, especially when they were angry.[34]

Domestic Violence against Slaves

Violence against slaves unquestionably resulted in death on many occasions.[35] Whatever the specific provocation, the precipitating factor was almost always the master's anger. As Seneca says in his *On Anger*, "How many slaves a master's anger has driven to flight, how many to death!" (3.5.4). The philosophical treatises on anger are an important primary but neglected source for instances of domestic violence, especially against slaves. According to Plutarch, "Newly purchased slaves inquire about their new master, not whether he is superstitious or envious, but whether he is quick tempered" (*On Calumny*, frg. 153 Sandbach; *Cohib. ira* 462a).

Although homicides involving slaves were statistically the highest in ancient households, in most instances the slaves were not killed but rather beaten. The severity of their injuries varied according to the nature of their offense, the character of the master, and other such factors. Sometimes the violence was a savage case of aggravated assault that stopped just short of

[33] S. Scott Bartchy, *MALLON CHRESAI: First-Century Slavery and the Interpretation of 1 Corinthians 7:21* (1973; repr. Eugene, Ore.: Wipf & Stock, 2003), 67–72, rightly notes that instances of both cruelty and kindness toward slaves are well documented.

[34] On the use of material from the Greco-Roman moralists to interpret social data supplied by other ancient sources and to illumine early Christian texts, see Abraham J. Malherbe, "Hellenistic Moralists and the New Testament," in *ANRW* 2.26.1: 267–333; and L. Michael White and John T. Fitzgerald, "*Quod est comparandum*: The Problem of Parallels," in *Early Christianity and Classical Culture: Comparative Studies in Honor of Abraham J. Malherbe* (ed. J. T. Fitzgerald, T. H. Olbricht, and L. M. White; NovTSup 110; Leiden: Brill, 2003; repr. Atlanta: Society of Biblical Literature, 2005), 13–39.

[35] One of the most shocking stories of domestic violence concerns the ex-slave Vedius Pollio, who had slaves thrown into a pond with flesh-eating fish. See Seneca, *On Anger* 3.40, and Cassius Dio, *Roman History* 54.23.

death, and sometimes masters used branding irons as a means of torture. In response to such extreme violence, some slaves chose suicide. The "tactless man" in the *Characters* of Theophrastus, for example, "stands watching while a slave is being whipped and announces that a boy of his own once hanged himself after such a beating" (*Char.* 12).[36] But more often it was a routine beating with a whip or rod or some other form of simple assault,[37] such as a blow with the hand.[38] The latter is precisely the form of beating anticipated by the author of 1 Peter, who uses the verb κολαφίζω ("to strike with the fist or knuckles" [κόλαφος = κόνδυλος]) to describe the master's anticipated battering of the slave (2:20).[39] Fetters were used to prevent flight—the slave's chief alternative to domestic violence other than murdering the master or launching a slave revolt.[40] But the bodies and especially the faces of slaves gave clear proof that they had been brutalized, often by angry masters. As Plutarch says in his *On the Control of Anger* (*Cohib. ira* 463a-b), "The tokens of savage and irascible men you will see on the faces of their servants and in the marks branded upon them and their fetters. 'The only music heard within the house' of an angry man 'is wailing cries,' as the stewards are being lashed within and the servant-maids being tortured."

Although there were masters who were kind and gentle, no one should suffer under the happy illusion that ancient slavery was a humane institution. Some of the ways in which hapless slaves were brutalized are absolutely chilling. To illustrate this, I shall give two excerpts from Galen's work on passions.[41] The first is as follows:

---

[36] The translation is that of James Diggle, *Theophrastus: Characters* (Cambridge: Cambridge University Press, 2004), 103.

[37] For whipping as the standard punishment for slaves, see Glenn R. Morrow, *Plato's Law of Slavery in its Relation to Greek Law* (Illinois Studies in Language and Literature 25; Urbana: University of Illinois, 1939), 66–71; and Virginia J. Hunter, *Policing Athens: Social Control in the Attic Lawsuits, 420–320 B.C.* (Princeton: Princeton University Press, 1994), 154–73.

[38] Plutarch, *Cohib. ira* 461b: "he who with rods and blows makes his servants at table hasten about running and crying out and sweating."

[39] On this verb, see John T. Fitzgerald, *Cracks in an Earthen Vessel: An Examination of the Catalogues of Hardships in the Corinthian Correspondence* (SBLDS 99; Atlanta: Scholars Press, 1988), 143–44 n. 89.

[40] Xenophon, *Oec.* 3.4: "in some households nearly all the servants are in fetters."

[41] Translations of Galen's work on the passions (= *Passions*) are those of Paul W. Harkins, *Galen: On the Passions and Errors of the Soul* (Columbus: Ohio State University Press, 1963), though I have occasionally made minor modifications to his renderings. References are to the book and chapter of Galen's treatise. I am indebted to Loveday Alexander,

> Other men, however, not only <strike> with their fists but kick and gouge out the eyes and stab with a stylus when they happen to have one in their hands. I saw a man, in his anger, strike a slave in the eye with a reed pen. The Emperor Hadrian, they say, struck one of his slaves in the eye with a stylus; and . . . the man lost his eye because of the wound (*Passions* 1.4).

The second excerpt concerns one of Galen's friends. This individual had a number of admirable qualities but was utterly incapable of controlling his rage when it came to his slaves:

> A friend of mine from Gortyna in Crete . . . was so prone to anger that he used to assail his servants with his hands and even sometimes his feet, but far more frequently with a whip or any piece of wood that happened to be handy. . . . When we had passed through Eleusis and were coming to the Thriasian Plain, he asked the [two] servants [who were with us] . . . about a piece of luggage, but they could give him no answer. He fell into a rage. Since he had nothing else with which to strike the young men, he picked up a good-sized sword in its scabbard and came down on the heads of both of them with the sword—scabbard and all. Nor did he bring down the flat side (for in this way he would have done no great damage) but struck with the cutting edge of the sword. The blade cut right through the scabbard and inflicted two very serious wounds on the heads of both—for he struck each of them twice. When he saw the blood pouring forth in abundant streams, he left us and quickly went off . . . to Athens (*Passions* 1.4).

The only silver lining in that despicable story is that this act of violence so upset Galen's friend that it led him finally to confront his problem. Slowly but surely, he began to gain control over his anger and make moral progress. But the problem of domestic violence toward slaves was not the simple result of individuals failing to keep their passions in check. To be blunt, the moralists' reductionistic solution simply overlooked other key factors.

A number of nonpsychological factors made domestic violence against slaves not only likely but also inevitable. Let me mention only two of these. First, "slaves were stereotyped as rascally, prone to excesses

---

"The Passions in the Novels of Chariton and Xenophon," for calling my attention to the importance of Galen's treatise on the passions and providing a helpful analysis of it. I have shamelessly borrowed a few of her fine turns of phrase. Her article is scheduled to appear in *The Passions and Moral Progress* (London: Routledge).

of drinking and eating, and dumb,"⁴² and those stereotypes made it easier for masters to think that they had to use physical force "to whip them into shape." Second, slaves were not only stereotyped as dumb and morally inferior but also dehumanized and often thought of as animals. This animalizing of slaves began early in Greek thought and even appears in early Christian literature.⁴³ As Keith Bradley has concluded, "The ease of association between slave and animal . . . was a staple aspect of ancient mentality, and one that stretched back to a very early period: the common Greek term for 'slave', ἀνδράποδον, 'man-footed creature', was built on the foundation of a common term for cattle, τετράποδον, 'four-footed creature'."⁴⁴ This animalizing of slaves is reflected even in how one was exhorted to feed them. In his treatise on household management, Xenophon discusses the issue of how to make slaves more obedient to their masters' orders. One of the participants in the dialogue, Ischomachus, makes the following argument: "But in dealing with slaves the training thought suitable for wild animals is also a very effective way of teaching obedience; for you will do much with them by filling their bellies with the food that they hanker after" (*Oec.* 13.9). In short, for Ischomachus, household slaves are to be treated just like domestic animals; give them as much food as they want, and they will behave. But what if they do not behave? The implication is clear: just as you reward colts and puppies when they obey you and punish them when they do not, you teach disobedient slaves by punishing them (*Oec.* 13.6–8). Seneca is more explicit. In condemning "cruel and inhuman conduct toward [slaves]," he affirms, "We maltreat them, not as if they were humans, but as if they were beasts of burden" (*Ep.* 47.5).

With some masters, the slightest provocation could occasion anger and thus subject the slave to punishment. As Galen notes, "Whenever a man becomes violently angry over little things and bites and kicks his servants, you may be sure that this man is in a state of passion" (*Passions* 1.2). Seneca chides such masters when he says, "We should not be exasperated by trifling and paltry incidents. A slave is too slow, or the water for the

---

⁴² Peter Garnsey, "The Middle Stoics and Slavery," in *Hellenistic Constructs: Essays in Culture, History, and Historiography* (ed. P. Cartledge, P. Garnsey, and E. Gruen; Berkeley: University of California Press, 1997), 159–74, esp. 160.

⁴³ See *Acts Thom.* 83: "Although you are men they lay burdens upon you, as upon the irrational beasts, because your lords think that you are not men like themselves." The translation is that of J. K. Elliott, *The Apocryphal New Testament* (Oxford: Clarendon, 1993), 480.

⁴⁴ See esp. Keith Bradley, "Animalizing the Slave: The Truth of Fiction," *JRS* 90 (2000): 110–25, esp. 110.

wine is lukewarm [i.e., rather than hot], or the couch-cushion disarranged, or the table too carelessly set—it is madness to be incensed by such things" (*Ira* 2.25.1), that is, trivial things that the slave had failed to do properly. Elsewhere he depicts a master dining "with a mob of standing slaves." While the master gorges himself with food, "the poor slaves may not move their lips, even to speak. The slightest murmur is repressed by the rod; even a chance sound—a cough, a sneeze, or a hiccup—is visited with the lash. There is a grievous penalty for the slightest breach of silence" (*Ep.* 47.3). In a similar way, Plutarch, in an attempt to persuade masters to delay the punishment of slaves so as not to do so in anger, asks,

> Which of us is so harsh that he scourges and chastises a slave because five or ten days ago he over-roasted the meat or upset the table or came too slowly at our bidding? And yet these are the very things which cause us to be excited and in a cruel and implacable mood at the moment they happen and are still fresh in our memory (*Cohib. ira* 459f-460a).

Again: "'No more unpleasant supper could there be' [Homer, *Ody.* 20.392] than that wherein household slaves are beaten and wife is reviled because something is burned or smoked or not salted enough, or because the bread is too cold" (461c; see also 461e).[45]

Both male and female masters beat their slaves, with Jewish and Christian households differing little in this regard from pagan ones.[46] Women were often viewed as even more susceptible to anger than men (Plutarch, *Cohib. ira* 457b), so it is not surprising that they are depicted as also beating their slaves. Galen, for example, praises his father but pours contempt on his mother and her "disgraceful passions." Not only did "she constantly shriek at my father and fight with him" but she also "was so very prone to anger that sometimes she bit her handmaids" (*Passions* 1.8). But Galen's mother was not alone in being abusive. In Tob 3:9, one of Raguel's female servant girls accuses his daughter Sarah of scourging them: "Why do you whip (μαστιγοῖς) us?" John Chrysostom (*Hom. Eph.* 15) makes clear that both pagan and Christian women beat their maids and verbally berated them. He adds that some women are

> so fierce and so savage as to lash them to such a degree that the bruises will not disappear with the day. For they will strip the dam-

---

[45] A similar list of trivial offenses by slaves that evoke anger is given by Martin of Braga, *On Anger* 7.

[46] For the story of Augustine's father whipping his slave-girls at his mother's insistence, see *Conf.* 9.9.20.

sels, and call their husbands for the purpose, and oftentimes tie them to the pallets. . . . Then if [the slave should] have occasion to go to the bath, there are bruises on her back when she is naked, and she carries about with her the marks of your cruelty. . . . [Furthermore,] some are come to such a height of indecency as to uncover the head and to drag their maidservants by the hair.[47]

Yet Chrysostom's discussion does not indicate the severity of the problem within the Christian community. More revealing is a decision made by a council at Elvira (Spain) in the first decade of the fourth century. At that council, "the bishops decided that if an enraged mistress whipped her maidservant so badly that she died within three days, 'and it is a question whether she killed her on purpose or by accident,' she was to do penance in order to be readmitted after five or seven years, depending on the circumstances."[48]

According to Seneca, Romans of his time were particularly abusive toward their slaves, acting in a manner that was "excessively haughty, cruel, and insulting" (*Ep.* 47.11). Thus it is not surprising that a Latin proverb of his time proclaimed, "[You have] as many enemies as you have slaves." Ever the moralist, Seneca comments, "They are not enemies when we acquire them; we make them enemies" (*Ep.* 47.5).

The popular philosophers and other moralists occasionally commented on the phenomenon of masters beating their slaves. They typically sought not to stop masters from punishing slaves but only to ensure that they did so when they were no longer angry. Although their comments sometimes express or imply a concern for the slaves' welfare, their main concern is thus not for the slave who is being abused but for the abusive master, who has been overcome by his angry emotions and no longer acts rationally. That is, even when the moralists comment directly on instances of domestic violence, they typically focus their attention on the master's moral slavery to the passions, not on his or her abuse of the legal slave.[49]

Galen belonged to the "don't flog while you're angry" school of thought, but added a novel twist befitting a physician:

> When I was a young man I imposed on myself an injunction that I have observed through my whole life, namely, never to strike any slave of my household with my hand. My father practiced

---

[47] All translations of Chrysostom are taken from the *NPNF* (slightly modified).

[48] Grant, *Early Christianity and Society*, 92–93.

[49] See, e.g., Xenophon, *Hell.* 5.3.7; Plutarch, *Cohib. ira* 459a–460c; Aulus Gellius, *Noct. att.* 1.26.4–9.

this same restraint. Many were the friends he reproved when they had bruised a tendon while striking their slaves in the teeth; he told them that they deserved to have a stroke and die in the fit of passion which had come upon them. They could have waited a little while, he said, and used a rod or whip to inflict as many blows as they wished and to accomplish the act with reflection. . . . So, too, you must exhort yourself never to strike a slave with your own hands, nor to assign the task to another while you are still angry; put it off until the next day. After your wrath has subsided, you will consider with greater prudence how many lashes should be given to the one who has merited the flogging (*Passions* 1.4–5).

Among Christian critics of the practice of whipping slaves, Chrysostom (*Hom. Eph.* 15) is the most eloquent. He strongly discourages the practice and finds the flogging of a naked female slave by the male master particularly monstrous. He prefers that slaves be corrected by flattery and acts of kindness. Yet even he ultimately allows a Christian woman to beat her slave-girl "with the rod and with stripes," though he insists that it must be done "neither frequently nor immoderately."

Let me conclude this discussion of violence toward slaves with the important caveat that not all slaves were brutalized, and that some slaves and their masters had affectionate regard for one another. Seneca, for example, argues that slaves should respect (*colant*) their masters rather than fear (*timeant*) them, and he explains that "respect means love (*amatur*)" and, in words that bring to mind 1 John 4:18, affirms that "love (*amor*) and fear cannot be mingled" (*Ep.* 47.18). In addition, he argues at length that slaves can provide benefits to their masters (*Ben.* 3.18–28) and gives an impressive collection of examples in support of his claim (*Ben.* 3.22–27). He defends dining with slaves (*Ep.* 47.2), calls them "unpretentious friends" (*Ep.* 47.1), and advises Lucilius to hunt for friends among his slaves at home (*Ep.* 47.16). "Associate with your slave on kindly, even on affable terms," he tells Lucilius; "let him talk with you, plan with you, live with you" (*Ep.* 47.13). "Treat your inferiors as you would be treated by your betters" (*Ep.* 47.11).[50] In addition, he praises Lucilius for living on friendly (*familiariter*) terms with his slaves (*Ep.* 47.1) and in not wishing

---

[50] Cf. Cicero, *Off.* 1.41: "We must have regard for justice even towards the humblest. Now the humblest station and the poorest fortune are those of slaves; and they give us no bad rule who bid us treat our slaves as we should our employees: they must be required to work; they must be given their dues." But see also 2.24: "those who keep subjects in check by force would of course have to employ severity—masters, for example, toward their servants, when these cannot be held in control in any other way."

to be feared by them (*Ep.* 47.19). But what implications does that kind of master-slave relationship have for the master's use of corporal punishment? As one might anticipate, corporal punishment has no place at all. Breaking radically with the ancient slave/animal equation, he tells Lucilius, "So I hold that you are entirely right in not wishing to be feared by your slaves, and in lashing them merely with the tongue; only dumb animals need the thong" (*Ep.* 47.19).

Seneca's discussion of how masters should treat their slaves finds an echo in 1 Pet 2:18, where the author describes some masters as "kind and considerate" (ἀγαθοῖς καὶ ἐπιεικέσιν).[51] It should be noted that he uses these highly positive terms of pagan masters, who are not the problem that he is confronting in this section. He focuses instead on the severe masters whose abuse of Christian slaves has occasioned his remarks. Unlike the household codes of Colossians (4:1) and Ephesians (6:9), the one in 1 Peter does not contain any instructions for Christian masters, apparently because there are no such masters in the Christian communities to which the author writes. If there had been, it would have been interesting to compare his exhortation to that of Seneca. Similarly, Seneca directs all his comments about slavery to slave-owners; not once, as far as we know, did he ever address himself directly to slaves.[52] Therefore, Seneca's call for humane treatment and 1 Peter's exhortation to good conduct and steadfast endurance are addressed to two quite different audiences.

Conclusion

Although this discussion has been limited, the results are quite revealing. The evidence suggests that ancient families, like our own, were often battle fronts rather than centers of refuge. The primary victims of domestic terrorism were household slaves whose words or deeds had angered their masters, both male and female, and who had to pay for their offenses with their bodies. Wives were also frequently victims of their husbands' rage, and to survive physically they were often forced to become servile in their attitudes and actions.[53]

---

[51] On ἐπιείκεια as a virtue, see the discussion of this term by Donald Dale Walker, *Paul's Offer of Leniency: Populist Ideology and Rhetoric in a Pauline Letter Fragment* (WUNT 2.152; Tübingen: Mohr Siebeck, 2002).

[52] I owe this point to Dimitris J. Kyrtatas, *The Social Structure of the Early Christian Communities* (London: Verso, 1987), 32.

[53] Anger was not the only emotion that occasioned domestic violence against wives. Jealousy did as well, sometimes in combination with anger. Plutarch, for instance, lists "the jealous man with his wife" as being among those people most prone to anger (*Cohib. ira*

As this essay has argued, early Christianity was a notorious domestic troublemaker, and the conversion of individual members of pagan households led to a new chapter in the history of domestic violence. To the long list of irritations that occasioned household violence, the Christian identity of slaves, wives, and children was now added. To combat the Christianization of his household, the pagan *paterfamilias* resorted to threats, intimidation, and acts of physical violence, which were traditional methods of exercising social control. This is the situation reflected in 1 Peter 2–3, where the author counsels battered slaves and wives in regard to the domestic terrorism that they were encountering. In some cases, he hoped that wives could lead their husbands to Christ by means of their conduct. In other cases, he hoped that the good conduct of both wives and slaves would minimize or eliminate the problem. In the final analysis, however, he knew that some Christians, wives as well as slaves, would suffer domestic violence for their faith in Christ, and to them he offered the example of Christ himself (2:21–24) and the assurance that it was both a blessing and a privilege to share Christ's sufferings (4:13).

457b). For an example of domestic violence occasioned by a combination of jealousy and anger, see Chariton's story of Chaereas and Callirhoe (see esp. 1.4.5).

3

The *Virtus Feminarum* in 1 Timothy 2:9–15

Abraham J. Malherbe

NEW Testament scholarship has not been kind to the Pastoral Epistles. Critics have denied the author any originality of thought, alleged that he had only a superficial knowledge of traditions he derived from Judaism, Christianity and paganism (especially popular philosophy), and judged him incapable of constructing a coherent system of his own.[1] However, of late some scholars have argued in detail that the author was more original and consistent in his thinking than has been thought,[2] and others have in general expressed a more favorable assessment of what he achieved.[3] In a couple of recent studies, I have proposed that the author

---

[1] E. g., A. T. Hanson, *The Pastoral Epistles* (NCBC; Grand Rapids: Eerdmans, 1982) 39, 42; L. R. Donelson, *Pseudepigraphy and Ethical Argument in the Pastoral Epistles* (HUT 22; Tübingen: Mohr Siebeck, 1986), 135–41; J. Roloff, *Der erste Brief an Timotheus* (EKK; Zurich: Benziger, 1988), 363–65; F. Young, *The Theology of the Pastoral Epistles* (Cambridge University Press, 1994), 50–55.

[2] E. g., K. Läger, *Die Christologie der Pastoralbriefe* (HThSt 12; Münster: Lit, 1996); A. Y. Lau, *Manifest in the Flesh: The Epiphany Christology in the Pastoral Epistles* (WUNT 2.86; Tübingen: Mohr Siebeck, 1996).

[3] E. g., Raymond F. Collins, *1 & 2 Timothy and Titus: A Commentary* (NTL; Louisville: Westminster John Knox, 2002); Carl R. Holladay, *Critical Introduction to the New Testament* (Nashville: Abingdon, 2005), 436–41. If the letters are examined individually rather than as a collection, and each is understood in terms of the circumstances reflected in each individual letter, greater coherence in the theology of each letter is likely to be discovered. For viewing the letters thus, see especially the work of Luke T. Johnson, e. g., *The First and Second Letters to Timothy* (AB 35A; New York: Doubleday, 2001). A growing tendency to

was more knowledgeable of contemporary philosophy than he has been thought to be, and that he adapted the philosophic paraenetic style to suit his own purpose.[4] Situating the Pastoral Epistles more firmly in their intellectual context, considerably illuminates the letters, which is not to claim, however, that their theological coherence has become crystal clear in the process.

Having recently discussed aspects of the letters' theology and style, in this paper I wish to focus on 1 Tim 2:9–15, which deals with ethics. It has been argued forcefully by some commentators that this section of text does not cohere literarily, but, including v. 8, is a cluster of five distinct pieces,[5] a contention that has been countered by others on both literary and thematic grounds.[6] Most commentators think that 2:8–15, although it is a new section, is connected to 2:1–7, even if only loosely.[7] The main reasons for these assessments are that the grammar is awkward, making for disjointed statements, and a number of traditions are employed without being developed in this context or shown to cohere with each other. In contrast, attempts have been made to identify themes that unite the entire chapter, such as worship or mission,[8] or to view it in light of classifica-

---

view the letters in this way is described well by Jens Herzer in a review article, "Abschied vom Konsens? Die Pseudepigraphie der Pastoralbriefe als Herausforderung an die neutestamentliche Wissenschaft," *TLZ* 129 (2004): 1267–82.

[4] Abraham J. Malherbe, "'Christ Jesus Came into the World to Save Sinners': Soteriology in the Pastoral Epistles," pages 331–58 in *Salvation in the New Testament: Perspectives on Soteriology* (ed. Jan G. van der Watt; NovTSup 121;Leiden: Brill, 2005); "Paraenesis in the Epistle to Titus," pages 297–317 in *Early Christian Paraenesis in Context* (ed. by James Starr and Troels Engberg-Pedersen; BZNW 125; New York: de Gruyter, 2004).

[5] E.g., James D. Miller, *The Pastoral Letters as Composite Documents* (SNTSMS 93; Cambridge: Cambridge University Press, 1997), 73.

[6] Ray Van Neste, *Cohesion and Structure in the Pastoral Epistles* (JSNTSSup 280; London: T. & T. Clark, 2004), 36–40.

[7] See the discussion in Van Neste, *Cohesion and Structure*, 83–85.

[8] More specifically, prayer: I. Howard Marshall, *A Critical and Exegetical Commentary on the Pastoral Epistles* (ICC; Edinburgh: T. & T. Clark, 1999), 415–16, but prayer associated with propagation of the gospel. Despite the confusion he observes in the "cluster," Miller (*Composite Documents*, 70) thinks that the catchword is προσεύχεσθαι (v. 8), and that the general issue addressed is "Directions for Public Worship." Jürgen Roloff (*Der erste Brief an Timotheus* [EKK; Neukirchen: Benziger,1988], 107–8) thinks that worship in the larger context of 2:1—3:13 has to do with conduct in the household of God.

tions of the larger section, 2:1—3:13, such as the first church order,[9] or a scheme of domestic duties.[10]

It is my contention in this paper that there is greater literary coherence to 2:9–15 than has been recognized, and that popular philosophical discussions of σωφροσύνη suggest that the text should be viewed within that rubric. The paper is a prolegomenon to exegesis of the passage.

The Literary Coherence of 1 Timothy 2:9–15

It will be useful to view the text schematically, beginning by observing the way in which the author sets up his treatment of the behavior of women, which is his major interest in chapter 2.

> (2:1) First of all, then, I urge that petitions, prayers, intercessions, and thanksgivings be made for all people, (2) for kings and all those in prominent positions, that we may lead a calm and quiet life with all godliness and dignity (ἵνα ἤρεμον καὶ ἡσύχιον βίον διάγωμεν ἐν πάσῃ εὐσεβείᾳ καὶ σεμνότητι). (3) This is good and acceptable in the eyes of God our Savior (τοῦτο καλὸν καὶ ἀπόδεκτον ἐνώπιον τοῦ σωτῆρος ἡμῶν θεοῦ), (4) who wishes all people to be saved (θέλει σωθῆναι) and come to know the truth. (5) For there is one God . . . [the creedal formulation and an autobiographical statement extend to v. 7].
>
> (8) I wish therefore that men pray in every place (of worship), raising holy hands without anger and dispute. (9) Likewise, (I also wish that) women adorn themselves (κοσμεῖν ἑαυτάς) with conduct that accords with order and decorum (ἐν καταστολῇ κοσμίῳ), with self-respect and moderation (μετὰ αἰδοῦς καὶ σωφροσύνης κοσμεῖν ἑαυτάς), (in particular), not (μὴ) with braided hair and gold, nor with pearls or extravagant dress, (10) but as befits (ἀλλ' ὃ πρέπει) women who profess reverence of God (θεοσέβειαν), (to adorn themselves) with good works (δι' ἔργων ἀγαθῶν). (11) A woman is to learn in quietness (ἐν ἡσυχίᾳ) and with full submission (ὑποταγῇ); (12) I do not (μὴ)

---

[9] So, briefly, Martin Dibelius and Hans Conzelmann, *The Pastoral Epistles* (trans. P. Buttolph and A. Yarbro; Hermeneia; Philadelphia: Fortress, 1972), 35; more extensively, Jerome Quinn and William C. Wacker, *The First and Second Letters to Timothy* (ECC; Grand Rapids: Eerdmans, 2000), who understand the apostolic exhortations of 2:1—3:13 as addressed to "the whole community of believers and their ministers."

[10] Which might make the section part of the topos "Obedience to the Authorities." So Norbert Brox, "*Die Pastoralbriefe: 1 Timotheus, 2 Timotheus, Titus* (RNT; Regensburg: Pustet, 1989), 121–22, on 2:1—3:16. *Contra* Roloff, *Der erste Brief an Timotheus*, 108–10.

permit a woman to teach or to exercise authority over a man, but (ἀλλὰ) she is to remain quiet (ἐν ἡσυχίᾳ). (13) For (γάρ) Adam was formed first, then Eve. (14) And Adam was not deceived, but the woman was deceived and fell into transgression. (15) But she will be saved (σωθήσεται δέ) through childbearing, if they continue in faith and love and holiness with moderation (ἐν πίστει καὶ ἀγάπῃ καὶ ἁγιασμῷ μετὰ σωφροσύνης).

The exhortation to pray (vv. 1–2) and the theological affirmation that follows (vv. 3–4) introduce terms that will be significant in vv. 9–15: quiet (ἡσύχιον), godliness (εὐσέβεια), and salvation (σωτήρ, σώζω). The first two describe conduct or demeanor, the third is part of the theological motivation for that conduct.

The literary coherence of the passage has been achieved in a number of ways. To begin with, the directive to men (v. 8) is brief, six times shorter than that to women. That they are to pray without being angry or disputatious is of a piece with the behavior described in vv. 1–2.

The author's real interest, the behavior of women, occupies him in three subsections (vv. 9–10, 11–12, 13–15). Each of these subsections picks up and gives behavioral specificity to the terms or their cognates introduced in vv. 2–4: θεοσέβεια (v. 10; cf. εὐσέβεια in v. 2); ἡσυχία (vv. 11–12; cf. ἡσύχιος in v. 2), σώζω (v. 15; cf. v. 4; σωτήρ in v. 3). There is therefore some literary coherence to the entire chapter.

The section on which this paper focuses, 2:9–15, exhibits similar coherence. It leads off with the command that women "adorn themselves (κοσμεῖν ἑαυτάς) . . . with self-respect and moderation (μετὰ αἰδοῦς καὶ σωφροσύνης)," and ends by urging that they "continue in faith and love and holiness with moderation (μετὰ σωφροσύνης)." This *inclusio* invites us to view the entire section as practical demonstrations of a woman's moderation or prudence.

This is not the only place in the Pastoral Epistles where σωφροσύνη is important in describing communal responsibilities. Titus 2:2–10 is particularly instructive. There, a list of communal responsibilities, replete with the philosophical virtues found in 1 Tim 2:1–2, 9–15, is shot through with σωφροσύνη and some of the other terms attention has been drawn to: Titus 2:2, σώφρονας; v. 4, σωφρονίζωσιν; v. 5, σώφροναν; v. 6, σωφρονεῖν; v. 2, σέμνος; v. 7, σεμνότης; cf. vv. 5, 9, ὑποτάσσομαι (cf. 1 Tim 2:11, ὑποταγῇ); v. 7, καλῶν ἔργων (cf. 1 Tim 2:10, ἔργων ἀγαθῶν); and the section ends by urging that slaves "adorn (κοσμῶσιν) the teaching of God our Savior in all respects (v. 10)." As will appear below, this is rather standard philosophical advice. Christian communal concerns, however, are revealed in the three ἵνα clauses in vv. 5, 8 and 10, and the directives are supported in vv. 11–15 by one of the major christological statements in the Pastoral Epistles. But even that statement, while containing traditional formulations, describes God's saving grace as having been manifested to educate people to live moderate, just, and godly lives (σωφρόνως καὶ δικαίως καὶ εὐσεβῶς, v. 12), which is a christianized form of the Greek cardinal virtues.[11]

In Titus 2:1–10, σωφροσύνη is to characterize various members of the Christian community, women (vv.3–5) and slaves (vv. 9–10) receiving most attention. In 1 Tim 2:9–15, the focus is entirely on women.

The first subsection (2:9–10) of the directives to women deals with a woman's personal demeanor. It is made up largely of philosophic commonplaces, and v. 9a contains the terms that provide the framework for vv. 9–15. The antithesis "not (μή) . . . but (ἀλλ')" need not be polemical, signaling social division caused by dress or personal decoration. The prescription is quite common, as is the antithesis, in which the stress rhetorically is on the second member.[12] The woman who professes reverence of God (θεοσέβειαν) adorns herself with good works. This is an instantiation of the life that is lived with all godliness and dignity (v. 2, ἐν πάσῃ εὐσεβείᾳ καὶ σεμνότητι), and is the first concrete way in which she adorns herself with self-respect and moderation (μετὰ αἰδοῦς καὶ σωφροσύνης).

The second subsection (2:11–12) takes up a quality of life that also derives from popular philosophy, and has a communal or social dimension. The subsection begins and ends with ἐν ἡσυχίᾳ ("in quietness," "quiet"), and the reference forms an *inclusio*. What is enclosed by the two brackets applies the notion of quietness to two aspects of a woman's conduct in the community. No grammatical connective ties the subsection to v. 10, so it is not immediately obvious whether it is a totally new, freestanding topic, or whether it is somehow related to what precedes. The latter is more likely the case. Like v. 10, vv. 11–12 also pick up from v. 2b, "a calm and quiet life with all godliness and dignity (ἤρεμον καὶ ἡσύχιον βίον . . . ἐν πάσῃ εὐσεβείᾳ καὶ σεμνότητι)," which suggests that quietness

---

[11] See Malherbe, "'Christ Came into the World to Save Sinners,'" 340–43.

[12] See Abraham J. Malherbe, *The Letters to the Thessalonians* (AB 32B; New York: Doubleday, 2000), Index of Major Subjects, s.v. antithesis. The serious pitfall of detecting a polemic behind every antithesis has not been avoided by much of New Testament scholarship. This antithesis points neither to social differences among the readers in view (so Lorenz Oberlinner, *Die Pastoralbriefe: Erster Timotheusbrief* [HTKNT; Freiburg: Herder, 1994], 90), nor to a contrast between modest Christian and ostentatious pagan women (so Marshall, *The Pastoral Epistles*, 449–50).

is a quality of behavior defined by godliness.[13] Two kinds of behavior are specified, namely, the acts of learning and teaching, and the relationship between husband and wife.

The third subsection (2:13–15) is connected to what immediately precedes by γάρ ("For"), which introduces the support for the directive given about the woman's ἡσυχία. This support utilizes Jewish-Christian tradition about the order of creation from which are derived Adam's priority and Eve's deception. But the woman will be saved (σωθήσεται) through childbearing (τεκνογονίας) if they (?) continue in faith and love and holiness with moderation or prudence (μετὰ σωφροσύνης). The subsection picks up the theme of salvation from vv. 3–4 and thus forms the second bracket of an *inclusio* which encompasses virtually the entire chapter. At the same time, it is also the second bracket of an *inclusio* that begins with v. 9, and provides the lens through which the woman's behavior appears as a life of σωφροσύνη.

This overview of the chapter demonstrates that structurally, the text coheres. It still remains to be determined whether the substance of the moral advice similarly coheres.

The Moderate Life

The advice in the chapter is of a sort that modern scholars describe as a bourgeois ethic,[14] the ethic representing the ideals of society, whose underpinnings were largely Stoic. New Testament scholars have detected a traditional quality to the advice. Sometimes they have been interested in relating 2:9 to 1 Pet 3:3, 5, and 2:11–12 to 1 Cor 14:33b–36 or have compared the use of the creation account in 2:11–14 with that in 1 Cor. 11:7–12. The interest of this paper is rather in the way 2:9–15 is illuminated by the philosophical traditions current in the first century.

The relevance of the philosophical material is not questioned by modern scholars, even though there is sometimes an unwarranted inclination to hold that such material came to the author via Hellenistic Judaism.[15]

---

[13] ἡσυχία can refer to social behavior (quietness, tranquility) or speech (silence). In 2:2b it has the former meaning, and it is likely that it does so in vv. 11–12 (esp. with ὑποταγή and αὐθεντεῖν). See Ceslas Spicq, *Les épitres pastorales* (EB; Paris: Gabalda, 1969) 1.388–90; idem, *Lexique théologique du nouveau testament* (Freiburg: Cerf, 1991) 688–94.

[14] Heinrich Julius Holtzmann (*Die Pastoralbriefe kritisch und exegetisch behandelt* [Leipzig: Engelmann, 1880], 307) originated the description. It was given wider currency by Dibelius and Conzelmann, *The Pastoral Epistles*, 8, 39–41. See also Brox, *Die Pastoralbriefe*, 124–25; Collins, *1 & 2 Timothy and Titus*, 54–59.

[15] So Martin Hengel in Hengel and C. K. Barrett, *Conflicts and Challenges in Early Christi-*

Hellenistic Jewish sources have not been used in this paper for lack of space, but also for another reason. These sources themselves appropriated the traditions under review here, and how they did so invites examination in its own right. It would be simplistic to assume that Hellenistic Judaism was the conduit through which Greek philosophical influence came to early Christianity. It is far more realistic to view Hellenistic Jewish and Christian literature vis-a-vis Hellenistic philosophy in terms of analogy rather than genealogy. A more complete study of the Pastoral Epistles will have to take those sources into consideration, but that is a task for another day.

A further caution is in order. The recognition that the Pastoral Epistles are indebted to philosophic traditions does not mean that one may presuppose that the philosophical argumentation that may underlie specific ethical instruction similarly underlies the moral instruction of the Pastoral Epistles where those traditions are used. The problem lies on both sides of the comparison. The literary character of the Pastoral Epistles does not contribute clarity to their argumentation. Howard Marshall has stated the matter well:

> There is a fair degree of unanimity in dividing up the epistles into their constituent small units, but there is little agreement on how to group the smaller units into larger wholes and trace a line of argument, or whether indeed this is the right way to understand the epistles at all.[16]

The same issues attend study of the philosophic material utilized by the Pastoral Epistles. Similar characteristics are illustrated, for example, by Plutarch's *Advice to Bride and Groom*, which is relevant to this inquiry. Plutarch does not provide philosophical arguments to buttress each bit of advice that he gives in this tractate, which begins with an epistolary salutation (138A), but he does emphasize the importance of philosophy to his ethical teaching and supposes that his young readers will remember what they had learned or what had been handed down to them.[17] We

---

anity (Harrisburg, Pa: Trinity, 1999). The commentaries by Roloff and Marshall sometimes tend in this direction. Collins (*1 & 2 Timothy and Titus*, 64–75) makes excellent use of the Old Testament as well as rabbinic traditions and Hellenistic Jewish writings in addition to the philosophic traditions to sketch a wide canvas against which the Pastoral Epistles are to be viewed.

[16] Marshall, *Pastoral Epistles*, 11.

[17] *Advice to Bride and Groom* 138C, 148BC; see Cynthia Patterson, "Plutarch's *Advice to Bride and Groom*: Traditional Wisdom through a Philosophic Lens," in *Plutarch's Advice to the Bride and Groom and a Consolation to His Wife: English Translations, Commentary, In-*

can, of course, situate most of his precepts within certain philosophical frameworks, but that is not of concern to him. Most of the material adduced below comes from attempts to classify or define philosophic themes or terms, or are exhortation to the moral life, rather than philosophical argumentation.

The Pastoral Epistles are similar in this respect to Plutarch and the kind of literature represented by his tractate (letter) on marriage. The Pastoral Epistles also refer constantly to teaching the readers are assumed to know, yet the letters are not known for robust theological argumentation.[18] The issues are not substantially different from those regarding paraenesis, understood as consisting of freestanding precepts.[19] For our present interest, however, it is important to note that the author does not simply make a collection of precepts devoid of any Christian element. So, the description of the Christian life in 2:2b is quite Hellenistic, but is said to be acceptable to God,[20] and its foundation is provided by the confession in vv. 5–6 and a reminder of Paul's apostolic appointment in v. 7. And the advice to women ends with traditional material in vv. 13–15. The two most extended christological formulations in the Pastoral Epistles also undergird instruction derived from the moral philosophers (Titus 2:11–14; 3:3–7), and are not mere appendages providing a theological sheen to rather prosaic moralizing.[21]

---

terpretive Essays, and Bibliography (ed. Sarah B. Pomeroy; Oxford: Oxford University Press, 1999), 128–37.

[18] The teaching function is important (2 Tim 4:2, διδαχή); it is κατ' εὐσέβειαν (1 Tim 6:3) and is to be followed or heeded (4:6, 13, 16; 2 Tim 3:10; 4:3); the tradition is to be handed on (2 Tim 2:2) and guarded (1 Tim 6:20; 2 Tim 1:14). For evaluation of the letters' theology, see above, esp. n. 1

[19] For extensive discussion of paraenesis, see Malherbe, *The Letters to the Thessalonians*, index, s.v. paraenesis; and idem, "Paraenesis in the Epistle to Titus".

[20] Cf. 1 Tim 5:4, where the formula again appears immediately after Hellenistic moral instruction. According to Marshall (*Pastoral Epistles*, 424) it is patterned after Deut 12:25, 28; 13:19; 21:9. For ἡσύχιος βίος, cf. Ps.-Pythagoras, *Epistle* 1(152, 2 Städele [*Die Briefe des Pythagoras und der Ptythagoreer*. Beiträge zur klassischen Philologie 115; Meisenheim: Hain, 1980), commentary 195. Plato's *Charmides* is of special interest. Its subject is σωφροσύνη, and it takes up many of the topics under review here. See 159B–161B for ἡσυχία, κοσμιότης, αἰδώς (160C: ἡσύχιος βίος) terms that occur in 2:9–15, and which will be discussed at greater length below.

[21] See Malherbe, "Christ Jesus Came into the World to Save Sinners"; Roloff (*Der erste Brief an Timotheus*, 127–28) thinks that the tradition behind 2:9–10 is superficially Christianized, as v. 10 shows: the virtues of v. 9 are understood as divine reverence expressed in good deeds.

All that having been said, the question remains whether we are ultimately left with no alternative but to view the three subsections of the advice to women in 2:9–15 as unrelated to each other, and at most to demonstrate the wide currency of the precepts by trawling for still more ancient parallels.[22] The structural analysis above suggests that more can be done. The section, 2:9–15, is enclosed by references to σωφροσύνη, and it is therefore methodologically natural to examine somewhat closely what was said about this virtue, especially as part of the complex of terms that are used in this passage.

What *Sophrosyne* Means

Σωφροσύνη possessed such a wide diversity of connotations that Helen North, in her magisterial study of the virtue, chose to transliterate the Greek word without italicizing it, and to use it as an English word.[23] I choose a middle way, using either the Greek or italicized transliteration. Modern New Testament scholars have similarly recognized the virtual impossibility of translating the word group; they have had to be content to render the Greek word according to the contexts in which it occurs, as meaning moderation, restraint, modesty, prudence, and self-control or to write summary accounts of its meaning.[24] The problem is not only a modern one; Cicero reflected the difficulty in 45 BCE, in his *Tusculan Disputations* (3.16–17), one of the works in which he interpreted Greek

---

[22] Collins (*1 & 2 Timothy and Titus*, 51–78) illustrates the procedure well. He does not give attention to how 2:9–15 fits into the literary structure of the chapter, as was attempted above, nor does he explore the interrelationship of the terms he so well places in the philosophic tradition, as will be attempted below. On the use of parallels in this kind of study, see L. Michael White and John T. Fitzgerald, "*Quod est comparandum*: The Problem of Parallels," in *Early Christianity and Classical Culture: Comparative Studies in Honor of Abraham J. Malherbe* (NovTSup 110; ed. by J. T. Fitzgerald, T. H. Olbricht, and L. M. White; Leiden: Brill, 2003) 13–39.

[23] Helen North, *Sophrosyne: Self-Knowledge and Restraint in Greek Literature* (Cornell Studies in Classical Philology; Ithaca: Cornell University Press, 1966), xi. See already, John Ferguson, *Moral Values in the Ancient World* (London: Methuen, 1958) 32–33. See also W. R. Lamb, in the introduction to his Loeb edition of the *Charmides* (1927) 3. Lisette Goessler, "Advice to the Bride and Groom: Plutarch Gives a Detailed Account of his Views on Marriage," in Pomeroy, *Plutarch's Advice*, 101 n. *.

[24] See Ulrich Luck, "σώφρων κτλ.," in *TDNT* 8 (1971): 1097, on the difficulty of translation; Collins, *1 & 2 Timothy and Titus*, index, s.v. *sophrosyne*; and Marshall, *Pastoral Epistles*, 182–84, under the rubric "self-control."

philosophy to his fellow Romans and created Latin philosophical terminology to render the Greek:[25]

> It is also probable that the temperate man (*temperans*)—the Greeks call him σώφρων, and they apply the term σωφροσύνη to the virtue which I usually call, sometimes temperance (*temperantiam*), sometimes self-control (*moderationem*), and occasionally also discretion (*modestiam*); but, it may be, the virtue could rightly be called "frugality (*frugalitas*)," the term corresponding to which has a narrower meaning with the Greeks . . . but our term has a wider meaning, for it connotes all abstinence and inoffensiveness . . . and embraces all the other virtues as well, (and in time) has come to include the three virtues of fortitude, justice and prudence . . . they are all mutually linked and bound together (trans. King, LCL).

W. R. Lamb draws attention to the intellectual element in the virtue: "The Greeks always tended to regard a moral quality as a state of the reasoning mind."[26]

Sophrosyne among the Virtues

Cicero could pile up somewhat equivalent terms, as he did elsewhere,[27] to describe expansively what the term means, and Stoicism allowed him to do so. My purpose here is not to offer an historical account of how *sophrosyne* was conceived (at various times) by the Stoics, but to demonstrate that the virtue was part of a congeries of terms. Stoics accepted the common notion of four cardinal virtues, prudence (φρόνησις), moderation (σωφροσύνη), justice (δικαιοσύνη) and courage (ἀνδρεία). To each of these primary virtues others were subordinated. To σωφροσύνη were subordinated εὐταξία (good order), κοσμιότης (decorum), αἰδημοσύνη (modesty), ἐγκράτεια (self-control).[28] This Stoic penchant for classifica-

---

[25] On the task, see *Tusc. Disp.* 1.1; *On the Nature of the Gods* 1.7–8, on which see the comments in *M. Tulli Ciceronis De Natura Deorum* (ed. A. S. Pease; Cambridge: Harvard University Press, 1955), 1:142–43; and for the problematic of the enterprise, see Kurt Scheidle, *Modus optumum. Die Bedeutung des "rechten Masses" in der römischen Literatur* (Studien zur klassischen Philosophie 73; Frankfurt: Peter Lang, 1993), 173–75.

[26] See n. 23 above.

[27] E. g., *On Duties* 1.15, 93, on which see Andrew R. Dyck, *A Commentary on Cicero, De Officiis* (Ann Arbor: University of Michigan Press, 1996), 241–51; North, *Sophrosyne*, 267–68; Scheidle, *Modus Optumum*, 181–83.

[28] Stobaeus, *Anthology* 2.59,4–60,2 Wachsmuth (*S. V.F.* 3.262, 264). For a more discriminating statement, see the discussion in A. A. Long and D. L. Sedley, *The Hellenistic Philosophers* (Cambridge: Cambridge University Press, 1987), 1:383–84.

tion did not lead to their isolating virtues from each other. Their "basic conception was that virtue was unitary and was simply given different names in the different spheres of activity."[29] They held that the virtues imply one another (ἀντακολουθεῖν ἀλλήλαις), "and that the possessor of one is the possessor of all, inasmuch as they have common principles."[30]

It was not only the Stoics who agglomerated such terms. This should caution us not to be too precise in our systematization. The treatise, *On Virtues and Vices*, falsely attributed to Aristotle but dating from the first century BCE or the first century CE, sums up the qualities of σωφροσύνη by saying that it is accompanied by εὐταξία, κοσμιότης, αἰδώς, εὐλάβεια (proper arrangement, orderliness, modesty, caution; 1250b12–13). We are obviously dealing with a common, basic understanding of *sophrosyne*, but Stoicism would continue to inform the popular conception of the virtue. The discussion that follows demonstrates that indebtedness.

A Royal Virtue

Sophrosyne was especially important to moral philosophers during the early Empire, and Musonius Rufus serves to illustrate how it was advanced in a discourse, *That Kings Too Should Study Philosophy*, addressed to a Syrian king.[31] Much of the discourse consists of commonplaces, but there is a marked Stoic element, especially in the second part.[32] Musonius argues that the king, the ideal man to the Stoics, should study philosophy, for it enables him to distinguish between virtue and vice, a capacity lying at the heart of his various royal functions. Musonius claims that the study of philosophy is required to be just and courageous, two of the four cardinal virtues, and says the following about the king's σωφροσύνη, the fourth virtue (he here omits wisdom):

> The king must, furthermore, himself exercise self-control (σωφρονεῖν) and teach his subjects self-control (σωφρονίζειν) so that he might rule with moderation (σωφρόνως) and they accept his rule with decorum (κοσμικῶς), neither party living self-indulgently. For the ruin of ruler and subject alike is self-

---

[29] Dyck, *De Officiis*, 242, with references; Scheidle, *Modus Optumum*, 182–83.

[30] Diogenes Laertius, *Lives of Eminent Philosophers* 7.125. Cf. Plutarch, *On Stoic Self-Contradictions* 1046E and p. 521 n. a in the Loeb Classical Library edition by Harold Cherniss.

[31] *Fragment* 8 (60–67 Lutz; 32–40 Hense).

[32] See North, *Sophrosyne*, 229–30; and esp. A. C. van Geytenbeek, *Musonius Rufus and Greek Diatribe* (Assen: van Gorcum, 1963), 124–29, for the Stoic elements.

indulgence (τρυφή). But how could someone be self-controlled (σωφρονήσειε) if he had not practiced controlling his desires (κρατεῖν τῶν ἐπιθυμιῶν), or an undisciplined person make others self-controlled (σώφρονας)? One can name no study (ἐπιστήμη) other than philosophy that develops self-control (σωφροσύνην). For it teaches us to live above pleasure and greed, to find contentment in a thrifty life and avoid extravagance. It makes people have respect (αἰδῶ ἔχειν) and to control their tongues (γλώττης κρατεῖν), and produces order (τάξιν), decorum (κόσμον) and propriety (εὐσχημοσύνην), and in general, what is fitting (πρέπον) in act and attitude.[33] When these qualities are present in a person they give him dignity (σέμνον) and self-control (σώφρονα), but when they are present in a king they make him godlike and worthy of respect (αἰδοῦς ἄξιος).[34]

Musonius praised *sophrosyne* more than any other of the cardinal virtues, and North claims that it "appears as a private, individual excellence ... Even in this instance the virtue remains entirely personal."[35] *Sophrosyne* is a virtue to be cultivated by all individuals, the king exemplifying the ideal.

In the texts so far adduced, terms appear in discussions about *sophrosyne* that are also used in 1 Tim 2 (κοσμιότης or cognates; αἰδημοσύνη or cognates; πρέπον or πρέπω; σεμνότης; and control of speech). For the sake of identifying a broader context, it will be useful to sketch how some of these terms or themes were used as they related to *sophrosyne* generally, as part of a recurring complex of terms, before examining them as descriptive of a woman's *sophrosyne*.

A Congeries of Virtues

Orderliness (κοσμιότης) and proper arrangement (εὐταξία) are subordinate to *sophrosyne*, and are defined respectively as "knowledge of decorous and indecorous movements" and "knowledge of when and in what order

---

[33] On πρέπον, cf. Fragment 18B (120, 6–7 Lutz; l04, 15 Hense): One should choose cheaper over expensive food because it is "more conducive to temperance and fitting to a good man" (σωφρονικωτέρα καὶ πρέπει ἀνδρὶ ἀγαθῷ). At table, "one should have regard for a fitting decorum and moderation" (κόσμου τε καὶ μέτρου). See further below.

[34] 62, 10–22 Lutz; 34,12–35,8 Hense. Musonius then goes on to speak of the king's fearlessness and ability in public discourse (62, 31–64, 9 Lutz; 36, 1–22 Hense). Women do not need this skill, and even in men he does not rank this ability highly (Fragment 4 [48, 20–23 L; 19, 8–11 H]).

[35] North, *Sophrosyne*, 229. It appears to me that this could not rule out a social dimension.

to perform actions."³⁶ They belong together and are the subject with which *sophrosyne* deals.³⁷ By them people exhibit their *sophrosyne*.³⁸ Orderliness and *sophrosyne*, in which temperance and self-control consist, are related so closely for Cicero that they are said to be one of the sources from which all that is morally right arises.³⁹

One of the things that this virtue produces, Musonius claims, is control over one's speech. Also for Cicero, orderliness, to be observed in all conduct, includes selecting the appropriate occasion and manner of speaking.⁴⁰ *Kosmos* can describe both the ordered world and adornment, and Plato calls *sophrosyne* "a kind of beautiful order (κόσμος πού τις)," an *ornatus vitae*, as Cicero would have it.⁴¹ This aspect of *sophrosyne* as adornment will receive more extensive treatment below.

Sophrosyne has a connection with αἰδώς (respect, self-respect, modesty, shame), which is constitutive for it. According to Musonius, it is philosophy that produces self-respect as well as *sophrosyne*. When boys and girls study philosophy, it produces prudence (φρόνησις) and they develop shame (αἰδώς) toward all things base. When these two qualities develop, the students are of necessity self-controlled (σωφρονεῖς).⁴² Musonius's student, Epictetus, mentions αἰδώς more often than he does, but once more Cicero will suffice to illustrate what was meant by the concept, here translated by *verecundia*:

> Since man is the only animal endowed with a sense of respect (*verecundia*) . . ., and with a concern to avoid any conduct un-

---

³⁶ Ibid., 219, translating *SVF* 3. 264 (see n. 26): ἐπιστήμη πρεπουσῶν καὶ ἀπρεπῶν κινήσεων and ἐπιστήμη τοῦ πότε πρακτέον καὶ τις μετὰ τί καὶ καθόλου τῆς τάξεως τῶν πράξεων. See Cicero, *On Duties* 1.142, who finds it particularly difficult to translate technical Greek terms at this point. See Dyck, *De Officiis*, 320–22

³⁷ Diogenes Laertius, *Lives of Eminent Philosophers* 7.125–26.

³⁸ Dio Chrysostom, *Discourse* 32.95.

³⁹ *On Duties* 1.15.

⁴⁰ *On Duties* 1.144. On the appropriate occasions for speaking, see Abraham J. Malherbe, "'In Season and Out of Season': 2 Timothy 4:2," *JBL* 103 (1984): 235–43; repr. in *Paul and the Popular Philosophers* (Minneapolis: Fortress, 1989), 137–45.

⁴¹ Plato, *Republic* 430E; Cicero, *On Duties* 1.93.

⁴² Musonius Rufus, Fragment 4 (48, 1–4 Lutz; 18, 4 Hense). The association of σωφροσύνη and αἰδώς is constant; see Spicq, *Lexique théologique du nouveau testament*, 1501 n. 3. See van Geytenbeek, *Musonius Rufus*, 26–27, who does not do justice to the intellectual element in Musonius' view, which is implicit in the role Musonius assigns to philosophy and his use of ἐπιστήμη. Cf. Cicero, *On Duties* 1.93–94, on which see the commentary by Dyck, *De officiis*, 249–50.

becoming, from this seed given by nature develops judiciousness, modesty, justice and moral virtue generally.[43]

Cicero made much of *verecundia*, which avoids giving offense, in *On Duties*.[44]

Self-respect is also clearly related to τὸ πρέπον, what is fitting. Musonius's king, the paradigm of *sophrosyne*, must behave, in act and attitude, in a manner that is fitting or appropriate (πρέπον).[45] This applies to the wise person's profession, that he will only do work that befits him and not violate his self-respect, the same principle applying also to what he eats and wears.[46] It is more than a matter of taste, etiquette or aesthetics, at least for Cicero, who translated πρέπον by *decorum*, whose essential nature is

> that it is inseparable from moral goodness; for what is proper is morally right, and what is morally right is proper. The nature of the difference between morality and propriety can be more easily felt than expressed. For whatever propriety may be, it is manifested only when there is pre-existing moral rectitude.

Propriety is inseparable from *sophrosyne*, for

> its relation to the cardinal virtues is so close, that it is perfectly self-evident and does not require any abstruse process of reasoning to see it. For there is a certain element of propriety perceptible in every act of moral rectitude; and this can be separated from virtue theoretically better than it can be practically.[47]

Propriety

> shines out in our conduct, engages the approbation of our fellow-men by the order, consistency, and self-control it imposes upon every word and deed.

---

[43] *On Ends* 4.18, translation by Robert Dobbin, *Epictetus, Discourses Book I.* (Oxford: Clarendon, 1998), 88; cf. *On Duties* 1.14; in 1.93, *verecundia* is used for σωφροσύνη. For Epictetus, cf. especially *Discourses* 1.28.19–23, and see B. L. Hijmans, *ASKHSIS: Notes on Epictetus' Educational System* (Assen: Van Gorcum, 1959) 27–30; Margarethe Billerbeck, *Epiktet: Vom Kynismus* (Philosophia Antiqua 34; Leiden: Brill, 1978), 67–69.

[44] North, *Sophrosyne*, 223.

[45] τὸ ἐν κινήσει καὶ σχέσει πρέπον (62, 20 Lutz; 35, 4–5 Hense). Cf. *SVF* 3.272, where the same phrase is used of κοσμιότης.

[46] Musonius, Fragment 11 (80, 19 Lutz; 104, 15 Hense); Fragment 18B (120, 6–9 Lutz; 104, 15 Hense); Fragment 16 (106, 14–15 Lutz; 88, 8–9 Hense).

[47] *On Duties* 1.94, 95 (trans. Miller, LCL).

In social relations, it even goes beyond justice, for while "it is the function of justice not to do wrong to one's fellow-men; of considerateness, not to wound their feelings; and in this the essence of propriety is best seen."[48]

The frequent references to Cicero have had a twofold purpose. They attempt to redress in a small measure the tendency to depend on Greek sources for philosophy at the turn of the eras. And, of immediate importance, Cicero allows us to observe the analysis that informed scholastic occupation with these virtues. Musonius is explicit about the role of philosophy in moral development, however, in the fragments of his discussions that have been preserved. He was practical rather than scholastic and used philosophical terms unself-consciously to describe the human condition and the way to virtue.[49] That is characteristic of the moral philosophers, including those who wrote about the *sophrosyne* of women.

The *Virtus Feminarum*

Sophrosyne was the primary virtue of women in antiquity, the most common one, often the only one, ascribed to women on tombstones.[50] In the thinking of philosophers of diverse persuasion, it was preeminently their virtue, the *virtus feminarum*.

Musonius, a Stoic, urges *That Women Too Should Study Philosophy*,[51] for it makes people, man or woman, live well. A woman especially must be σώφρων, which means self-controlled and pure in sexual behavior and moderate in appearance and dress. The person, man or woman, who lives in the way philosophy inculcates, will be the most well-ordered (κοσμιώτατος). Philosophy enables women to run their households well. In serving her husband, a wife will be an ornament (κόσμος) to her relatives. Philosophy claims that self-respect or modesty (αἰδώς) is the

---

[48] Cicero, *On Duties* 1.98, 99.

[49] For Musonius, see further below; see also Ps.-Plutarch, *On Education* 7D-F; Dio Chrysostom, *Discourses* 32.15–16.

[50] See Richmond Lattimore, *Themes in Greek and Latin Epitaphs* (Urbana: University of Illinois Press, 1962), 290–91, 335–37; A.-M. Vérilhac, "L'image de la femme dans les épigrammes funéraire grecques," in *La Femme dans le monde méditerranéen*, Collection des travaux de la Maison de l'Orient, 19 (ed. A.-M. Vérilhac; Lyon: GDR 1985), 85–112, esp. 92, 102.

[51] Fragment 3 (38,25–42,29 Lutz; 8,15–13,3 Hense).

greatest good, and teaches the greatest moderation (καταστολή)⁵² and self-control (σωφρονεῖν).⁵³

One difference between men and women is that women do not require skill in speaking, like men do,⁵⁴ for they pursue philosophy as women.⁵⁵ Musonius, as usual, states the matter more positively than the traditional view of women. So Plutarch (*On Talkativeness* 507B) can assume that a woman lacked *sophrosyne* because she could not hold her tongue,⁵⁶ and Sophocles (*Ajax* 586) assumed that a woman's *sophrosyne* consisted in her silence: "Do not question, do not ask; *sophronein* is good." Euripides (*The Children of Heracles* 476–77) thought that the combination of silence (σιγή), modesty (σωφρονεῖν), social quietism (ἥσυχον) and staying at home were best for a woman.⁵⁷

We have taken note above of the connection between orderliness and *sophrosyne*. *Kosmos* and its cognates were utilized in countless comments on a woman's clothing and physical appearance, playing on the two meanings of "order" and "ornament" or "decoration." In his *Advice to Bride and Groom*, Plutarch repeatedly commends inner qualities rather than outward appearance. It is *sophrysone*, not outward appearance that counts (141D); the *sophron* woman wears self-respect (αἰδώς) in place of clothes; a woman adorns herself with wise sayings from great ancient women (145DF), and so on. One of the gnomic statements of Antiphanes excerpted by Stobaeus for his collected sayings on marriage reads: "Wish not to brighten your body with cosmetics, but your heart with pure works and habits."⁵⁸ Parallels from Greek and Roman as well as Jewish texts to 1 Tim 2:9 and 1 Pet 3:3–4 are found in all good commentaries, and need not be repeated here.⁵⁹ Of interest to our present purpose are two texts

---

⁵² Cf. Epictetus, *Discourses* 2.10.15, αἰδώς καταστολή, ἡμερότης; *Encheiridion* 40: Girls should be taught that they are honored for nothing but their orderly behavior (εὐκοσμία) and self-respect (αἰδημοσύνη).

⁵³ Cf. Ps.-Hippocrates, *Epistle* 13 (64, 21–24 Smith): σωφροσύνη and κοσμιότης are expected of a wife. Stobaeus, *Anthology* 4.22.54 (4.597.6–7 Hense): The κόσμος of a wife reflects on her husband.

⁵⁴ Fragment 8 (62, 31–64, 9 Lutz; 36, 1–22 Hense). Cf. n. 32.

⁵⁵ Fragment 4 (48, 20–23 Lutz; 19, 8–11 Hense).

⁵⁶ In his description of the king, evidently a loquacious man as well as a woman does not have σωφροσύνη.

⁵⁷ Cf. Aeschylus, *Suppliants* 724–25, ἡσύχως ... σεσωφρονισμένως.

⁵⁸ Fragment 264 Kock (Stobaeus, *Anthology* 4.23.3 [4.569, 14–15 Hense]).

⁵⁹ See the texts and discussion in Bruce W. Winter, *Roman Wives, Roman Women: The Appearance of New Women and the Pauline Communities* (Grand Rapids: Eerdmans, 2003),

that have to do with Crates, the Cynic philosopher (fourth-third century BCE).

In *Advice to Bride and Groom* 141E, Plutarch recounts an anecdote about Lysander, tyrant of Sicily, who refused to accept finery and jewels for his daughters. He justifies his refusal with what purports to be a quotation from Crates:

> "Adornment (κόσμος)," says Crates, "is what adorns (τὸ κοσμοῦν); and what adorns a woman is what makes her better ordered (κοσμιωτέραν) not gold or emerald or scarlet, but whatever gives an impression of dignity (σεμνότης), good order (εὐταξίας), and self-respect (αἰδοῦς)."[60]

The play on the two meanings of κόσμος is basic to a paraenetic letter erroneously attributed to Crates, perhaps written in the first or second century CE:

> Do not abstain from the most beautiful ornament (κόσμου), but adorn (κόσμει) yourself every day so that you may stand out. The most beautiful ornament (κόσμος) is the one that decorates (κοσμῶν) you most beautifully, but the one that decorates you most nobly is the one that makes you most decorous (κοσμιωτάτην), and it is orderliness (κοσμιότης) that makes you most decorous (κοσμιωτάτην). Both Penelope and Alcestis, I think, adorned (κεκοσμῆσθαι) themselves with it and even now they are praised and honored for their virtue. In order, then, that you, too, might become like them, try to hold fast to this advice.[61]

Neopythagoreans were particularly interested in the subject of women, and two texts, purportedly written by women, add to the picture.

The first is a treatise, *On a Woman's Sophrosyne*, by Phintys, preserved in two fragments.[62] According to Phintys, a woman's chief virtue

97–122.

[60] Translation by Donald Russell in Pomeroy, *Plutarch's Advice to Bride and Groom*, 9 (modified).

[61] Ps.-Crates, *Epistle* 9, trans. Ronald F. Hock (slightly modified), in *The Cynic Epistles*, (ed. Abraham J. Malherbe; SBLSBS 12; Missoula, Mont.: 1977) 61.

[62] The authorship and date of the work are disputed. The text, preserved in Stobaeus (*Anthology* 4.588,17–593,11 Hense), is reprinted in Holger Thesleff, *The Pythagorean Texts of the Hellenistic Period* (Acta Academiae Aboensis, Humaniora 24/3. Abo: Abo Akademi, 1961) 151–54, to which the citations refer. English translations are available in *The Pythagorean Sourcebook and Library* (comp. and trans. Kenneth Sylvan Guthrie; Grand Rapids: Phanes Press, 1987) 263–64 (Guthrie paraphrases Thomas Taylor's original translation); Vicki Lynn Harper, in *A History of Women Philosophers* (ed. Mary Ellen Waithe;

is σωφροσύνη (152, 3–4). There are virtues that are particularly appropriate to men (152, 9–10), and some to women, such as those having to do with domestic matters (152, 10–11) and pleasing her husband, and some men and women have in common (bravery, justice, prudence (152, 11). But σωφροσύνη is particularly appropriate to women (152, 17–18). Among the ways by which a woman learns this virtue are, most important, the holiness and godliness (ὁσιότητός τε καί εὐσεβείας) of the marriage bed (152, 20–21, 25), for procreation (τέκνων γενέσει; 153, 1–2), and bodily adornment (152, 21–153, 2–28), which should be simple and unostentatious.[63]

The other document is a pseudonymous letter probably dating from the early Empire:[64]

> It appears to me that on your own accord you have acquired considerable noble qualities. For that you eagerly wish to hear what adorns (εὐκοσμίας) a woman justifies the hope that that you will grow old in virtue. The temperate (σώφρονα), freeborn woman must live with her legal husband adorned with quietness (ἡσυχία κεκαλλωπισμένην),[65] clad in neat, simple, white dress without extravagance or excess. She must avoid clothing that is either entirely purple or is streaked with gold, for that kind of dress is worn by hetaerae when they stalk the masses of men. But the adornment

---

Dordrecht/Boston/Lancaster: Martinus Nijhoff, 1987) 1:26–31. For adornment and *sophrosyne* elsewhere in the Neopythagoreans, see David L. Balch, "Neopythagorean Moralists and the New Testament Household Codes," *ANRW* 2.26.1 (1992) 399–401; Johan C. Thom, *The Pythagorean Golden Verses* (Religions in the Graeco-Roman World 123; Leiden: Brill, 1995), index, s.v. σωφροσύνη.

[63] It is instructive to compare Plutarch, *The Dialogue on Love* 767E, who thinks of σωφροσύνη as "a mutual self-restraint which is a principal requirement of marriage." He then contrasts the temperance that comes from without and through usage is imposed by shame or fear, to Love (Eros), who "has in himself enough self-control (ἐγκρατείας), decorum (κόσμου), and mutual trust (πίστεως), so that if he ever but touches the heart even of a profligate, he turns him from his other lovers, drives out insolence, humbles pride and intractability, and brings in modesty, silence, and calm (αἰδῶ, σιωπήν, ἡσυχίαν). He clothes him with the robes of decorum (κόσμιον) and makes him deaf to all appeals but one" (trans. Helmbold, LCL). The examples that he goes on to adduce show that he thought the same thing of women (768A-D).

[64] Pseudo-Melissa, *Letter to Clearata*. My translation is from the Doric text in Städele, *Briefe des Pythagoras,* 160–62. The translation is available in Abraham J. Malherbe, *Moral Exhortation: A Greco-Roman Sourcebook* (Library of Early Christianity 4; Philadelphia: Westminster, 1986), 83. A Koine version, P. Haun. II 13, with English translation, has been published in E. A. Judge, "A Woman's Behaviour," *New Docs* 6 (1992): 18–23.

[65] I accept P. Haun. II 13's reading of ἡσυχία for αἰσχύνα (modesty), approximating αἰδῶ, which also makes sense in a context like this.

(κόσμος) of a woman who wishes to please her own husband is her character and not her clothing. For the freeborn woman must be beautiful to her own husband, not to the men of the neighborhood.

You should have a blush on your cheeks as a sign of modesty (αἰδοῦς) instead of rouge, and should wear nobility, decorum (κοσμιότατα) and temperance (σωφροσύναν) instead of gold and emeralds. For the woman who strives for virtue must not have her heart set on expensive clothing but on the management of her household. She must please her husband by doing what he wishes, for a husband's wishes ought to be an unwritten law to an orderly wife (κοσμίᾳ γυναικί), and she should live by them. She should be of the opinion that, together with herself, she brought to him her orderly behavior (εὐταξίαν) as the most beautiful and largest dowry. For she must trust more in the beauty and riches of her soul than of her face or money. For envy and illness can strip away the latter, but the former continue to death.

Phintys connects *sophrosyne* to marriage for the sake of procreation. This is part of the fabric of domestic responsibilities inculcated in the Neopythagorean writings, and also in many other texts.[66] Not all philosophers thought that to be married was the best way of life, at least not for individuals who committed themselves to the philosophic life.[67] Some did hold that one reason for marriage was that nature intended sexual relations to result in procreation.[68] Musonius held the view that sexual intercourse-

---

[66] For example, Antipater of Tarsus (apud Stobaeus, *Anthology* 4.509, 9; 510, 3–5 Hense [*SVF* 3.255, 9; 256, 4–6]; trans. in Will Deming, *Paul on Marriage and Celibacy: The Hellenistic Background of 1 Corinthians 7* [2d ed.; Grand Rapids: Eerdmans, 2004], 225, 227), assumes a husband is to teach his wife about household management. Philo (*Special Laws* 3.169–171) has much in common with Phintys (see David L. Balch, *Let Wives be Submissive: The Domestic Code in 1 Peter* (SBLMS 26; Chico: Scholars, 1981), 52–54.

[67] See O. Larry Yarbrough, *Not Like the Gentiles: Marriage Rules in the Letters of Paul* (SBLDS 80; Atlanta: Scholars, 1985), 32–41; Deming, *Paul on Marriage and Celibacy*, 50–107.

[68] The subject is pursued in Musonius, Fragments 13A, 13B, 14, and 15, on which see van Geytenbeek, *Musonius Rufus on Greek Diatribe*, 62–71). The popularity of the topic is reflected in the extensive treatment it receives in the popular handbook by Hierocles (*On Duties*, excerpted by Stobaeus, translated in Malherbe, *Moral Exhortation*, here, pp. 100–4). See also the medical writer, Soranus (*Gynecology*, 1.40). For early Christian writers, see Carolyn Osiek and David Balch, *Families in the New Testament World: Households and House Churches* (Louisville: Westminster John Knox, 1997), 149–51. For the philosophical background to procreationism, see Kathy Gaca, *The Making of Fornication: Eros, Ethics, and Political Reform in Greek Philosophy and Early Christianity* (Hellenistic Culture and Society 40; Berkeley: University of California Press, 2003).

was to be confined to married couples, and even then, only to procreate.[69] It is not surprising then, that having many children was thought highly desirable by some.[70]

Conclusion

Helen North has drawn attention to "Paul's" use of *sophrosyne*:

> To Paul sophrosyne usually signifies self-control and mastery of the appetites. He associates it with *aidos* (I Tim 2.9), with *enkrateia* (Titus 1.8), one of the Gifts of the Spirit (Gal. 5.23), with sobriety (Titus 2.2, 6; I Tim 3.2), and in the case of women, with conjugal love (*philandria*: I Tim 2.9; Titus 2.2, 5). Although, like most moralists in the Greek world, he construes sophrosyne as the essential virtue of women (Titus 2.6; I Tim 2.9), he also enjoins it upon men of every age (Titus 2.2, 6) and specifically lists it among the qualifications of a bishop (Titus 1.8; I Tim 3.2).[71]

She claims further that the function of *sophrosyne* in the Pastoral Epistles conforms to contemporary pagan usage, but that it is christianized.[72]

The evidence laid out above shows her to be correct with respect to women, whose behavior and demeanor are described in 1 Tim 2:9–15 under the rubric of *sophrosyne*. The details of that behavior have a place in conventional Greco-Roman discussions of the virtue: order/adornment, quietness/silence, self-respect/modesty, appropriateness of behavior, marital relations and having children.

There is a philosophical background to this congeries of terms, but philosophical argumentation is not constitutive to the fabric of discourse when the purpose is moral exhortation, as is the case with 1 Tim 2:9–15. The individual details are like the tesserae in a mosaic; they contribute to the whole picture, but their functions in doing so are determined by the design or pattern to which they contribute. The image of a mosaic also captures the static nature of the individual parts, and the fact that they are to be seen in relation to the whole.

---

[69] Musonius, Fragment 12 (86, 4–6 Lutz; 64, 1–4 Hense).

[70] See references to Musonius and Hierocles in n. 68. But other comments as well as legislation to increase the birth rate point to an unwillingness to have many children. See Beryl Lawson ed., *The Family in Ancient Rome: New Perspectives* (Ithaca: Cornell University Press, 1987), 1–57, 170–72.

[71] *Sophrosyne*, 317.

[72] *Sophrosyne*, 316, 317, 318. See at n. 11 above.

These are features we should do well to heed in working with texts like the one before us. Marshaling the evidence as has been done in this article is only the first step. The effort is justified because *sophrosyne* is such an important quality of character in the Pastoral Epistles. But questions remain that must still be addressed. Why did the author choose the conventions he did, how does he use them, and why does he use them in this way? The answers to those questions can only be gained through exegesis of 1 Tim 2:9–12, which has not been the purpose of this paper, and which I have, in fact, studiously avoided.[73] What has been done here is preliminary to that exegesis, and, I would say, is its *sine qua non*.

---

[73] The exegetical task will be carried out in my commentary on the Pastoral Epistles for the Hermeneia series.

4

Mark and the Inclusion of the Gentiles

Allan J. McNicol

In the famous incident of Jesus confronting the temple authorities in Jerusalem shortly before his arrest Mark records a graphic word of Jesus:

> Is it not written, "My house shall be called a house of prayer for all the nations"? But you have made it a den of robbers.

There is one major difference between this record of Mark 11:17 and the parallels in both Matthew 21:13 and Luke 19:46; Mark alone records the prophetic word of Isaiah 56:7 (LXX) that the house of prayer will be "for all the nations." Besides the fact that Mark's quote reflects directly the Greek Septuagint, one may well inquire whether this is a mere accidental Marcan composition or whether Mark meant to say something more about the temple than Matthew and Luke. Only through a wider study of how Mark treats the mission of Jesus and the role of the Gentiles in God's plan will we be able to decide.

In this essay we address the wider question. We will attempt to show that concern for the Gentiles is an important subtext within Mark's narrative of the Jesus story. At the same time this concern is never worked out at the expense of Israel. Rather, the emphasis comes on Gentile and Jew being united together in a new community under the lordship of Christ.

Furthermore, based on the presupposition that Mark first circulated within Roman Christianity, we are interested in determining its significance for the church in the context of its development toward the end of the first century.[1] Procedurally, we will start with the context of Jesus' last week in Jerusalem and then follow these strands throughout the rest of the gospel. As we approach the end of this study we will attempt to fit the results of our study into the framework of what we know was taking place in the church at that time. Our goal in reading Mark through the mirror of the mission to the Gentiles is to gain deeper insight into the word Mark brought to the church of his time.

The End of the Temple Era

A considerable segment of Mark (chaps. 11–16) covers the last week of Jesus' ministry. There is truth to the oft-expressed dictum that Mark is a "passion account with a long introduction." When we begin to look more closely at this section we see that it falls into two parts. There is the arrest, trial, crucifixion, and vindication of Jesus (14:12—16:20).[2] But this comes only after the grounds for the arrest are carefully prepared. Primarily, this preparation comes about in 11:1—14:11. A strong case can be made that Mark viewed Jesus' critique of the temple and his announcement that it would be replaced by "another, not made by hand" (14:58) as the pre-

---

[1] The provenance of Mark is still debated. As part of an international research team, the author has recently published on this matter in David B. Peabody, Lamar Cope, and Allan J. McNicol, *One Gospel from Two: Mark's Use of Matthew and Luke* (Harrisburg, Pa.: Trinity, 2002), 55–63. We make the case for a Roman provenance. For an exhaustive discussion of the case for a Roman provenance see C. Clifton Black, *Mark: Images of an Apostolic Interpreter* (Columbia: University of South Carolina Press, 1994). In a brief summary article of this project ("Was Mark a Roman Gospel?" *ExpTim* 105 [1993–1994]: 39), Black tentatively concludes that the tradition of the ancient church for a Roman provenance is correct. See also John Donahue, "Windows and Mirrors: The Setting of Mark's Gospel," *CBQ* 57 (1995): 1–26. For a recent argument favoring the major alternative of a Galilean origin, Joel Marcus, *Mark 1–8: A New Translation with Introduction and Commentary* (AB 27; New York: Doubleday, 1999), 25–34.

[2] Both the beginning and end of this division may be contested. Commentators usually view the passion account as beginning at 14:1–2 with the reference of the desire of the chief priests and scribes to arrest Jesus. F. J. Maloney, *The Gospel of Mark: A Commentary* (Peabody, Mass.: Hendrickson, 2002), x. However, in several earlier verses (Mark 3:6; 11:18; 12:12) Mark intimates that the authorities are seeking to destroy Jesus, so this is not exactly a new development. We contend that Mark 14:1–9 is linked to a complex structural pattern of intercalation, commencing in 12:37b, and that this link takes precedence. There is an analysis of both this pattern and the whole contentious issue of where Mark ends in *One Gospel from Two*, 235, 330–35. I argue that Mark ended his gospel with a now lost resurrection account. Our present 16:9–20 has been incorporated into a late recension. This is somewhat similar to the conclusion of the recent massive study of James A. Kelhoffer, *Miracle and Mission: The Authentication of Missionaries and their Message in the Longer Ending of Mark* (WUNT 22.112; Tübingen: Mohr Siebeck, 2000).

cipitating factor for his arrest. Structurally and thematically there are good reasons for the claim.

Structurally, Mark 11:1—14:9 is dominated by two major units both of which feature the temple. First, Mark 11:11–25 (26)[3] constructs an elaborate literary edifice that intercalates the curse of the fig tree with a critique of the temple.[4] Jesus' curse of the fig tree in 11:12–14 and its fulfillment in 11:20–26 serves as a metaphor for his withering critique of the temple establishment which occurs in 11:15–19. Jesus' carefully calculated actions at the temple were designed to hinder the routine procedures for offering sacrifices. When viewed in connection with the fate of the fig tree, this can mean only that he is intimating that the old order, centering on the temple, is about to die in order that something new will emerge from its destruction. This theme reemerges toward the end of the unit in Mark 12:37b–14:11. Again, in a massive use of intercalation, Mark constructs Jesus' discourse (13:3–37) after the prediction of the destruction of the temple (13:2). The frame consists of two accounts of poor women acting honorably over against the treachery of powerful temple leaders (12:38–44; 14:1–9). In the midst of this treachery, which will incorporate the end of the temple (13:2), Jesus exhorts his disciples to remain faithful (13:5–23). Thus, the action in Mark's account of Jesus' visit to Jerusalem, prior to the passion narrative itself, is dominated by the theme of the end of the old order anchored in the temple. Throughout this unit Mark entertains a similar theme. Systematically, the "Parable of the Wicked Tenants" (12:1–12) fires against the temple establishment. The authorities perceived this clearly (12:12). A critique of other leaders in Israel who also accept the centrality of the temple for Jewish life follows (12:13–34). Jesus answers those who ask about his authority (11:27–33) that only one greater than David can bring this to fulfillment (12:35–37). Thus, in the Marcan scheme of things, this critique of the temple was anathema to the prevailing authorities and furnished the reason for Jesus' arrest.

Thematically, the critical unit of 11:1—14:11 argues that the era of temple worship has come to an end and will be replaced by a community of people characterized by faith. This can be shown in the clear composi-

---

[3] Most modern English translations omit Mark 11:26 because it does not occur in many of the Egyptian witnesses. However, there is strong attestation for this verse in a broad spectrum of other ancient manuscript traditions. We believe these witnesses are sufficient evidence for the acceptance of Mark 11:26 as a received text.

[4] For a recent summary of Mark's important use of the literary device of intercalation, Timothy J. Geddert, *Mark: Believer's Church Bible Commentary* (Scottsdale, Pa.: Herald, 2001), 416–17.

tional differences between Mark, on the one hand, and Matthew and Luke on the other.

Returning to the critical text of Mark 11:15–19, we find Jesus in the market along the southern wall of the temple complex.[5] Here Jesus' actions can only be interpreted as having the express intention of halting the commerce essential for the regular operation of the temple. Mark parallels either Matthew or Luke in 11:15. Then, in keeping with the word of Zech 14:21, that on the eschatological day vendors would be excluded from the house of the Lord, Jesus drives out the traders. In addition, he turns over the tables of the moneychangers and those selling doves for sacrificial purposes (Matt 21:12; Luke 19:45).[6] But in the next verse (11:16), Mark adds that Jesus bans the vessels from being carried through the temple. This verse is unique to Mark. Jesus' action is not a protest against commerce. Mark knew that under normal circumstances commerce was necessary for the temple to operate. Rather, Mark avers that the time for usual temple activity is over. Something else will have to replace it.

Mark begins 11:17 with a characteristic compositional construction, "and he began to teach them."[7] Along with the other imperfect verb, "he was saying to them," various forms of which are found in Matt 21:13 / Luke 19:46, Jesus pronounces the scriptural justification for this action. The scripture is Isa 56:7 (cf. Jer 7:11).[8] Compared with the parallels in Matthew and Luke, as already noted, Mark is closer to the Septuagint version of Isaiah. Particularly striking is Mark's note that the house of prayer is for "all the Gentiles." This reference puzzles some commentators who presuppose the priority of Mark. Why would Luke, who was much in favor of the Gentile mission, omit this reference? But our question is why it is in the text of Mark? We answer that it is not simply an unthought-

---

[5] Jostein Adna, "Jesus' Symbolic Act in the Temple (Mark 11:15–17)," in *Gemeinde ohne Tempel: Zur Substituierung und Transformation des Jerusalemer Tempels und seines Kults im Alten Testament, antiken Judentum und frühen Christentum* (eds. Beate Ego, Armin Lange, and Peter Pilhofer; WUNT 2.118; Tübingen: Mohr Siebeck, 1999), 463, gives an excellent description of the actual layout of the outer precincts of the Herodian temple. Our interpretation is based on this analysis. He has put to rest the view still common in commentaries that the market stretched out across the court of the Gentiles.

[6] John's account is more vigorous. He has Jesus use a whip to drive out the vendors along with sheep and oxen (John 2:15). The next verse may also echo Zech 14:21.

[7] Mark 1:21; 2:13; 4:2; 9:31; 10:1. David Barrett Peabody, *Mark as Composer: New Gospel Studies* (Macon, Ga.: Mercer University Press, 1987), 62, 122–23, 163.

[8] In the context of Isa 56:1–8 the reference is to a promise of acceptance to all faithful "eunuchs and foreigners" normally excluded from full participation in the people of God.

ful carry-over of the quotation from Isaiah, but a deliberate usage by the author of the second Gospel.

On the basis of the conduct of the chief priests and scribes (12:38–40), and reports of others profiting excessively from the temple establishment, Mark could easily have connected this saying with Jesus' echo of Jer 7:11, "den of robbers," in order to conclude that economic pursuits had eclipsed the spiritual focus of the temple. But even if one understands the reference to "robber's den" differently as an allusion to a misdirected view of the temple as a zone of safety free from the Lord's prosecution, Mark's emphasis lies elsewhere. The major emphasis of Mark 11:17 is on replacement, not merely as the second temple was of the first, but something of an entirely different order. It will be a house that includes "all nations." As such, Mark intimates that the new temple may well be comprised of people, not a place.

This interpretation is reinforced by the connection Mark makes between the fate of the Jerusalem temple and the image of the fig tree's destruction in Mark 11:22–26. In 11:22–26 Jesus begins to sketch the outline of his ideal temple community. It will not be a physical structure. It will be a people. And these people will be those characterized by faith, forgiveness, and prayer.[9] Thus we are claiming that the saying on prayer (11:24–25) is intimately linked with the reference to the "house of prayer" in 11:17.[10] The people of faith and prayer are the temple "not made with hands" (Mark 14:58). This theme of replacement develops through the rest of this unit.

First, in the Parable of the Wicked Tenants Mark once again highlights, over against Matthew and Luke, the depth of the perfidy of the rebellious tenants. Mark alone (12:5) refers to many others being beaten and killed by the tenants. But what is especially striking is that the owner of the vineyard (God) will take the vineyard from the rebellious tenants and give it to "others" (Mark 12:9//Luke 20:16). Mark, like Luke, lacks the wording of Matthew 21:44, which states that the kingdom of God will be taken from the Jerusalem leadership and given to "another people" who

---

[9] Note *One Gospel from Two*, 246–47, for a discussion of Mark's compositional activity in these verses. Of special interest is the argument that Mark deliberately highlights themes in the Lord's Prayer as being central to the spiritual vision that the book commends. This would indicate that Mark is familiar with the Lord's Prayer, even though he does not include the full version in his Gospel.

[10] Donald Juel, *Messiah and Temple* (SBLDS 31; Missoula, Mont.: Scholars, 1977), 135. In short, God's house will be people: "living stones" (cf. 1 Pet 2:4–10).

can lead Israel better.[11] In the context of Mark the vineyard will come to be the community of faith and prayer. It will no longer be defined either by its structure (the temple), nor will it be a particular ethnic community. Its capstone will be Jesus himself (Acts 4:11; 1 Pet 2:7).

A second important indicator of the nature of the new temple occurs in Mark 12:28–34 where the scribe asks about the greatest commandment. Especially striking is the wording of Mark 12:32b–34, which does not occur in the parallels of Matt 22:34–40 and Luke 10:25–28, 20:39–40. In the conversation with the scribe, Jesus defines the essence of Torah (Mark 12:29–31). The scribe responds positively using similar terminology (Mark 12:32–33). Interestingly, the scribe's response in 32b expresses a concern for monotheism (a point of interest to a community that incorporates Gentiles). Then in 12:33b the scribe attaches a comment to the commandment on love of neighbor: "it is much more than all whole burnt offerings and sacrifices." This signature response is a deliberate Marcan composition. In response Jesus says, "You are not far from the kingdom of God." Jesus commends the scribe for understanding that the centerpiece of the faith is no longer the temple but a people characterized by love of God and neighbor.

Finally, Mark announces explicitly what has been implicit in this unit: The temple will be destroyed (Mark 13:2). As with Matthew and Luke, Mark spends considerable time on this matter. The focus is not on the destruction of the temple itself but the horrors that will precede its end (Mark 13:5–23, 28–31).[12] Mark's point can be stated concisely. The end of the temple will come within a generation. But this is not the end of the age. One does not know when the Son of Man will come (Mark 13:24–27; 32–37). In the meantime the new mission begun among the Gentiles bringing the gospel to all nations will continue (Mark 13:10). Unlike Matthew 24:14, Mark does not connect the mission with the eschaton. The horrors that accompany the proclamation in Mark 13:9–13 appear to be an abiding reality for the new community. Jesus suffered from Jewish and Gentile authorities. His followers will not escape similar harassments. The "living stones" of the new temple of Jew and Gentile are called simply to remain faithful to the end (Mark 13:13). If found faith-

---

[11] See the excellent explanation by Anthony J. Saldarini, *Matthew's Christian-Jewish Community* (Chicago: University of Chicago Press, 1990), 60–61. Matthew's account refers to a change of leadership within the Jewish community.

[12] Allan J. McNicol, *Jesus' Directions for the Future* (Macon, Ga.: Mercer University Press, 1996), 151–92.

ful, they will be gathered from the ends of the earth when the Son of Man comes in his glory (Mark 13:27).

Intimations of Gentile Inclusion in the Galilean Ministry

At the center of Mark's narrative is a riveting focus upon the life of Jesus. It is important to remember that, as with any biographer, Mark must follow a principle of selectivity in portraying his subject.[13] At the heart of the activity of Jesus, before the fateful week in Jerusalem, is the Galilean ministry. As late as Mark 9:12 and 10:1, Jesus appears in Galilee. For Mark, Jesus' proclamation of the good news of the kingdom in Galilee has a generally positive tone (Mark 1:14, 38–39, 45; 3:14; 5:2; 6:12; 7:36). On the other hand, as in Matthew, Jerusalem is not a positive place for Jesus. Not only is he crucified there, but even while he is in Galilee, his enemies come "from Jerusalem" (Mark 3:22; 7:1).[14] Moreover, the focus on the Galilean mission has other overtones. Galilee was populated by both Jews and Gentiles and was traversed by a major route to Damascus and Greater Syria. Christianity won acceptance very early among Gentiles in Syria.[15] Although the political scene in Galilee had changed considerably from the time of Jesus' ministry to the writing of Mark, the Jewish-Gentile population mix remained relatively stable. As such, Jesus' fortunes in Galilee

---

[13] For example, Mark (at least in our received form) has no account of the birth of Jesus nor a record of his formative early years, features that are central to most biographies in the Hellenistic world. Moreover, as already noted, to undergird the theological claim that he is the crucified Son of God, Mark highlights the last days of Jesus culminating in his agonizing death. Indeed the crucifixion casts a shadow over the entire Marcan story.

[14] Donald Senior and Carroll Stuhlmueller, *The Biblical Foundations for Mission* (Maryknoll, N.Y.: Orbis, 1983), 218. Nevertheless, this is not the total story. As pointed out by Andreas J. Köstenberger and Peter O'Brien (*Salvation to the Ends of the Earth* [Downers Grove, Ill.: Apollos/InterVarsity, 2001], 85), Galilee does not always appear in a favorable light. Jesus certainly suffered rejection there even from his own family (Mark 6:1–6), and misunderstanding by his disciples. The most detailed treatment of the whole issue in recent times is the work of Zenji Kato, *Die Völkermission im Markusevangelium: Eine Redaktionsgeschichtliche Untersuchung* (Bern: Lang, 1986). Kato takes the position that the Marcan message of Jesus himself (i.e., gospel) is an overlay of earlier traditions. The overlay conveys the reality of the experience of the first century church in taking the gospel to the Gentiles.

[15] As noted by W. R. Farmer (*Jesus and the Gospel* [Philadelphia: Fortress, 1982], 138–40) Matthew uses the Isaianic quote (Isa 9:1–2), incorporating Galilee of the Gentiles, as the framework for his account of Jesus' ministry (Matt 4:12–25; 13:1–3; 15:29–30; 17:22–23; 19:1–2). Thus an association of Gentiles and Galilee is embedded in both the Gospel tradition and early Christian mission.

could serve as a template for what happened in other Jewish and Gentile communities (including the Roman church) after receiving the gospel of Jesus. Thus, the Galilean ministry functions for Mark as a deliberate construct. The course of Jesus' ministry not only is preparatory for the events in Jerusalem, but also becomes a crucial resource whereby the end-time people of God may learn about the appropriate place of Jew and Gentile in the kingdom. We will briefly note some of these lessons that emerge in Mark 1–10.

Jesus' ministry commences with the announcement of the coming of God's new world (Mark 1:14–15). Jesus' mission centers on teaching that realistically includes his exorcisms and healings (cf. Mark 1:21–28). The early emphasis on calling disciples (1:16–20; 2:13–14) culminates in the call of the Twelve (3:7–19). The formation of the Twelve is generally accepted as an announcement that through his ministry Jesus viewed the re-formation or restoration of Israel as taking place. Thus, for Mark, the destiny of Israel occupies a very prominent place in Jesus' mission.

No sooner does he announce Israel's restoration than Jesus' ministry begins to follow a strange new course. With opposition coming from the heart of Israel (3:22) the account underscores that the true follower of Jesus is not identified by family or ethnic connection, but only by doing the will of God (Mark 3:31–35; 6:1–6). Only insiders will know the truth of Jesus' ministry (Mark 4:11–12). But as the ministry unfolds, even the closest insiders (the Twelve) do not fully comprehend what is taking place (Mark 4:33–41). And that cloud of misunderstanding does not dissipate until the empty tomb. In the meantime, Mark gives an early indicator that Jesus' ministry will have an impact beyond Israel. In a lengthy account, he narrates the exorcism of the Gerasene demoniac (Mark 5:1–20). News of this incredible event spreads through the heavily Gentile cities of the Decapolis where this man seems to be well known (Mark 5:20).

After Jesus' rejection in his hometown (Mark 6:1–6), the Twelve, the nucleus of the new Israel, are sent forth in mission (Mark 6:7–30).[16] Mark is almost silent about what happened. Rather, he goes into a long recitation about the perfidity of Herod Antipas in killing John the Baptist. This seems to function both as an anticipation of the death of Jesus and as a reminder of the brutality of some of the Roman imperial authorities. The

---

[16] Noticeably in comparison with the parallel instructions to the Twelve in Matt 10:5–10, Mark omits any reference to a prohibition against going among the Gentiles (Matt 10:5–6). There may be a faint echo of this in Mark 7:27, but, even here, the Gentile as well as the Jew is the beneficiary of Jesus' mission.

kingdom will not come from the power of the nation-state, whether it be Israelite or Gentile.

Now we come to a crucial juncture in Mark (6:30—8:21). Much of the activity of Jesus centers around the Sea of Galilee. Commentators have long noted that in this section Jesus seems to oscillate between entering Jewish and Gentile regions.[17] What is less readily noticed is another aspect of the unit that highlights the disciples. Herod (Mark 6:14–24) and the Pharisees (Mark 7:1–23) are pictured as opponents. In the heart of the narrative are the two great feedings of the multitudes in 6:31–44 and 8:1–10. Then toward the end of the unit in 8:14–21 a very important incident occurs. Embarking into the boat Jesus begins to warn his disciples about the leaven of Herod and the Pharisees (Mark 8:15). To the Marcan reader this can only mean to "watch out" for the leaven (pervading influence) of the already identified traditional power structures of the time. The confounded disciples wonder whether they are being rebuked for not bringing enough bread. But the perceptive reader views matters on a different level. Jesus reminds the disciples that the feeding of the five thousand led to massive amounts of bread being left over (Mark 8:19). The same was true with the four thousand (Mark 8:20). At this point, full understanding by the disciples is withheld (Mark 8:21; cf. 6:52; 8:17). But in the retrospective view of a reader a generation after the cross there is insight: the feeding stories indicate that with the new world coming with Jesus' mission, in contrast to ordinary reality and political leadership, there abundant resources exist for all, both Jew and Gentile.

Clearly, in Mark 6:30–44, Jesus feeds a massive number. Ever since Mark 5:21 it appears that the focus of Jesus' ministry is among the Jewish people. This culminates with the feeding of the 5000, who are usually thought to be from Israel.[18] Yet shortly after, in Mark 6:53, the focus shifts.

---

[17] An influential analysis is Werner Kelber, *The Kingdom in Mark: A New Place and a New Time* (Philadelphia: Fortress, 1974), 45–65. Technically speaking, Mark seems to organize the unit into a trip starting and ending at Bethsaida (Mark 6:45; 8:22).

[18] G. H. Boobyer, "The Miracles of the Loaves and the Gentiles in St. Mark's Gospel," *SJT* 6 (1953): 77–87, arguing against this consensus, contends that the recipients of both feeding incidents were Gentiles. This is only the tip of an iceberg of a long-standing discussion among scholars, involving, of all things, Marcan geography. There are many interpreters who claim that Mark is saying that when Jesus is on the west bank of the Sea of Galilee (the Feeding of the Five Thousand) he affirms his mission to Israel. When he is on the east bank (the Feeding of the Four Thousand) he is among Gentiles. Boobyer argued that both feedings took place on the east bank. In my view, this line of reasoning is too esoteric because the geographical references are unclear. Rather, Mark's emphasis in the feeding stories is that there is plenty of food (both material and spiritual) for both Jew and for Gentile. Thus,

The people of Gennesaret (Gentile territory?) receive Jesus well (Mark 6:53–56). Then, in the presence of the Pharisees, Jesus declares all foods clean (Mark 7:19). Immediately following this incident, Jesus accepts a Gentile woman on the basis of her great faith (Mark 7:24–30).[19] Clearly, Mark evinces a growing interest in Gentiles.

Within this significant unit (Mark 6:30—8:22), the disciples have seen amazing things. Indicative of the feeding stories, Jesus provides abundantly for both Jew and Gentile. At this stage his followers are prevented from full understanding (Mark 6:52). In the unit 8:22—10:52 they must learn that the basis for this unification of Jew and Gentile will be the way of the cross.[20] To the sensitive reader of Mark, the disciples are transparencies. Through the learning experience of the disciples, Mark is telling believers throughout the Greco-Roman world that, on the basis of faith, the ground at the foot of the cross is equal for both Jew and Gentile. This point comes fully into the light of day in the Passion Narrative.

The Founding of a New Community as God's Temple

Mark, of course, concludes his narrative with the Passion account (Mark 14:12—16:8[20]). As already noted, at the beginning of the momentous last week in Jerusalem, Mark focuses on a withering critique of the Jerusalem temple and its replacement. Indeed, a pericope at the end of this unit affirms this claim (Mark 14:3–9). Jesus enters the house of a leper. An unknown woman intrudes and pours expensive ointment upon him. This is interpreted as both an anticipation of his anointing, in view of a premature death, and a prefiguration of the announcement of his kingship at the cross (Mark 14:3, 8; 15:26). Then Jesus makes a momentous announce-

---

although there is a definite shift toward the Gentiles in this unit, it cannot be conclusively determined in the feeding stories.

[19] Indeed, the next incident of the healing of the deaf and speech-impaired man in Mark 7:31–37 takes place in the Decapolis. See *One Gospel from Two,* 179–80. In the Matthean parallel, the Decapolis is not mentioned (Matt 15:29–31). Also Matthew refers to the woman by the traditional derogatory term of "Canaanite" (Matt 15:22). For Mark, the woman was a "Greek," by birth, "Syrophoenecian" (Mark 7:26). Nevertheless, even in this place of great concern for a Gentile, the Jewish mission ("to the Jew first" of Rom 1:16) is not lost (Mark 7:27).

[20] This is most clearly indicated in Mark 8:31–38; 9:30–37; 10:32–45 which set forth the controlling pattern of this unit three times. Jesus announces his coming destiny (crucifixion and resurrection). The disciples misunderstand. Jesus gives a word of clarification that true discipleship involves taking up the way of the cross.

ment. This woman will be remembered wherever the gospel is proclaimed throughout the entire world (Mark 14:9). Mark (unlike Matthew or Luke) regularly uses "gospel" in an absolute sense for the proclamation about Jesus' vindication through his death, burial, and resurrection. Linking up with 13:10, Mark envisions the proclamation of the word to all humans from Jesus' death until the Parousia. The existence of a community of believers behind the gospel is a necessary presupposition for the task. It will be composed of Jew and Gentile in order to bring this word to the whole world.

An additional link to the Gentile mission comes at Jesus' trial before the Jewish council (Sanhedrin). The earlier activities of Jesus at the temple (Mark 11:15–18) will again come to light and play a crucial role in the proceedings. After his arrest by the temple authorities Jesus appears before the council (Mark 14:53–72). The whole episode has many jarring features and is clearly puzzling. Some even question whether the trial ever had a basis in historical fact.[21] Following the narrative, however, one of the oddest features of this pericope occurs in 14:55–59. The temple authorities are seeking testimony against Jesus worthy of a capital offense (Mark 14:55). Finding none, some bring false testimony; and, most oddly, it is contradictory. This can only mean that Mark pictures the entire scene as chaotic. In the middle of this chaos, a significant theme emerges. Certain ones testify that they have heard Jesus say, "I will destroy this temple made by hand, and in three days I will build another, not made by hand" (Mark 14:58). Donald Juel provided insight by pointing out that this is a scene filled with irony.[22] Strictly speaking, if one follows the narrative, Jesus had not said that he would destroy the temple and build another in three days.[23] Yet, on a deeper level, Jesus' earlier critique in 11:15–17 and 13:2 indicates that such a charge is true, although not in the way the opponents understand it. God was about to put an end to the temple; and in three days (clearly a reference to the resurrection), there would emerge another temple, not made by hand.[24]

---

[21] E.P. Sanders, *Jesus and Judaism* (Philadelphia: Fortress, 1985), 299.

[22] Juel, *Messiah and Temple*, 205.

[23] John 2:19 is aware of a saying that comes close but refers the temple to Jesus' body. See also Matt 26:61.

[24] Juel, *Messiah and Temple*, 205, identifies this temple as "the Christian church." Juel's wording should be nuanced. Probably we come closer to Mark's position by stating the physical temple's replacement in terms of Pauline terminology. The risen Christ inaugurates the eschatological community of Jesus' disciples and fills it as a body with power. The charge "made by hand" is clearly negative. See Raymond Brown, *The Death of the Messiah*

Significantly, the charge against Jesus in Mark 14:58 is the first time that the Greek word for the "inner sanctuary" of the temple, as opposed to the general word for "temple premises," is used in Mark. Since the inner sanctuary is the locale of God's special presence this deepens the charge against Jesus. It remains in the minds of those who taunt Jesus while he is on the cross (Mark 15:29). And, finally, in 15:38 the curtain concealing God's presence in the inner sanctuary is ripped from top to bottom at the moment of Jesus' death. The point of irony is complete. Jesus' prophetic activity, set in full motion when he comes into the city, has borne fruit. The temple made by hand is rendered profane. The time for its replacement, the revealing of the end-time people of God is at hand. The title on the cross, ironically true, screams "King of the Jews" (Mark 14:26). But even this is not the full truth. In his death Jesus builds a new and living temple that is open for both Jew and Gentile. The culminating point comes in the remark of the Gentile centurion, "Surely, this man was the Son of God!" (Mark 15:39). Through his committed ministry, culminating in his death, Jesus has made known the depth of God's love; he is prepared to give his life as a sign of that commitment.

A reader of Mark who views the Gospel as ending at 16:8 is not presented with a pretty picture. The disciples have fled. The fearful women are in panic, unable to bring word about the empty tomb. But, by no means is this the end of the story. Reconciliation will take place in Galilee (Mark 16:7). This has to be the correct reading because throughout the passion narrative Mark goes out of his way to show that Jesus was a prophet and what he said comes to pass as true. Key pieces of this puzzle are the passion predictions (Mark 8:31; 9:30–31; 10:32–34). Intimately connected with these predictions are the words spoken at the prophecy of Peter's denial, "But after I have risen, I will go ahead to Galilee" (Mark 14:28). Similar words occur in Mark 16:7. Given this superstructure, the reader of Mark must believe that reconciliation between Jesus and his disciples occurs in Galilee (cf. Matt 28:10, 16–20).

A number of years ago C. F. Evans gave considerable reflection on the use of the Greek word "to go before" in Mark.[25] After lengthy analysis that covers some, but by no means all, of the territory negotiated in this article, Evans concludes there are only two options for solving this conundrum. Either one understands this to be a reference to the Parousia,[26] or

(ABRL 1; New York: Doubleday, 1994), 438–44.
[25] C.F. Evans, "'I Will Go Before You Into Galilee'," *JTS* 5 (1954): 3–18. Mark 14:28 and 16:7 are the key passages.
[26] Thus, W. Marxsen, *Mark the Evangelist* (trans. Roy A. Harrisville et al.; Nashville:

one should understand it to mean "he is leading you to the Gentiles."[27] In light of our discussion, one may offer a slight reformulation. The return to Galilee is really the first step in a worldwide mission where Jesus will incorporate both Jew and Gentile into his new temple. There we will meet him. Or, to echo Paul, God is no longer a God of the Jews only, but has brought both Jew and Gentile into a universal community (Rom 3:29–30). The outcome of Jesus' life proves God to be One God of all.

Mark and the Church in Rome

How would the church in Rome hear Mark's narrative account of Jesus' life? The question, asked many times, may never be definitively answered.[28] Many pieces of the puzzle of the early years of the church at Rome still remain to be put in place.[29] Recently the English translation of Peter Lampe's massive study of Christianity at Rome in the first two centuries of our era has reinvigorated the issue.[30] Heavy on prosopographic investigations, it has made one thing clear: the tensions between Jew and Gentile reflected in Paul's letter to the Romans were embedded in the constituencies of the small group of house churches that constituted the early decades of Roman Christianity. Lampe makes some useful comments about how social structure affected the organization of the church in Rome well into the second century[31] but mainly eschews theological issues. Clearly, however, Paul's letter to the Romans reveals that there were considerable tensions. And *1 Clement*, written in the latter part of the first century, indicates that they continued.[32] Within this context of ethnic tension, betrayal by fellow believ-

---

Abingdon, 1969), 54–95.

[27] C.F. Evans, "I Will Go Before You Into Galilee," 18.

[28] Some question that the audience for the gospels can be restricted to a community in a relatively small area. Richard Bauckham, "For Whom Were the Gospels Written?" in *The Gospels for All Christians: Rethinking the Gospel Audiences* (ed. R. Bauckham; Grand Rapids: Eerdmans, 1998), 9–48. This perspective has some plausibility. But, one must remember that the church at Rome, even in the first century, was not entirely unrepresentative of the small struggling Christian communities outside of Judea.

[29] David Dungan ("The Purpose and Provenance of the Gospel of Mark according to the 'Two Gospel' [Owen-Griesbach] Hypothesis" in *New Synoptic Studies* [ed. William R. Farmer, Macon, Ga: Mercer University Press, 1983], 411–40) would be the first to agree.

[30] Peter Lampe, *From Paul to Valentinus: Christians at Rome in the First Two Centuries* (ed. Marshall D. Johnson; trans. Michael Steinhauser; Minneapolis: Fortress, 2003).

[31] Lampe, *From Paul to Valentinus*, 397–412.

[32] *1 Clement* 5–6. See Raymond E. Brown and John P. Meier, *Antioch and Rome: New Testament Cradles of Catholic Christianity* (New York: Paulist, 1982), 159–83. On conflict in Rome, see Donahue, "Windows and Mirrors," 24–25.

ers and subsequent demoralization in the church, even after the Neronian persecutions had passed, an irenical account of Jesus' mission as inclusive of both Jew and Gentile would be plausible—even if it may not be welcome in all quarters. Paul's plea for the conversion of all Israel (Rom 9–11) now has subsided. The concern for the church is primarily internal unity, not the conversion of Israel. For this situation Mark is an excellent reminder that in the life of Jesus the true gospel has come. Jesus has formed both Jew and Gentile into a new temple. To ensure that it not be profaned, every believer should take up the way of the cross, living a life of faith, forgiveness, and prayer. The Marcan life of Jesus is a model for this way of discipleship.

Some years ago James Thompson addressed similar issues in an informative exegetical study of Mark 13:10.[33] This essay contends that the theme of an inclusive mission pervades the totality of Mark. I offer this study on the grounds of both our long friendship and appreciation for the many exegetical insights that are clearly evident in the work he has produced over the years.

---

[33] James W. Thompson, "The Gentile Missions as an Eschatological Necessity," *ResQ* 14 (1971): 18–27.

Traditions in Texts

5

The Rhetoric of Adventure
Deuteronomy 1:19–46 and Gilgamesh III

Mark W. Hamilton

How did ancient Near Eastern rhetors persuade audiences? What rules did they follow? Although rhetorical criticism of their ancient texts has received much attention over the past century, especially for biblical studies since Muilenburg's programmatic 1969 essay,[1] much remains to be done, especially when we think of the rhetorical event as something more than the structure of texts or their aesthetic dimensions.[2] Unlike our colleagues in New Testament studies or Greco-Roman antiquity in general, who may draw on ancient handbooks and monographs from Plato to Cicero to Quintilian, we must resort to mirror reading of texts. Still progress can occur.

As a contribution to the larger project of examining ancient Near Eastern approaches to persuasion, I offer the following comparative study of two texts: (1) parts of the Standard Babylonian Tablet III of the "Epic of Gilgamesh," which recites speeches by Gilgamesh to the elders of Uruk,

---

[1] James Muilenburg, "Form Criticism and Beyond," *JBL* 88 (1969): 1–18.

[2] For a criticism of the tendency of biblical scholars to think of rhetoric in structural and aesthetic terms, that is, to work primarily as *literary* critics, see the handbook of Phyllis Trible, *Rhetorical Criticism: Context, Method, and the Book of Jonah* (GBS; Minneapolis: Fortress, 1994), 48–52; but Alan Hauser, "Rhetorical Criticism of the Old Testament," in *Rhetorical Criticism of the Bible: A Comprehensive Bibliography with Notes on History and Method* (ed. Duane Watson and Alan Hauser; BibInt 4; Leiden: Brill, 1994), 4; Mark Gray, *Rhetoric and Social Justice in Isaiah* (LHBOTS 432; London: T. & T. Clark, 2006) 4–10.

who must, at some level, approve of his and Enkidu's mission to slay the giant Humbaba; and (2) Deuteronomy 1:19–46, which recounts a speech by the character Moses[3] recounting the failure of Israel to take the land from "a great people, one taller than we, with cities great and fortified in the sky, yes sons of the Anaqim" (עַם גָּדוֹל וָרָם מִמֶּנּוּ עָרִים גְּדֹלֹת וּבְצוּרֹת בַּשָּׁמָיִם בְּנֵי עֲנָקִים; 1:28). While no genetic relationship between the stories exists, and in many respects they breathe different atmospheres (one the world of epic and heroism, the other of moral instruction), nevertheless they share narrative elements (a hero contemplating a fight with giants, the search for divine approval, the validation of other humans of their quest), and they illustrate different options for speechmaking in the ancient Near East. While the precise extent of Israel's knowledge of Gilgamesh remains disputed, we do know that the epic was known throughout the Levant and did have some measurable impact upon the biblical tradition.[4] We also know that Deuteronomy knew, if not the epic itself, then the Mesopotamian literary traditions. Both texts interact with widespread ancient Near Eastern conceptions of heroism and kingship,[5] if in radically different ways. Both texts rework older traditions (either JE or the Old Babylonian version of the epic and even older discrete stories). Thus a comparison of the two texts, identifying both points of similarity and of contrast, is an appropriate way of studying the rhetorical options of the ancient Near East.

Each document includes several speeches, or oral, communication events involving more than two persons and addressing issues of public interest. The following analysis of these texts draws on contemporary argumentation theory, especially as articulated by Toulmin[6] and Perelman

---

[3] It goes without saying that reference to Moses as speaker in Deut 1 is a literary device of a much later author.

[4] See, e.g., the discussion in Alexander Heidel, *The Gilgamesh Epic and Old Testament Parallels* (Chicago: University of Chicago Press, 1949); Hans-Peter Münster, "Parallelen zu Gen 2f and Ez 28 aus dem Gilgamesch Epos," *ZAH* 3 (1990): 167–78; but Karel van der Toorn, "Echoes of Gilgamesh in The Book of Qoheleth? A reassessment of the Intellectual Sources of Qohelet," in *Veenhof Anniversary Volume* (ed. W. H. Van Soldt; Leiden: Nederlands Instituut voor het Nabije Oosten, 2001), 503–14.

[5] On the world of the hero, see the recent work of Gregory Mobley, *The Empty Men: The Heroic Tradition of Ancient Israel* (ABRL; New York: Doubleday, 2005).

[6] Stephen Toulmin, *The Uses of Argument* (1958; rev. ed.; Cambridge: Cambridge University Press, 2003). See a survey of the literature in Frans H. van Eemeren, "Argumentation Theory: An Overview of Approaches and Research Themes," in *Rhetorical Argumentation in Biblical Texts: Essays from the Lund 2000 Conference* (ed. Anders Eriksson, Thomas Olbricht, and Walter Übelacker; Harrisburg, Penn.: Trinity, 2002), 9–26.

and Olbrechts-Tyteca and some of their successors.[7] By examining the nature of the arguments on offer and their sequencing, it is possible to understand more fully ancient speech-making. As Perelman and Olbrechts-Tyteca noted, the ordering of arguments can help or hurt an audience's acceptance of them when "the self-evidence of the axiom is a preoccupation, and where, in the choice of steps, one is preoccupied with the relative intelligibility of particular orders of demonstration."[8] Arguments must move from the accepted to the disputed, at least in principle, if the audience is to accept them. In addition to the hoary Aristotelian categories of ethos, logos, and pathos (and the concomitant focus upon the character of the rhetor culminating in Quintilian), a study of the content, shape, and ordering of arguments reveals the rhetor's perception of the shifting moods of audiences (even literarily constructed ones as in the texts at hand) and the needs of the speaker himself or herself.[9] This is especially true when a speech event can be situated in a network of such events, or, in other words, when a particular speech demonstrably draws upon, recasts, reuses, or otherwise engages with an identifiable tradition of ideas, beliefs, or literary motifs, as is the case with the two texts at hand. Let us examine first Gilgamesh and then Deuteronomy.

Gilgamesh III

The Standard Babylonian[10] edition of Gilgamesh was edited in the late second millennium BCE and circulated widely in Mesopotamia throughout the first millennium, where it was apparently a popular text in both Assyria and Babylonia. Tablet III includes a number of speeches, if, again, we define "speech" as an oral communication event involving one or more speakers and an audience of more than a handful of persons (although even here the boundary between conversation and speech is fluid). Unsurprisingly, Gilgamesh himself is usually the speaker, though Enkidu, Ninsun, Humbaba, and the officials of Uruk also sometimes make orations. These speeches concentrate in the first five tablets, though perhaps

---

[7] Chaïm Perelman and L. Olbrechts-Tyteca, *The New Rhetoric: A Treatise on Argumentation* (Notre Dame, Ind.: University of Notre Dame Press, 1969). For a critical analysis, see Christopher Tindale, *Rhetorical Argumentation: Principles of Theory and Practice* (Thousand Oaks, Cal.: Sage, 2004), esp. 66–69.

[8] Perelman and Olbrechts-Tyteca, *New Rhetoric*, 490.

[9] See ibid., 494.

[10] On the relationship of the Standard Babylonian edition to the Old Babylonian version, see A. R. George, *The Babylonian Gilgamesh Epic* (2 vols.; Oxford: Oxford University Press, 2003), 1:192–216.

others have not survived. The audience of the speech may include large crowds, or sometimes a deity. On one occasion, Enkidu addresses a door, though of course his "real" audience is the audience of the epic itself. The following table illustrates the use of speeches in the narrative of the epic.

Text	Speaker	Audience	Subject
I. 84–91(?)	the gods	Anu	Pleading for Gilgamesh's subjects against him
I.94–98	the gods	Aruru	Fashion Enkidu!
II.260–71	Gilgamesh	Young men (*eṭlūtu*)	Boasting of trip of Uruk
II. 272–86	Enkidu	Elders (*šībūtu*)	Advice against Gilgamesh's trip
II.287–99	Senior advisors (*malikē rabbūtu*)	Gilgamesh	Advice against Gilgamesh's trip
III.1–12	Enkidu(?), elders(?)	Gilgamesh	Let Enkidu go first
III.23–34	Gilgamesh	Ninsun	A prayer
III.35–99	Ninsun	Shamash	A prayer for Gilgamesh's success
III.202–11	Gilgamesh	Officials of Uruk	Charge to protect Urukians
III.212–27	Officials (*šakkanakkū*, etc.)	Gilgamesh	Repeating old advice
V.86–94	Humbaba	Gilgamesh/ Enkidu	Taunt of friends
V.145–55	Humbaba	Gilgamesh/ Enkidu	Plea for life

Text	Speaker	Audience	Subject
V.175–80	Humbaba	Gilgamesh/ Enkidu	Plea for life
VI.172–78	Gilgamesh	Serving girls of palace (*muttabilātiša bītišu*)	Boasting of prowess
VII.39–63	Enkidu	A door	Reverse of building dedication
VIII.3–56	Gilgamesh	Men of the city	Obsequy for Enkidu
VIII.67–91	Gilgamesh	Call to all the land	Call to people to mourn

Here I wish to examine part of the deliberations surrounding Gilgamesh's decision to hunt down Humbaba, the giant in the Cedar Forest, a section beginning in II.260 and extending to the end of Tablet III. The section consists of eleven recognizable units as well as two significant breaks (one of two lines and the other of sixty-six)

A. A speech by Gilgamesh advocating the assault on Humbaba (II.260–71)
B. A speech by Enkidu opposing the adventure (II.272–86)
C. An identical speech by the elders of Uruk first opposing and then supporting the adventure (II.287—III.12)[11]
D. A request by Gilgamesh asking Enkidu to join him in appealing to Ninsun (III.13–22)
E. A prayer by Gilgamesh to Ninsun (III.23–34)

[11] While Ronald T. Ridley ("The Saga of an Epic: Gilgamesh and the Constitution of Uruk," *Orientalia* 69 [2000]: 341–67, esp. 365) may be right to posit a distinction between the elders and the younger men in older stages of the epic, the SB edition seems to use the two groups in parallel. The precise function of the council remains obscure in the SB version, though apparently Gilgamesh must win their approval for his mission.

F. A prayer/speech by Ninsun to Shamash (III.35–99)
G. A second prayer/speech by Ninsun to Shamash (III.100–10)
H. Lacuna (III.111–12)
I. A blessing by Gilgamesh and Enkidu by Ninsun (III.113–35)
J. Extensive lacunae (III.136–201)
K. A farewell address by Gilgamesh to the elders of Uruk (III.202–11)
L. A speech in response by the elders to Gilgamesh (III.212–27)
M. A speech by Enkidu (III.228—end [broken])

Sections B and C, A and D, and D and L correspond closely, often verbatim, although the repetition of lines does not imply a lack of rhetorical movement. The second appearance of given lines may bear a significantly different meaning and suasory impact than the first appearance.

Although many lines are missing from the manuscripts of Tablet III, enough survives to give a sense of the rhetorical strategies used in the (fictive) speeches employed. Since a full analysis of the tablet would takes us far afield, let us focus chiefly on Gilgamesh's opening and closing speeches advocating the adventure against Humbaba and then the arguments against his trip.

First, II.260–71 and III.23–34 contain the same speech with only minor variations: "I will face an unknown battle, ride an unknown road. . . . I will return and perform the *akitu* festival twice in a year. . . ." The repetition of the speech, first to Gilgamesh's subjects in Uruk and then to his mother the goddess Ninsun, recognizes his need to persuade both human and divine stakeholders. Gilgamesh boasts of his passion for the trip (*agdapuš allak*) and then of his future actions. First, he will take the trip to the Cedar Forest by dangerous roads and battle the giant. Then he will return home to celebrate the Akitu festival, the New Year's celebration in which the monarch played an important role.[12] Gilgamesh thus argues that he will return home and carry out the duties of kingship, thus making

---

[12] For the first millennium evidence, which mutatis mutandis bears on the older situation, see Beate Pongratz-Leisten, *Ina Šulmi Īrub: Die kulttopographische und ideologische Programmatik der akitu-Prozession in Babylonien und Assyrien im 1.Jahrtausend v. Chr.* (Mainz: von Zabern, 1994), 109–11. Chronistic texts correlate royal inactivity with the gods' immobility and the noncelebration of the Akitu; see e.g., Chronicle 16.4 (BM 86379); Chronicle 17.ii.1–5 (BM 35968) mentions a royal celebration of the Akitu in Babylon, though with apparent ritual abnormalities. For the texts, see the critical edition of A. K. Grayson, *Assyrian and Babylonian Chronicles* (repr. ed.; Winona Lake, Ind.: Eisenbrauns, 2000).

his adventure not an escape from his responsibilities, but the carrying out of them on a higher plane. He highlights those elements of his adventure that most bear upon his subjects' needs, thus selecting aspects that will make his case most persuasive, or, as Perelman and Olbrechts-Tyteca put it, the rhetor displays "certain elements on which" he "wishes to center attention in order that they may occupy the foreground of the hearer's consciousness."[13] Gilgamesh downplays the Urukians' highlighting of the adventure's danger to him and implicitly to themselves, since they risk losing their king. He emphasizes instead the glory that will accrue to himself, his city, and his gods.

Although the speeches to the Urukians and to Ninsun are essentially identical, they have different purposes. The first functions as deliberative speech (to use Aristotle's terminology), i.e., it seeks to persuade a reluctant audience of the validity of the speaker's proposed actions. The second, however, functions both to persuade Ninsun to appeal to the higher deity, Shamash, for aid (which Ninsun obligingly does), but also to celebrate in advance appropriate rituals, which would honor both Ninsun and Shamash. Thus the second speech borders on epideisis. It is a prayer for one deity to pray to another.

While the rhetoric of prayer is largely unexplored territory,[14] it seems to me that such a prayer as Gilgamesh's functions much like the offer to praise at the conclusion of many psalms of lament in the Bible. The repetition of the various arguments for Gilgamesh's trip to a series of increasingly significant audiences both leverages the sensory networks of the characters' world of the epic, and makes those arguments more persuasive to the implied hearers of the Epic itself. Since the two audiences (the Urukians and Ninsun) will experience the Akitu differently, the mention of it functions differently in the two iterations of these (identical at a surface level) speeches. As Pongratz-Leisten points out, the mythological elements of the Akitu concretized the antecedent ritual.[15] In the "Gilgamesh Epic," the movement becomes still more complex, as narrative underwrites ritual, which in turn gives meaning to the narrative.

Second, Ninsun's speeches to Shamash (III.46–99 and 101–10) seek Shamash's approval for an action that will anger some deities and will pose

---

[13] Perelman and Olbrechts-Tyteca, *New Rhetoric*, 142.

[14] A rare study of the rhetoric of prayer is by Patrick Miller, "Prayer as Persuasion: The Rhetoric and Intention of Prayer," in *Israelite Religion and Biblical Theology* (JSOTSup 267; Sheffield: Sheffield Academic Press, 2000), 337–44.

[15] Pongratz-Leisten, *Ina Šulmi Īrub*, 109–11.

danger to Gilgamesh and Enkidu.[16] Moreover, as god of justice, Shamash has some stake in Gilgamesh's actions as a king, since the monarch must guarantee justice. Ninsun opens by blaming Shamash for giving Gilgamesh an "unsleeping heart" (*libbu lā ṣalālu*; l. 46), arguing that the deity must take responsibility for her son's rashness. She then cites his earlier speech about traveling unknown paths and fighting Humbaba, whom, however, she labels "the wretched thing you hate" (*mimma lemnu*[17] *ša tāzerru*; l. 54), thus labeling the hero's intended victim as one deserving death and implying an enthymeme: the god of justice hates Humbaba; he must therefore be evil; the role of the king (Gilgamesh) is to destroy evil (cf. Psalm 101; DT 1[18]); therefore Gilgamesh is justified in killing Humbaba. Her second speech adds a further argument, i.e., that Gilgamesh is destined to share heaven with Shamash (ll. 101–10). The precise theological point is unclear,[19] but the statement clearly states an implied enthymeme: since Gilgamesh is fated to work alongside Shamash, the deity ought to protect him. Ninsun also assumes what all Mesopotamians assumed, viz., that, as Benjamin Foster puts it in another context, "useful knowledge was transmitted vertically, from above to below."[20] Persuasion in this context is merely reminder; Shamash, at least notionally, persuades himself.

Third, the final extant speech in Tablet III (ll. 215–27) comes from the Urukians, who have granted Gilgamesh permission to leave them in order to play the hero, with certain conditions. Their advice draws inspiration from Ninsun's appointment of Enkidu to the leadership of the expedition (ll. 124–33), even if we do not know how they knew what she had done (the text is broken). In any case, they begin by counseling Gilgamesh

---

[16] In the Old Babylonian version, Gilgamesh speaks directly to Shamash. The introduction of an intermediary in the Standard Babylonian version arguably fits the later move to question the hero's ability to master the world (see the general discussion, not of this text, in Thorkild Jacobsen, *The Treasures of Darkness: A History of Mesopotamian Religion* [New Haven: Yale University Press, 1976], 223–26). But rhetorically, the introduction of Ninsun introduces a voice that can make arguments for the adventure that Gilgamesh himself cannot make, since he is not privy to certain information or relationships.

[17] George (*Gilgamesh Epic*, 2: 812) notes that *mimma lemnu* is a technical term for an unknown evil entity in exorcistic and medical texts.

[18] This is the late Neo-Assyrian text that W. G. Lambert (*Babylonian Wisdom Literature* [Oxford: Clarendon, 1960] 110–15) calls "Advice to a Prince," a manifesto for low taxation and the honoring of ancient customs in southern Babylonia. This is the closest Mesopotamian equivalent to the *Fürstenspiegel* of Ps 101.

[19] See George, *Gilgamesh Epic*, 2: 814.

[20] Benjamin R. Foster, "Transmission of Knowledge," in *A Companion to the Ancient Near East* (Malden, Mass.: Blackwell, 2005), 245.

to return home in safety (*ina šulmi*), the unstated assumption being that his return will further his rule.

They then insist that he should allow Enkidu to lead the fight, making several arguments: a warrior should not rely only on himself, but (to quote an apparent proverb), "He who goes in front (*ālik māḫri*) rescues a colleague; let him who knows the way protect (*liṣṣur*) his companion." Here the Standard Babylonian edition recasts its Old Babylonian antecedent while following the basic structure of the older speech. The Old Babylonian proverb (OB III.255–56) makes more sense: "He who goes in front brings his colleague safety (*tappa ušallim*); the one whose eyes gleam (*šuwura*)[21] guards his own life (*pagaršu iṣṣur*)." The Old Babylonian version of the Urukian's speech is much longer and more elegant than the Standard Babylonian version and deserves more attention than I can give it here. Yet the Standard Babylonian revision at this point, while preserving the structure and many of the words of the older version, underscores more saliently Enkidu's role as companion on the road. The Standard Babylonian aphorism, because it states a commonplace that needs no warrant, serves as a warrant for the Urukians' argument (even though in a different context, it might argue for Gilgamesh's going first to save Enkidu).

Their argument continues with a description of Enkidu. Although the text's celebration of Enkidu's warriorly prowess applies equally to Gilgamesh, the speakers do not allow for the possibility that their argument could be subverted.

Why? Because the final speech in Tablet III does not function as deliberative oratory, but as epideictic oratory, to use Aristotle's terminology. That is, the narrative has moved from a period in which Gilgamesh must persuade his audience to allow him to go fight Humbaba, to a situation in which all have agreed on the appropriateness of the fight and are now celebrating it. The skill with which the epic does this is, of course, one more mark of its greatness as literature. But more than that, we see here evidence of options in Babylonian speech-making and speech-hearing and of an internal awareness of such options. Not only can the tradents of the epic assume that their audience understands speeches at multiple, subtle levels, but at least some ancient persons approached the threshold of theorization about rhetoric. Just as the Mesopotamians had an advanced understanding of mathematics and astronomy (being able to predict eclipses and measure plane geometric figures with such notions as the Pythagorean

---

[21] George (*Gilgamesh Epic*, 1:205) more idiomatically renders the phrase "the one whose eyes were peeled."

theorem), even though they did not write formulas or otherwise reduce their knowledge to principles, just so they seem to have been able to think sophisticatedly about rhetoric, even though they did not produce handbooks comparable to those of Aristotle, Cicero, or Quintilian.

These speeches create (1) rhetors who skillfully arrange arguments broadly conceived, using language and imagery effectively, and (2) an audience that attends to such arrangements to make "right" decisions. This is heroic speech, the sort of thing that Deuteronomy deliberately deconstructs.

Deuteronomy 1:19–46

If such self-awareness and ability to create elaborate rhetorical products was true of Mesopotamia, it was also true of ancient Israel. A fictive rhetorical event comparable to the "Epic of Gilgamesh" on at least that point, Deuteronomy presents itself as a series of speeches by Moses on the Plains of Moab addressing the Israelites about to enter the promised land. Although the composition history of the text is complex and debatable at various points,[22] the fictive nature of the rhetorical setting is clear. Given the fluid boundary between written and oral texts,[23] and this text's self-presentation as a speech, the author must have had reason to believe that an ancient audience would have judged his speech verisimilitudinous, and thus we can derive from it a sense, however imperfect, of what an ancient Israelite speech should be. An audience in the exilic era or perhaps earlier in the late monarchy heard "Moses" arguing for contested beliefs and behaviors, using their historical experiences as warrants.[24] The text reshapes (resequences, supplements, deletes, rephrases) older material and fits it into larger argumentation structures in order to persuade its audience.

---

[22] See the discussion in, e.g., Moshe Weinfeld, *Deuteronomy 1–11* (AB 5; New York: Doubleday, 1991), 9–13; Jeffrey Tigay, *Deuteronomy* (Philadelphia: Jewish Publication Society, 1996), xxiv–xxvi; Richard Nelson, *Deuteronomy* (OTL; Louisville: Westminster John Knox, 2002), 3–9.

[23] See the discussion in William Graham, *Beyond the Written Word: Oral Aspects of Scripture in the History of Interpretation* (Cambridge: Cambridge University Press, 1987).

[24] See the remarks of Timo Veijola, "Principal Observations on the Basic Story in Deuteronomy 1–3," in *A Song of Power and the Power of Song: Essays on the Book of Deuteronomy* (Winona Lake, Ind.: Eisenbrauns, 1993), 137–46; on the place of these chapters in the DH, see Martin Noth, *Überlieferungsgeschichtliche Studien* (Tübingen: Mohr/Siebeck, 1967), 3:14; Lothar Perlitt, "Deuteronomium 1–3 im Streit der exegetischen Methoden," in *Das Deuteronomium: Entstehung, Gestalt und Botschaft* (ed. Norbert Lohfink; Leuven: Peeters, 1985), 149–63; Antony Campbell and Mark O'Brien, *Unfolding the Deuteronomistic History* (Minneapolis: Fortress, 2000), 43–46.

Without reviving Gerhard von Rad's conjectures about Levitical preaching,[25] or thinking of Deuteronomy as a true speech,[26] we can examine speeches within the book for clues to rhetorical strategies.

The pericope at hand serves this purpose well. Indeed, the pericope contains one speech event within another, and we should examine the text on at least two levels. At one level, Moses and the children of Israel in the wilderness deliberate on a possible invasion of Canaan, a story that also appears in a P account with JE elements in Numbers 13–14.[27] The genetic relationship among these versions of the story is far from clear, however, and the final version of the P story may presume Deuteronomy.[28] On a second level, Moses many years later (in the world of the narrative) rehearses this episode for different rhetorical purposes. The rhetorical (and temporal) levels interlock at a third level, that of the book's argument for its view of Israelite communal norms. Yet it is possible to separate the various levels of argumentation, and here I wish to focus on the first two.

The Speeches in the Wilderness

The first level consists of an interchange of addresses, not set speeches but excerpts of them set in the wilderness, cited by the speech on the Plains of

---

[25] Gerhard von Rad, "The Levitical Sermon in I and *II Chronicles*," in idem, *The Problem of the Hexateuch and Other Essays* (trans. E. W. Trueman Dicken; New York: McGraw-Hill, 1966), 267–80; see the remarks of Bernard Levinson and Douglas Dance, "The Metamorphosis of Law into Gospel: Gerhard von Rad's Attempt to Reclaim the Old Testament for the Church," in *Recht und Ethik im Alten Testament* (ed. Bernard Levinson and Eckart Otto; Altes Testament und Moderne 13; Münster: LIT, 2004), 103–9.

[26] Marc Brettler, "A 'Literary Sermon' in Deuteronomy 4," in *"A Wise and Discerning Mind": Essays in Honor of Burke O. Long* (ed. Saul Olyan and Robert Culley; Providence, R.I.: Brown Judaic Studies, 2000), 33–50.

[27] Ludwig Schmidt ("Die Kundschafterzählung in Num 13–14 und Dtn 1,19–46," *ZAW* 114 [2002]: 40–58), has recently attempted to isolated the JE elements, but it is difficult to know precisely the direction of dependence between P and JE, nor is a direct line between JE and Deuteronomy readily discernible. Also, Norbert Lohfink, Darstellungskunst und Theologie in Dtn 1,6–3,29," *Biblica* 41 (1960): 107–10; Mittmann, Siegfried, *Deuteronomium 11–63 literarkritisch und traditionsgeschichtlich untersucht* (BZAW 139; Berlin: de Gruyter, 1975), 42–64. (who envisions a multistaged, back-and-forth process of development, JE to D to JEDPR).

[28] Even this is difficult. See the detailed analysis of David Frankel, *The Murmuring Stories of the Priestly School* (SVT 39; Leiden: Brill, 2002), 119–201, esp. 145–60. On the broader issues, Cees Houtman, "Zwei Sichtweisen von Israel als Minderheit inmitten der Bewohner Kanaans: Ein Diskussionsbeitrag zum Verhältnis von J und Dtr(G)," in *Deuteronomy and Deuteronomic Literature* (FS Brekelmans; ed. M. Vervenne and J. Lust; Leuven: Peeters, 1997), 213–31.

Moab for different purposes. Vv. 20–21, after a travelogue notice in v. 19, introduce Moses' two arguments for taking the land: YHWH is giving the land to Israel (נתן יהוה אלהיך [20] אשר יהוה אלהינו נתן לנו לפניך את הארץ [21]), and YHWH has told (דבר) Israel to go. A further backing of these warrants appears when v. 21 calls YHWH אלהי אבתיך ("God of our ancestors"), thus alluding to Deuteronomy's memorial culture and the recurrent theme of the promise to the ancestors.[29] The call to take the land rests on a long-standing divine promise.

This argument resumes in v. 29 with what Nelson calls a "sacral war sermon"[30] after an interlude in which Israelites contest the easy claims to divine protection, an interchange to which we will return momentarily. Moses must shore up his argument by both repetition and extension. V. 29 thus charges Israel not to fear the inhabitants of the land, while vv. 30–31 offer several warrants[31] for this position:

(1) יהוה אלהיכם ההלך לפניכם
("YHWH your God is going before you")

(2) הוא ילחם לכם ככל אשר עשה אתכם במצרים לעיניכם
("He will fight for you just as he did with you in Egypt in your sight")

(3) ובמדבר אשר ראית נשאך יהוה אלהיך
("and in the desert, where you have seen YHWH your God carry you")

(4) כאשר ישא איש את בנו
("just as a man carries his son")

The sequencing of arguments shows authorial care. "Moses" does not mention warfare until the people have first objected to his call to take the land by mentioning fortifications and the prowess of the autochthonous population in v. 28. Moreover, the claim that "YHWH your God goes before," though a rare locution in the Pentateuch (Exod 13:21; Deut 31:6, 8)

---

[29] On which see Georg Braulik, *The Theology of Deuteronomy* (North Richland Hills, Tex.: BIBAL, 1994) 183–98. Deuteronomy mentions the אבות in 1:8, 11, 21, 35; 4:1, 31, 37; 5:3, 9; 6:3, 20, 18, 23; 7:8, 12, 13; 8:1, 18; 9:5; 10:11, 15; 11:9, 21; 12:1; 13:7, 18; 18:8; 19:8; 24:16; 26:3, 7, 15; 27:3; 28:11, 36, 64; 29:12, 24; 30:5, 9, 20; 31:7, 16, 20 (in addition to several instances of אב in the singular). See the study of Norbert Lohfink, *Die Väter Israels in Deuteronomium* (OBO 111; Göttingen: Vandenhoeck & Ruprecht, 1991).

[30] Richard Nelson, *Deuteronomy*, 28–29.

[31] On warrants and backing, see Toulmin, *Uses of Argument*, 89–100.

both frames this section (see also v. 33) and sets the stage for the next two arguments, which necessarily flesh it out. The second and third warrants draw the imagined audience's attention to the stories of the exodus and wilderness wanderings. Moses refutes the Israelites' arguments by appeal to accepted notions about the divine warrior, culminating in an emotional appeal to divine benevolence.

The fourth warrant is perhaps the most interesting, because the commonplace of parental care appears to clinch the argument for divine benevolence by an appeal to pathos. If presented earlier, this warrant would have begged the question: Israel questions YHWH's caring instincts, not the Divine Warrior's prowess. Yet the immediately preceding warrants foreclose distrustful analyses of divine activity. Thus the appeal to emotion—pathos—works rhetorically because it appeals to emotions properly grounded in a certain way of receiving the Israelite tradition. As Perelman and Olbrecht-Tyteca put it, ad hominem arguments work with particular audiences because such arguments share the audience's assumptions about structures of reality.[32] To put things differently, the arrangement of arguments in vv. 29–31 fashions an audience, so to speak, by appealing to two semiotic plains simultaneously, the tradition of wilderness and exodus on the one hand, and the sentiments of family relations on the other. Neither layer of emotional appeal can stand alone, but their juxtaposition creates something larger than the sum of the parts.

The appeal to emotion in the Hebrew Bible deserves far more attention than it has received,[33] even though ancient Greco-Roman rhetorical theorists topicalized the emotional aspects of speech-giving and speech-hearing as a factor in persuasion.[34] Here the appeal to pathos serves

---

[32] Perelman and Olbrechts-Tyteca, *New Rhetoric*, 110–14.

[33] On emotional display in general, see Gary Anderson, *A Time to Mourn, a Time to Dance* (University Park, Penn.: Pennsylvania State University Press, 1991); Mayer Gruber, *Aspects of Nonverbal Communication in the Ancient Near East* (StPohl 12/1–2; 2 vols.; Rome: Biblical Institute Press, 1980); Mark Smith, "The Heart and the Innards in Israelite Emotional Expression: Notes from Anthropology and Psychobiology," *JBL* 117 (1998): 415–26; M. L. Barré, "'Wandering About' as a *Topos* of Depression in Ancient Near Eastern Literature and the Bible," *JNES* 60 (2001): 177–87; J. S. Kselman, "'Wandering About' and Depression: More Examples," *JNES* 61 (2002): 275–77; Paul Kruger, "Depression in the Hebrew Bible: An Update," *JNES* 64 (2005): 187–92.

[34] Aristotle *Rhet.* 1.10; see the discussion in Simo Knuuttila and Juha Sihvola, "How the Philosophical Analysis of Emotions was Introduced," in The Emotions in Hellenistic Philosophy (Dordrecht: Kluwer, 1998): 1–19; Simo Knuuttila, *Emotions in Ancient and Medieval Philosophy* (Oxford: Clarendon, 2004), esp. 1–110; Thomas H. Olbricht, "*Pathos* as Proof in Greco-Roman Rhetoric," in *Paul and Pathos* (ed. Thomas H. Olbricht and Jerry L. Sumney; SBLSymS 16; Atlanta: Society of Biblical Literature, 2001), 7–22.

character development by painting YHWH as the benevolent parent and, conversely, Israel as the recalcitrant child. The figure thus accomplishes something new in the argument, the creation of sentiment for the rightness of the call to conquest.

Israel, of course, has contested this call. The counterarguments in vv. 27–28, which vv. 29–31 refute, push in the opposite direction. The people refuse to enter the land on several grounds:

(1) בשנאת יהוה אתנו הוציאנו מארץ מצרים
("in hatred YHWH brought us from the land of Egypt")

(2) לתת אתנו ביד האמרי להשמידנו
("to give us into the hand of the Amorites,
to slaughter us")

(3) אנה אנחנו עלים אחינו המסו את לבבנו
("Where can we go? Our brothers have melted our heart")

(4) עם גדול ורם ממנו ערים גדלת ובצורת בשמים
וגם בני ענקים ראינו שם
("there are a people greater and taller than we, large cities fortified to the sky—and we even saw the children of the Anaqim")

The first warrant, unsubstantiated by the tradition and perhaps, as Tigay argues, calculated to "display the people's perversity and ingratitude,"[35] nevertheless serves rhetorically to state a controversial thesis. The absence of the substantive אלוהנו ("our God") with יהוה tellingly rejects the Israelite tradition and thus Moses' original arguments. The second, third, and fourth warrants build cumulatively to form an enthymeme: the might of the indigenous population and the power of their fortresses will necessitate at best massive bloodshed and risks defeat; thus a deity who leads us to such pain must wish to destroy us; thus he must hate us. The argument is all the more startling, or rather perverse, once we recognize that for ancient Near Easterners, gods were typically understood to call the nation to warfare;[36] the rebels thus subvert a widely accepted cultural assumption.

---

[35] Tigay, *Deuteronomy*, 16.

[36] For examples, see Bustanay Oded, "'The Command of the God' as a Reason for Going to War in the Assyrian Royal Inscriptions," in *Ah, Assyria…: Studies in Assyrian History and Ancient Near Eastern Historiography Presented to Hayim Tadmor* (ed. Mordechai Cogan and

The third warrant shifts the blame for cowardice onto the spies, while the fourth justifies the spies' report as plain common sense, even though it removes the divine warrior from political calculation and exaggerates the power of the cities and their inhabitants. By highlighting the inhabitants' gigantism[37] and claiming that their fortifications reached the sky and thus the realm of the gods,[38] the Israelites contest Moses' notion of space and thus of divine activity and competence. Presumably the author has in mind Iron Age fortifications and not the reused Middle Bronze fortifications used in the Late Bronze Age[39] and recalled by Iron I Israelites, and thus the elaborate system of gatehouses, solid city walls, and battlements that probably lay in ruins at the time of the chapter's composition in the postexilic period. If so, then the Israelites' argument serves to erase their entire history from "settlement" to "exile."

The Speech on the Plains of Moab

Yet the audience of the speech of Deut 1–3 of which 1:19–46 is a segment cannot accept this argument because at the second level of speech event Moses has already prepared them to reject the Israelites' arguments. As early as 1:4 the text highlights the vulnerability of the Amorites. The pericope at hand can be outlined in several ways, none entirely convincing.[40] Structural complexity does not imply confusion, however, but a careful

---

Israel Eph'al; Scripta Hierosolymitana 33; Jerusalem: Magnes, 1991), 223–30.

[37] On gigantism, see Lothar Perlitt, "Riesen im Alten Testament: Ein literarisches Motiv im Wirkungsfeld des Deuteronomismus," in idem, *Deuteronomium-Studien* (FAT 8; Tübingen: Mohr/Siebeck, 1994), 205–46; more generally, Cristiano Grottanelli, "The Enemy King is a Monster," in idem, *Kings and Prophets: Monarchic Power, Inspired Leadership, & Sacred Text in Biblical Narrative* (New York: Oxford University Press, 1999), 47–72.

[38] Tigay (*Deuteronomy*, 17) cites an Assyrian parallel, but the rhetorical function in Deuteronomy is different. See the study and photographs in David Ussishkin, *The Conquest of Lachish by Sennacherib* (Tel Aviv: Tel Aviv University, Institute of Archaeology, 1982).

[39] See the survey in Ze'ev Herzog, "Fortifications: Bronze and Iron Ages," *OEANE* 3 (1997): 324–25; Shlomo Bunimovitz, "The Middle Bronze Age Fortifications in Palestine as a Social Phenomenon," *Tel Aviv* 19 (1992): 221–34; Israel Finkelstein, "Middle Bronze Age 'Fortifications': A Reflection of Social Organization and Political Formations," *Tel Aviv* 19 (1992): 201–20; on the gate as a locus of royal (and thus state) power and justice (thus monopolization of violence), see Rüdiger Schmitt, "Der König sitzt im Tor: Überlegungen zum Stadttor als Ort herrschaftlicher Repräsentation im Alten Testament," *UF* 32 (2002): 475–85.

[40] E.g., Christensen (*Deuteronomy*, 30) finds two examples of the *Numeruswechsel* (1:21–31 and 1:32—2:1), while Nelson (*Deuteronomy*, 26–31) finds a series of narrative scenes (1:19–21, 22–25, 26–28, 29–33, 34–40, 41–44), and Lohfink ("Darstellungskunst," 120–23) identifies concentric circles of speeches.

layering of argumentation in the form of story-telling. The stories include such elements as: travelogue; quoted speech of Moses, Israel, and YHWH; third person narration of the characters' emotional state (e.g., ותרגנו באהליכם ["and you sulked in your tents"; v. 27] or יקצף ["and he was angry"; v. 34]); confession; and curses. The piling of up of such genres not only creates an interesting story. It also creates a skein of arguments supporting Moses' argument for entering the land, and conceivably the postexilic author's plea for a repetition of that event. Since figures frequently serve as arguments in speeches,[41] it does make sense to identify some that contribute to the flow of argument in Deut 1:19–46.

Although a complete analysis of the rhetorical moves of the speech unit is impossible within the scope of this essay, it is instructive to examine a few elements. First, notice the use of the second person address to Israel. On one hand, this usage is a non sequitur: the murmurers all died in the wilderness. Yet the speech's imagined audience identifies with them both genetically (they are their descendants) and emotionally (they also fear entry into the land), while the actual audience of the book of Deuteronomy (in the exile) can make the same identifications. Therefore, the use of the second person verbs constructs the audience's self-view.

תקרבון   ("and you drew near"; v. 22)
ותאמרו   ("and you said"; v. 22)
ולא אביתם   ("but you did not agree"; v. 26)
ותמרו   ("but you embittered"; v. 27)
לא תערצון   ("but you should not tremble"; v. 29)
ותיראון   ("nor should you fear"; v. 29)
ראית   ("you have seen"; v. 31)
אינכם מאמינם   ("are you not rejecting?"; v. 32)
תלכו בה   ("you should go in it"; v. 33)

The verbs in which Israel acts are uniformly negative, while those by which they are acted upon are universally positive. The stark contrast between their actions and attitudes on the one hand, and YHWH's on the other thus creates a rhetorical environment in which their arguments against

---

[41] Tindale, *Rhetorical Argumentation*, 59–87; Perelman and Olbrechts-Tyteca, *New Rhetoric*, 167–83.

conquest cannot be convincing. They become cowards in the presence of the ever victorious divine warrior.

Second, this rhetorical rigging, so to speak, continues in the description of Moses' response and YHWH's final judgment on him. Moses accedes to the plan to send the spies because the Israelites' apparently innocuous and commonsensical request to investigate the cities and the land (v. 23) met his approval (וייטב בעיני הדבר). Although Deuteronomy does not share P's conviction that YHWH planned for the spies (Num 13:1–2), neither does it object to the arrangement on principle. Yet when Israel refuses to see the land's prosperity as warrant for belief in YHWH's beneficence and thus the plan for conquest, but rather focuses only upon the perils facing them, Moses finds that YHWH is angry with him (גם בי התאנף יהוה בגללכם; v. 37) and forbids him to enter the land. Unlike the P story in Numbers 20, Deuteronomy does not identify Moses' sin, leading many interpreters to explain his punishment as substitionary for the people.[42] Yet this is difficult, as many others have noted, not least because it posits a role for Moses difficult to find elsewhere in the Pentateuch. Indeed, Moses, in sharp contrast to Gilgamesh, remains passive in this story, functioning merely as the intermediary between YHWH and the people.

Another possibility arises when we consider the shaping of the divine decree in vv. 35–40. YHWH's sentence of Moses sits in the center of a chiasmus:[43]

> A. The present generation will not see the land (v. 35)
>
> B. Caleb will inherit the land (v. 36)
>
> C. Moses will not enter the land (v. 37)
>
> B'. Joshua will enter the land (v. 38)
>
> A'. The next generation will enter the land (v. 39)

---

[42] Christensen, *Deuteornomy*, 32; Weinfeld, *Deuteronomy*, 150; Nelson, *Deuteronomy*, 29–30; Tigay, *Deuteronomy*, 19–20, 425 (with some rabbinic references); JSB.

[43] On concentric circles as structural patterns throughout Deut 1:19–46, see Christensen, *Deuteronomy*, 31. On the theology of the decree, see Patrick Miller, "The Wilderness Journey in Deuteronomy: Style, Structure, and Theology in Deuteronomy 1–3," in *Israelite Religion and Biblical Theology: Collected Essays* (JSOTSup 267; Sheffield: Sheffield Academic, 2000), 576–78.

V. 40 adds a final element, a command. The condemnation of Moses thus stands in contrast to the fate of Caleb and Joshua as he identifies with one instantiation of the nation rather than another.

Moreover, the references to Caleb and Joshua contain explanations for their destinies. While the text may assume the JE account,[44] it is still necessary to read the rationale for their entries in the context of Deuteronomy. Thus Caleb may enter the land יַעַן אֲשֶׁר מִלֵּא אַחֲרֵי יהוה ("because he was utterly loyal to YHWH"), while Joshua can be counted on to appropriate the land (יַנְחִלֶנָּה). In other words, as warriors they form an inseparable pair (much like Enkidu and Gilgamesh). Moses, in contrast, accedes to the people's plans and then, despite his best efforts, fails to persuade them to take the land. Thus his rhetorical failures account for his failure to enter Canaan.

Third, the preparation for this verdict on Moses' earlier speech begins with v. 19, which introduces the setting of the deliberative speeches in the Wilderness. The excerpts of those speeches serve the second speech event level as a series of figures leading to the conclusion in which Israel may take the land only after a forty-year probation. Moses bears some responsibility for the end result because he allows a reconsideration of his own speech in vv. 21–22. Though Weinfeld is technically right to point out that v. 22 proposes only that the spies find the best road into the land and to its principal cities,[45] in the context of the entire speech in 1:19–46, the counsel proves susceptible to multiple interpretations. The people's apparent sagacity and bravery, at first glance so similar to the Urukians' advice to Gilgamesh and Enkidu, in the end highlights the Israelite congregation's rebellion, as they reject divine leadership and thus undercut any viable notion of heroism. This multivalence of meaning must be deliberate for it allows the narrator to prepare us for the wild-eyed description of those cities in v. 28 and thus the ultimate rejection of Moses' charge to take the land. Unlike Gilgamesh, Moses cannot persuade his audience to defeat the giants, nor does he lead them there himself. The deconstruction of the hero (whether Moses or Israel) goes well beyond the widespread reconfiguration of the heroic tradition that Israelites often practiced, and of which many texts give evidence.[46]

---

[44] Nelson, *Deuteronomy*, 26. Certainly Deuteronomy does not prepare for his appearance in 1:36. But Deuteronomy does not distinguish among the spies as does Numbers.

[45] Weinfeld, *Deuteronomy 1–11*, 145.

[46] See Mobley, *Empty Men*, 48–74.

All of this raises the question of genre for the speech on the Plains of Moab. The speeches in the Wilderness fit nicely into Aristotle's category of deliberative rhetoric, i.e., speech that exhorts to or dissuades from (Συμβουλῆς δὲ τὸ μὲν προτροπὴ τὸ δὲ ἀποτροπή) particular actions in the audience's future (ὁ μέλλων).[47] Yet the larger speech in 1:19–46 describes past events. Nor is it obvious that the rhetorical aim of the unit in its role at the beginning of the Deuteronomistic History is the resettlement of the land either in the sixth century or earlier (depending again on how one dates this material). Rather, the speech in the Plains of Moab seems to fit better Aristotle's category of epideictic speech, i.e., speech that praises or blames present realities (τὰ ὑπάρχοντα).

Reading the text this way explains several curious aspects of the story, in particular the fact that YHWH does not make speeches except through his intermediary Moses. On the one hand, Deuteronomy distances the deity from the events, and goes to great lengths to show that the failure of Moses' rhetoric (and thus of YHWH's!) was due to the obstinacy of the audience who could not accept reasonable arguments. Far from compromising the supernal speaker's ethos, as one might expect, for the composer of these chapters, Israel's reaction in the wilderness only enhances YHWH's standing for his actual (postexilic) audience. God, or rather the author portraying speeches about God, uses absence and even nonpersuasiveness as ceremonial, which, as Perelman and Olbrechts-Tyteca put it, is "a technique that enhances a speaker's glamour by emphasizing rank [and] can promote persuasion if the listeners consider it a ritual in which they themselves also take part."[48]

Perelman and Olbrecht-Tyteca criticize an overly aesthetic orientation toward epideictic oratory, seeking to place it instead within the realm of argumentation. The orator in this case seeks to "establish a sense of communion centered on particular values recognized by the audience."[49] Their notion of communion is not beyond criticism,[50] but its value lies in the recognition that speakers operate from an assumed knowledge about the thought world of their hearers. Thus Deuteronomy does not need to persuade its audience of the rightness of its basic positions on all sorts of issues, but rather the book (hence the speech in 1:19–46) shares a set of views with the audience. If this is correct, then the speech serves not to

---

[47] Aristotle *Rhet* 1.3.3–4 (1358b).
[48] Perelman and Olbrechts-Tyteca, *New Rhetoric*, 321.
[49] Ibid., 51.
[50] Tindale, *Rhetorical Argumentation*, 66–69.

persuade Israel to *do* anything, but rather to confirm it in its basic self-understanding. Deliberative speech at the first level of discourse (the period of the speeches in the Wilderness) becomes epideictic speech at the second and third levels (the speech on the Plains of Moab and the final version of Deuteronomy).

Conclusion

In this essay, I have tried to indicate approaches to persuasion in two texts that, though separated by centuries and even understandings of the structure of human society and religion, nevertheless share common assumptions and strategies. Doubtless much remains to be said about these texts and about ancient Near Eastern rhetoric more broadly, the study of which is in its infancy. Still it is possible to identify some features of rhetoric in these texts that may deserve further study in other texts.

First, these texts pay careful attention to the audience and its assumptions about the nature of reality. In building argumentation, both Gilgamesh and Moses (or rather the composers of their literary speeches) seek to understand their hearers' plausibility structures and to interact with them. The interaction may be critical, even astringent, but it is nevertheless careful and emphasizes common values as the rhetor seeks agreement. Second, argumentation takes multiple forms. Syllogism is comparatively rare but enthymeme is not. Pathos constitutes argument. Third, the ethos of the speaker, though contestable in both of these texts, figures significantly in the argument. The character of the speaker is itself a part of the argument for and against the deliberations of the audience. Fourth, persuasion results from communion between speaker and audience. The rhetor must find common ground with the audience's perceived values and desires. Fifth, the human audience does not exclude the divine audience. This factor deserves far more attention than I can give it here, but we should not assume that ancient persons forgot the transmundane in their speechmaking. Certainly Assyrian letters to the gods and other forms of ancient Near Eastern prayer (as in both Gilgamesh and to a lesser extent in Deuteronomy) are rhetorical forms. Sixth, both texts offer versions of events that are otherwise well-known in their respective contexts, and thus offer contestable interpretations of those events. The Humbaba/Huwawa story reflects third millennium (or earlier) notions of the hero, just as Deuteronomy's giants lived long before the real audience of the book.

Finally, as Frans van Eemeren has noted, argumentation is (1) a "complex speech act" that occurs in a (2) particular social setting with

(3) "commitments created by the performance of this speech act" that (4) aims at rectifying differences of opinion.[51] Whatever one's view of van Eemeren's overall program, surely he is correct that a rhetorical analysis of any speech-event, in this case of two ancient texts, must pay attention to both the surface structure of the text itself and to its social setting, or in other words, the complex network of symbols of which it is a part. This brief essay has shown, I believe, that despite numerous differences in the world views of first-millennium Israel and second-millennium Mesopotamia, it is possible to identify patterns of persuasion common to both. Gilgamesh's speech succeeds because he can cast the notion of the hero in his culture in his own favor. Yahweh's (!) fails to persuade because Israel cannot imagine itself in a heroic position. The arguments are not dissimilar, but they are contestable. Israel's refusal to accept the heroic possibility, based on its failure to reason correctly, leads to its downfall. And in their failure to attend to the "correct" arguments lies all the difference.

---

[51] Frans H. van Eemeren, "Argumentation Theory: An Overview of Approaches and Research Themes," in *Rhetorical Argumentation in Biblical Texts: Essays from the Lund 2000 Conference* (ed. Anders Eriksson, Thomas Olbricht, and Walter Übelacker; Emory Studies in Early Christianity 8; Harrisburg, Pa.: Trinity Press International, 2002), 18.

6

Hebrew Poetics and Biblical Interpretation:

Insights from Psalm 120

Rick R. Marrs

PSALM 120 belongs to that corpus of fifteen psalms (120–134) entitled the שירי־המעלות. In earlier Psalm studies, the primary interest in these psalms concerned this superscription. However, their apparent use of poetic parallelism also received mention. The older literature generally regarded these psalms as having an inordinate amount of "repetitive parallelism," although little discussion was given to determining and delineating the precise nature and effect of this parallelistic feature. Psalm 120 has received little material discussion. If mentioned at all, Ps 120:1 has received passing mention, for it presents an affirmation that sits uneasily with the lamenting remainder of the psalm. Thus, discussion has ensued regarding the proper translation of v. 1, proposed scenarios for the sequence of v. 1 vis-à-vis vv. 2–7, and the genre of this poem. Little attempt has been made to relate the poetic dynamics of the poem to these interrelated issues of translation (v. 1) and genre.

Before analyzing the poetic style of Psalm 120, a note is in order. Anyone who engages in stylistic analysis makes a conscious (or perhaps subconscious) decision regarding the definition of style and what constitutes style. Often this underlying discussion of style focuses upon the relationship between style and content. That one can distinguish between what a person says, and the manner in which he or she says it affirms a distinction. This relationship is often conceived metaphorically: stylisticians argue whether the relation of style and content parallels that of clothing to the body, or that of flesh and bones to the body.¹

The nature and function of repetition in poetry has received considerable attention over the past few decades.² In modern literary studies, F. W. Bateson argues that repetition occurs not for memorability, but for synthesization. Repetition allows a poem to cohere, linking the several parts of the poem together into a unified whole.³ E. Stankiewicz, another modern literary critic, argues that repetition produces an interplay between sequence and simultaneity. Simultaneity presents successive elements in their simultaneous present, allowing an integrated structure in which each part is perceived as an autonomous part of a sequence and as a dependent part of a whole.⁴ Similarly, Bateson speaks of the multidimensionality of poetic language. Repetition allows a poem to say several things at once, resulting in an integrated whole.

The concern for integration and cohesion is a primary issue in stylistic analysis, since in the final analysis a poem is an integrated, cohesive unit. Cohesion can be accomplished through several means: repetition (i.e., semantic or syntactic patterning), metaphor or rhetorical figures.⁵ Determining the interrelation of these several aspects or techniques to pro-

---

¹ The former metaphor understands style as something external and nonessential to the poem (i.e., something appended to provide ornamentation), while the latter conceives of style as an organic and essential part of the poem (i.e., inherent and integral).

² See James Kugel, *The Idea of Biblical Poetry* (New Haven: Yale, 1981); Michael O'Connor, *Hebrew Verse Structure* (Winona Lake: Eisenbrauns, 1980); Adele Berlin, *The Dynamics of Biblical Parallelism* (Bloomington: Indiana University Press, 1985); W. G. E. Watson, *Classical Hebrew Poetry* (JSOTSup 26; Sheffield: Sheffield, 1984); Luis Alonso-Schökel, *Estudios de Poetica Hebrea* (Barcelona: Juan Flors, 1963); David L. Petersen and Kent Richards, *Interpreting Hebrew Poetry* (GBS; Minneapolis: Fortress, 1992).

³ *English Poetry* (New York 1966), 44–46.

⁴ "Structural Poetics and Linguistics," *Current Trends in Linguistics* 12/2 (1974): 643–44.

⁵ R. Wellek and A. Warren (*Theory of Literature* [New York: Harcourt Brace Jovanovich, 1977], 178) correctly note that one cannot simply assume that a particular stylistic figure functions identically in each occurrence. E.g., in contemporary stylistics, figures are frequently categorized haphazardly as intensifying figures, reflecting "sublime" style). They deny that specific figures must in all cases have specific effects or "expressive values." This insight is relevant to our study. We cannot simply assume that the repetition in the שירי־המעלות functions identically to that in other psalms (especially much earlier psalms).

duce an integrated, cohesive unit results in an increased understanding and appreciation of the message of the poem itself.[6]

To my knowledge, little attempt has been made to relate the poetic dynamics of Psalm 120 to the form critical and redaction critical concerns created by v 1. This article suggests that the poetic dynamics of this psalm are relevant to its form critical understanding and possible redaction history. If the poetic presentation of a psalm is not merely ornamentation, but provides cohesiveness and coherence, then the poetic structure (specifically the repetitive style) may contribute meaningfully to the focus and purpose of the psalm.

Psalm 120

1. When I was in distress I cried out to Yahweh
   and he answered me.

2. Yahweh, deliver me from lying lips,
   from a deceitful tongue.

3. How much more will he requite you,
   [O] Deceitful tongue!

4. A warrior's sharpened arrows, with fiery coals
   of broomwood.

5. I am undone, for I sojourn in Meshech,
   I dwell among the tents of Qedar!

6. For too long have I dwelt among warmongers.

7. Indeed, whenever I propose peace,
   they are for war.

---

[6] E. Stankiewicz ("Structural Poetics," 649) notes the frequent interplay in a poem between similarity at one level with simultaneous dissimilarity at another level. This interplay between similarity, which produces a patterning effect at one level, and dissimilarity, which results in variation, produces a noteworthy stylistic achievement. A. Berlin ("Grammatical Aspects of Biblical Parallelism," *HUCA* 50 [1979]: 17–43) has analyzed such interplay between different stylistic elements in Hebrew poetry. This interplay, when successfully done, results in an intermeshing of diverse parts into an integrated whole.

Form and Redaction Critical Matters

H. Gunkel[7] first noted the inappropriateness of an apparent "answer" (v. 1) introducing an ensuing lament (vv. 2–7). To solve this dilemma, he translated v. 1 to express potential reality rather than current reality:

> In my distress I cry to the Lord,
> *That* he may answer me.

However, Gunkel's solution has received little following.[8] More customary has been the solution of F. Crüsemann, who regards Psalm 120 not as an individual lament (so Gunkel), but as an individual song of thanksgiving.[9] The psalmist harks back to a distressing situation (vv. 2–7) that has now been resolved. Thus, there is a (perhaps lengthy) time gap between v 1 and vv. 2–7. V. 1 depicts the psalmist's current situation; vv. 2–7 detail the psalmist's former predicament.[10]

Building upon Crüsemann's form critical assessment, a few scholars have attempted to flesh out possible scenarios and settings in life for this psalm. H.-J. Kraus theorizes that v. 1 assumes the psalmist now present at the sanctuary to pay his vow. He looks back to a former time of distress (depicted in vv. 2–7). For Kraus, vv. 5–7 confirm the correctness of this interpretation.[11]

---

[7] *Die Psalmen* (Göttingen: Vandenhoeck & Ruprecht, 1968), 537–39.

[8] Note, however, the RSV and NRSV.

[9] *Studien zur Formgeschichte von Hymnus und Danklied in Israel* (WMANT 32; Neukirchen: Neukirchen-Vluyn, 1969), 155ff.

[10] Numerous interpretations simply resolve the tension between v. 1 and vv. 2–7 by considering v. 1 a later insertion, ill-suited to the remainder of the psalm. E.g., O. Loretz (*Die Psalmen* [Neukirchen: Neukirchen-Vluyn, 1979]) considers v. 1 a gloss that has been transposed from its original setting at the end of the psalm, since an introductory answered request has no known literary parallel. However, convincing explanations for an editor's insertion of such a problematic opening for a lament are sorely lacking. Alternately, scholars have understood this verse to refer to a past event (A. Weiser, *The Psalms* [OTL; Philadelphia: Fortress, 1962); H.-J. Kraus, *Psalmen 60–150* [BKAT 15.2; Neukirchen: Neukirchen-Vluyn 1978]); a past event recited for a present situation (C. Keet, *A Study of the Psalms of Ascents* [Greenwood, S.C.: Mitre, 1969]; M. Dahood, *Psalms 101–150* (AB 17A; New York: Doubleday, 1970]); a present event (W. M. L. DeWette, *Commentar über die Psalmen* [Heidelberg: Mohr, 1856]; R. Kittel, *Die Psalmen* [KAT; Leipzig: Deichert, 1914]); or a future event (C. Briggs, *The Psalms* [ICC; New York: Scribners, 1907–8]).

[11] Kraus (*Psalmen*, 1009) considers the use of the term גּוּר ("sojourn") and the use of the perfect tense in v. 6 crucial evidence supporting his interpretation. (However, Kraus does acknowledge that Gunkel's interpretation has the advantage of concreteness, especially in conjunction with Ps 55:18–19.)

Although utilizing the same form critical assumptions of F. Crüsemann, L. Allen reconstructs a rather different scenario. Given the grammatical nature of vv. 1–4, he considers vv. 3–4 a continuation of the thanksgiving begun in vv. 1–2. Thus,

> The precise form of the psalm appears to be a thanksgiving for heard prayer rather than for a transformed situation. The situation remains the same, but the psalmist has received priestly assurance that Yahweh has heard his prayer, and for this he gives thanks.[12]

For Allen, the psalmist's situation remains materially unchanged; however, because of his appeal to Yahweh for deliverance, his religious outlook has changed dramatically. Though currently at the sanctuary, he exits confidently, knowing that Yahweh will rectify the dire circumstances that await him on his return from the sanctuary.[13]

K. Seybold reconstructs a quite specific background for this psalm. He speculates that Ps 120 depicts a soldier accused of treason while fighting alongside Bedouin mercenaries. This warrior comes to the temple for a divine verdict on the charges.[14]

Although creative readings of this brief psalm, none of these reconstructions addresses in any detail its unusual poetic nature, nor provides an entirely satisfying solution to the anomalous location of v. 1 in relation to the lament in vv. 2–7. I suggest that an analysis of the poetic dynamics of the psalm may elucidate the rather striking arrangement of the verses.

---

[12] *Psalms 101–150* (WBC 21; Waco: Word, 1983), 147. Allen cites the circumstances of Ps 6 (where for him vv. 9–11 [ET 8–10] follow the complaint of vv. 2–8 [ET 1–7]). For a similar scenario, see also R. Davidson, *The Vitality of Worship* (Grand Rapids: Eerdmans, 1998), 405.

[13] For Allen (148) vv. 5–7 evidence not a quotation from an earlier complaint, but "represent a plight which but for the implementation of the divine assurance still awaits him on return from the sanctuary." He concludes that the worshiper leaves the temple, having poured out his complaint before God and received a priestly blessing assuring him of God's favorable response. He theorizes that the psalmist would no doubt return to the sanctuary to render full thanks when the actual deliverance occurs.

[14] Seybold (*Die Wallfahrtpsalmen* [BTS 3; Neukirchen: Neukirchen-Vluyn 1978], 54) reads אדבר (v. 7) with a forensic nuance (cf. Ps 127:5); he also associates this psalm with other temple entrance psalms. His analysis seems overly precise given the scant information provided in this psalm. Interestingly, A. Ceresko ("Psalm 121: a prayer of a warrior?" *Bib* 70 [1989]: 496–510) considers Ps 121 a "warrior psalm."

Stylistic Analysis of Psalm 120

The poetic nature and structure of Psalm 120 has generated little substantive discussion among scholars. As previously mentioned, two assumptions generally prevail: (1) the psalm manifests little development or cohesion; or (2) v. 1 is inappropriately located since it diverges from the normal form of an individual lament. A stylistic analysis of this psalm shows that both assumptions are ill-founded. In actuality, the poem develops in three directions. V. 1 introduces the three themes: בצרתי לי ("in my distress");[15] קראתי ("I called"); ויענני ("and he answered me").[16] קראתי is elaborated in v. 2; ויענני is developed in v. 3; בצרתה לה is expanded in vv. 5–6.

The first instance of parallelism occurs in v. 2: מלשון רמיה // מספר שקר.[17] This semantic doubling produces intensification. The two

---

[15] צרה and its verbal counterpart צרר appear frequently in conjunction with the prepositions ב and ל. However, the form occurs only here. Although numerous explanations have been given for this morphological phenomenon, none appear overwhelmingly convincing. For (ה)צר + ל, see Gen 32:8; Isa 49:20; 1 Sam 28:15; Pss 31:10; 59:17; 69:18; 102:3; for (ה)צר + ב, see Pss 18:7; 81:8; 91:15. For a list of feminine nouns with this morphology, see *GKC* 90g; *B-L* 65t-u. This form also occurs in Ugaritic. *GKC* consider this form an old accusative of intention or direction, which has become simply an emphatic poetic feminine, without syntactic meaning. *B-L* argue that the תה ending was added when the original meaning of –*a* was lost, often to express exclamation. Dahood considers this form an accusative based on an original **saratu*. The expected genitive does not occur since case endings are no longer in use and correct forms have been forgotten. H. Finley ("A Stylistic Approach to the Chronology of Selected Psalms: an Analysis of Psalms 67, 77, 93, 120–127, 129, 133, and 134" [Ph.D. diss., The Johns Hopkins University, 1956], 80–81) considers צרתה an archaic fossilized form utilized for metrical sake. Significantly, he fails to mention the meter. All of these hypotheses are quite speculative and less than convincing. This form, which appears elsewhere in the שירי־המעלות (see 124:4; 125:3), may in this context simply reflect a later hypercorrection. The LXX correctly translates this colon: ἐν τῷ θλίβεσθαί με (the LXX regularly translates בצר(ה) ל this way: Pss 18:7; 106:44; 107:6, 13, 19, 28). In Biblical Hebrew, the temporal aspect of this construction is often specifically indicated through the addition of a time indicator (usually either עת or ביום).

[16] The word pair קרא and ענה are well attested in biblical Hebrew and need not be documented in detail. In some instances God calls to obtain an answer, while in other cases a human calls to God for a response. In several of these passages it is quite difficult to determine a time frame. Typical examples include: Pss 50:15; 81:8; 86:7; 102:3. At Bethel Jacob builds an altar to אל הענה אתי ביום צרתי (Gen 35:3). In contrast, in 1 Kgs 18:26 Baal is typified as a god who does not answer (ענה).

[17] Both the LXX and the Syriac insert a conjunction (*kai*; *w-*) before the MT רמיה מלשון, which is reflected in some translations (e.g., NEB; JB). The syntax of רמיה מלשון has generated considerable discussion. Although difficult, the MT vocalization of this phrase is retained, even though this results in a grammatical variation with שקר

elements (מלשון רמיה; מחפת שקר) intend synonymity; the repetition adds nothing syntactically or thematically to the line.[18] A similar repetition occurs in v. 3: מה יסיף לך // מה יתן לך.[19] The doubling also provides intensification and is strengthened by the fact that נתן and יסף occur frequently as word pairs.[20] This doubling is followed by a reiteration

---

מספה. Kraus considers רמיה to be in apposition to לשון (i.e., "the tongue, which is falsehood"), citing GKC 131c in support. Dahood considers this a dialectic peculiarity (he cites Prov 6:24 [לשון נכריה] in support; however, his suggestion is confusing, since Prov 6:24 does not correspond syntactically with Ps 120:2). Moving in a different direction, D. Grossberg (*Centripetal and Centrifugal Structures in Biblical Poetry* [SBLMS 39; Atlanta: Scholars, 1989], 23) links רמיה to the archery imagery in the psalm. For him, this dual nuance of רמיה (from *רמה [Qal: "to shoot"]) leads the reader to reprocess the information of vv. 2–3 in two directions: speech; arrows.

[18] The semantically synonymous doublet לשון רמיה // ספר שקר is grammatically varied (NcN // NappN). Like v 1, this verse is composed of traditional language. The word pair לשון + שפת is well attested in biblical Hebrew and Ugaritic. In most instances שפת precedes לשון. When these nouns occur with modifiers (suggesting falsehood), שפת almost exclusively occurs with שקר, while לשון occurs with a variety of modifiers (e.g., רמיה, מרמה, שקר). See *Ras Shamra Parallels* (AnOr 49, 50; ed. L. Fisher; Rome: Pontifical Biblical Institute, 1972, 1975), I.ii.579 (hereafter *RSP*) for a representative listing of the various syntactical relationships in which שפה and לשון occur. (Cf. the following: (')ספתי שקר [Ps 31:19; Prov 10:18; 12:22; 17:7; cf. v. 4]; שפת מרמה [Ps 17:1]; לשון Jer 9:2, 4; Ps 109:2; Prov 6:17; 12:19; 21:6; 26:28]; לשון רמיה [Mic 6:12]; לשון מרמה [Ps 52:6 {cf. v 4: עשה רמיה]; עשה רמיה // דבר שקרים [Ps 101:7]; מרמה // שקר [Amos 8:5]; שקרים מרמה [Prov 12:17]. Often מלשון רמיה is omitted as dittography from v. 3 (so S. Mowinckel, *Real and Apparent Tricola in Hebrew Psalm Poetry* [Oslo: Aschehoug, 1957], 69). Others omit יהוה (so Baethgen), or place it at the end of v. 1 (so Briggs). It has been suggested the מלשון מרמה be read on the basis of the LXX. However, מרמה and רמיה are translated indiscriminately by δόλος and δόλιος in the LXX. There is no textual warrant for emendation in v. 2.

[19] The difficulty of this verse is evidenced in the Versions and in the variety of interpretations among commentators. The construction מה . . . מה is well attested in biblical Hebrew, both with an interrogative nuance and with an exclamatory nuance. (See *RSP* I.ii.345, for examples of both nuances. The exclamatory nuance is attested elsewhere in the שירי־המעלות in Ps 133:1). This construction occurs in contexts charged with intense emotion:

Job 6:25:   מה נמרצו אמרי ישר
            ומה יוכיח הוכח מכם
Job 26:2–3: מה עזרת ללא כח
            מה יעצת ללא חכמה
Jer 2:33:   מה תיטבי דרכך לבקש אהבה
Jer 2:36:   מה תזלי מאד לשנות את דרכך

[20] The vocalization of יֻתַּן and יֹסִיף have caused considerable discussion. The LXX and Syriac translate both verbs as passives. (The LXX reads δοθείη and προσδοθείη respectively. The Syriac reads *ntlwn* and *nwspwn*; apparently the impersonal plurals are func-

of the final phrase of the preceding line (לְשׁוֹן רְמִיָּה). When vv. 2–3 are viewed together, an orderly positional arrangement emerges:

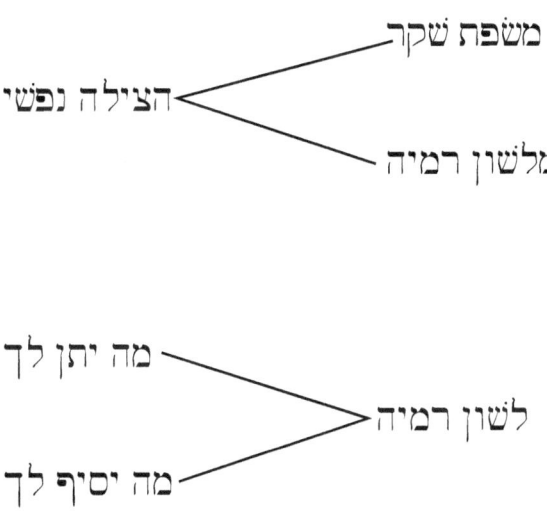

Verse 2 opens with a single imperative followed by dual prepositional phrases. Verse 3 opens with two verbal phrases followed by a single vocative.[21]

---

tioning as passives.) Consequently, יִתֵּן and יֹסִיף are often revocalized יֻתַּן and יֻסַף (so BHK; BHS; Gunkel). These emendations are far from certain. The LXX and Syriac may simply reflect an attempt to understand an obscure line, or may exhibit an effort to de-emphasize Yahweh's direct responsibility. The LXX regularly translates the Hiphil of יסף with προστίθημι. Interestingly, Hiphil forms in Isa 10:20; 52:1; Joel 2:2; Prov 9:11 are translated passively in the LXX. Thus, the LXX may reflect stylistic variation rather than textual variation. The subject of this line is best understood as Yahweh with the exclamation directed toward the slanderous tongue.

[21] For Grossberg (*Centripetal Structures*, 23) the direct repetition forces the reader's attention to the figures of speech. "The reiteration and the specific term reiterated both exert a unifying and centralizing force on the psalm." Numerous scholars (e.g., Weiser; Kraus; Gunkel; Mowinckel, *Psalmenstudien* [Kristiania: Dybwad, 1921–22], 1: 89; 5:133]) have attempted to related this line to a well attested prosaic oath formula: . . . וְכֹה יֹסִיף . . . כֹּה יַעֲשֶׂה לְ (see Ruth 1:17; 1 Sam 3:17; 14:44; 20:13; 25:22; 2 Sam 3:9, 35; 19:14; 1 Kgs 2:23; 2 Kgs 6:31). It is argued that this formula was taken over by the psalmist, but reformulated with the exclamatory מַה to express the intensity of the assertion. From this context the variation לָךְ . . . לְכָה is explained. In the oath formula, the preposition לְ

Repetition occurs again in vv. 5–6.[22] The repetition occurs in a tripartite elaboration with semantic and syntactic interplay:[23]

גרתי [24]   משך [25]

---

regularly occurs after the first verb. (The only exceptions are 1 Sam 14:44 [where it does not occur] and 2 Sam 3:9 [where it occurs after both verbs]). Familiar with the formula, a ל was placed after יתן, although incorrectly pointed. The correct pointing is reflected in לְךָ, making clear the reference to לשׁון. Comparison of v 3 with the prosaic oath formula seems ill-founded. In reality, only one term from the oath formula is attested (יֹסִיף). Significantly, in the oath the first verb is always עשׂה. Also, the oath is always directly followed by אם or כי (once כי אם). It is preferable to understand this line simply as an intense exclamation (see above, Job 6:25; 26:2, 3; Jer 2:33, 36). Significantly, in the Joban and Jeremian passages this construction (מה . . . מה) also conveys a sense of irony and ridicule. Job mockingly praises the advice and helpfulness of his three friends. Jeremiah scorns the wanton flagrancy of Judah's sinfulness. Similarly, one may not be mistaken to see a note of scorn and ironic rebuke in the psalmist's assertion against his adversaries.

[22] The precise relationship of this line to v 3 and to the larger context is difficult to ascertain. Clearly the image of the tongue as a deadly weapon is a common metaphor in biblical Hebrew (Jer 9:7; Pss 57:5b; 64:4; cf. also Prov 25:18; 26:18, 19; Sir 51:5, 6). V. 4 is best understood as a specification of the punishment desired by the psalmist in v. 3. The psalmist exclaims that his enemies will be afflicted by the same devastation and destruction their own speech wrought. This is preferable to interpreting v 4 as the answer to a question in v. 3 or the reflex of an oath (so Gunkel; Buttenwieser, *The Psalms* [New York: KTAV, 1969]; Keet; Weiser). In theophanies Yahweh appears wielding arrows and fiery coals (see especially Ps 18:7–20). The psalmist expectantly envisions a punishment equal to their crime (viz., deadly arrows and burning coals). The above translation presupposes two images (viz., arrows and coals). Dahood's suggestion that the preposition of the second colon (עם) performs double duty, is dubious, since nowhere in biblical Hebrew does עם carry an agential nuance. Conversely, H. Fuhs ("גחל *ghl*," *TDOT* II [Grand Rapids: Eerdmans, 1973], 461–65) translates this line: "arrows . . . sharpened on coal-fire." Many scholars unnecessarily interpret these images metaphorically (e.g., Buttenwieser: "fierce and endless strife," the latter alluding to a hot fire retaining heat; Weiser: "murder and fire," i.e., death and destruction).

[23] As elsewhere, the psalmist employs a common formula but uses an unusual form. The phrase אוי ל כי is common (cf. 1 Sam 4:7; Isa 6:5; Jer 4:13, 31; 6:4; 15:10; 45:3; 48:46; Hos 7:13; Lam 5:16); the interjection אויה occurs only here.

[24] In this line the LXX and Syriac diverge significantly from the MT. Apparently both read a nominal form for גרתי and a verbal form for משך. LXX: ἡ παροικία μου ἐμακρύνθη ("my sojourn is prolonged"); Syriac: *twtbwty 'grt* ("my sojourn has been lengthened"). Conjecture concerning the text behind the LXX and Syriac is difficult, since a nominal of גור occurs only in Jer 41:17 (גרות: apparently meaning a lodging place, rather than conveying a notion of temporal abstraction [e.g., "stay"]). If משך is repointed as a passive participle (the verb is well attested in references to prolonged status [see *BDB*, 604]), it disagrees in gender with גרתי (theoretically a feminine; note, however, Briggs, who reads גורי [unattested]).

[25] This line has been interpreted variously: (1) retaining the MT, many understand here a reference to the Mushku (Greek: Moschoi) who inhabited the region between the Caspian

שׁכנתי	עִם אָהֳלֵי קֵדָר[26]
שָׁכַנְתִּי לָהּ נַפְשִׁי[27]	עִם שׂוֹנֵא שָׁלוֹם.[28]

The cola of v. 5, while semantically synonymous, are syntactically varied. The cola of vv. 5c, 6, while semantically varied, are syntactically similar. The initial phrases in each colon (viz., שָׁכַנְתִּי, נַפְשִׁי לָהּ שָׁכְנָה) parallel closely, while the final phrases (שׂוֹנֵא שָׁלוֹם; עִם אָהֳלֵי קֵדָר), though

---

Sea and Black Sea); (2) several scholars emend מֶשֶׁךְ. The Mushku are well attested in the Assyrian annals of Tiglath-Pileser and Sargon. For further discussion of the Mushku, see: M. Mellink, "Meshech," *IDB* 3 (1962): 357–58; F. Weissbach, "Zu den Inschriften der Sale im Palaste Sargon's II von Assyrien," *ZDMG* 72 (1918): 161–85; M. Streck, *Assurbanipal und die letzten assyrischen Königen bis zum Untergange Ninevehs* (Leipzig: Hinrichs, 1916); A. Olmstead, *History of Assyria* (New York: Scribners, 1923); H. Saggs, "The Nimrud Letters, 1952 – Part IV," *Iraq* 20 (1958) 182–212. This geographical interpretation of Meshech virtually nullifies a literal interpretation, since the distance between Meshech and Qedar is substantial. However, understanding the term as a metaphor for barbarians is less than satisfying, since in the Assyrian annals the Mushku are renowned only for their distance from Assyria, not their barbarism. This may provide the clue for the mention in Psalm 120—the psalmist is lamenting his *distance* from his homeland. (Grossberg [*Centripetal Structures*, 24] finds a merismus here – Mesek and Qedar express the totality of the menacing diaspora.) Gunkel, seeking to retain a geographical name, emends מֶשֶׁךְ to מַשָּׂא. Massa, in close proximity to Qedar, gives a more concrete tie to the passage (in Gen 25:13–14 Massa and Qedar are sons of Ishmael). For a fuller discussion of Massa, see W. F. Albright, "The Biblical Tribe of Massa' and Some Congeners," in *Studi Orientalistici in Onore di Giorgio Levi della Vida* (Rome: Istituto per l'Oriente, 1956), 1–14. Alternately, some scholars suggest emending מֶשֶׁךְ to מֹשֵׁךְ and inserting קֶשֶׁת (so Briggs; *BHK;* Mowinckel, *Psalmenstudien*, 2:193). According to Briggs, "one drawing (the bow)" parallels שׂנא (v. 6). In support of this emendation Isa 21:17 is cited: "Few of Qedar's stalwart archers shall remain . . . ." The parallelism with Qedar speaks against the last emendation.

[26] The Qedarites, a nomadic tribe of the Arabian peninsula, appear frequently in first millennium annals. The effect a geographical locale might have on one's faith was a special concern to the psalmists (cf. Pss 15:1; 65:5; 78:55, 60).

[27] This construction contains a pleonastic ethical dative (*GKC* 119s). Ps 123:4 presents an exact syntactical parallel: רַבַּת שָׂבְעָה לָּהּ נַפְשֵׁנוּ. Psalm 94:17 provides another striking parallel: לוּלֵי יְהוָה עֶזְרָתָה לִּי כִּמְעַט שָׁכְנָה דוּמָה נַפְשִׁי. The form עֶזְרָתָה לִּי morphologically parallels בְּצָרָתָה לִּי (v. 1); כִּמְעַט syntactically parallels רַבַּת.

[28] Lit.: "those who hate peace." A plural (שׂוֹנְאֵי) is read with the Versions rather than the singular of the MT. (Dahood retains the singular, arguing that a shift from singular to plural is characteristic of the heated language of laments.) The phrase שׂנא(י) שָׁלוֹם clearly parallels אָהֳלֵי קֵדָר. The participial form of שׂנא is found in construct with several nouns: תּוֹכַחַת (Prov 12:1; 15:10); טֹב (Mic 3:2); צִיּוֹן (Ps 129:5); מִשְׁפָּט (Job 34:17); צַדִּיק (Ps 34:22); יְהוָה (2 Chr 19:2). F. Crüsemann (*Hymnus*, 172) argues that this phrase represents a typical designation for the enemy of the individual. It always refers to inner Israelite party strife, rather than external enemies (except for Ps 106:10, 41). Significantly, Ps 120 renders such a hypothesis dubious.

syntactically equivalent (=P + NcN), are quite varied semantically. Vv. 5–6 display a noteworthy development. Initially it appears that the psalmist is lamenting his geographical setting (מֶשֶׁךְ; קֵדָר). However, in v. 6 it becomes clear that the lament primarily stems from the character of the inhabitants of his surroundings (שׂוֹנֵא שָׁלוֹם [cf. v 7]).[29] Appropriately, the phrase אָהֳלֵי קֵדָר reflects both aspects: it reiterates the unsuitability of the geographical setting (מֶשֶׁךְ // קֵדָר) and anticipates the reason for this unacceptable situation (אָהֳלֵי . . . שׂוֹנֵא שָׁלוֹם).

In its larger structure Psalm 120 develops and elaborates its opening line: בְּצָרָתָה לִּי קָרָאתִי וַיַּעֲנֵנִי. Thematically, v. 2 details the psalmist's cry (קָרָאתִי) for deliverance from adversaries of deceitful speech. The doubling heightens the intensity of the cry. V. 4 formulates specifically the desired punishment (the line continues and completes the thought of the preceding line [v. 3], while simultaneously recalling וַיַּעֲנֵנִי of v. 1. Vv. 5–6 detail the distress in which the psalmist finds himself. Again, repetitive elaboration gives evidence of the severity of the situation. The gravity of the situation is underscored not only through repetition, but also through rhetorical flourish. V. 5 opens with an exclamation: אוֹיָה לִי). This exclamation sets the tone for the developed description of the situation, which climaxes in v. 6: רַבַּת שָׁכְנָה לָּהּ נַפְשִׁי עִם שׂוֹנֵא שָׁלוֹם. The conclusion (v. 7) summarily contrasts the psalmist and the adversaries. Semantic parallelism (antithetic: שָׁלוֹם vs. מִלְחָמָה) occurs with grammatical variation (הֵמָּה מִלְחָמָה vs. אֲנִי שָׁלוֹם).

The three phrases of v. 1 provide a thematic overview and introduction to the psalm.[30] Positioned between the elaborations of these themes

---

[29] I.e., the hostile exilic environment the psalmist experiences manifests itself specifically in slanderous attacks from his neighbors (see R. Clifford, *Psalms 73–150* [Nashville: Abingdon, 2003], 218).

[30] Nowhere else in the Psalter does a lament begin with an expression of confidence affirming the successful outcome of the situation. Elsewhere such assertions occur toward the middle or end of the poem. The closest structurally parallel psalm to Ps 120 is Ps 40, a psalm which opens with an extended affirmation of God's gracious intervention, but concludes with a rather extended lament. Significantly, Ps 40 has been interpreted in several ways. For Ps 120, the opening expression of confidence functions admirably as an overarching thematic organizer and anticipatory summation of the remainder of the psalm. Interestingly, Jonah 2 contains a poem which begins similarly to Ps 120:1. Although the poem in Jonah is most likely an insert, it nonetheless demonstrates one context in which such language functions: קָרָאתִי מִצָּרָה לִי אֶל יְהוָה וַיַּעֲנֵנִי (2:3). Jonah exults in his deliverance from death (drowning), while yet far away from complete safety. Ps 120 envisions a similar situation. The psalmist confidently asserts his deliverance as actual, even though the rescue has yet to be realized.

are two exclamations (vv. 3, 5a).³¹ The first pronouncement is lengthy, the second pronouncement briefer. The first concerns the adversaries; the second concerns the psalmist. The conclusion starkly contrasts the psalmist and the adversaries; the former, espousing peace, dwells among treacherous warmongers. Because of the adversaries' refusal to accept peace, the psalmist invokes an appropriate punishment (arrows and coals = war weapons).³² Verse 1 announces the themes (with a confident vision of the outcome), which vv. 2–6 elaborate. The conclusion boldly contrasts the psalmist and his antagonists (in language appropriate to the preceding description).

Conclusion

Though replete with difficult lines and phrases, Psalm 120 evidences in its own right numerous parallelistic phenomena. Not surprisingly, many of these phenomena are manifested elsewhere in the שִׁירֵי־הַמַּעֲלוֹת, with similar intentions. In Psalm 120 the varied repetitive phenomena result in a cohesive and coherent poetic piece. Stylistic analysis suggests an alternate understanding of the opening verse, allowing interpretation to go beyond strictly form critical concerns. The suggestions of Bateson and Stankiewicz concerning modern literary analysis seem appropriate to our psalm. Repetition allows a poem to cohere, linking its several parts together into a unified whole. Repetition produces an interplay between sequence and simultaneity. Simultaneity presents successive elements in a common present, allowing an integrated structure in which each part is perceived as an autonomous part of a sequence and as a dependent part of a whole. Repetition thus allows a poem to say several things at once.

---

³¹ The first pronouncement (מַה יִּתֵּן לְךָ וּמַה יֹּסִיף לָךְ), set between the elaboration of קָרָאתִי (v 2) and וַיַּעֲנֵנִי (v 4), precedes an assertion of the coming punishment; the second pronouncement (אוֹיָה לִי) precedes a lengthy description of the lamentable situation.

³² The psalmist's affirmation ("I am [for] peace") functions not only as the psalmist's statement of innocence, but also serves as that ironic trait that now justifies the psalmist's "call to arms" (cf. J. Eaton, *The Psalms* [London: T. & T. Clark, 2003], 423).

7

The Faith (Faithfulness) of Jesus in Hebrews

Thomas H. Olbricht

> *The understanding of Jesus' faith in Hebrews is a more fully developed understanding of what many scholars now understand Pauline "faith of Christ" to mean—the absolute fidelity of Christ to the will of God and its fully exemplary character for other believers.*[1]

IN chapter 11, the Hebrews writer identified fifteen persons of faith from the Hebrew Bible and heralded multiple others unnamed. Yet the noteworthy exemplar of faith is Jesus, about whom the author wrote: "looking to Jesus the pioneer and perfecter of our faith who for the sake of the joy that was set before him endured the cross, disregarding its shame, and has taken his seat on the right hand of God" (Heb 12:2).

The Hebrews writer placarded the faith of Jesus as an example for those who later come to have faith in him. What is transparent in Hebrews, however, for the past two decades has been a matter of considerable controversy in respect to Paul. The question is whether Paul ever refers to the faith of Jesus, or only to faith in Jesus.

I dedicate this essay to James W. Thompson who has published both on Hebrews and Paul. I will first set forth the controversy regarding the

---

[1] Carl R. Holladay, *A Critical Introduction to the New Testament: Interpreting the Message and Meaning of Jesus Christ* (Nashville: Abingdon, 2005), 463.

faith of Jesus in the writings of Paul, assess the characteristics of that faith (faithfulness), and then turn to Hebrews so as to ascertain the manner in which the book perceives the attributes of Jesus' faith (faithfulness).

The Controversy Regarding the Faith (Faithfulness) of Jesus in the Writings of Paul

As Thomas H. Tobin notes in regard to the Pauline controversy, "The recent discussion of this issue began with Richard B. Hays, *The Faith of Jesus Christ*."[2] Philip F. Esler sets the context for the debate internationally. In his recent book on Romans he commented on Rom 3:21–26 in which the phrase διὰ πίστεως Ἰησοῦ Χριστοῦ (3:22) is translated, "through faith in Jesus Christ". The NRSV proposes an alternate reading "through the faith of Jesus Christ." In verse 26 the phrase δικαιόντα τὸν ἐκ πίστεως Ἰησοῦ, translated "justifies the one who has faith in Jesus" the NRSV alternate reading is, "who has the faith of Jesus." Esler wrote:

> The traditional interpretation of these expressions, which is still dominant in Great Britain and Europe, ably championed by J. D. G. Dunn, is that they are objective genitives and carry the meaning, as in the translation above of "faith in Jesus Christ" and "faith in Jesus." On this view Jesus/Jesus Christ is the object of faith. Since the 1980s, however, a different interpretation, that the genitives are subjective, meaning "the faith of Christ Jesus" and "the faith of Jesus," has become popular in North America, where it may now well be the majority view; on this interpretation Jesus/Jesus Christ becomes the model of faith.[3]

---

[2] Thomas H. Tobin, *Paul's Rhetoric in Its Contexts: The Argument of Romans* (Peabody, Mass.: Hendrickson Publishers, 2004), 132 n. 11. A collection of articles representing a spectrum of differences on the controversy appears in David M. Hay and E. Elizabeth Johnson, eds., *Romans* (vol. 4 of *Pauline Theology*; SBLSymS 4; Atlanta: Scholars, 1997). Some earlier proponents of the reading "the faith of Jesus" were Richard N. Longenecker, *Paul the Apostle of Liberty* (New York: Harper and Row, 1964), 149–52; A. G. Hebert, "Faithfulness and Faith," *Theology* 58 (1955): 373–79; T. F. Torrance, "One Aspect of the Biblical Conception of Faith," *ExpTim* 68 (1957): 111–14. For an up-to-date bibliography see Hung-Sik Choi, "PISTIS in Galatians 5:5–6: Neglected Evidence for the Faithfulness of Christ," *JBL* 124 (2005): 467–90.

[3] Philip F. Esler, *Conflict and Identity in Romans: The Social Setting of Paul's Letter* (Minneapolis: Fortress, 2003). On Dunn's declaration see J. D. G. Dunn, "Once More PISTIS CHRISTOU," in Hay and Johnson, *Romans*, 61–81. Those who favor the faith of Jesus include Luke Timothy Johnson, "Rom. 3:21–26 and the Faith of Jesus," *CBQ* 44 (1982): 77–90; Sam K. Williams "The *Pistis Christou* Formulation in Paul," *NovT* 22 (1980): 248–63; and idem, "Again *Pistis Christou*," *CBQ* 49 (1987): 431–47.

Other Pauline texts with the same construction are Gal 2:16, 20; 3:22; Eph 3:12; and Phil 3:9.

A number of New Testament scholars, at least since the Reformation, seem uncomfortable about discussing Jesus as a person of faith.[4] These same scholars, however, are not reluctant to write about the teaching and action of Jesus. Most observe that his life consisted of words and works. The works of Jesus are an expression of his obedience to the will of his Father. "For I have come down from heaven, not to do my own will, but the will of him who sent me." (John 6:38)[5] Scholars likewise are not reluctant to write about the expectations of Jesus that his disciples exhibit works. The works of the believers, however, express gratitude for the salvation that comes from God. Salvation is not of works lest anyone should boast; salvation is a great gift from God (Eph 2:8). Humans are justified by faith in Jesus Christ. Faith in Christ, many contend, is not generated from human resources, but is given by the grace of God through his Holy Spirit.

A consensus rejection of the nineteenth-century liberal Jesus now prevails among New Testament scholars.[6] Late nineteenth- and early twentieth-century liberals perceived Jesus, not so much as the crucified savior, but as the moral and ethical exemplar for humankind. As a result, many New Testament scholars at the beginning of this new millennium are reluctant to set forth Jesus as a model for Christian works, and some of the believer's faith. Rudolf Bultmann, despite rejecting aspects of the claims of his liberal professors, nevertheless assigned a nontraditional salvific role to Jesus. For Bultmann, Jesus was the ultimate exemplar of authentic faith as reconfigured in Heideggerian phenomenology.[7] Not many New Testament scholars currently, however, embrace his view that Jesus was the originator of authentic existential (i. e. Heideggerian) faith.

The storm center for discussion of Jesus' faith now focuses on Paul. Some linguistic and contextual reasons exist for translating διὰ πίστεως

---

[4] Karl Barth is an exception, *The Epistle to the Romans* (London: Oxford University Press, 1933), 96. See also Thomas Torrance, "One Aspect of the Biblical Conception of Faith," *ExpTim* 68 (1957): 111–14. For pre-Reformation interpretations, see Ian G. Wallis, *The Faith of Jesus Christ in Early Christian Traditions* (SNTSMS, Cambridge: Cambridge University, 1995), esp. chap. 6.

[5] So Rudolf Bultmann, *Theology of the New Testament* (trans. Kendrick Grobel; New York: Scribner's, 1951), 1:314.

[6] H. K. McArthur and R. F. Berkey, "Jesus, Quest of the Historical," in *DBI* 1: 578–85.

[7] Ibid., 1:314–29, 2:70–92; Robert Morgan, "Bultmann, Rudolf Karl (1884–1976)," in *DBI* 1:148–49.

Ἰησοῦ Χριστοῦ "the faith of Jesus Christ." Those who argue for the translation "the faith of Jesus" have in mind especially his faithfulness in complying with the expectations of the Father rather than his inner trust in God. If his faith, or better faithfulness, is exhibited through his actions, the faith of Jesus therefore cannot be an exemplar for human faith, at least, in the conception of Paul, so the objectors claim. The human faith that justifies is not faithfulness, but inner trust in Jesus as Lord, which is in fact, in the thinking of some, not generated at all by the believer but is a gift of God through his Holy Spirit. The result is that many Pauline scholars in Great Britain and on the continent resist any suggestion that a few of Paul's phrases διὰ πίστεως Ἰησοῦ Χριστοῦ may be translated "the faith of Jesus" (e. g. Rom 3:22, 26; Gal 2:20). The rejection is ostensibly not, however, on christological (or perhaps more appropriately soteriological), but linguistic grounds.[8]

This resistance does not extend to the Hebrews writer since statements as to Jesus' faith are explicit. Though this point is not often made, one might expect a passing remark, that after all, one of the reasons for rejecting the Pauline authorship of Hebrews is its emphasis upon the faith of Jesus.[9] Even though scholars do not explicitly deny that Hebrews sets out Jesus as an exemplar for the believer's faith, little is often made of this declaration in the commentaries.

The Faith of Jesus in Paul

Three recent studies on Romans take up the question of whether in any case Paul's construction should ever be translated the faith (or faithfulness)

---

[8] Charges that positions regarding the faith of Jesus result from christological predilections rather than linguistic considerations flow from both sides. Hays has charged that the objection of some to "'the faith of Jesus' may be rooted in an implicitly docetic Christology." Richard B. Hays, "PISTIS and Pauline Theology: What is at Stake?" in E. Elizabeth Johnson and David M. Hay, eds., *Pauline Theology*, vol. 4: *Looking Back, Pressing On* (SBLSymS 4; Atlanta: Scholars, 1997), 55. Philip F. Esler has countered that "such a reduction in the status of Christ is arguably a movement in a proto-Arian direction, in that this position is far more comfortable with Christ as a creature rather than as the creator" (Esler, *Conflict and Identity in Romans*, 158). As I will argue in more detail later, however, the whole matter is more tied in with a perspective on justification by faithfulness.

[9] Lindars wrote of the Hebrews author's perspective on faith, "Hebrews contributes a new definition of the virtue of faith as action in the light of assurance concerning the future. This is a valuable counterweight to Paul's use of faith, which is easily misunderstood as an attitude of passivity"; Barnabas Lindars, *The Theology of the Letter to the Hebrews* (Cambridge: Cambridge University Press, 1991), 127.

of Jesus. Philip Esler discusses this reading in respect to Rom 3:22, 26.[10] Esler points out that Richard Hays believed that a narrative regarding the salvific work of Jesus lies behind Paul's observation. He further observes that such a narrative was posited by Rudolf Bultmann in regard to a redeemer myth, a view that has now largely been rejected.[11] One can grant Esler's conclusion in regard to the narrative proposed by Hays and still be justified in thinking that the translation "the faith of Christ" is warranted on theological and possibly linguistic grounds. Esler quotes Williams to the effect that "Christ is not the object of such faith, however, but rather its supreme exemplar—indeed its creator."[12] Esler attributes Williams's view to the liberalism of a century ago that Barth himself could not shake off.[13] One does not need to support the model christology of liberal theology, however, to hold that Paul did in some sense perceive Jesus as an exemplar, for example, "Be imitators of me, as I am of Christ" (1 Cor 11:1) or that Christ in his obedience, certainly affirmed by Paul in Romans, exhibited his faithfulness. It is perhaps not accidental that in his index Esler does not include the word "faithfulness" which is a characteristic of God (Rom 3:3) and is a dimension of God's righteousness.

More recently Thomas H. Tobin published a major work on Romans in which he comes out adamantly against any translation of Paul's statements as "the faith of Christ."[14] Tobin argues that the issue is not grammatical since πίστις can be followed by either the subjective or objective genitive, though the subjective genitive is more common in both the New Testament and elsewhere. Tobin claims that in all these special cases the genitive is objective because if subjective in some instance Jesus Christ would be the subject of the verb πιστεύω which he asserts does not happen. He also points out that the adjectival πίστις is used of God four times, and once each to Abraham, Paul himself, Paul and Apollos, Timothy, and to a believer versus an unbeliever.[15] But never once does it adjectivally refer to Christ. This is an interesting argument, but it might cut both ways. For example, the subjective genitive in some cases might refer to the faith of Christ. Tobin does not perceive the righteousness of God from the perspective of God's covenant faithfulness, that is, his cov-

---

[10] Esler, *Conflict and Identity in Romans*, 157–59.

[11] Ibid., 158.

[12] Williams, "Again *Pistis Christou*," 446.

[13] Esler, *Conflict and Identity in Romans*, 159.

[14] Thomas H. Tobin, *Paul's Rhetoric in Its Contexts*, 132–37.

[15] Ibid., 132.

enant righteousness. Since he gives little emphasis to God as faithful in covenant, so it seems that he likewise wishes to rule out Christ's contribution to God's faithfulness.

The third study, which I find more insightful, is N. T. Wright's commentary on Romans in the *New Interpreter's Bible*. In his discussion of Rom 3:21–31 Wright argues that the righteous of God is the revelation of "God's salvific covenant faithfulness."[16] God's faithfulness therefore is especially revealed through "the faithfulness of Jesus the Messiah."[17] It is through Christ's obedience unto death that sins are forgiven, justification is secured, and the global covenant community is created:

> Paul is not speaking of Jesus' "faith" either in the sense of the things Jesus believed, or Jesus' exemplary trust in God, or Jesus' religious experience. Nor is he suggesting that Jesus' "obedience" was somehow meritorious, so that by it he earned "righteousness" on behalf of others. That is an ingenious and far-reaching way of making Paul's language fit into a theological scheme very different from his own. Rather he is highlighting Jesus' faithful obedience, or perhaps we should say Jesus' obedient faithfulness, to the saving plan marked out for Israel, the plan by which God would save the world. On the cross Christ accomplished what God had always intended the covenant to achieve. Where Israel as a whole had been faithless, he was faithful: 3:22 answers to 3:2–3.[18]

The translation of certain texts in Paul as the faith of Jesus therefore has specifically a focus upon Jesus' contribution to the faithfulness of God in respect to his covenant promise through the obedience of Jesus. The preferred translation of διὰ πίστεως Ἰησοῦ Χριστοῦ is therefore "through the faithfulness of Jesus" as Choi has, I believe, successfully demonstrated.[19]

In this essay I am interested in that of which the faith of Jesus consists as a possible topic in Paul, but especially in the book of Hebrews. Is Jesus' faith simply an inner trust in the hegemony of God? Or does it consist of his faithful execution of the will of God, and therefore is most appropriately translated faithfulness? Or does the faith of Jesus, in fact, participate

---

[16] N. T. Wright, "The Letter to the Romans," in *The New Interpreter's Bible* (ed. Leander Keck et al.; Nashville: Abingdon, 2002), 10:465.

[17] Ibid., 467.

[18] Ibid.

[19] Hung-Sik Choi, "PISTIS in Galatians 5:5–6: Neglected Evidence," 471, 483, 486, 490.

in dimensions of both? As an answer to this question in Paul, I will primarily refer to an essay by Luke Timothy Johnson.[20]

I have not discovered scholars, Luke Timothy Johnson excepted, who discuss what the attributes of the faith of Christ might be. Johnson locates the faith of Christ in the context of his obedience.[21] He quotes Bultmann, "Paul understands faith primarily as obedience; he understands the act of faith as an act of obedience."[22] Johnson declares that in Paul's vision, Jesus responded "in his earthly life to the mystery of God with that obedience which Paul calls faith."[23] Paul declared in Phil 2:8, "he humbled himself and became obedient to the point of death—even death on a cross." From this Johnson concluded,

> The obedience of Jesus is a model for the Philippians' obedience. We might also suggest that Jesus' obedience was the *ground* for their own obedience. He made it possible for them to be obedient. If we transpose this obedience language to that of "faith," we can suggest that the "faith" of Jesus in God was the ground of possibility for their "faith" in God. The final expression of that faith in the death on the cross opened up that possibility by revealing the paradoxical power of God to save in weakness, i. e., it revealed his way of making humans righteous before him.[24]

Johnson further argued that Paul made the same claim in Rom 3:22 and 5:18–19.[25] Choi furthermore, argued that Gal 5:5–6 is "a *crux interpretum* for the πιστις Χριστου at least in Galatians."[26] "For through the Spirit, by faith, we eagerly wait for the hope of righteousness. For in Christ Jesus neither circumcision nor uncircumcision counts for anything; the only thing that counts is faith working through love" (Gal 5:5–6). It denotes the "faithfulness of Christ."

The Faith (Faithfulness) of Jesus in Hebrews

We shall first look at faith and Christology in Hebrews through the early work of James Thompson, *The Beginnings of Christian Philosophy: The*

---

[20] Luke Timothy Johnson, "Rom. 3:21–26 and the Faith of Jesus," 77–90.

[21] Ibid., 85–90.

[22] Bultmann, *Theology of the New Testament*, 1:324.

[23] Johnson, "Rom. 3:21–26," 87.

[24] Ibid., 88.

[25] Ibid., 88–90.

[26] Hung-Sik Choi, "PISTIS in Galatians 5:5–6," 490.

Epistle to the Hebrews.²⁷ Scholars up until the 1980s had explained some aspects of Hebrews from the perspective of Gnosticism, Platonism, Philo, and apocalypticism. Thompson concludes that it may be particularly fruitful to examine Hebrews against the backdrop of Middle Platonism.²⁸ Whereas those of the Hellenistic age presented catalogues of exemplars, their heroes were persons of courage, virtue, and rationality, not as with the Hebrews writer persons of faith. Faith was not an admired trait among the Hellenists, nor was a willingness to suffer.

> It is well known that the critique of Christianity which was offered by Platonist philosophers was directed largely at the Christian' insistence on πίστις. Πίστις was the state of mind of the uneducated, who believe things on hearsay without being able to give reasons for their belief. In fact, what astonished pagan observers was the very behavior which is praised in Hebrews: the willingness to suffer for the undemonstrable.²⁹

But as Middle Platonism unfolded there was "a growing tendency to give to faith an indispensable role in one's relation to the divine."³⁰

For Philo, according to Thompson, faith is belief in a real heavenly country. The person of faith is a sojourner in a world of physical realities who aspires to transcend the body and the senses. God is the occupant of the fatherland. Platonism and Stoicism hold a similar view. However, philosophers do not commonly employ πίστις for this phenomenon until later. Hebrews is different in that faith is directed toward God's reliable oath and promise.³¹ Furthermore, the rewards for this confidence lie not in this life but in that beyond (Heb 10:35–39), giving faith an obvious eschatological dimension involving hope.³² Reward accrues through faithfulness, that is, endurance.³³ God himself is the enduring one, and so also is his city to which the believer travels. Whatever God promises, whatever happens in the realm of God, such as the taking of Christ's blood into the

---

²⁷ James W. Thompson, *The Beginnings of Christian Philosophy: The Epistle to the Hebrews* (Washington, D.C.: Catholic Biblical Association, 1982). The monograph draws upon his 1974 dissertation at Vanderbilt University.

²⁸ Thompson, *Beginnings of Christian Philosophy*, 15–16.

²⁹ Ibid,, 53. See also E. R. Dodds, *Pagan and Christian in an Age of Anxiety* (New York: Norton, 1965), 120.

³⁰ Ibid., 56.

³¹ Thompson, *Beginnings of Christian Philosophy*, 59–60

³² Ibid., 74.

³³ Ibid., 63.

heavenly tabernacle endures forever.[34] Despite the criticism of the early pagan authors the meaning of πίστις in Hebrews has to do with proof, reality, and knowledge that are based upon experience, though not, for the most part, subjective experience.[35] The Hebrews writer in this regard is closer to Philo than to others of his contemporaries.[36] For Plato, seeing is knowledge. For the Hebrews writer and Philo, seeing leads to faith.[37] Faith is exhibited through endurance in suffering, not as in Platonism or Stoicism in asceticism.[38]

Craig Koester in his recent commentary on Hebrews takes up the question of how best to understand faith that book. He first observes that the noun faith occurs in Hebrews thirty-two times and the verb twice, the majority in Hebrews 11.[39] He proposes that faith has "two dimensions of meaning."[40] The first meaning is trust. "One properly responds to a promise by trusting that the God who made it will keep it (10:23; 11:11) and reward those who seek him (11:6, 26)."[41] Though trust is an inner decision the focus does not lie with the inwardness (in the language of Koester, "state of mind"[42]), but with the objective promise that God has made. Koester appropriately does not even mention the inwardness of trust. Interestingly, Jesus is said to trust in God in Heb 2:13 in a quote, apparently from Isa 8:17, in which the prophet is encouraged to trust the "testimony" of God.

The second meaning proposed by Koester is faithfulness. This has to do with perseverance, that is, holding fast without wavering (6:12, 10:23). "Faith manifests itself in steadfast assurance in the face of threats, as Moses and his parents defied the king's wrath in order to do what was right (11:23, 27)."[43] Faithfulness is also the chief dimension of the faith of Jesus.

---

[34] Heb 9:12 cf. Thompson, *Beginnings of Christian Philosophy*, 67.

[35] Ibid., 71–72.

[36] Ibid., 74.

[37] Ibid., 78.

[38] Ibid., 74.

[39] Craig R. Koester, *Hebrews* (AB 36; New York: Doubleday, 2002), 125.

[40] Ibid.

[41] Ibid., 125–26.

[42] Ibid., 472. Koester rejects the translation of Luther and Tyndale "sure confidence" which he takes to be a state of the mind.

[43] Ibid., 126.

Thus Jesus, "the pioneer of faith," endured the cross and despised its shame (12:2). Former leaders of the Christian community provide examples of faithfulness to be imitated (13:7). To live by faith is to be faithful, as Jesus and Moses proved to be (2:17; 3:2, 5). Concepts related to faith include striving (4:11; 6:11) and boldness before God and other people (3:6; 4:16; 10:19, 35).[44]

As a summary Koester wrote,

> Jesus exemplified faith by confessing his trust in God (2:13) and by faithfully enduring suffering and shame in the confidence that God would bring him to everlasting joy.... Jesus makes faith possible, for his death and exaltation convey God's faithfulness to his promises, and God's faithfulness is the basis for human faith."[45]

Major Texts on the Faithfulness of Jesus in Hebrews

I will now examine in some detail in the faithfulness of Jesus in respect to Heb 2:5–18, 5:5–10, 7:22–28, 12:1–4, and 13:12–13.[46]

Hebrews 2:5–18

The faithfulness of Christ in Hebrews is more detailed and nuanced than in the writings of Paul. Though the work of God and Christ are set in a covenant context in Hebrews, the focus is not on God's righteousness in respect to the covenant promise as in Romans, but on the faithful action of the Son on the behalf of humankind. For example, there is no reference to the righteousness of God in Hebrews, though God is declared faithful (11:11), nor do "just", "justified" or "justification" occur. Righteousness and faithfulness are rather assigned to the Son; his righteousness in 1:9 and his faithfulness in 2:17, 3:2, 6.

---

[44] Ibid.

[45] Ibid., 127.

[46] For my views on the purpose, structure and audience of Hebrews, see Thomas H. Olbricht, "Hebrews as Amplification," in *Rhetoric and the New Testament: Essays from the 1992 Heidelberg Conference* (eds. Stanley E. Porter and Thomas H. Olbricht; Sheffield: Sheffield Academic, 1993), 375–87; and idem, "Anticipating and Presenting the Case for Christ as High Priest in Hebrews," in *Rhetorical Argumentation in Biblical Texts: Essays from the 2000 Lund Conference* (eds. Anders Eriksson, Thomas H. Olbricht, and Walter Übelacker (Harrisburg, Penn.: Trinity Press International, 2002), 355–72.

God is inextricably involved in the work of the Son according to the Hebrews writer. Attridge observed, "Christ the ἀρχηγός is God's instrument in God's action of 'leading' ἀγαγόντα many to glory."⁴⁷ It was God who made Jesus "a little lower than the angels" (2:9). It was God who "crowned [Jesus] with glory," and by whose grace Christ "tasted death for everyone." It was God who made Jesus "the pioneer of their salvation perfect through sufferings" (2:10).⁴⁸ It was God finally, who appointed Jesus high priest because of his faithful obedience as a human to his God assigned tasks (5:5).

Heb 2:5–18 likewise clearly declares Jesus' faithfulness to be the result of his submissive acceptance of the will of God. Christ demonstrated by tasting death for all (2:9). Because of his obedience to the will of God, Jesus became perfect through suffering (2:10). In regard to the perfectibility of Jesus through suffering, Walters wrote, "Despite his sinlessness Jesus was not incapable of ethical growth. He kept his sinlessness only by way of his faithfulness to the upward call of God; Christ had to undergo a process of perfection."⁴⁹

> Jesus' life was continually beset with opposition, increasing opposition. He offered many prayers and petitions in the course of his earthly life, but all the prayers, all the loud cries, all the obedience he rendered became focused in the final great prayer and the final great act of obedience. Because he submitted to the will of God at the end as at the beginning and at every point in between, his prayer was heard . . . . He might not have seen the cross before him until opposition had reached a critical point. The statement Hebrews makes is that Jesus learned obedience; he learned as he went along the obedience that was required of him. His response to faith carried him forward to ever greater challenges; the tension of his ethical position was as real as of his eschatological position.⁵⁰

---

⁴⁷ Harold W. Attridge, *The Epistle of Hebrews* (Hermeneia; Philadelphia: Fortress, 1989), 88.

⁴⁸ James Thompson (*The Letter to the Hebrews* [Austin, Tex.: Sweet, 1971], 41) wrote, "The ultimate purpose of God is in bringing many sons to glory. Here one notices that the purpose of this detailed discussion is to relate their experience to the whole plan of God." See also David A. DeSilva, *Perseverance in Gratitude: A Socio-Rhetorical Commentary on the Epistle to the Hebrews* (Grand Rapids: Eerdmans, 2000), 112–15.

⁴⁹ John R. Walters, *Perfection in New Testament Theology: Ethics and Eschatology in Relational Dynamic* (Lewiston, N.Y.: Mellen Biblical Press, 1995), 127.

⁵⁰ Ibid., 129.

Jesus made it possible for those sanctified to be one with himself, and therefore also with the Father. "For the one who sanctifies and those who are sanctified all have one Father" (2:11). Lindars observed, "The sacrifice of Jesus is permanently effective: 'For by a single offering he has perfected for all time those who are sanctified' (10:14), whereas the sacrifices under the Law 'can never . . . make perfect those who draw near.'"[51] For this reason Jesus is not ashamed to call them brothers and sisters (2:11). These perspectives are absent in Paul, though for him Christ became the firstborn of the new humanity, as opposed to the old humanity through Adam (Romans 5). In willingly becoming lower than the angels, Jesus put his trust in God (2:13). Jesus took on human flesh and thereby shared the very nature of humankind (2:17). By his death, he destroyed death through defeating the one who has the power over death, that is, the devil, and released his brothers and sisters from the fear of death (2:14–15).[52] (The release from the fear of death Paul also declared in 1 Corinthians 15:54–57). Christ came to help and rescue the descendants of Abraham, not angels (2:16).

Through his suffering and willing death, Christ became a high priest in the service of God, appointed by him (2:17). It was in order to take up this priesthood that he was perfected. His being perfected did not situate the Son on a higher moral ground. Rather, he sacrificed himself on behalf of humankind (2:17). Because he was tested, he is able to help those being tested (2:18). Attridge wrote, "Christ 'is able' (δύναται) to give aid because as a fellow sufferer, he is merciful and sympathetic, but also because, by his suffering, he has been brought to that position of honor and glory whence true help comes."[53] In all of these ways Jesus was faithful to God and to his sisters and brothers. His faith (faithfulness) was demonstrated through his obedient salvific actions.

Hebrews 5:5–10

Hebrews 1:8–9 declares the righteousness of Jesus in his rule [scepter] and life, but the point seems not to refer to right action in covenant since

---

[51] Barnabas Lindars, *Theology of the Letter to the Hebrews*, 45.

[52] Talbert points out that Jesus in 2:9–18 shares with humans (1) suffering (2:10–18), (2) temptation (2:18), and (3) death (2:9, 14). Thus is his salvific work in which he demonstrates his faith, that is, his faithfulness. In so doing he (1) becomes the pioneer of faith (2:10–13), (2) overpowers the devil (2:14–15), and (3) becomes the merciful high priest (2:16–18). Charles H. Talbert, *Learning through Suffering: The Educational Value of Suffering in the New Testament and in Its Milieu* (Collegeville, Minn.: Liturgical, 1991), 61–62.

[53] Attridge, *Hebrews*, 96.

righteousness in this case contrasts with wickedness. Jesus was faithful in accepting the flesh of humanity so that he could be a faithful priest on behalf of humans (2:17). He "was faithful to the one who appointed him," just as Moses also "was faithful in all God's house" (3:2). The Son, like Moses, likewise will be faithful to the believers who comprise God's house that is established through himself. "Christ, however, was faithful over God's house as a son, and we are his house if we hold firm the confidence and the pride that belong to hope" (3:6).

Jesus was a special priest after the order of Melchizedek as declared in Psalm 110. The Levitical priests through a sacrifice for their sins obtained the "power" to forgive the sins of the people (5:3). Jesus, through the sacrifice of himself attained this power. The death he died was that of a human. In this manner he addressed human death and also the right to be a special priest of God. "In the days of his flesh, Jesus offered up prayers and supplications, with loud cries and tears, to the one who was able to save him from death, and he was heard because of his reverent submission" (5:7). About these actions Talbert remarked that Christ's sufferings no doubt included the Gethsemane experience, but in addition this text incorporates the general diversities of his life.[54] Here Hebrews spells out the details of Christ's faithfulness in far more detail that in any depiction in Paul. Jesus' faithful submission to God was recognized and rewarded. About this Thompson wrote, "The cries and tears intensify the author's interest in Jesus' humanity. Jesus participated in the human situation so completely that he experienced the natural human fear at the prospect of death."[55] First, he was rewarded through his appointment to the priesthood.[56] Second, his brothers and sisters were rewarded. "Although he was a Son, he learned obedience through what he suffered; and having been made perfect, he became the source of eternal salvation for all who obey him, having been designated by God a high priest according to the order of Melchizedek" (5:8–10).[57]

---

[54] Talbert, *Learning through Suffering*, 63; Attridge, *Hebrews*, 149–52.

[55] Thompson, *Letter to the Hebrews*, 77.

[56] Talbert (*Learning through Suffering*, 66–67) observed that through his suffering Jesus was perfected for priestly service through his earthly ministry and ultimately through his entry into heaven (64). Jesus learned the "shocks" of human existence through his suffering. The result was that it qualified him to be the high priest for humankind.

[57] On the obedience of Christ see: Richard N. Longenecker, "The obedience of Christ in the Theology of the Early Church," in *Reconciliation and Hope: New Testament Essays on Atonement and Eschatology Presented to L. L. Morris on his 60th Birthday* (ed. Robert Banks; Grand Rapids: Eerdmans, 1974).

David Peterson wrote about the perfection of Christ, "His life of obedience, his sacrificial death and heavenly exaltation are the means by which he was perfected. Believers in turn are perfected by the very actions and accomplishments that perfect Christ." [58]

> The personal preparation of Christ to offer his once-for-all sacrifice and to be a merciful and faithful heavenly high priest is particularly emphasized in 4:14—5:10. His experience of suffering and temptation was not only for the purpose of acquainting him with the situation of his "brothers", so that he could achieve perfect sympathy with them and show "mercy" and "grace to help in time of need". It was also to show men "how far God ought to be submitted to and obeyed: and so that he himself might "learn" to carry out the task of the *ebed Yahweh* to its end"[59]

Specifically, Jesus was perfected, not because of his ethics and morals, but for his service as a never-dying priest for humankind. He likewise became the model extraordinaire for those who sought to replicate his life of faithfulness.

Hebrews 7:26–28

Hebrews 7:26–28 summarizes the claims about Christ as priest especially from chapter 5. Christ was holy, blameless, undefiled, and separated from sinners throughout his earthly Sonship. As the result of this faithfulness he was exalted above the heavens (7:26). He did not need to offer animal sacrifices as did the Levitical high priests, but he made a once for all sacrifice of himself (7:27). The law appointed priests who, because of their weaknesses had first to sacrifice on their own behalf. But the word of oath, that is, Psalm 110 regarding Melchizedek, appointed "a Son who has been made perfect forever" (7:28). Jesus obviously was faithful to both God and humans in the sacrifice of himself. Koester wrote,

> In one sense Christ's movement from suffering to completion in glory is exemplary, offering hope that since God exalted the Son who suffered, he will exalt his other sons and daughters who suffer. In another sense, Christ's completion is unique, for from his position at God's right hand his is singularly able to minister on behalf of others.[60]

---

[58] David Peterson, *Hebrews and Perfection: An Examination of the Concept of Perfection in the 'Epistle to the Hebrews'* (Cambridge: Cambridge University Press, 1982), 186.

[59] Ibid., 103.

[60] Craig R. Koester, *Hebrews*, 374.

Hebrews 12:1–4

After placarding several Old Testament persons of faith, the Hebrews writer finally rests his case by hailing Jesus as the exemplar par excellence. He is the pioneer of a new and perfected faithfulness. He "endured the cross, disregarding its shame . . . " (12:2). He did this "for the sake of the joy that was set before him" and as the result, "has taken his seat at the right hand of the throne of God" (12:2). He "endured such hostility against himself from sinners" (12:3). Most of all Jesus endured, and in like manner those who believe in him should endure—"not grow weary or lose heart." The endurance of Jesus was a primary exhibition of his faithfulness. Three times, Hebrews emphasizes Jesus' endurance (11:2, 3, 13:13). He was also declared faithful three times (2:17, 3:2, 6). Believers in Jesus are those who come to have faith in Jesus because of the faith or faithfulness of Jesus. Jesus was faithful all the way to his glorification. In this manner he exceeded all those before him and thus became the perfect exemplar of faith.

N. Clayton Croy particularly focused upon the connection between suffering and endurance.[61] He argues, correctly, I think that the suffering in Hebrews is not punishment for sin, but the enduring of hardship.

> Lastly, the list of exemplars in chapter 11, especially with Jesus as the culmination 12:1–3, lionizes not persons who have endured punishment for sin, but those who have endured (undeserved) hardship, privation, and mistreatment. If the readers of the epistle were suffering God's punishment for sin, they would not have a sense of solidarity with the luminaries of Israel's past as the author has described them. Similarly, the list in chapter 11, while certainly including martyrs (vss 35–8), primarily highlights those who have remained faithful in difficult times. The forward-looking, or promissory, emphasis of chapter 11 is strong. Again, the call is to endure, not to die.[62]

Croy wrote of faithfulness in terms of Jesus' experience. He says that the Hebrews author in 12:1–3 only highlights those experiences of Jesus that are relevant to the readers. There are four aspects: (1) joy, (2) endurance, (3) shame, and (4) hostility.

> In summary then, Hebrews 12:1–3 presents Jesus not so much as a martyr or a model of self-renunciation, but as the paradigm of

---

[61] N. Clayton Croy, *Endurance in Suffering: Hebrews 12:1–13 in its Rhetorical, Religious and Philosophical Context* (Cambridge: Cambridge University Press, 1998).

[62] Ibid., 3.

faithful endurance who has completed the course in advance of all others. In creating this image, the author has employed a long-established tradition of athletic agon which enables him to underscore endurance in suffering as a quality needed by the readers.[63]

Croy argues that though punitive suffering appears in biblical texts, and I add, especially in the Old Testament though also in the New, the suffering found in Hebrews is nonpunitive.[64]

Recognizing the importance of Jesus' faith, Walters sets out the manner in which it superceded that of the past heroes. The perfection proposed by the Hebrews writer was corporate, but could not be perfected by the past heroes until the breakthrough of Jesus for believers as his sisters and brothers. As Croy puts it,

> The worthies of the past by faith beheld the Promise and made it their own, but they came to enjoy it only afterward. They were not perfected until the others could join them. This shows very clearly the assumption on the part of the author that perfection is corporate, unlike the individual's quest in the speculative philosophy of Hellenism. Only one individual could pursue it without the aid of others, the Son who was perfected by God through sufferings (2:10). And he had it in mind all along to bring his sisters and brothers with him. Here is another example of ethical futurity. The heroes of old kept faith with God and responded to the commands given them, but it would only be later that the pioneer would come who would be called upon to go the extra distance no one else had gone. Until that part of the divine provision had been executed, perfection for everyone else was out of the question. That level of relationship with God was not yet opened.[65]

Hebrews 13:12–13

At the close of the treatise the writer declares that Jesus faithfully "suffered outside the city gate in order to sanctify the people by his own blood" (13:12). He exhorts the readers with "Let us then go to him outside the camp and bear the abuse he endured" (13:13). On this text Talbert commented that Jesus offered his own blood in the heavenly holy of holies so as to secure eternal forgiveness. His body was offered outside the gates of Jerusalem, just as the priests offered the bodies of bulls and goats, in the

---

[63] Ibid., 76.
[64] Ibid., 219.
[65] Ibid., 152–53.

temple. Therefore believers, though pilgrims with their eyes on the heavenly Jerusalem, offer their own earthly selves in service to others away from the heavenly gates.[66]

Conclusion

According to Hebrews then, the faith(fulness) of Jesus in its concreteness is the ultimate exemplar of faith(fulness) for the believer. Jesus was faithful in taking on the flesh of humankind, meeting human challenges and temptations, dying humanity's death, and in his glorification serving as their priest forever. Especially in the events leading to his death and in his death his faithfulness serves as a model for human faithfulness. For the Hebrews writer salvation is attained, not so much by faith in Jesus Christ, but through the Son's faithfulness, and Christians' replication of that faithfulness.

---

[66] Talbert, *Learning through Suffering*, 68–69.

Christ Our Pasch
Shaping Christian Identity in Corinth

Jeffrey Peterson

James W. Thompson has observed that in the hortatory appeals of Paul's letters, the apostle "builds his case for appropriate conduct on the basis of the community's memory of his missionary preaching."[1] There has of course been a good deal of previous work on the question of Pauline "missionary proclamation."[2] Important work remains to be done, however, inasmuch as (1) significant evidence for the topoi of Paul's formative instruction has been left unexploited and, even more importantly, (2) many scholars have not been as perceptive as Thompson in discerning the extent to which each of Paul's letters to his churches constitutes a moment in a continuing conversation about the implications and interpretation of this formative teaching.[3] This essay represents an initial probe into one piece of evidence to which Thompson draws attention

---

[1] James W. Thompson, *Preaching Like Paul: Homiletical Wisdom for Today* (Louisville: Westminster John Knox, 2001), 49–50.

[2] Thompson notes especially the influential work of C. H. Dodd and largely accepts his summary of the contents of the kerygma; ibid., 46 and n. 15.

[3] See ibid., 21–60, esp. 40 (e.g., "The epistles are, in fact, the continuation of a conversation"). The conversational metaphor itself is of course widespread. Calvin Roetzel (*The Letters of Paul: Conversations in Context* [4th ed.; Louisville, Kent.: Westminster John Knox, 1998]) is typical in that, while mentioning Paul's missionary proclamation as "the first stage in each conversation between Paul and the various churches" (80–81), he concentrates on the letters as responses to challenges posed by Paul's churches rather than the churches' appropriation and interpretation of the Pauline kerygma.

as an example of an epistolary appeal to Paul's prior proclamation, viz., 1 Cor 5:7–8.[4]

For purposes of historical description, it may be more helpful to refer to Paul's "formative instruction" than his "missionary proclamation," for at least two reasons. First, Paul's aim in imparting his εὐαγγέλιον was the formation of a community, a fact sometimes neglected in scholarly reconstructions of the kerygma. Second, Paul's use of εὐαγγέλιον, κήρυγμα, and related vocabulary is metaphorical; Stanley Stowers has shown that Paul did not literally stand in the agora or at the street corner and announce, "The end of the present evil age is at hand!" Rather, Paul taught people his messianic dogma in private settings, most often in homes, the social institution in which the Pauline communities subsisted.[5] The formative instruction imparted by Paul and accepted by his Gentile converts in the founding of a household community offered them a new identity, a share in the heritage of Israel.[6]

In a recent study of "Rhetorical Shorthand in Pauline Argumentation," Margaret Mitchell has recognized 1 Cor 5:7 as an instance of Paul's use of synecdoche. In the statement "our Passover offering has been sacrificed, namely Christ" (τὸ πάσχα ἡμῶν ἐτύθη χριστός), Paul explicitly refers only to Jesus' crucifixion; as a synecdoche, however, this paschal clause (as I will call it) makes allusion to one element of the more extensive gospel narrative that is presupposed if the allusion is to be intelligible to the letter's recipients.[7]

---

[4] Ibid., 77. It is a pleasure to offer this essay in honor of James Thompson, mentor and friend, in appreciation of his exemplary scholarship in the service of the church.

[5] Stanley K. Stowers, "Social Status, Public Speaking, and Private Teaching: The Circumstances of Paul's Preaching Activity," *NovT* 26 (1984): 59–82.

[6] Recent studies undertaken in connection with the Paul and Politics Section of the Society of Biblical Literature have shown that an adequate consideration of this process cannot ignore its political dimensions; see the two collections edited by Richard A. Horsley (*Paul and Empire: Religion and Power in Roman Imperial Society* [Harrisburg, Pa.: Trinity, 1997]; *Paul and Politics: Ekklesia, Israel, Imperium, Interpretation: Essays in Honor of Krister Stendahl* [Harrisburg, Pa.: Trinity, 2000]). The most important of these dimensions is the consciousness that Paul's proclamation fostered in the communities brought into being in response to it that they form part of a new political entity (cf. Phil 3:20). An earlier version of this essay was presented to this section on 21 November 2005 at the SBL Annual Meeting in Philadelphia; I am grateful for the occasion to interact with these scholars in their concern to uncover the political implications of Pauline rhetoric.

[7] Margaret M. Mitchell, "Rhetorical Shorthand in Pauline Argumentation: The Functions of 'the Gospel' in the Corinthian Correspondence," in *Gospel in Paul: Studies on Corinthians, Galatians and Romans for Richard N. Longenecker* (JSNTSup 108; ed. L. Ann Jervis and Peter Richardson; Sheffield: Sheffield Academic, 1994), 70–72.

Mitchell's description of the dynamic between missionary catechesis and the argument of an individual letter is similar to Thompson's: "Once the contextual meaning of 'the gospel' was fully established, as by Paul's missionary teaching, it was then possible at a second and later stage of reflection to invoke that known quantity in shorthand, either by a brief phrase, a synecdochical reference, or a metaphorical allusion."[8] Mitchell derives the three categories of brevity, synecdoche, and metaphor from the ancient rhetorical discussion of tropes. The categories, while heuristically useful, are not watertight. Indeed, while Mitchell herself treats the paschal clause of 1 Cor 5:7 only as an instance of synecdoche, it fits well under all three of her rhetorical headings: a five-word statement that evokes the whole of the gospel narrative by metaphorical reference to one of its elements, Christ's crucifixion, as a paschal offering.

Mitchell's consideration of the paschal clause is itself an example of the phenomenon she is studying, as it is brief. This is entirely appropriate in a study treating the use of brevity throughout 1 Corinthians, yet concentrated attention on 1 Cor 5:7–8 affords a fuller picture of how Paul undertook to shape a new identity for his converts in Corinth based on the founding narrative of Jesus' death, resurrection, and impending advent. Paul presented this narrative as the fulfillment of Israel's ancestral hopes recorded in the Scriptures, in which non-Jews had now received a stake by the grace of God. As we will see, this narrative clearly involved a challenge to the ultimacy of the Roman order, but Paul's focus in his attempts to shape Corinthian identity centered on the ordering of the new community's internal life according to norms derived from the Jesus narrative and the Scriptures that he understood it to fulfill.

We can begin our examination by broadening our focus from the paschal clause itself to include its immediate context. The clause appears in the middle of a pericope (vv. 6b–8) that critiques the Corinthian community's response to the sexual behavior of one of its members; Paul labels their "boasting" as "not good" (οὐ καλὸν, v. 6a)—that is, by litotes, as "very bad." He then undertakes to support this judgment through the comparison of immoral behavior with leaven developed in vv. 6b–8. The paschal clause constitutes one element of this supporting argument and depends for its significance on the surrounding web of associations.

Johannes Weiss amply demonstrated the degree to which this argument depends on an acquaintance with Passover ritual as detailed in

---

[8] Mitchell, "Rhetorical Shorthand," 69. See also Larry W. Hurtado, *Lord Jesus Christ: Devotion to Jesus in Earliest Christianity* (Grand Rapids: Eerdmans, 2003), 127.

Exodus 12. Weiss notes that in v. 7a the adjective παλαιός is superfluous to the exhortation; "it would of course be sufficient to say, 'Sweep out the leaven.'"⁹ The addition of παλαιός reflects the Passover practice of purging one's house of leaven from the first day of the festal week (ἀπὸ δὲ τῆς ἡμέρας τῆς πρώτης, Exod 12:15 LXX); it also evokes the ethical transformation of the παλαιὸς ἄνθρωπος that Paul presents as a result of conversion to his gospel (cf. Rom 6:6). That this transformation is in view is confirmed by the description of the purified community as, not a "pure" or "unleavened" lump of dough, but a "new" one, as also by the characteristic juxtaposition of imperative ("clean out the old leaven") and indicative ("as indeed you are unleavened").¹⁰

The evocation of Passover ritual is deepened in the paschal clause itself, in v. 7b. In the transitional καὶ γάρ, καί is often left translated (as in NRSV), but Weiss suggests the translation "for indeed our Passover lamb is also [already] sacrificed: Christ."¹¹ Weiss's translation appears to give καί both emphatic and augmentative force (*ja auch*); I would suggest that καί is best read simply as emphatic and propose rendering the paschal clause "for indeed our Passover lamb is [already] sacrificed, [namely] Christ."¹² Following on the exhortation to purge out the old leaven, the significance of the metaphor is that the Corinthians' paschal sacrifice is now slaughtered, as it were, and ready to be brought into the house, from which the leaven should have already been removed.¹³ Weiss holds that one should interpret the appeal to "celebrate the festival" (ὥστε ἑορτάζωμεν, v. 8a) figuratively, in keeping with the earlier figurative references to the "old leaven," the "new lump," "purge out," and "unspoiled."¹⁴ He neglects to note

---

[9] "*Es würde ja genügen, zu sagen: fegt den Sauerteig aus*" (Johannes Weiss, *Der erste Korintherbrief* [Göttingen: Vandenhoeck & Ruprecht, 1910], 134). Translations of Weiss are mine.

[10] Weiss, *Korintherbrief*, 135.

[11] Weiss, *Korintherbrief*, 135: "*denn es ist ja auch (schon) unser Passahlamm geschlachtet: Christus.*"

[12] The use of θύειν in 1 Cor 5:7 echoes Exod 12:21 LXX (θύσατε τὸ πάσχα) as well as the uses of the root with τὸ πάσχα as object in Deut. 16:2, 5, 6 LXX.

[13] For first-century practice in this respect, see Josephus *Ant.* 2.317 and discussion in Maurice Casey, *Aramaic Sources of Mark's Gospel* (SNTSMS 102; Cambridge: Cambridge University Press, 1998), 221–22. Paul's point is vividly captured in Paula Fredrikson's paraphrase: "it's already 14 Nisan and there's still *chometz* in the house" ("Ultimate Reality in Ancient Christianity: Christ and Redemption," in *Ultimate Realities: A Study of the Comparison of Religious Ideas* [ed. Robert C. Neville, John Berthrong, and Peter Berger; Albany: SUNY Press 2000], 64).

[14] Weiss, *Korintherbrief*, 136. See however below, n. 24.

that ἑορτάζωμεν supplies a final evocation of Exodus 12 (ἑορτάσετε αὐτὴν ἑορτὴν κυρίῳ, Exod 12:14 LXX; cf. ἑορτάσεις κυρίῳ τῷ θεῷ σου, Deut. 16:15 LXX), occasioning a transition from the sacrificial vehicle back to the moral tenor and so closing the circle that Paul opened at v. 6b.

Weiss's interpretation of the passage focuses on the authorial perspective and does not consider the rhetorical situation as Mitchell rightly encourages us to do. Here we may note that in order for an audience to follow the argument even minimally, they must be acquainted with the festival that Jews call πάσχα (its native Aramaic name) and above all they must recognize the removal of leaven from the home and the use of "unleavened loaves" (vv. 7, 8) as elements of the festival's celebration.[15] If Weiss's analysis is correct, for Paul's exposition to have its full impact on his auditors, they must further be aware that the paschal celebration begins with the removal of leaven before the offering of the eponymous sacrifice. Paul gives no explanation of any of these terms for an audience that, significantly, he characterizes as converted Gentiles in 12:2 (cf. 6:9–11), and not as Jews, for whom such familiarity could be assumed.

Moreover, Paul expects the Corinthians to recognize in Jesus' execution (presented as such through the use of σταυρός and σταυρόω in 1 Cor 1:13, 17–18; 2:2, 8) "their" paschal offering, in distinction from the Passover sacrifice that annually unites Israel. That is, Paul expects his converts to be familiar not only with the Jewish festal practice in some detail but also with an interpretation of the death of Christ in light of this festival as constitutive of the community into which Paul's preaching has introduced them. We thus should conclude that 1 Cor 5:6–8 presupposes that the Corinthians have acquired knowledge of the paschal ritual and its application to Christ from Paul or his missionary associates in the course of the community's initial formation.

This reminds us of Paul's own summary of his formative instruction as a proclamation of Jesus' death for "our" sins and his resurrection "on the third day," and both of these theologoumena "in accordance with the Scriptures" (κατὰ τὰς γραφάς, 1 Cor 15:3–4). Paul's neglect of a footnote detailing the texts of Jewish Scripture that he presented Jesus' death and resurrection as fulfilling is of course a great disappointment to the scholar. After much inconclusive debate, many have recently elected to make a virtue of necessity and assert that Paul intended no particular

---

[15] Fredrikson assumes rhetorical incompetence on Paul's part here and suggests that his remark "would probably panic a trained Pharisee more than this audience" ("Ultimate Reality," 64).

texts as fulfilled.[16] I have elsewhere offered the suggestion that we should rather envision Paul's missionary catechesis as introducing his converts to a catena of scriptural texts linked in his imaginative presentation of the founding narrative of Jesus' salvific death, resurrection, enthronement, and anticipated *parousia* and grounding this narrative in the ancestral traditions of Israel.[17] The presupposition of familiarity with paschal imagery in 1 Cor 5:7 provides evidence that Exodus 12 was among the texts Paul employed to interpret the death of Jesus in missionary catechesis.

For confirmation of this suggestion we may turn to 1 Cor 11:23–26, which Helmut Koester has recently argued belongs with 15:3–5 as traditions that were foundational to the Pauline churches.[18] The starting point for evaluation of the Last Supper tradition retailed by Paul is the recognition of its overlap in content with the Synoptic accounts of this supper, and especially with the Marcan and Matthaean accounts, which exhibit the same bread-cup structure in the context of a meal.[19] There are of course differences between the Pauline and Synoptic accounts, but (as in the source criticism of the Synoptics themselves) it is first of all the similarities that demand an explanation in terms of tradition history. Here the similarities suggest that the Pauline and Synoptic accounts derive from a common tradition.

Maurice Casey has shown that the Passover setting of the Last Supper in Mark 14:12–26 is not merely a redactional contribution of the evangelist. Rather, incidental details throughout the pericope confirm that the pre-Marcan tradition presented the supper as a Passover meal.[20] Similarly,

---

[16] See Gordon D. Fee, *The First Epistle to the Corinthians* (NICNT; Grand Rapids: Eerdmans. 1987), 725, 727–728; Anthony C. Thiselton, *The First Epistle to the Corinthians: A Commentary on the Greek Text* (NIGTC: Grand Rapids: Eerdmans; Carlisle: Paternoster, 2000), 1195–97.

[17] See Jeffrey Peterson, "The Extent of Christian Theological Diversity: Pauline Evidence," *ResQ* 47 (2005): 3 n. 10; a more extensive treatment is forthcoming under the title "The Pre-Pauline Christological Catena in 1 Cor 15:3–4."

[18] See Helmut Koester, "The Memory of Jesus' Death and the Worship of the Risen Lord," *HTR* 91 (1998): 343–48.

[19] The shorter Lucan recension is prior to the longer and represents the evangelist's redaction of the Marcan account (Bart D. Ehrman, *The Orthodox Corruption of Scripture: The Effect of Early Christological Controversies on the Text of the New Testament* [Oxford: Oxford University Press, 1993], 197–209). The parallels with Paul in the longer Lucan recension reflect assimilation of the resulting distinctive narrative to the developing liturgical tradition and to the Pauline text on which it drew.

[20] Casey, *Aramaic Sources*, 228–29, 236–47. One need not find convincing Casey's contention that Mark originated in Aramaic or his detailed reconstruction of this hypothetical *Vorlage* to recognize the value of his exegetical observations, the vast majority of which can

the Pauline version of the tradition exhibits details that are best explained if Paul presented Jesus as having instituted the supper in a Passover context.[21] Thus (1) Jesus' blessings over bread and wine are recalled as having taken place at "night," as also at Mark 14:17, in accordance with the requirement of Exodus 12 and Deuteronomy 16 that the Passover be eaten after sundown. (2) Paul associates the tradition with the anticipation of eschatological salvation (1 Cor 11:26), as does also Mark 14:25; this fits well in the context of expectations of national deliverance associated with Passover observance (on which see below). (3) Jesus' words of interpretation would be particularly unusual at an "ordinary" meal and would be more intelligible at one in which interpretation of elements was expected, even if the interpretation itself was novel. (4) The specifically atoning significance ascribed to the bread and the wine also commends a paschal context.

Such an interpretation of these elements of the meal is often taken to count against a Passover setting, as commentators frequently note that the Passover was not presented as an atonement sacrifice in the Hebrew Bible or in later Judaism. But Jon Levenson has observed that "the unclassifiable passover sacrifice of Exodus 12 . . . [has] much in common with a sin offering, for it is through the blood of the lamb that lethal calamity is deflected, as the mysterious Destroyer is prevented from working his dark designs upon the Israelite first-born (vv 21–23)." Levenson further suggests that "in the heated apocalyptic Judaism that served as the matrix of Christianity, the Destroyer [could easily have been] transmuted into a personification of the Israelites' own mortal sins, and the blood of the paschal lamb . . . seen as effecting not only escape from death, but purification from moral pollution as well."[22] (5) Finally, this mention of atonement comes in connection with reference to a "new covenant," evocative of Jer 31:31. The allusion to this text suggests a parallel with God's covenant with Israel initiated at Passover and completed at Sinai. All these details of the tradition that Paul details commend a recognition that he introduced Jesus' last supper to his converts as a Passover meal and made them aware of its significance.

---

be made out from the Greek text of Mark.

[21] Casey is thus hasty to declare that in 1 Cor 11:23–26, in contrast to Mark 14:12–26, "there is no mention of Passover" (*Aramaic Sources,* 248).

[22] Jon D. Levenson, *The Death and Resurrection of the Beloved Son: The Transformation of Child Sacrifice in Judaism and Christianity* (New Haven: Yale University Press, 1993), 208–9.

We should note also that in 10:1–13, Paul presupposes that the details of the exodus narrative are familiar enough that he can allegorize them straightaway. These passages strongly suggest that some version of a paschal/exodus narrative and its fulfillment in Christ were among the traditions Paul had imparted to the Corinthians in the course of his founding and formative instruction in the community. When considered in light of 1 Cor 15:3–4, it is strongly tempting to conclude that the bedrock of Pauline missionary theology (the communal foundation that he laid, as he puts it in 1 Cor 3:10–11) involved a narrative of Jesus' death and resurrection as a universal Passover offering that sealed God's eschatological covenant and inaugurated the fulfillment of prophetic hopes for a new exodus in which all the nations would be participants in addition to Israel.

Inculcating this foundational narrative in converts from non-Jewish backgrounds involved a considerable degree of resocialization. 1 Corinthians is itself one of our most informative sources for the dimensions of this process and the various aspects of life under Roman rule on which it impinged. Paul invites the Corinthians to think of themselves as no longer Gentiles (ὅτε ἔθνη ἦτε, 12:2). Rather, they are among those who are receiving deliverance (οἱ σῳζόμενοι, 1:18) through the divine power vouchsafed by the message that Paul epitomizes as "the message of the cross." As such they constitute a distinct group from those who are in the process of perishing (οἱ ἀπολλύμενοι), i.e., Jews and Greeks, or Gentiles, who for varying reasons take offense at the proclamation of a royal messiah (initially) shamed through execution at the hand of imperial functionaries (1:22–23).[23] Conversely, the former group, to which the Corinthians belong, embraces Jews as well as Greeks who have been invited by God to receive in the service of the crucified Messiah a measure of divine power and wisdom unavailable elsewhere and surpassing the power and wisdom of humans (1:24–25), doubtless including human rulers. Here again Paul assumes a considerable background in messianic lore on the part of his auditors, especially an understanding of the role of the "crucified Messiah" in the divine project of rescue and the resulting division between those embracing this deliverance and those rejecting it.[24]

---

[23] I take it that the present participles describing some people progressively experiencing deliverance (οἱ σῳζόμενοι) and others meeting their end (οἱ ἀπολλύμενοι) in the present refer to those living through the apocalyptic transition between the present evil aeon and the aeon to come. On the political implications of such rhetoric, see the suggestive comments of Horsley, "Rhetoric and Empire—and 1 Corinthians" (in Horsley, ed., *Paul and Politics*), 96–101.

[24] See the suggestive sketches by Nils Alstrup Dahl, *Jesus the Christ: The Historical Origins*

The resocialization of the Pauline churches involved the adoption of certain folkways of Palestinian Jewish messianists. These include the use of ἀμήν as a response to prayer (1 Cor 14:16), the acclamation μαράνα θά (1 Cor 16:22), and the invocation of God as αββα, which we may infer as general practice in Pauline and non-Pauline churches from Gal 4:6 and Rom 8:15. This appears to have extended to the use of the Jewish calendar, at least for purposes of orientation, as is clearly the case with Pentecost in 16:8, and perhaps also with Passover in 5:7, as certainly in later Christian history.[25]

How may the appropriation of Passover tradition have served in this new way of locating one's identity within a new way of bisecting the world, a bisection not between Jew and Gentile or Greek and barbarian or Roman and provincial, but between messianist and antimessianist?[26] Baruch Bokser notes the function of Passover in constituting Israel as a people distinct from the Gentiles (Exod 12:43–50), and this function may be reflected in Paul's use of the supper as establishing the community's boundary in 1 Cor 10:14–22.[27] Such a use of Passover tradition to define

---

of Christological Doctrine (Minneapolis: Fortress 1991), 27–47, 65–79; the ambitious interpretation of Paul's message as anti-Roman polemic in Neil Elliott, "The Anti-Imperial Message of the Cross" (in Horsley, ed., *Paul and Empire*, 167–183); and the cautionary remarks of Christopher Bryan, *Render to Caesar: Jesus, the Early Church, and the Roman Superpower* (Oxford: Oxford University Press, 2005), 55–64.

[25] The conclusion that Paul's reference to Passover and its celebration is strictly metaphorical (Weiss, *Korintherbrief*, 136) is rash. For the possibility that the paschal image is occasioned by the time of the letter's composition (or, perhaps more to the point, of its anticipated declamation in Corinthian house churches within a week or two thereafter, cf. Michael B. Thompson, "The Holy Internet: Communication Between Churches in the First Christian Generation" in *The Gospels for All Christians: Rethinking the Gospel Audiences* (ed. Richard Bauckham; Grand Rapids: Eerdmans, 1998), esp. 61; see Thiselton, *First Epistle to the Corinthians*, 407–408. In light of the questions raised by Horsley and others (see above, nn. 6 and 23), it might be asked whether inculcating such folkways represented a challenge to acquiescing in one's political identity as a subject of Rome. For example, were the Jewish festal observances advocated in preference to the Roman festal calendar *as Roman*, perhaps registering a protest against political or economic oppression experienced under the imperial order? Or was the Roman calendar simply rejected as non-Israelite, as differing from the calendar that the God of Israel had revealed in Torah for observance by his people, now reconstituted through the death and resurrection of his Messiah?

[26] It seems clear from the description of 1:23 that Paul envisions the division between those being rescued and those perishing as made subsequent to a declaration for or against the crucified Messiah, not prior to this decision. Thus it seems justified to describe "the perishing" also as "those rejecting the gospel of the crucified Messiah."

[27] Baruch M. Bokser, "Unleavened Bread and Passover, Feasts of," in *ABD* 6 (1992): 757–58. It is possible that this text, which excludes uncircumcised males from the Passover observance, was a factor in the separation of Jewish from non-Jewish messianists in Antioch

the boundaries between the partisans of the crucified Messiah and his opponents is implied by the designation of Jesus as "*our* paschal offering"—a cultic observance in which those being rescued must participate and in which those perishing may not.

The degree to which such an understanding of Passover may have been foundational to the nascent Corinthian community is suggested by Levenson's examination of midrashic treatments of the binding of Isaac, beginning with Jubilees 17–18. In a narrative inspired by the prologue to Job, Jubilees commends Abraham as "faithful in all affliction" (17:15), whereupon Prince Mastema, noting Abraham's love for his son proposes that God command him to offer Isaac as a burnt offering so as to test the patriarch's faithfulness (17:16). With characteristic precision, Jubilees records this exchange as taking place "in the first month . . . on the twelfth of that month" (17:15), i.e., three days before the time appointed for the offering of the paschal lamb, "at twilight after the fourteenth" (Exod 12:6; Lev 23:5).[28] After the three-day journey of Gen 22:4, Isaac thus becomes (prospectively) the first paschal offering, and Israel's seven-day "feast of the LORD" is in consequence celebrated in the first month (the seven days representing the full extent of Abraham's journey—three days to the mountain, three days from the mountain, and one Sabbath on which Abraham and his party did not travel).[29] Later sources, which may preserve exegetical traditions contemporary with or earlier than Paul, identify "the blood of the binding of Isaac" with the blood of the first paschal sacrifice and identify Abraham's mountain "in the land of Moriah" (Gen 22:2) with "Mount Moriah," on which Solomon built the temple (2 Chr 3:1).[30] These midrashic traditions provide a suggestive context for Paul's appeal to

---

(Gal 2:11–14); if the communal meals observed by the Messianists in Antioch had paschal associations (as the treatment of 1 Cor 11:23–25 in the text above may suggest)—or if at least the particular meal recounted in Gal 2:11–14 did—"those from James" perhaps counseled "separate but equal" messianic meetings to allow for literal compliance with the requirement that only the circumcised participate in the Passover. For other aspects of the controversy at Antioch, see now Richard Bauckham, "James, Peter, and the Gentiles," in *The Missions of James, Peter, and Paul: Tensions in Early Christianity* (ed. Bruce Chilton and Craig Evans; NovTSup 115; Leiden and Boston: Brill, 2005), 121–35.

[28] Levenson, *Death and Resurrection*, 176.

[29] Ibid., 177.

[30] Ibid., 180–81. As Levenson notes, the name Moriah in the text of 2 Chr 3:1 (or, alternatively, of Gen 22:2 if the latter is an interpolation) is itself likely an inner-biblical midrash encouraging the same conclusion (174).

Genesis 22 in Rom 8:32, which probably played a larger role in his formative instruction than this scant allusion would suggest.[31]

Such fanciful exegesis might seem far removed from political realities. In fact, the zeal for the temple and the paschal sacrifice expressed in the desire to find them warranted in the life of father Abraham was the engine of political revolt in Judea. More concretely, the festal assembly at the temple provided the occasion for action against Rome, as also for Rome's exercise of vengeance on rebels. In John Drury's memorable phrasing, "zeal and idealism [as exemplified by Jubilees] are as much a part of the historical actuality of Passover as the vast crowd centered on the temple. The mixture of the two was volatile."[32] Passover was at root the festival commemorating the divine deliverance by which Israel was freed from slavery to Egypt (Josephus *B.J.* 4.402; 5.99; *A.J.* 2.313; 2.317; 3.248; 17.213)—and the prayers of all Israel at the temple might result in yet another deliverance from the situation aptly described in the confession of Neh 9:36–37: "Here we are, slaves to this day—slaves in the land that you gave to our ancestors to enjoy its fruit and its good gifts. Its rich yield goes to the kings whom you have set over us because of our sins; they have power also over our bodies and over our livestock at their pleasure, and we are in great distress." Israel might nourish the hope of one day regaining ἐλευθερία, the freedom to order national life according to the traditions of the fathers (Josephus *A.J.* 12.302–303).[33] Josephus details the results when some Jews went beyond hope and prayer to act on their convictions (as in *B.J.* 5.98–

---

[31] Dahl, *Jesus the Christ*, 137–151; Douglas A. Campbell, *The Quest for Paul's Gospel: A Suggested Strategy* (JSNTSup 274; London: T. & T. Clark, 2005), 85–87, holding that "[o]nly this much-neglected story can account for all the motifs that Paul deploys" in Romans 5–8, viz., "a story of a descent by a Father's own Son through obedience to suffering and death, a story that also speaks of love" (86) and noting (86 n. 23) that it also explains allusions in 1 Corinthians, "where paschal connections are important," citing "on the third day" in 1 Cor 15:3, as well as the curse on "everyone who is laid on wood" (Gal 3:13). On the value of the major topics treated in Romans for the recovery of Paul's formative instruction (as suggested by Rom 15:15), see Peterson, "Extent of Theological Diversity," 9–10.

[32] John Drury, "'Christ Our Passover,'" in *Crossing the Boundaries: Essays in Biblical Interpretation in Honour of Michael D. Goulder* (ed. Stanley E. Porter, Paul Joyce, and David E. Orton; Leiden: Brill, 1994), 226.

[33] Louis H. Feldman, "Josephus' Portrayal of the Hasmoneans Compared with 1 Maccabees," in *Josephus and the History of the Greco-Roman Period: Essays in Memory of Morton Smith* (ed. Fausto Parente and Joseph Sievers; Leiden: Brill, 1994), 46. It is noteworthy that life according to the traditions of the fathers is precisely the ideal from which God called Paul to proclaim Christ among the nations (Gal 1:14–16) and which Paul willingly abandoned for the sake of that calling (Phil 3:4–11).

105) and Rome responded with the ferocity it thought necessary to secure her imperial interests (*B.J.* 6.420–434).[34]

Here we meet perhaps the starkest contrast between Paul and those Jews who took up arms for the liberation of the temple and the land. Paul offered his converts a new identity in continuity with that of Israel (cf. οἱ πατέρες ἡμῶν, 1 Cor 10:1). He introduced them to the service of the universal Lord Jesus Christ (1 Cor 1:2–3, 7–10; 8:6; 12:3) and inculcated in them an expectation of his royal advent (1 Cor 1:7–8) when he will overthrow every power hostile to his Father, so that ultimately "God will be all in all" (1 Cor 15:23–28). In the meantime, Paul encourages the members of his churches to anticipate their future deliverance (or alternatively to reflect on the present, heavenly subsistence of the kingdom that awaits earthly revelation, as in Gal 4:26; Phil 3:20–21) and engage themselves with the process of moral transformation that Paul urges on his converts, inviting them to live by the power of the divine Spirit in the present evil age under the will of the eventual sovereign.[35] Paul and the leaders who revolt in Judea differed from each other not in anticipating divine deliverance from earthly oppression (among other ills), but in the role they ascribed to present human acts of revolt in effecting this deliverance. It is thus typical that the paschal clause is deployed toward the end of ordering the community's internal life as part of the goal of being sustained "blameless until the end, unaccused in the day of our Lord Jesus Christ" (1 Cor 1:8), a phrase that recapitulates in brief the substance of the message of "Christ our Pasch" preached by Paul and embraced by Gentile converts in Corinth, the message in conformity with which Paul sought to reshape his converts' perception of the world and their responsibilities within it.

---

[34] Josephus' references to Passover are canvassed and discussed in Federico M. Colautti (*Passover in the Works of Josephus* [JSJSup 75; Leiden: Brill, 2002]) and helpfully tabulated at 145–47 (with contemporaneous sources surveyed at 155–90) but with disproportionate attention to questions of source criticism (cf. 13–21) and insufficient consideration of the political setting, even in the section devoted to contextualizing Passover observance (191–235); the brief, impressionistic survey in Drury, "'Christ our Passover,'" 226–27, is a useful supplement, albeit inadequately documented.

[35] See the account of Paul's pastoral preaching within an eschatological horizon in Thompson, *Preaching Like Paul*, 85–106.

9

The First Theologian
The Originality of Philo of Alexandria

Gregory E. Sterling

There are a surprising number of concepts that appear first in the writings of Philo of Alexandria. For example, Philo is the first to attest the *via negativa* in the full form that denies the possibility of naming or comprehending God.[1] He is the first to argue that when we use names for God or make statements about God, we are speaking katachrestically, i.e., using language illegitimately for one who is beyond naming or description.[2] He is the first to use the expression "the intelligible cosmos."[3] He is the first to suggest that the "ideas" are God's thoughts.[4] He is the first to maintain that piety is the "queen of the virtues," the virtue from which all other virtues spring.[5] He is the first to speak of the "law of nature."[6] He is

---

[1] For example, he held that God was "unnameable" (ἄρρητος) at least three times (*Mut.* 14–15; *Her.* 170; *Somn.* 1.67) and "uncomprehensible" (ἀκατάληπτος) numerous times (*Cher.* 97; *Det.* 89; *Post.* 15; *Conf.* 138; *Mut.* 10; *Somn.* 1.67; *Spec.* 1.47). For further terms see below. Unless otherwise indicated, all translations of Philo are my own.

[2] See *Sacr.* 101; *Post.* 168; *Mut.* 11–14, 27–28; *Somn.* 1.229; *Abr.* 120 *De Deo* 4.

[3] *Opif.* 15.

[4] *Opif.* 16. See §§15–25.

[5] *Spec.* 4.147. See also *Decal.* 119; *Spec.* 4.135; *Virt.* 95.

[6] For the expression "law of nature" (νόμος φύσεως) see *Post.* 185; *Plant.* 132; *Abr.* 135; *Ios.* 31; *Mos.* 2.7, 245; *Spec.* 3.32; 4.205; *Praem.* 42, 108; *Prov.* 2.23; *QE* 2.19. The plural expression, "laws of nature," occurs in *Opif.* 13; 171; *Ebr.* 47; *Somn.* 2.174; *Mos.* 2.48, 82; *Decal.* 132; *Spec.* 1.155, 202, 306; 3.112; *Contempl.* 59; *Aet.* 59. Cf. also *On numbers* F 35.

the first to cultivate the image of philosophy as the handmaid of theology.[7] He is the first to use the paradox "sober intoxification."[8] The list could be expanded, especially if we considered literary forms as well as concepts. It is, however, sufficient to raise the issue of Philo's originality.

There have been diverse responses to the issue. The most famous advocate of the originality and significance of Philo is unquestionably Harry Austryn Wolfson. At the end of his *magnum opus* he wrote: "This fundamental departure from pagan Greek philosophy . . . appears first in Hellenistic Judaism, where it attains its systematic formulation in Philo." He then affirmed: "Philo is the founder of this new school of philosophy, and from him it directly passes on to the Gospel of John and the Church Fathers from whom it passes on to Moslem and hence to medieval Jewish philosophy." He concluded: "Philo is the direct or indirect source of this type of philosophy which continues uninterruptedly in its main assertions for well-nigh seventeen centuries, when at last it is openly challenged by Spinosa."[9] The other end of the spectrum is represented by Richard Goulet who argued in a similarly massive treatment that Philo reworked an existing allegorical commentary that had an ethical emphasis but lacked any interest in creation. Whereas Wolfson attempted to deny Philo's inconsistencies in his systematization of the Alexandrian's thought, Goulet championed them as a means for uncovering Philo's polemic against the earlier and, in his view, superior, commentary.[10]

The views of most scholars fall somewhere between these two extremes. In recent years, some have attempted to assess Philo's contributions to the exegetical tradition that he inherited. Like Goulet, they recognize that Philo worked with a tradition; however, they view Philo as the apex of the tradition rather than its nadir.[11] Others have concentrated on one of the "firsts" listed above without contending that Philo was a systematic thinker in the way that Wolfson did. Was Philo the originator or tradent of the concept that he first attests? The evidence is often ambiguous as a re-

---

[7] *Congr.* 79.

[8] For the expression μεθὴ νηφάλιος see *Opif.* 71.

[9] H. A. Wolfson, *Philo: Foundations of Religious Philosophy in Judaism, Christianity, and Islam* (2 vols.; Cambridge: Harvard University Press, 1947), 2:457.

[10] R. Goulet, *La philosophie de Moïse: Essai de reconstitution d'un commentaire philosophique préphilonien du Pentateuque* (Histoire des doctrines de l'antiquité classique 11; Paris: Vrin, 1987).

[11] The most important contribution is that of T. J. Tobin, *The Creation of Man: Philo and the History of Interpretation* (CBQMS 14; Washington D. C.: Catholic Biblical Association, 1983).

sult of the fragmentary nature of the philosophical material in this period. It is, therefore, hardly surprising to discover that while Hans Lewy suggested that Philo was the originator of the concept of sober intoxification (μεθὴ νηφάλιος),[12] David Winston pointed out that he had overlooked an epigram that suggests an origin in Bacchic circles.[13] Similarly, Helmut Koester thought that Philo had created the concept of the law of nature (νόμος φύσεως)[14] a suggestion that Richard Horsley successfully challenged.[15] Roberto Radice argued that Philo was the catalyst for the concept of the ideas as God's thoughts,[16] an argument that has failed to convince David Runia who thinks that Radice has given Philo too much credit.[17]

While each of these debates is useful, I prefer to take a different tack. I suggest that rather than assessing Philo's place in the archaeology of exegesis or his status within ancient philosophy, we should understand his greatest contribution to lie in the sphere of theology. Wilhelm Bousset was the first to make this observation. He wrote: "The Jewish philosopher Philo is the first theologian of faith, the first who develops a detailed psychology of faith."[18] Bousset's assessment has been echoed several times. Isaak Heinemann opened his famous monograph on Philo's *Bildung* with an endorsement of Bousset's judgment.[19] Jean Daniélou more pointedly wrote: "he (Philo) is a theologian—and unquestionably the first theologian to treat fully of the divine transcendence."[20] More recently, David Runia has

---

[12] H. Lewy, *Sobria Ebrietas* (Giessen: Töpelmann, 1929).

[13] D. Winston, *Philo of Alexandria, The Contemplative Life, The Giants, and Selections* (The Classics of Western Spirituality; New York: Paulist, 1981), 358 n. 341.

[14] H. Koester, "ΝΟΜΟΣ ΦΥΣΕΩΣ: The Concept of Natural Law in Greek Thought," in *Religions in Antiquity: Essays in Memory of Erwin Ramsdell Goodenough* (ed. Jacob Neusner; SHR 14; Leiden: Brill, 1968), 521–41.

[15] R. Horsley, "The Law of Nature in Philo and Cicero," *HTR* 71 (1978): 35–59.

[16] R. Radice, "Observations on the Theory of the Ideas as the Thoughts of God in Philo of Alexandria," *SPhA* 3 (1991): 126–34.

[17] D. T. Runia, *Philo of Alexandria, On the Creation of the Cosmos according to Moses* (PAC 1; Leiden: Brill, 2001), 151–52.

[18] W. Bousset, *Kyrios Christos: A History of the Belief in Christ from the Beginnings of Christianity to Irenaeus* (trans. J. E. Steely; Nashville: Abingdon, 1970), 200.

[19] I. Heinemann, *Philons griechische und jüdische Bildung: Kulturvergleichende Untersuchungen zu Philons Darstellung der jüdischen Gesetze* (Breslau: Marcus, 1929–32; repr., Hildesheim: Olms, 1962), 5.

[20] J. Daniélou, *A History of Early Christian Doctrine before the Council of Nicaea*, vol. 2: *Gospel Message and Hellenistic Culture* (trans. J. A. Baker; Philadelphia: Westminster, 1973), 326.

defended Bousset's epithet on grounds similar to those of Daniélou.[21] I began considering this possibility while exploring the significance of piety (εὐσέβεια) in Philo.[22] The suggestion is thus not new; however, no one has attempted to work out the bases for this claim in a comprehensive fashion. This contribution represents an initial effort.

I will frame the question broadly. In what ways could we consider Philo a theologian? Unfortunately, we do not have an adequate ancient presentation of theology (θεολογία) by which we can assess Philo. I will use two categories that are attested in ancient texts. While I will touch on the issue of the originality of a specific point at times, I am more interested in how Philo subsumes specific concepts in his larger system than whether he is the originator of a specific concept. I believe that his greatest contributions lay in the development of his central framework and the *modus operandi* for the development of that framework rather than in specific concepts.

The Ontological Priority of God

Theology, as the word itself suggests, should begin with a discussion of God. Aristotle initiated the formal discussion.[23] In his discussion of causes, the Stagirite wrote: "So then there are three speculative philosophies: mathematics, physics, and theology." He explained: "For it is clear that if the Deity is present anywhere, it is present in such a category and the most honorable science must deal with the most honorable class."[24] Discussions of the gods were relatively common among Hellenistic philosophers. A number of figures wrote treatises entitled *On the Gods* or something

---

[21] D. T. Runia, "Naming and Knowing: Themes in Philonic Theology with Special Reference to the *De mutatione nominum*," in *Knowledge of God in the Graco-Roman World* (ed. R. van den Brack, T. Baarda, and J. Mansfield; EPRO 112; Leiden: Brill, 1988), 69–91, esp. 82–89; reprinted as in *Exegesis and Philosophy: Studies on Philo of Alexandria* (Variorum Collected Studies Series 332; Aldershot: Variorum, 1990), xi; and idem, "Philo the Theologian," in *The Dictionary of Historical Theology* (2000): 424–26.

[22] I first presented this material in a paper for the Hellenistic Moral Philosophy and Early Christianity Group of the Society of Biblical Literature in Novmerber of 1999. It will appear as "The Queen of the Virtues: Εὐσέβεια in Philo of Alexandria," *SPhA* 18 (2006): forthcoming.

[23] For a survey of theology within Hellenistic philosophy see J. Mansfeld, "Theology," in *The Cambridge History of Hellenistic Philosophy* (ed. K. Algra, J. Barnes, J. Mansfeld, and M. Schofield; Cambridge: Cambridge University Press, 1997), 452–78.

[24] Aristotle, *Metaph.* 6.1 (1026a); cf. Plato, *Resp.* 379a-b for God as a cause.

similar: Epicurus,[25] Cleanthes,[26] Chrysippus,[27] Antipater of Tarsus,[28] and Cicero.[29] Jewish and Christian authors followed suit and used the term to denote their understanding of God. Josephus argued that the Egyptians who worshipped animals "were not capable of reaching the solemnity of our theology."[30] In his *Praeparatio evangelica*, Eusebius suggested that the term Hebrew came from an eponymous ancestor Heber whose name is related to the verb "to cross over." This is appropriate in the bishop's eyes since it represents those who cross over from things in this world to things divine. Hebrews are thus those who pass over to the "theology about the creator and demiurge of all."[31] While we may debate the bishop's etymology,[32] his understanding of theology (θεολογία) is beyond challenge. This suggests that the first task for a theologian is to speak about God.

The dominant impression that a reader has when working through the Philonic corpus is the theocentric nature of his thought. This is not a coincidence: Philo uses θεός more than any other noun. It appears 2480 times in his corpus. The next most frequent noun is ψυχή which appears 1814 times or 27% less frequently. The third most common noun is unsurprisingly λόγος which appears 1413 times or 43% less often.[33]

More important than this quantitative observation is the way in which Philo presents the Deity. Virtually every treatment of Philo's understanding of God notes his emphasis on divine transcendence. For our purposes, I prefer to speak of the ontological priority of God. By ontological priority I mean that Philo consistently subordinated everything to God and considered God to be the basis for all that is good. Let me illustrate by

---

[25] Diogenes Laertius 10.27.

[26] Diogenes Laertius 7.175.

[27] Plutarch, *Stoic rep.* 1052b.

[28] Plutarch, *Stoic rep.* 1051 e-f.

[29] *On the Nature of the Gods*.

[30] Josephus, *C.Ap.* 1.225.

[31] Eusebius, *Praep.ev* 11.6 (520 c).

[32] Eusebius thus understood עברי to come from עבר. The actual etymology is a point of debate.

[33] All counts are based on P. Borgen, K. Fuglseth, and R. Skarsten, *The Philo Index: A Complete Greek Word Index to the Writings of Philo of Alexandria* (Leiden: Brill/Grand Rapids: Eerdmans, 2000). The following represents a descending order of the most frequent nouns in Philo. I have included nouns that appear at least 500 times: θεός (2480), ψυχή (1814), λόγος (1413), φύσις (1342), ἄνθρωπος (1172), σῶμα (998), ἀρετή (955), γῆ (849), μέρος (699), νόος (686), κόσμος (634), βίος (611), πατήρ (586), αἴσθησις (567), πάθος (536), γένος (535), νόμος (535), ἀρχη (523), and ἀνήρ (511).

examining how Philo handles the most important text relating to God's transcendence in the LXX.

Exodus 3:14

As is well known, the LXX of Exodus 3:14 contains the famous "I am the Self-Existent" (Ἐγώ εἰμι ὁ ὤν).[34] Philo alludes to this text many times and cites it verbatim at least four times.[35] The allusions are largely his references to the Deity.[36] Based on the phrase "I am the Self-Existent" (ἐγω εἰμι ὁ ὤν) of the LXX and his Platonic understanding of reality he calls God "Being" (ὁ ὤν),[37] "the God who is actually Being (ὁ ὄντως ὢν θεός),[38] or "truly Being" (ὁ ὢν πρὸς ἀλήθειαν),[39] and a number of expressions in which he converts ὁ ὤν to the Platonic τὸ ὄν "Being" (τὸ ὄν),[40] "actual Being" (τὸ ὄντως ὄν),[41] "true Being" (τὸ πρὸς ἀλήθειαν ὄν),[42] The citations are even more forceful. We will take them up individually.

The first citation occurs in the course of Philo's explanation of the Tent of Testimony, a tent that he understands as the virtue of God, in *The Worse Attacks the Better*. The Torah exegete comments: "he says that this tent is called the tent of testimony, very precisely, since the tent of the Being (τοῦ ὄντος) exists and is not merely named. For among the virtues, God's virtue is real (πρὸς ἀλήθειαν), existing in being (κατὰ εἶναι σουνεστῶσα)." He explained: "God alone exists in being (ἐν τῷ εἶναι ὑφεστάναι). For this reason he will necessarily say of him: 'I am

---

[34] For a more detailed treatment of this text in Philo see D. Wyrwa, "Über die Begegnung des biblischen Glaubens mit dem griechischen Geist," *ZTK* 88 (1991): 29–67, esp. 39–47.

[35] *Det.* 160; *Mut.* 11; *Somn.* 1.231; *Mos.* 1.75.

[36] For details see L. A. Montes-Peral, *Akataleptos Theos: Der unfassbare Gott* (ALGHJ 16; Leiden: Brill, 1987), 48–74.

[37] *Sacr.* 10; *Det.* 92; *Mut.* 82; *Abr.* 121. Cf. also the genitive τοῦ ὄντος in *Det.* 159; *Plant.* 26; *Mut.* 57; *Somn.* 1.234; 2.227, 237, 292; *Spec.* 1.81.

[38] *Det.* 139. Cf. also the genitive τοῦ ὄντως ὄντος in *Her.* 70.

[39] *Mut.* 11.

[40] *Det.* 153, 154; *Post.* 2, 9, 15, 21, 28, 168, 175; *Gig.* 52; *Deus* 4, 33, 52, 55, 69, 81; *Agr.* 171; *Plant.* 21, 22, 72, 86; *Ebr.* 43, 86, 108, 117; *Conf.* 65, 95, 97; *Her.* 170, 229; *Congr.* 8; *Fug.* 78, 89; *Mut.* 7, 8, 9, 10, 14, 17, 87, 182; *Somn.* 1.35, 157, 182, 184, 218, 230; 2.237; *Abr.* 270; *Mos.* 2.161; *Spec.* 1.209 (*bis*), 307; *Virt.* 185, 215; *Praem.* 27, 56; *Prob.* 43; *Contempl.* 2.

[41] *Det.* 161; *Deus* 11; *Ebr.* 83; *Congr.* 51.

[42] *Abr.* 80 and *Mos.* 2.67.

Being' (ἐγώ εἰμι ὁ ὤν)" (Exodus 3:14). Philo then contrasted God with everything else: "those things after him are not in the realm of being (οὐκ ὄντων κατὰ τὸ εἶναι) but are only thought to exist by opinion."[43] There is an ontological divide between God and everything else, a divide that Exodus 3:14 makes clear. God is therefore unique in the strict sense of the term.

The second text takes place in the course of Philo's exposition of Genesis 17:1 in *On the Change of Names*. In his explanation he introduced Exodus 33:13 as a subordinate lemma. The text records Moses' request to see God. Philo explained God's response to Moses that he would only see "what is behind me" (τὰ ὀπίσω μου) (Exodus 33:23) to indicate that we can not perceive God, only the things below God. He extended the thought: "Therefore it follows that it is not possible for a proper name (ὄνομα κύριον) to be given to the true Being (τῷ ὄντι πρὸς ἀλήθειαν)." The Alexandrian cited Exodus 3:14 in support: "Don't you see that when the curious prophet asked how he should answer those who inquired about his name, he said 'I am Being' (ἐγώ εἰμι ὁ ὤν), which is the equivalent to: my nature is to be, my nature is not to be named?"[44] The juxtaposition of the denial that God has a proper name (ὄνομα κύριον) with Exodus 3:14 suggests that Philo denied that κύριος was God's proper name. This is a striking statement since Philo used κύριος for the Tetragrammaton.[45] He proceeded to concede that katachrestically we may call God κύριος ὁ θεός.[46] He based his concession on the following verse (Exodus 3:15) in which God is identified as κύριος ὁ θεός. However, Philo pointed out that the final clause of Exodus 3:15 imposed strict limits on the name: "my name is an age-long name, a memorial for generations of generations" (τοῦτό μού ἐστιν ὄνομα αἰώνιον καὶ μνημόσυνον γενεῶν γενεαῖς). Philo explained the three key terms as follows: it was "an age-long name" (ὄνομα αἰώνιον), that is, it existed in an age not prior to time; it was "a memorial" (μνημόσυνον), it was within human memory rather than beyond memory; and it was "for generations" (γενεαῖς), it was intended for mortals. This led him to Exodus 6:3 which in the LXX reads: "I appeared to Abraham, Isaac, and Jacob being their

---

[43] *Det.* 160.

[44] *Mut.* 11.

[45] See J. R. Royse, "Philo, κύριος, and the Tetragrammaton," *SPhA* 3 (1991) 167–83, esp. 176–77. See also F. Shaw, "The Emperor Gaius' Employment of the Divine Name," *SPhA* 17 (2005): 33–48, esp. 41–46.

[46] *Mut.* 12–13. On this text see Runia, "Naming and Knowing," the most important treatment of the entire text under consideration.

God. I did not disclose my name Lord (τὸ ὄνομά μου κύριος) to them." Philo read the final clause as "I did not disclose my proper name (ὄνομά μου τὸ κύριον) to them." He made two changes to the text of Exodus 6:3 to sustain his point: first, he converted the nominative κύριος to the accusative κύριον, thereby transforming the noun ("Lord") into an adjective ("proper"). Second, he suggested that the definite article was out of place. He may have taken his cue from the unusual order of the Greek. At least the *hyperbaton* required some explanation. He thus placed the definite article before the adjective rather than the noun. The shift in case of κύριος and the rearrangement of the noun-adjective syntax altered the meaning of the underlying Hebrew, which uses the Tetragrammaton, as well as the literal rendering of the LXX and brought the text into line with Philo's point that God is unnameable. The expositor then introduced Genesis 32:29 in which God refused to disclose his name to Jacob. He concluded: "If in fact God is unnameable (ἄρρητος), then he is also inconceivable (ἀπερινόητος) and uncomprehensible (ἀκατάληπτος)."[47] Here we have a clear articulation of Philo's negative theology.[48] He held that God was unnameable (ἄρρητος), a term that he used to refer to God in two other texts.[49] It is a synonym with ἀκατονόμαστος.[50] Based on God's unnameability, he argued that God is inconceivable (ἀπερινόητος)[51] and uncomprehensible (ἀκατάληπτος).[52] The former is part of a group of terms that begin with "in-" (ἀπερι-) that Philo may have developed in his effort to emphasize God's inconceivability. In other texts he claimed that God was indescribable (ἀπερίγραφος)[53] and incomprehensible (ἀπερίληπτος).[54] The last term is closely related to the final term in

---

[47] *Mut.* 15.

[48] On Philo's negative theology see Wolfson, *Philo*, 2:110–26; D. Baer, "Incompréhensibilité de Dieu et théologie négative chez Philon d'Alexandrie," *Présence Orthodoxe* 8 (1969): 38–46; Daniélou, *Gospel Message*, 323–38, esp. 326–27; D. Carabine, *The Unknown God: Negative Theology in the Platonic Tradition: Plato to Eriugena* (Louvain Theological and Pastoral Monographs 19; Louvain: Peeters/Grand Rapids: Eerdmans, 1995), 191–221; and C. Noak, *Gottesbewusstein: Exegetische Studien zur Soteriologie und Mystik bei Philo von Alexandria* (WUNT 2.116; Tübingen: Mohr Siebeck, 2000), esp. 63–67.

[49] These are cited in n. 1 (*Her.* 170; *Somn.* 1.67. Cf. *Mut.* 14–15).

[50] *Somn.* 1.67, where it appears along with ἄρρητος.

[51] See also *Fug.* 141.

[52] These are cited in n. 1 (*Cher.* 97; *Det.* 89; *Post.* 15; *Conf.* 138; *Mut.* 10; *Somn.* 1.67; *Spec.* 1.47).

[53] *Sacr.* 59 (*bis*).

[54] *Her.* 229.

our text, "uncomprehensible" (ἀκατάληπτος), a privative adjective that came to play an important role in the thought of Plotinus.[55] It is not critical for us to determine whether Philo was the first to develop this negative theology or was only a tradent of it. It is important to understand that he used it because it was essential for his understanding of God. He could not make a positive statement about God because, as David Runia has pointed out, an attribute would, in a Platonic context, add to Being. If Philo acknowledged a name for God, he would by necessity include predication (e.g., the good God = God is good) which would entail plurality since it requires a relationship with something else (e.g., God is good with respect to something else).[56] Philo understood what was at stake. He therefore rejected any name because he rejected predication and by extension plurality with respect to God.

The third and fourth texts largely repeat the same material in abbreviated form. The third is found in *On Dreams* 1, where Philo drew the same conclusions from the same juxtaposition of texts. Only now he began with Exodus 6:3 and then moved to 3:14. He introduced Exodus 6:3 by saying "In another place when he inquired whether there was a certain name of the Being, he came to understand clearly that he has no proper name (κύριον μὲν οὐδέν). Whatever someone may use, he uses katachrestically. For by nature he can not be named, but the Being by nature is (μόνον εἶναι τὸ ὄν)." This led him to cite Exodus 3:14 where no name is given, only the statement 'I am Being' (ἐγώ εἰμι ὁ ὤν).[57]

The fourth is part of the narrative of *On the Life of Moses* in which Philo recounted Exodus 3. He summarized the text in this way: "He said, 'First tell them that 'I am Being' (ἐγώ εἰμι ὁ ὤν) so that they may learn the distinction between Being and not Being and, in addition may be taught that no name at all may be properly used of me to whom alone belongs the quality of being (τὸ εἶναι)."[58] The only time that Philo wavers from this assertion is in *On Abraham* where he says that "Being" (ὁ ὤν) is God's "proper name" (κύριον ὄνομα).[59] Although I would not want to accuse Philo of consistency, I think that he is making an accommodation

---

[55] On the term and its importance for the understanding of God in Philo see Montes-Peral, *Akataleptos Theos: Der unfassbare Gott*.
[56] Runia, "Naming and Knowing," 77.
[57] *Somn.* 1.230–32. The sentence that follows the citation of Exodus 3:14 is problematic.
[58] *Mos.* 1.75.
[59] *Abr.* 121.

in this instance. Being is the only proper name for God and, I think that we may add, it is not a proper name.

Implications

The implications of this exegesis for Philo's exegesis of other texts should not be overlooked. We have already seen how his insistence on God's transcendence required a negative theology. Let me give two other examples to illustrate how the ontological priority of God affected Philo's interpretation of scripture.

In his account of creation, Philo argued that God created the intelligible cosmos on day one[60] or alternatively, in the first account of creation.[61] In his account of day one, Philo compares God's activities to an architect who plans a city before he builds it. "Then having taken up the imprints of each (τοὺς ἑκάστων . . . τύπους) in his soul as if on a wax tablet, he carries around the intelligible city as an image." From this image he builds the city "like a good builder (δημιουργός ἀγαθος), keeping his eye on the model (τὸ παράδειγμα), he begins to construct the city out of stones and lumber, making sure that the corporeal substances correspond to each of the incorporeal forms (ἑκάστῃ τῶν ἀσωμάτων ἰδεῶν)."[62] Philo then applied this to God. He wrote: "when he had decided to establish the megalopolis, he first conceived its imprints (τοὺς τύπους αὐτῆς). From these, after he formed the intelligible cosmos (κόσμον νοητόν), he completed the sense-perceptible, using the former as a model (παραδείγματι χρώμενος ἐκείνῳ)."[63]

In this description Philo has drawn on the Platonic tradition that posited the ideas as the thoughts of God. Xenocrates thought that the supreme god was an intellect.[64] It was a natural extension to think of the ideas as the deity's thoughts. While we cannot be sure that this took place as early as the Old Academy, the possibility cannot be ruled out. It was widely held among Middle Platonists. A statement from Varro suggests that Antiochus held a version of this.[65] Alcinous included it in his *Handbook on Platonism*. In his exposition of forms he said: "A form in its relation to God is his thinking (νόησις αὐτοῦ)." Again, "the forms are

---

[60] *Opif.* 15–35.
[61] *Opif.* 129–30.
[62] *Opif.* 17–18.
[63] *Opif.* 19.
[64] Fr. 15 (Heinze).
[65] In Augustine, *CD* 7.28.

the eternal and perfect thoughts of God."[66] It appears that Philo knew and embraced an accepted Platonic position. Why? Unlike Plato, for whom the ideas could have an independent ontological status, Philo needed to subordinate them to God, who had ontological priority. Philo did this by considering the ideas to be God's thoughts.

The second example is Philo's treatment of piety (εὐσέβεια). Prior to Philo it was common for philosophers to consider piety as either a co-ordinate or a secondary virtue to justice. Plato had Euthyphro make the point: "This is what I think, Socrates, one part of justice is piety and holiness, namely the part concerning service to the gods; the remaining part of justice is the part concerning service to humans."[67] It is hardly a surprise to hear Aristotle call justice (δικαιοσύνη) "perfect virtue," "the chief of virtues," and "the whole of virtue."[68] Piety was accordingly a secondary virtue for Theophrastus[69] and the Peripatetic tradition[70] as well as for the Stoa.[71] Zeno, the founder of the Stoa considered prudence (φρόνησις) to be the central virtue.[72] The situation is quite different in Philo. The Jewish exegete called piety (εὐσέβεια) "the queen of the virtues,"[73] "the queen of the dance,"[74] "the greatest,"[75] "the leading and greatest virtue,"[76] "the finest and most profitable,"[77] and "the source of the virtues."[78] Similarly, he labeled religiosity (θεοσέβεια) "the greatest virtue"[79] and "the perfect

---

[66] Alcinous 9. For a detailed analysis see J. Dillon, *Alcinous, The Handbook of Platonism* (Clarendon Later Ancient Philosophers; Oxford: Clarendon, 1993), 93–100, esp. 94–95.

[67] Plato, *Euthyphr.* 12E.

[68] Aristotle, *Eth. nic.* 5.1 (1129b26–1130a10).

[69] Theophrastus, in Stobaeus 3.3.42 (Fortenbaugh, *Theophrastus of Eresus*, no. 523).

[70] Cf. Pseudo-Aristotle, *On Virt. vit.* 1250b 20–24 (5.2–3).

[71] *SVF* 3.64.14–25. Sometimes the Stoics simply listed εὐσέβεια in a list of virtues, e.g., *SVF* 2.304 16–31.

[72] Plutarch, *Virt. mor.* 440E–441D; *Stoic rep.* 1034C–E.

[73] He used two different terms: ἡγεμονίς *Decal.* 119 [with ὁσιότης]; *Spec.* 4.135 [with ὁσιότης]; *Virt.* 95 [with φιλανθρωπία]; amd *QG* 2.38) and βασιλίς *Spec.* 4.147).

[74] Philo, *Praem.* 53.

[75] *Spec.* 4.97.

[76] *Abr.* 60.

[77] *Mos.* 1.146.

[78] *Decal.* 52.

[79] *Opif.* 154 (θεοσέβεια is parallel to εὐσέβεια in 155); *Abr.* 114.

good."⁸⁰ Conversely, he called impiety (ἀσέβεια) "the greatest evil"⁸¹ and "the endless evil."⁸²

How do we explain the shift? There are several possibilities. We might attribute Philo's emphasis to an understanding of the fear of God as the beginning of wisdom in the LXX.⁸³ However, this does not seem likely since he did not draw from Proverbs 1:7. Another option would be to attribute his emphasis to an attempt to make piety consistent with the Middle Platonic *telos* of "likeness to God" (ὁμοίωσις θεῷ).⁸⁴ While this may have been a factor, it does not seem to have been the dominant concern. Philo does not make a specific connection between "likeness to God" (ὁμοίωσις θεῷ) and piety (εὐσέβεια). Further, other Middle Platonists did not share his emphasis on piety, a point that we would expect if the connection were internal to the Platonic tradition. Rather, I suggest that the theocentric nature of Philo's thought and his unrelenting accentuation of the ontological priority of God led him to this position. For Philo it was largely a question of the ultimate source: "The supreme source of all that exists is God; just as piety is (the supreme source) of the virtues."⁸⁵ The rationale for the analogy between God as source and piety as source is that the physical and moral worlds are both the creations of God: piety toward God governs both our concept of the creation and the ordering of our lives. Everything, including ethics, begins with a proper belief in the existence of God and the divine governance of the cosmos. Philo made the point explicitly in the second "credo" at the conclusion of *On the Creation of the World*. If someone believes "that God is and exists and that he is the One existing Being; that he created the cosmos and made it one, having made it, as was said, similar to himself in singularity; and that he always exercises providence over what has come into existence," then, "he will live a blessed and happy life, having been engraved with the teachings of piety and holiness."⁸⁶ The credo serves both to conclude the account of creation and to set the reader up for the exposition of the laws that will follow. In this way piety is a presupposition for ethics.

---

⁸⁰ *Congr.* 130.

⁸¹ *Congr.* 160.

⁸² *Fug.* 61.

⁸³ So Wolfson, *Philo*, 2:215; Lohse, *Religion und Kultur*, 105.

⁸⁴ Kaufmann-Büchler, "Eusebeia," 994.

⁸⁵ *Decal.* 52. Cf. also *Abr.* 114.

⁸⁶ *Opif.* 172.

These examples illustrate Philo's unswerving commitment to God's ontological priority. This commitment in part, leads me to call him a theologian. It is not simply that he speaks about God; many others did as well. What sets Philo apart is his unyielding insistence on God's transcendence and the way that God's ontological priority controls his thought.

Philosophia theologiae ancilla

I said that this focus justifies the sobriquet in part. Commitment to God's transcendence alone would not justify us in bestowing the title "theologian" on Philo. A philosopher could share the same commitment without crossing over to theology. What distinguishes Philo from a philosopher is his commitment to scripture as the primary source for his reflections. While he wrote at least eight treatises that we consider to be philosophical in nature, these are hardly comparable in scope to the three commentary series that he composed in approximately fifty-seven treatises. Valentin Nikiprowetzky was correct to consider Philo an exegete, an assessment shared by most Philonists today.[87] This raises the issue of the relationship between philosophy and scripture in Philo.

The Encyclical Studies, Philosophy, and Theology

Philo dealt with this very question in his allegory of Sarah and Hagar, an allegory that he developed most fully in *On the Preliminary Studies*.[88] Philo understood Sarah to represent wisdom or virtue[89] and Hagar the encyclia.[90] He explained the relationship between the two in a text that heavily influenced later generations: "it is necessary to understand that the introductions of great themes must be great. The greatest theme is virtue. For it deals with the greatest matter, the entire human life." He continues, "Naturally therefore it will not make use of limited introductions but grammar, geometry, astronomy, rhetoric, music, and every other intellectual discipline. Hagar, the handmaid of Sarah is a symbol of these." Philo accordingly understood Sarah's order for Abraham to go to her handmaid

---

[87] V. Nikiprowetzky, *Le commentaire de l'écriture chez Philon d'Alexandrie: Son caractère et sa portée, observations philologiques* (ALGHJ 11; Leiden: Brill, 1977). The most important recent discussion is P. Borgen, *Philo of Alexandria: An Exegete for his Time* (NovTSup 86; Leiden/New York: Brill, 1997).

[88] *Congr.* 1–70.

[89] He moves back and forth between Sarah and Hagar. See *Congr.* 2–3 and 12–13 for examples.

[90] E.g., *Congr.* 11, 12, 13, 14 κτλ.

to mean that he should embrace the encyclia.[91] This is a preliminary step to the embrace of wisdom or virtue. Later in the treatise, Philo introduced philosophy as a middle term. He explained: "In fact just as the encyclia contribute to the taking up of philosophy, so also philosophy contributes to the acquisition of wisdom." He then defined each: "For philosophy is the pursuit of wisdom and wisdom the knowledge of things divine, human, and their causes.[92] Therefore just as the preliminary division is the servant of philosophy, so philosophy is the servant of wisdom."[93] The final clause became the basis for the famous aphorism of the medieval world: "philosophy is the handmaid of theology" (*philosophia theologiae ancilla*).[94]

The precise relationship between philosophy and Scripture in Philo is a matter of debate. There are a number of statements in the Philonic corpus that suggest that Philo believed that philosophy grasped the same realities as Scripture. Let me provide a couple of examples. In the opening sections of *On the Creation of the Cosmos*, Philo suggested that Moses had two sources for his understanding of the cosmos. He wrote: "But Moses had both reached the very summit of philosophy and had been instructed in the many and most essential concepts of nature by means of oracles. . . ."[95] In this statement Philo indicated a harmony between human reason as it is cultivated in philosophy and divine revelation vouchsafed through oracles. He is even more forthcoming in his comments about understanding God in *On the Virtues*: "For what comes to the adherents of the most esteemed philosophy, comes to the Jews through their laws and customs, namely the knowledge of the highest and most ancient Cause of all and the rejection of the deception of created gods."[96] The most interesting aspect of this statement is the point at which philosophy and Jewish scriptures converge, the understanding of God.

How then was philosophy a servant? Why could Philo not simply equate the encyclical studies with Hagar and philosophy with Sarah and leave it at that? The fundamental problem was that he took his *aphorme* from Scripture, not philosophy. Unlike Plato, Aristotle, Chrysippus, or

---

[91] *Congr.* 11–12.

[92] This is the standard Stoic definition of philosophy. See Cicero, *Off.* 2.5; Seneca, *Ep.* 89.5; and Sextus, *M.* 9.13 (*SVF* 2.36).

[93] *Congr.* 79.

[94] On the importance of Philo for the later tradition see A. Heinrichs, "Philosophy, the Handmaiden of Theology," *GRBS* 9 (1968): 437–50.

[95] *Opif.* 8.

[96] *Virt.* 65.

Antiochus, who used reason to theorize about reality, Philo had an authoritative source. Philosophy offered the intellectual framework through which he read Scripture; however, it could not displace the revelation of Moses as the primary source for reflection.

Scripture

This leads us to consider the use of Scripture in Philo's theologizing. It is important to understand that Scripture both served as the basis for and—to a noteworthy extent—governor of Philo's thought. The Alexandrian stated the principle clearly at the outset of *On the Creation of the Cosmos*: "But on behalf of the God-beloved author it is necessary that we dare to speak, even if it is beyond our ability, stating nothing from our own resources," rather he would make "only a few observations rather than many, those to which it is reasonable for the human mind to reach when it is possessed by a love and desire for wisdom."[97] We might discount this statement as standard rhetoric. After all, Philo also began his presentation of the Therapeutae with a similar claim which had no reference to Scripture.[98] We might also remember that Josephus opened his *magnum opus* with a famous claim not to "add or omit anything" to the biblical text, and then proceeded to make massive alterations.[99] These examples show that the claim could be a rhetorical trope.

Before we dismiss it out of hand, however, we should remember that Philo repeated the claim in his exegetical treatments and offered justifications for it. So, for example, he summarized his presentation of the intelligible world with the statement: "someone might say that the intelligible cosmos is nothing other than the Logos of God as he is creating the cosmos." He continued: "This is Moses' teaching not mine." He justified the latter claim with a reference to Genesis 1:27: "As he describes the genesis of the human being in the following narrative, he explicitly notes that the human being was formed in the image of God (κατ' εἰκόνα θεοῦ)." He then concluded: "If the part is an image of an image (i.e., humans are in the image of the Logos who is the image of God), it is clear that it is also true of the whole." He continued: "Now if the entire sense-perceptible cosmos which is greater than the human, is a copy of the divine image (μίμημα θείας εἰκόνος), it is clear that the archetypal seal, which we say is the intelligible cosmos, would itself be the model (παράδειγμα), the

---

[97] *Opif.* 5.
[98] *Contempl.* 1.
[99] Josephus, *AJ* 1.17.

archetypal idea of the ideas, the Logos of God."[100] Philo's case rests on his understanding of "in" (κατά). While we may disagree with his reading of Genesis 1:27, we must give him credit for a close reading of the text. Philo made a similar case when he explained God's charge to Moses to build the tabernacle according to the model or type that he saw on the mount. The charge occurs four times in Exodus.[101] Philo consistently argued that the text referred to the Platonic ideas. For example he explained Exod 26:30 as follows: "Again, he indicates the paradigmatic essences of the ideas by saying 'according to the appearance which was shown to you on the mountain.'"[102] While we may demur, Philo was convinced that he had found the Platonic ideas in Moses.

I am therefore inclined to take Philo's claim more seriously than I might have at first glance. An initial reading leads most to think that Philo could manipulate the text through allegory to mean anything that he wants. While allegory gave him the capacity to read the text in ways that we do not, he must still justify his reading by the text. In this way the text exercised a degree of control over his allegories. The language of Scripture determined the topics that he treated: he needed a basis in the biblical text in order to read it philosophically. The sequence of the biblical narrative determined the order of the topics in Philo: he conscientiously followed the sequence and always returned to it after his digressions. The variations in the biblical narrative determined to some extent the nature of Philo's exegesis: inconcinnities and inconsistencies in the biblical text make for creative exegetical moves. *In nuce*, we must always remember that Philo's basic task was to explain Scripture and that the messiness of his thought is due in no small part to the nature of the text that was the basis for his reflections.

This realization helps us to understand some of the limits of Philo's thinking. The Torah exegete does not provide us with a full treatment of an issue. We are always forced to search through the whole of his corpus when we want to know what he thought about a given topic. Even when we have done this, there are often a number of unanswered issues. Why? His observations are always comments on a biblical text. While he can and does introduce excurses into his exposition, they are just that, excurses, not full treatments. This also helps us to understand Philo's inconsistencies.

---

[100] *Opif.* 24–25.
[101] Exod 25:8 (9 MT), 40; 26:30; 27:8.
[102] *QE* 2.90 on Exod 26:30. Cf. also *QE* 2.52 on Exod 25:8 (9 MT); *QE* 2.82 on Exod 25:40. *Mos.* 2.74, 76 explains Exod 25:8 (9 MT), 40. The section that deals with Exod 27:8 is missing.

Sometimes he preserved different exegetical traditions. He appears to have accepted a polyvalent text and typically did not argue for one interpretation to the exclusion of all others. At other times, he either changed his mind or followed the lead of the biblical narrative with the result that he contradicted what he had previously said.

Conclusions

There are thus at least two bases for calling Philo a theologian: his unswerving commitment to the ontological priority of God and his commitment to Scripture as the record of revelation. Are these adequate bases for such a designation? We should remember that Philo considered what he did philosophy, reflecting a broad understanding of the term. He was first and foremost a follower of Moses, but he understood Moses within a Platonic framework. It was, however, not philosophy in the sense that professional philosophers conceived of philosophy.[103] It is also not much help in addressing the issue of his originality, unless we are reduced to the affirmation that his originality lay in the creative combination of Hellenistic philosophy and Torah exegesis through allegorical interpretation. Philo was certainly not the first Jewish interpreter to do this. We could hold him out as the apex of a tradition and claim originality for the tradition that he attests.

There is another way to reflect on the question. Suppose we considered Philo against the tradition that he most heavily influenced, Christianity.[104] Could the Christian appropriation of Philo's works help us to think of his contribution? We might begin by comparing him to two significant early Christian thinkers: Paul and Origen. Was Paul a theologian? I would answer negatively. Paul was committed to the ontological priority of God, although his thought is not as theocentric as Philo's. What really sets him apart from Philo is his function: he was principally an apostle, i.e., a missionary and a religious thinker. He wrote letters to churches addressing immediate concerns and did not engage in systematic reflection on the Scriptures through the lens of Hellenistic philosophy. The result was that

---

[103] For texts along with discussions of his place in philosophy see G. E. Sterling, "Platonizing Moses: Philo and Middle Platonism," *SPhA* 5 (1993): 96–111, esp. 99–103, and D. T. Runia, "Was Philo a Middle Platonist? A Difficult Question Revisited," *SPhA* 5 (1993): 112–40. Cf. also the responses to these two presentations by D. Winston (141–46), T. Tobin (147–50), and J. Dillon (151–55).

[104] There is an enormous bibliography on the Christian appropriation of Philo. The most important survey is D. T. Runia, *Philo in Early Christian Literature: A Survey* (CRINT 3.3; Minneapolis: Fortress, 1993).

Paul composed letters that later became Scripture rather than commentaries on Scripture. I am not denying that he reflected on Scripture or provided interpretations of it, but this was not his principal task. From our vantage point, the apostle belongs to the first order rather than to the second. Origen, like Philo and Paul, was unambiguously committed to the ontological priority of God. Unlike Paul but very much in keeping with his Alexandrian Jewish predecessor, he was passionately committed to the systematic exposition of Scripture and even outstripped the Torah exegete in volume–no small accomplishment. He read Scripture through a philosophical lens and, in particular, was deeply influenced by Middle Platonism. Unlike Philo or Paul, Origen wrote a systematic treatment of his faith, *On First Principles*. This work, along with Irenaeus' *Against All Heresies*, was among the first systematic expositions of the Christian faith. For these reasons, most would consider Origen a theologian. If Origen is a theologian in the strict sense and Paul is not, where should we situate Philo? I would place him between the two, though closer to Origen than Paul. The two Alexandrians are more closely aligned in intellectual orientation and function than either is to Paul.

We might think of the same issue along slightly different lines. James Thompson argued that when the author of Hebrews adopted a Platonic metaphysic from the intellectual world attested by Philo, the step marked the transition to Christian philosophy.[105] There is a sense in which this is true. However, the impact of Philo on Christianity lay more in theology than philosophy. The distinct orientation and *modus operandi* of Philo made his thought attractive to Clement and Origin who took it up and bequeathed to later generations of Christians where it became distinct from philosophy. It became theology proper. This is Philo's greatest legacy.

In a recent novel Ann Rice has captured the significance of Philo by suggesting that while Jesus was a boy living in Egypt he attended the school of Philo.[106] While a historical connection between Philo and Jesus is pure fiction, the story captures the importance of Philo for early Christianity: he stands at the beginning of Christian theology. It is in this light that we may rightfully call him "the first theologian."

---

[105] J. Thompson, *The Beginnings of Christian Philosophy: The Epistle to the Hebrews* (CBQMS 13; Washington, D.C.: Catholic Biblical Association, 1982), esp. 152–62. I am pleased to be able to contribute this essay in honor of James Thompson.

[106] A. Rice, *Christ the Lord. Out of Egypt: A Novel* (New York: Knopf, 2005).

10

Rhetorical Strategy in Isaiah 1–5

John T. Willis

From J. G. Eichhorn (1783)[1] and W. Gesenius (1821)[2] until the 1970s, the typical approach to the book of Isaiah was diachronic. Scholars distinguished authentic from spurious material. They believed genuine oracles of the prophet Isaiah were limited to chs. 1–39, and unauthentic material in these chapters exceeded genuine. They dated Isaiah 40–66 much later than the prophet Isaiah. They viewed these chapters together until 1892, when B. Duhm separated Deutero-Isaiah (chs. 40–55; 540–536 BCE) from Trito-Isaiah (chs. 56–66; 536 to 444 BCE).[3]

Coherence of the Book of Isaiah

Beginning in the 1970s, several scholars, approaching the book of Isaiah from redactional, canonical, and new literary perspectives, have attempted to determine the flow of thought and structure of the book or portions thereof in its final form. B. S. Childs contends the book is a unity whose parts are interrelated canonically. Its diverse materials originated much earlier than its final form, but "the canonical editors of this tradition em-

---

[1] J. G. Eichhorn, *Einleitung in das Alte Testament,* 3rd ed. (Leipzig: Weidmann, 1803), 3:50–55.

[2] W. Gesenius, *Philologisch-kritischer und historiker Commentar über den Jesaja* (3 vols; Leipzig: Vogen, 1821).

[3] B. Duhm, *Das Buch Jesaia übersetzt und erklärt* (4th ed.; Göttingen: Vandenhoeck & Ruprecht, 1922), xii.

ployed the material in such a way as to eliminate almost entirely those concrete features and to subordinate the original message to a new role within the canon."[4]

R. E. Clements defends the coherence of the book, admitting that materials from various chronological periods appear in it, but contending that redactors (= authors) arranged these materials purposefully to communicate certain theological ideas. Isa 13:1—14:23 is a microcosm of the entire book. As it reflects Israel's fortunes in the Neo-Assyrian and Neo-Babylonian empire over two centuries, the book covers Israel's wider political fortunes from the eighth to fifth centuries BCE. The themes of God's people's blindness and deafness (6:9–10; 29:18; 32:3; and 35:5 in 42:16, 18–20; 43:8; 44:18); Yahweh's rejection of his people, stated in 2:6 and assumed in the extrinsic expression "this people" (6:9–10; 8:6, 12; 28:14; 29:13; 30:9); and the return of Yahweh's faithful people to Zion (11:12–16; 19:23; 27:12–13; 35), a theme permeating chs. 40–55, suggest the final redactors/authors of the book intended to prepare the hearers/readers for chs. 40–55 in chs. 1–39. Redactors/Authors of Isaianic material linked announcements of judgment on Jerusalem in chs. 1–39, in particular 2:6—4:1, with the Babylonian destruction of Jerusalem in 587 BCE. They incorporated ch. 39 to associate Jerusalem's overthrow and the Davidic monarchy with Isaiah's prophecies. The book's composers incorporated chs. 40–66 to counterbalance threats with promises. Isaiah 40–55 complement chs. 1–35. From their inception, Isaiah 40–55 were intended to develop and enlarge upon prophecies of Isaiah of Jerusalem, to supplement earlier material and to influence the way hearers understood it. Further, the proto-apocalyptic chs. 56–66 highlight the way in which promises of chs. 40–55 began to take effect. They carry forward the prophetic word declared on the eve of Babylon's overthrow in chs. 40–55. Isaiah 62:6–12 is a significant end point in a series of declarations of Yahweh's word concerning Jerusalem in chs. 1–39 and 40–55.[5]

---

[4] B. S. Childs, *Introduction to the Old Testament as Scripture* (Philadelphia: Fortress, 1979), 325, 334; idem, *Isaiah* (OTL; Louisville: Westminster John Knox, 2001), 4.

[5] R. E. Clements, "The Prophecies of Isaiah and the Fall of Jerusalem in 587 B.C.," *VT* 30 (1980): 421–36; idem, "The Unity of the Book of Isaiah," *Int* 36 (1982): 117–29; idem, "Beyond Tradition-History. Deutero-Isaianic Development of First Isaiah's Themes," *JSOT* 31 (1985): 95 113; idem, "Patterns in the Prophetic Canon: Healing the Blind and the Lame," in *Canon, Theology, and Old Testament Interpretation* (ed. G. M. Tucker, D. L. Petersen, and R. R. Wilson; Philadelphia: Fortress, 1988), 189–200; idem, "The Prophecies of Isaiah to Hezekiah concerning Sennacherib: 2 Kings 19.21-34 // Isa. 37.22-35," in *Prophetie und geschichtliche Wirklichkeit im alten Israel: Festschrift für Siegfried Herrmann zum 65. Geburtstag* (ed. R. Liwak und S. Wagner; Stuttgart: Kohlhammer, 1991), 65–78;

R. Rendtorff argues that the final form of the book of Isaiah reflects a literary and theological coherence due to the intentional efforts of its redactors/authors. He follows P. R. Ackroyd and R. F. Melugin in noting a contrast between judgment speeches and salvation assurances in Isaiah 1–39 and 40–55. The proclamation of divine "comforting" is prominent throughout the book (12:1; 40:1; 51:12; 66:13). Many words and phrases recur throughout the book (Yahweh's "glory," "Behold," "guilt" and "sin"), as do repeated themes (Zion/Jerusalem, the Holy One of Israel, justice and righteousness). Isaiah 40–55 form the heart of the book as a unified and self-contained literary work, and authors/ redactors have shaped chs. 1–39 and 56–66 in light of this section. Stages of redaction and composition antedate the book, but its authors have produced a coherent whole. As Rendtorff puts it, "The common starting point among scholars interested in the formation of the book of Isaiah is the conviction, or at least the assumption, that the present shape of the book is not the result of more or less accidental or arbitrary developments but rather that of deliberate and intentional literary and theological work."[6]

W. Brueggemann argues that social processes and dynamics in the community that gave the book of Isaiah its final shape explain its present form. Isaiah 1–39 are a sustained critique of the culture oppressing the community. They denounce the contrived positivism of the powerful, whose motivations and actions are self-serving, designed for their own advantage, unconcerned about others. This critique facilitates the community's public embrace of pain, consisting of guilt at responsibility for denied value and lost and irretrievable grief, and the emergence of hope rooted in memories of old stories in the community's life, in Isaiah 40–55. The public embrace of pain releases the social imagination of the community, giving it freedom, energy, and courage to envision an alternative world, in Isaiah 56–66. "Thus the parts of the Isaiah tradition are dynamically related to each other. Each is thus better understood out of the preceding which permitted it and/or the following element permitted by it."[7]

---

idem, "'Arise, Shine; For Your Light Has Come': A Basic Theme of the Isaianic Tradition," in *Writing and Reading the Scroll of Isaiah: Studies of an Interpretive Tradition* (ed. C. C. Broyles and C. A. Evans; VTSup 70/1; Leiden: Brill, 1997), 441–54; idem, "'Who is Blind but My Servant?' (Isaiah 42:19): How Then Shall We Read Isaiah?" in *God in the Fray: A Tribute to Walter Brueggemann* (ed. T. Linafelt and T. K. Beal; Minneapolis: Fortress, 1998), 143–56.

[6] R. Rendtorff, "The Book of Isaiah: A Complex Unity. Synchronic and Diachronic Reading," in *Society of Biblical Literature 1991 Seminar Papers* (ed. E. H. Lovering, Jr.; Atlanta: Scholars, 1991), 9.

[7] W. Brueggemann, "Unity and Dynamic in the Isaiah Tradition," *JSOT* 29 (1984): 102.

J. Vermeylen and O. H. Steck argue, Isaiah 56–66 was never a separate work, but the chapters' author(s) was (were) responsible for the composition of Isaiah 1–55 in its present form, and wrote chs. 56–66 as a continuation and conclusion of this work.[8]

E. W. Conrad argues that the beginning (Isa 8:16–20) and end (Isa 30:8) of the vision of Isaiah suggest that the book provides the context and occasion for reading another book, the book of Isaiah's vision (chs. 6–39). By surrounding Isaiah 6–39 with chs. 1–5 and 40–66, the composer(s) of the surrounding material made chs. 6–39 easy to read for his (their) contemporaries, because it reflects contemporary social conventions. The royal narratives concerning Ahaz (6:1—9:6 [Eng. 7]) and Hezekiah (chs. 36–39) play an important role in the book's structure. After the announcement of Assyrian devastation of Judah in the Ahaz narrative (8:7–8), a war oracle (10:24–27) promises deliverance from Assyria; after the announcement of Babylonian devastation of Judah in the Hezekiah narrative (39:5–7), war oracles (41:8–16; 43:1–4, 5–7; 44:1–5) promise deliverance from Babylon. "The former things" and "the things to come" (41:22–23; 43:9, 18; 44:7; 46:9; etc.) concern Babylon and future salvation. Based on the Hezekiah narrative (esp. 37:21–29), those desiring deliverance from Babylon may trust Yahweh to accomplish what he promised long ago. The composition's audience was an international community of survivors with minority status, suffering, threatened, believing legal and religious institutions around it are morally bankrupt, and imagining a society where the people will be king.[9]

C. R. Seitz argues that earlier material in the book of Isaiah was the basis for the later. Yahweh's promise that he would deliver Jerusalem/Zion from Assyria under Sennacherib in 701 BCE as he had "determined long ago" (37:26) is the foundation of his promise that he would deliver Jerusalem/Zion from Babylon who devastated the city in 587 BCE as he announced "from the beginning" (40:21; 46:10), "from of old" (44:7–8;

---

[8] J. Vermeylen, "L'unité du livre d'Isaie," in *The Book of Isaiah: Le livre d'Isaïe. Les oracles et leurs relectures* (BETL 81; ed. J. Vermeylen; Leuven: Peeters, 1989), 11–53; O. H. Steck, "Autor und/oder Redaktor in Jesaja 56–66," in *Writing and Reading the Scroll of Isaiah: Studies of an Interpretive Tradition* (ed. C. C. Broyles and C. A. Evans; VTSup 70/1; Leiden: Brill, 1997), 219–59.

[9] E. W. Conrad, "The Community as King in Second Isaiah," in *Understanding the Word: Essays in Honor of Bernhard W. Anderson* (ed. J. T. Butler, E. W. Conrad, and B. C. Ollenburger; JSOTSup 37; Sheffield: Sheffield Academic, 1985), 99–111; idem, "The Royal Narratives and the Structure of the Book of Isaiah," *JSOT* 41 (1988): 67–81; and idem, *Reading Isaiah* (OBT; Minneapolis: Fortress, 1991), esp. 155–58.

45:21; 46:9), "long ago" (48:3, 5).[10] "You [Yahweh] have made heaven and earth" (37:16) is the basis for:

> I am Yahweh, who made all things,
> who alone stretched out the heavens,
> who by myself spread out the earth (66:24).[11]

H. G. M. Williamson argues Deutero-Isaiah was never a separate work, but a reinterpretation of Proto-Isaiah for a later community: e. g., the announcement that Yahweh's servant will be "exalted and lifted up" and "very high" (52:13) and the description of Yahweh as "the high and lofty one" who dwells in "the high and holy place" (57:15) derive from the vision of Yahweh as "high and lofty" (6:1); and the promise Jerusalem that will be "inhabited" (44:26) and the references to Zion's "waste and desolate places" and "devastated land" (49:19) allude to "cities lying waste without inhabitant" and the "land [being] utterly desolate" (6:11). These and additional illustrations suggest that the book of Isaiah is coherent.[12]

M. A. Sweeney insists that one concentrate on the redaction of the entire book of Isaiah. The structure of chs. 1–39 is due not only to issues and concerns in these chapters, but also in chs. 40–66. The structure of chs. 1–39 anticipates chs. 40–66, so issues and concerns of chs. 40–66 are dominant in determining the structure of chs. 1–39. Chs. 40–66 develop themes from chs. 1–39, but the author(s) of chs. 40–66 does (do) not understand these themes exclusively from their context in chs. 1–39, but also in relation to historical events and theological ideas of his/their own situation. The author(s) of chs. 40–66 introduced themes in chs. 1–39 not there originally, and removed others that were, but ceased to be theologically relevant for his/their own situation. Isaiah 1–39 are the product of the final redaction of the entire book, and they function as a preface to chs. 40–66, the literary goal of the work. Isaiah 13–14, 36–39, 40–55 portray Babylon as the dominant world power and anticipate her fall, which is Deutero-Isaiah's perspective. Deutero-Isaiah applies the Davidic promises and covenant to all God's people. The author(s) of Isaiah 36–39 idealize(s) faithful Hezekiah in contrast to faithless Ahaz, and emphasize(s) Yahweh's positive response to Hezekiah's faith. Isaiah 36–39 provide the context for chs. 40–66. Isaiah 35 is transitional, drawing motifs of the exodus and the

---

[10] C. R. Seitz, *Zion's Final Destiny: The Development of the Book of Isaiah, A Reassessment of Isaiah 36–39* (Minneapolis: Fortress, 1991), 199–200.

[11] Ibid., 85.

[12] H. G. M. Williamson, *The Book Called Isaiah: Deutero-Isaiah's Role in Composition and Redaction* (Oxford: Clarendon, 1994), 38–39, 52–53.

blind and deaf from chs. 40–66 and 1–34. Isaiah 1 summarizes the major themes of the book, especially sin, punishment, and salvation. The corresponding themes and vocabulary in chs. 1 and 65–66 suggest that these chapters form an inclusio around the book. Sweeney thinks the book's basic structural division is between ch. 1, the prologue that summarizes Isaiah's message, and chs. 2–66, the body. Chs. 36–39 form a bridge between two major sections: the "Assyrian" section (chs. 1–35) which anticipates judgment by Assyria followed by restoration, and the "Babylonian" section (chs. 40–66) which presupposes judgment by Babylon and announces restoration. In chs. 36–39, Hezekiah serves as a paradigm for Judah. As Yahweh delivers Hezekiah from illness yet Hezekiah dies fifteen years later, so Yahweh delivers Judah from Assyria yet Babylon will execute Yahweh's judgment on Judah. The authors of the book of Isaiah composed it to support the reforms of Ezra in the late fifth century BCE.[13]

W. A. M. Beuken and J. Blenkinsopp add another argument for intentional redactional arrangement of the book of Isaiah. Deutero-Isaiah emphasizes "the servant of Yahweh," and Trito-Isaiah, "the servants of Yahweh." Isaiah 40–55 prepare hearers for chs. 56–66. Isaiah 53:10 states Yahweh's servant "shall see his offspring" = the servants of Yahweh, while Isa 54:17 promises the children of the city will live as the servants of Yahweh on their own heritage.[14]

Coherence of Isaiah 1–12

Several scholars argue that sections of the book of Isaiah are coherent (chs. 36–39, 40–55, 56–66, and 1–12 or portions thereof). R. J. Marshall and P. R. Ackroyd defend the coherence of Isaiah 1–12; A. H. Bartelt, that of Isaiah 2–12, and M. A. Sweeney, that of Isaiah 1–4 (see discussion above).

R. J. Marshall argues that in Isaiah 1–12, disciples of Isaiah preserved his genuine oracles, added material, and shaped it into a unity, because: (a) a sociological continuity underlies the growth of Isaiah 1–12; (b) genuine Isaianic material and editorial material fit well together; and (c) Isaiah

---

[13] M. A. Sweeney, *Isaiah 1–4 and the Post-Exilic Understanding of the Isaianic Tradition* (BZAW 171; Berlin: de Gruyter, 1988), esp. 1–30; idem, "The Book of Isaiah as Prophetic Torah," in *New Visions of Isaiah* (ed. R. F. Melugin and M. A. Sweeney; JSOTSup 214; Sheffield: Sheffield Academic Press, 1996), 50–67.

[14] W. A. M. Beuken, "The Main Theme of Trito-Isaiah: 'The Servants of YHWH'," *JSOT* 47 (1990): 67–87; J. Blenkinsopp, "The Servant and the Servants in Isaiah and the Formation of the Book," in *Writing and Reading the Scroll of Isaiah. Studies of an Interpretive Tradition* (ed. C. C. Broyles and C. A. Evans; VTSup 70/1; Leiden: Brill, 1997), 155–75.

1–12 contain clues as to the organizational pattern of these chapters.[15] The clues include exaltation of Jerusalem and the temple (2:2–5 and 4:2–6), overthrow of the sinful monarchy and ensuing restoration (8:21—9:6 [ET 7]; 10:33—11:16), and covenant theology connected with king and temple. They betray literary organization: the structure of the covenant lawsuit (Isa 1:2–20) from judgment (vv. 2–17) to promise (vv. 18–20) indicates the basis for the relationship of judgment and promise in the body of the prophecy, 1:21—12:6; introductory formulas, refrains, and content connect Isa 5:8–30 with 9:7(ET 8)–10:4, suggesting 6:1—9:6 (ET 7) were inserted to break their connection; two oracles predicting the exaltation of Jerusalem and the temple with intervening judgments precede these chapters, and two songs anticipating the coming of the Davidic king with intervening judgments follow them; 10:5—12:6 take a turn, indicating progression; two darkness figures anticipate the first Messianic passage in 9:1–6 (ET 2–7); and two forest figures, the second in ch. 11; and progression of thought involving the ensign appears in 5:26; 11:10, 12.[16]

P. R. Ackroyd argues that recurring vocabulary, expressions, and themes in Isaiah indicate the book's coherence. The structure of Isaiah 1–12 indicates why much material was connected with the prophet Isaiah. 1:2—2:4(5) is not an introduction to the book, but stands alongside other units in Isaiah 1–12, viz., 2:6–22; 3–4; 5 + 9:7(ET 8)–10:4; 6:1—9:6 (ET 7); 10:5—11:16; 12, setting the tone for the entire book. Isaiah 1–12 presents Isaiah as a messenger of doom and salvation. When the final redactor of Isaiah 1–12 summons his hearers/readers to look back to Isaiah, his concern is not a history of Isaiah's activity, but the basis for accepting present application of Isaiah's authoritative message, supported by his divine commission and fulfillment of his words, so that the hearer/reader can see the authentication of Isaiah's message rests on applicability to new situations.[17]

A. H. Bartelt argues that Isaiah 2–12 constitute a separate coherent unit in the book. Subject matter, syllable counting, stress counting, prose particles, and lineation determine subunits. Isaiah 6:1—8:23a are the center around which 5:25–30 and 9:7 (ET 8)–10:4 form the inner inclusio, and 5:8–24 and 10:5ff. the outer. 5:1–7 and 8:23b—9:6 (ET 7) are transitional. Chs. 2–4 precede 5:1—10:4, and 10:5—12:6 follow

[15] R. J. Marshall, "The Unity of Isaiah 1–12," *LQ* 14 (1962): 21–38, esp. 21–22.
[16] Ibid., 30–33; idem, "The Structure of Isaiah 1–12," *BR* 7 (1962): 19–32, esp. 26–31.
[17] P. R. Ackroyd, "Isaiah I-XII: Presentation of a Prophet," in *Congress Volume: Göttingen, 1977* (VTSup 29; Leiden: Brill, 1978), 16–48 = *Studies in the Religious Tradition of the Old Testament* (London: SCM, 1987), 79–104.

them. Each pair of units surrounding the center forms concentric circles. 5:1—10:4 are a coherent redactional whole whose theme is Yahweh the real king. Therefore, Ahaz must trust in Yahweh rather than in Assyria. 10:5—12:6 are a unit declaring Yahweh will punish Assyria and deliver a remnant of Israel; then Zion will praise Yahweh and make known his deeds to the nations. Likewise, Isaiah 2–4 are coherent, announcing that human arrogance will be humbled and Yahweh alone will be exalted, while Yahweh will restore his purified remnant.[18]

Rhetorical Criticism and the Book of Isaiah

James Muilenburg initiated rhetorical criticism for interpreting the Hebrew Bible in 1968.[19] Subsequently, several scholars have used rhetorical criticism in interpreting portions of the Hebrew Bible, understanding and applying it diversely.

Rhetorical criticism may help interpret Isaiah 1–5. Presumably, the author(s) of the book of Isaiah felt compelled to address situations the audience was encountering.[20] He/they composed this work for oral performance by well-trained, professional speakers/rhetoricians.[21] His/their purpose was to persuade the audience to think and act appropriately in response to situations it faced. He/They took great care in *what* he/they said (content) and *how* he/they said it (structure, vocabulary, etc.). The author(s) and his/their audience share a common perspective which makes communication possible.[22]

The purposes of rhetoric may be to teach, persuade, or please or inspire.[23] New Testament scholars use classical Graeco-Roman rhetoric and rhetorical theory dating from the fifth to first centuries BCE to interpret

---

[18] A. H. Bartelt, *The Book around Immanuel: Style and Structure in Isaiah 2–12* (ed. W. H. Propp; Biblical and Judaic Studies from the University of California, San Diego 4; Winona Lake: Eisenbrauns, 1996), 133–36, 182–88, 237–43.

[19] James Muilenburg, "Form Criticism and Beyond," *JBL* 88 (1969): 1–18.

[20] See Karl Möller, *A Prophet in Debate: The Rhetoric of Persuasion in the Book of Amos* (JSOTSup 372; Sheffield: Sheffield Academic, 2003), 38.

[21] See H. J. B. Combrink, "The Rhetoric of Sacred Scripture," in *Rhetoric, Scripture and Theology: Essays from the 1994 Pretoria Conference* (ed. S. E. Porter and T. H. Olbricht; JSNTSup 131; Sheffield: Sheffield Academic, 1996), 108–9.

[22] See Y. Gitay, "Rhetorical Criticism," in *To Each Its Own Meaning: An Introduction to Biblical Criticisms and Their Application* (ed. S. R. Haynes and S. L. McKenzie; Louisville: Westminster John Knox, 1993), 139, 143.

[23] See Phyllis Trible, *Rhetorical Criticism: Context, Method, and the Book of Jonah* (GBS; Minneapolis: Fortress, 1994), 7–9, esp. the chart on 9.

NT works. Hebrew Bible scholars, however, deduce the nature of rhetoric in the Hebrew Bible from its content and ancient Near Eastern literature. This is not necessarily less precise, because any author must use structure, vocabulary, and so on, to communicate, and modern interpreters must determine what these are by studying texts.[24] Karl Moller on Amos, C. S. Shaw on Micah, T. Renz on Ezekiel, B. Wiklander on Isaiah 2–4, and Y. Gitay on Isaiah 1–12, among others, have used rhetorical criticism to interpret prophetic materials.[25]

Bitzer defines rhetoric as "a mode of altering reality . . . by the creation of discourse which changes reality through the mediation of thought and action."[26] G. A. Kennedy proposes that a rhetorical-critical analysis of biblical materials must include five elements. (1) Determine rhetorical unit(s) from smallest to entire book. (2) Determine the rhetorical situation addressed. (3) Identify the rhetorical genre, which may be judicial, in which the author summons her/his hearers to judge past events; deliberative, in which the author invites the audience to deliberate on expedient actions for future performance; or epideictic (demonstrative), in which the author envisions the audience as spectators. (4) Analyze the author's rhetorical strategy. (5) Assess the rhetorical effectiveness of the unit or book to address the situation.[27] The present study applies these principles to Isaiah 1–5 in modified form, and suggests the function of these chapters in the book.

There is a growing scholarly consensus that the book of Isaiah is a composition addressing a small but complex Judean community in and around Jerusalem between 450–400 BCE near the time of Ezra and Nehemiah, consisting of factions struggling to survive under Persian rule, but warring over socio-politico-religious issues.[28] Assuming this kind of

---

[24] D. Patrick and A. Scult, *Rhetoric and Biblical Interpretation* (Bible and Literature Series 26; JSOTSup 82; Sheffield: Sheffield Academic Press, 1990), 13.

[25] Möller, *A Prophet in Debate*; C. S. Shaw, *The Speeches of Micah: A Rhetorical-Historical Analysis* (JSOTSup 145; Sheffield: JSOT Press, 1993); T. Renz, *The Rhetorical Function of the Book of Ezekiel* (VTSup 76; Leiden: Brill, 1999); B. Wiklander, *Prophecy as Literature: A Text-Linguistic and Rhetorical Approach to Isaiah 2–4* (ConBOT 22; Malmö: Gleerup, 1984); and Y. Gitay, *Isaiah and His Audience: The Structure and Meaning of Isaiah 1–12* (StSN 30; Assen: Van Gorcum, 1991).

[26] L. F. Bitzer, "The Rhetorical Situation," in *Rhetoric: A Tradition in Transition. In Honor of Donald C. Bryant* (ed. W. R. Fisher; East Lansing, Mich: Michigan State University Press, 1974), 250.

[27] G. A. Kennedy, *New Testament Interpretation through Rhetorical Criticism* (Chapel Hill: University of North Carolina Press, 1984), 33–38.

[28] See C. R. Seitz, "Isaiah, Book of (Third Isaiah)," in *ABD* 3:501–6; J. Blenkinsopp, *Isa-*

setting, this essay suggests the author(s) of the book of Isaiah intended to encourage the faithful to trust in Yahweh's power and compassion in difficult times, and concurrently to deflect and transform the feelings and actions of the rebellious detrimental to the community's physical, social, economic, and spiritual health. Isaiah 1–5 play a significant role in the rhetorical strategy of this (these) author(s).

Coherence of Isaiah 1–5

Three lines of evidence suggest Isaiah 1–5 are a coherent section in Isaiah 1–12 and the entire book: (1) structure, (2) subject matter, and (3) recurrence of words and expressions. Isaiah 6 begins a new section in the book.

Structure of Isaiah 1–5

Isaiah 1–5 are chiastic.

> A. Call to Repent = To do justice and righteousness (1:2–31).
>
> > 1. Relatively long doom oracle (*rib*) against God's people for injustice and unrighteousness (1:2–20).
> > 2. Relatively short doom oracle against leaders of God's people for injustice and unrighteousness (1:21–31).
>
> B. Prophetic announcement that God will be exalted and arrogant human beings will be humbled (2–4).
>
> > 1. Short conditional hope oracle announcing God will be exalted (2:1–5).
> > 2. Doom oracle announcing the arrogant people of God will be humbled (2:6–22).
> > 2'. Doom oracle announcing arrogant leaders of God's people will be humbled (3:1–15).
> > 2". Doom oracle announcing arrogant women of God's people will be humbled (3:16—4:1).
> > 1'. Short conditional hope oracle announcing God will redeem the penitent remnant of his people (4:2–6).
>
> A'. Announcement that God will punish his people for injustice and Unrighteousness (5).

---

iah 56–66 (AB 19B; New York: Doubleday, 2003), 51–54.

2'. Relatively short doom oracle against God's people for injustice and unrighteousness (5:1–7).

1'. Relatively long doom oracle (six "alas" or "woe oracles") against leaders of God's people for injustice and unrighteousness (5:8–30).

The central section of Isaiah 1–5 (B) begins and ends with short "conditional" hope oracles: God will exalt Jerusalem *if* a remnant repents and returns to him (2:1–5 and 4:2–6). The first hope oracle contrasts with the following doom oracle, which denounces God's people for arrogance because of foreign alliances, military strength, wealth, and foreign gods. The second hope oracle contrasts with the preceding doom oracle, proclaiming that restoration of the remnant will occur after Yahweh has washed away the filth of the daughters of Zion (4:4) denounced in that oracle. These hope oracles form an integral part of chs. 2–4. The three doom oracles denounce groups characterized by arrogance: God's people (2:6–22), her leaders (3:1–15), and her influential women (3:16—4:1). The message of chs. 2–4 is that Yahweh will humble his arrogant people, and will be exalted by establishing the temple mount as the highest of the mountains (2:1–5) and by cleansing and protecting Mount Zion (4:2–6).

Each outer unit of Isaiah 1–5 contains two pericopes. Chapter 1 has a relatively long pericope denouncing God's people for substituting rituals for righteous living (1:2–20) followed by a relatively short pericope reproving leaders of God's people for treating widows and orphans unrighteously and for adopting foreign religious practices (1:21–31). Conversely, ch. 5 has a relatively short pericope emphasizing Yahweh's disappointment over his people's unrighteousness (5:1–7), followed by a relatively long pericope containing six "alas" or "woe oracles" denouncing unrighteous practices (5:8–30).

Chiasmus occurs frequently in the Hebrew Bible. Roland Meynet comments that one characteristic of the rhetoric of the Hebrew Bible

> is the specific manner in which it composes . . . concentrical arrangements [i.e., chiasmus]. Instead of developing its argumentation in a linear way, in the Graeco-Roman fashion, to a conclusion which is the point of resolution of the discourse, it is organized most of the time in an involutive manner around a centre which is the focal point, the keystone, through which the rest finds cohesion.[29]

---

[29] R. Meynet, *Rhetorical Analysis: An Introduction to Biblical Rhetoric* (ed. D. J. A. Clines and P. R. Davies; JSOTSup 256; Sheffield: Sheffield Academic Press, 1998), 175–76.

NT writers follow the rhetoric of the Hebrew Bible, not classical Graeco-Roman rhetoric. Several passages in the Gospels illustrate this: Matt 5:3–12; 26:57—27:26; Mark 14:53—15:20, Luke 18:31—19:46; 5:17–26; 1:57–66.[30] Two books listing studies on chiasmus in the Bible (and nonbiblical literature), published in 1981 and 1999, show the extent of chiasmus in the Bible.[31] Evidence suggests that biblical peoples thought and spoke chiastically, and enjoyed composing and experiencing chiastically-arranged works.

Subject Matter of Isaiah 1–5

There is a common theological focus in Isaiah 1–5. These chapters confront the spirit of self-righteous arrogance among God's people (2:6–22) and their leaders (3:1—4:1). Yahweh, whose people have reduced to insignificance, will be exalted to sovereign supremacy; and Yahweh's people, who have elevated themselves, will be humbled. 2:9, 11, 17; 5:15–16 summarize:

> The haughtiness of people shall be humbled, and the pride of everyone shall be brought low, and Yahweh alone will be exalted on that day.

Yahweh will take away from Jerusalem and Judah the highly esteemed and leaders (3:1–3), replacing them with "boys," "babes," and other incapable leaders (3:1–8b),

> because their speech and their deeds are against Yahweh, defying his glorious presence (3:8c-d).

He will afflict Zion's "haughty" women, and remove all manifestations of their pride (3:16—4:1). By contrast, Yahweh will elevate the temple mountain; all nations will stream to it that he might teach them his ways (2:2–4); Yahweh will restore the remnant of his people from whom "the filth of the daughters of Zion" is washed away (4:2–6). Yahweh will humble the arrogant and exalt the subdued.

The "covenant lawsuit" (3:13–15) at the center of the doom oracles in this central section of Isaiah 1–5 (3:1—4:1) suggests the leaders' arrogance manifests itself when they use their power to oppress the poor.

---

[30] Meynet, *Rhetorical Analysis*, 317–50.

[31] J. W. Welch et al, *Chiasmus in Antiquity* (Hildesheim: Gerstenberg, 1981); J. W. Welch and D. B. McKinlay, *Chiasmus Bibliography* (Provo: Research Press, 1999).

This condemnation of unrighteousness is strong in chs. 1 and 5 (1:15–17, 21–24; 5:7, 8–10, 22–23).

Isaiah 1–5 contain many announcements of punishment for sin (1:5–8, 20, 24–25, 28–31; 2:9–21; 3:1, 4–5, 9,11–12; 3:17—4:1; 4:4; 5:5–6, 9–10, 13–15, 24–30). Most announce future punishment, but some refer to the past (1:5b–8; 2:9; 3:9, 12; 5:13–15). The purpose of divine judgment is to remove evil to restore good (1:9, 18–19, 25–27; 2:2–5, 11c, 17c; 3:10; 4:2–6; 5:16–17).

The picture of Yahweh is consistent in Isaiah 1–5. Yahweh has always blessed an undeserving people like a father rearing helpless children (1:2–4), a vinedresser preparing, protecting, and tending his vineyard (5:1–2), a shepherd sustaining his flock (5:17), or a teacher instructing his students (2:3; 5:24). Hence, when Israel rebels, Yahweh's wrath is kindled and he comes to punish them, terrifying the earth (1:24–25; 2:10, 19, 21; 5:25). Yet, gracious and merciful, he does not completely destroy (1:9; 4:3–4).

Recurrence of Words and Expressions in Isaiah 1–5

The recurring themes in Isaiah 1–5 are reinforced by repeated words and expressions. Additional words and expressions appear twice or more in these chapters, suggesting they belong together. ארץ occurs 13x: 4x of the world (1:2; 2:19, 21; 5:26); 8x of the land of Judah (1:7, 19; 2:7 [2x], 8; 4:2; 5:8, 30); 1x of the ground (3:26). The summons to earth (and heavens) to hear Yahweh's lawsuit against his people at the beginning of chs. 1–5 (1:2), and Yahweh's summons to "a people (Assyrians) at the ends of the earth" at the end (5:26) form an inclusio around this unit. Yahweh's theophany to punish, then to restore, affects the earth (2:19, 21) and the land of Judah (punishment—1:7; 5:30; restoration—4:2). ידע, "know," of human beings knowing God and his plan, appears 4x: 2x each in chs. 1 (v. 3 [2x]) and 5 (vv. 13, 19).

Words for "sin" occur 10x: חטא, "sin," 3x (1:4, 18; 3:9); עון, "iniquity," 2x (1:4; 5:18); and רע, "evil," 5x (1:4, 16; 3:9, 11; 5:20). The idea that Yahweh's people "despise" (נאץ) him or his word appears 2x (1:4; 5:24). "Holy One of Israel" describes Yahweh 3x (1:4; 5:19, 24); 5:16 declares Yahweh is "holy;" 4:3 says those who remain in Jerusalem will be called "holy." "Daughter of Zion" for Jerusalem (1:8) and "daughters of Zion" for influential women of Jerusalem (3:16, 17; 4:4) occur 4x. Roots meaning "to be left, remain," indicating the remnant, occur 4x (יתר—1:8, 9; 4:3; שאר—4:3). "Vineyard" occurs 8x: 1x literally (1:8), 7x metaphorically for God's people (3:15; 5:1 [2x], 3, 4, 5, 7).

"People" appears 15x: 3x for foreign nations (2:3, 4; 3:13 [MT]), 11x for God's sinful, impenitent people (1:3, 4, 10 ["you people of Gomorrah"]; 2:6; 3:5, 7, 12 [2x], 14; 5:13, 25), 1x for the poor whom the wicked oppress (3:15). "Nation" occurs 5x: 1x for Judah (1:4), 4x for foreign nations (2:2, 4 [2x]; 5:26). Three passages compare Jerusalem's sin and punishment with that of Sodom and Gomorrah (1:9, 10; 3:9). Three passages refer to Yahweh's "law" or "instruction" (תורה) parallel with "word" (דבר [1:10; 2:3]; אמרה [5:24]). "Yahweh of hosts" appears 9x (1:9, 24; 2:12; 3:1, 15; 5:7, 9, 16, 24). "Hand" occurs 10x: 1x of Yahweh doing mighty works (5:12); 3x of Yahweh's power (1:25; 5:25 [2x]); 1x of one's rule over his people (3:6); 4x describing evil activities (1:12, 15; 2:8; 3:11); 1x of spreading forth palms (כף) in prayer (1:15). "Eye" occurs 7x: 1x of God hiding his "eyes" (1:15); 1x of God seeing evil (1:16); 1x of God's people provoking Yahweh's eyes (3:8); 4x describing the arrogant (2:11; 3:16; 5:15, 21).

שפט "to judge, justice," appears 12x: 1x of Yahweh's arbitration between nations (2:4); 2x of favoring an orphan in a lawsuit (1:17, 23); 1x of deciding who is right in court (5:3); 2x of governmental officials (1:26; 3:2); 5x of treating others justly (1:17, 21, 27; 5:7, 16); 2x of divine punishment (3:14; 4:4). צדק, "to be righteous, righteous," occurs 8x: 2x of righteous persons (3:10; 5:23); 6x of right living (1:21, 26, 27; 5:7, 16, 23). "Sword" as a military weapon occurs 4x (1:20; 2:4 [2x]; 3:25).

סור, "to take away," appears 4x: 1x of the wicked "taking away" rights of others (5:23); 3x of Yahweh "taking away" valuables from his people as punishment (1:25; 3:1, 18). בער, "to burn," occurs 4x: 1x of the wicked oppressing the poor (3:14); 3x of Yahweh's punishment (1:31; 4:4; 5:5). הוי, "woe, alas, ah", occurs 8x (1:4, 24; 5:8, 11, 18, 20, 21, 22). "Zion" appears 8x (1:8, 27; 2:3; 3:16, 17; 3:3, 4, 5); "Jerusalem" 9x (1:1; 2:1, 3; 3:1, 8; 4:3 [2x], 4; 5:3). "Mountain" occurs 6x: 3x of mountains around Jerusalem (2:2, 14; 5:25); 3x of the temple mount (2:2, 3; 4:5). "House" (בית) occurs 11x: 2x of the temple (2:2, 3), 3x of God's people (2:5, 6; 5:7); 1x of one's clan (3:6); 4x of a private dwelling (3:7, 14; 5:8, 9); 1x in "houses of the soul"="perfume boxes" (3:20). שחח, "to be humbled," and שפל, "to be brought low," occur in synonymous parallelism 4x (2:9, 11, 17; 5:15); שפל appears alone in 2:12. הדר, "glory," occurs 4x: 1x of Jerusalem's glory (5:14); 3x of Yahweh's glory (2:10, 19, 21). כבוד "glory" appears 6x: 2x of "honorable" persons (3:5; 5:13); 1x meaning "heavy" (with iniquity) (1:4); 1x of the "branch of the Lord" (4:2); 1x of restored Jerusalem (4:5); 1x of Yahweh's glory (3:8). גבה appears 6x: 5x of human pride (2:11, 15, 17; 3:16; 5:15); 1x of Yahweh's "exaltation" (5:16). שַׂר, "prince," occurs 4x (1:23; 3:3, 4, 14), קָצִין, "ruler," 3x of high officials (1:10; 3:6, 7). Isaiah 1–5 condemn "deeds" of the wicked 2x (1:16; 3:8), and commend "deeds" of the righteous 1x (3:10). עָשָׂה, "to do, make," appears 16x: 3x of "making" idols (2:8 [2x], 20); 6x of Yahweh's "deeds" (3:11; 5:4 [2x], 5, 12, 19); 6x of a vine "bringing forth" grapes (5:2 [2x], 4 [2x], 10 [2x]); 1x of a woman's "well set" hair (3:24). רִיב, "to bring a lawsuit, lawsuit," occurs 3x (1:17, 23; 3:13). The "day of Yahweh" occurs 10x: 8x of divine punishment (2:11, 12, 17, 20; 3:7, 18; 4:1; 5:30); 2x of divine restoration of the remnant (2:2; 4:2).

Function of Isaiah 1–5 in the Book

In 1962, G. Fohrer published an influential article arguing that Isaiah 1 is the prologue to the entire book, theologically summarizing its message.[32] Many scholars have accepted this hypothesis. This essay proposes that this is correct but incomplete. If it is true that Isaiah 1–5 are arranged chiastically, that their subject matter is coherent, and that key words and expressions recur at significant points, then the final editors/authors of the book of Isaiah intended the audience to hear Isaiah 1 in conjunction with chs. 2–5. Hence, they composed Isaiah 1–5 symmetrically as the theological introduction to the entire book, presenting the main themes of the book in summary form. There are five major themes in the book, each a vital part of Isaiah 1–5.

First, human sin has kindled Yahweh's wrath, and he punishes Israel (or nations) for their sins. This punishment may be past (1:4–9), present (36:1–22), or future (28:1–22); it will happen on the Day of Yahweh to his people (2:6–22; 3:7, 18; 5:30; 22:1–14), Babylon (13:1–19), and Syria (Aram [with North Israel], 17:1–11), among others.

Second, arrogance or pride is the fundamental human sin, whether of Ephraim and Samaria (9:7–11 [Eng. 8–12]; 28:1, 3), Assyria (10:5–19), Babylon (13:11, 19; 14:9–15; 46:1; 47:7, 10), Moab (16:6; 25:11), Tyre (23:9), or the enemies of his people (26:5). Yahweh blesses those who are contrite and humble in spirit (57:15; 66:2).

In contrast to declarations that Yahweh will humble the arrogant, the book of Isaiah proclaims Yahweh as the only true God, while idols are nothing. According to Isaiah 1–39, Yahweh is creator of heaven and earth, universal king, in control of nations (37:14–29). God's people will

---

[32] G. Fohrer, "Jesaja 1 als Zusammenfassung der Verkündigung Jesajas," *ZAW* 74 (1962): 251–68.

denounce oaks and gardens where Baal is worshiped (1:29–31). When Yahweh judges his people, they will throw away their idols (2:18–21; 31:7). When Yahweh appears, the idols of Egypt will tremble (19:1, 3). According to Isaiah 40–55, Yahweh is creator and sustainer of the universe (40:18, 21–31; 44:6–8); idols are lifeless wooden objects covered with silver and gold (40:19–20; 44:9–20). Yahweh lays waste mountains and hills, dries up rivers and pools; idol worshipers will be put to shame (42:15–17; 45:20–21; 48:3–5). According to Isaiah 56–66, humanity is Yahweh's work (64:8). Yahweh's awesome deeds demonstrate there is no God besides him (64:3–4). Israel provokes Yahweh by engaging in idolatrous practices: sacrificing in gardens, offering incense on bricks and reviling him (57:13; 65:2–7; 66:17). None of their sacrifices is acceptable to Yahweh (66:3).[33]

Third, the editors/authors of the book of Isaiah emphasize that God's people must practice "justice" and "righteousness" toward others. This is much more important than observance of rituals. According to Isaiah 1–39, defending orphans and widows takes precedence over many sacrifices (1:10–17). The elders and princes of God's people stand condemned because they crush the poor (3:13–15). The good grapes God expects from his vineyard (Israel) are justice and righteousness (5:7). Yahweh pronounces "alas" or "woe oracles" on those who acquit the guilty for a bribe and deprive the innocent of their rights (5:22–23), who deny justice to the needy (10:1–4). Yahweh will restore Zion by laying the sure foundation of trust in him and making justice the plumbline and righteousness the plummet for erecting his spiritual building (28:16–17). Currently, God's people draw near to him with their mouths and honor him with their lips, but their hearts are far from him (29:13–14). The prophet envisions a time when justice and righteousness will be dominant in Jerusalem (32:1, 7, 16; 33:5). According to Isaiah 40–55, Yahweh's servant will bring justice to the nations (42:1–7; 51:4). According to Isaiah 56–66, Yahweh calls on his people to maintain justice and righteousness (56:1). Yahweh denounces his people who fast and keep the Sabbath, but do not practice justice and righteousness (Isa. 58:1—59:19).[34]

---

[33] On the themes of human arrogance and Yahweh's exaltation, see D. W. Gowan, *When Man Becomes God: Humanism and Hubris in the Old Testament* (Pittsburgh: Pickwick, 1975); and G. Stansell, "Isaiah 28–33: Blest be the Tie that Binds (Isaiah Together)," in *New Visions of Isaiah* (ed. R. F. Melugin and M. A. Sweeney; JSOTSup 214; Sheffield: Sheffield Academic, 1996), 73–74, 80–82.

[34] On the themes of justice and righteousness, and of widows, orphans, aliens, and the poor, see E. W. Davies, *Prophecy and Ethics: Isaiah and the Ethical Tradition of Israel* (JSOT-

Fourth, the book of Isaiah stresses interaction between Zion/Jerusalem and the nations. Yahweh is Creator of the universe (40:26, 28), including all nations; he uses nations to accomplish his "plan" or "work" (5:12, 19; 28:21; 30:1): Assyria (1:7–9; 5:24–30; 8:5–8; 10:5–19), Babylon (47:6), Persia (13:17–19; 44:24—45:7), Syria (Aram) and Philistia (9:11–12 [Heb. 10–11]). Before Yahweh, the nations are like "a drop [hanging] from a bucket," "dust on the scales" (40:15), "grasshoppers" (40:2), "less than nothing and emptiness" (40:17).

In every section of the book, Zion/Jerusalem sustains one of four relationships to the nations. (1) Yahweh uses nations to punish Zion/Jerusalem for her sins (in chs. 1–39: 1:2–9; 5:8–30; 10:5–19; 37:26–29; chs. 40–55: 42:22–25; 47:5–7; chs. 56–66: 60:13–14; 63:18; 64:10–11). (2) Yahweh defends Zion against nations, and uses Zion to overthrow hostile nations (chs. 1–39: 10:12, 15–19, 24–27b; 14:4–23; 29:5–8; 31:4–9; 37:21–29, 33–38; chs. 40–55: 40:15–17, 22–23; 41:15–16; 47:8–15; 51:22–23; chs. 56–66: 63:1–6). (3) Yahweh uses nations to restore penitent Zion/Jerusalem (chs. 1–39: 11:10–14; 14:1–2; chs. 40–55: 49:22–23; chs. 56–66: 60:5–6, 8–9, 11–14; 61:5–6). (4) Yahweh uses Zion/Jerusalem as his "witness," "light," "messenger," to bring the nations to him (chs. 1–39: 2:2–5; 19:18–25; chs. 40–55: 42:5–7; 43:8–13; 49:1–7; chs. 56–66: 56:2–8; 60:1–3; 66:18–23).[35]

Fifth, Yahweh punishes the unfaithful not to destroy but to redeem. Ultimately, a "remnant" will survive and be Yahweh's "people" on earth (chs. 1–39: 1:8–9; 4:2–4; 6:13; 7:21–22; 10:20–23; 11:11–16; 28:5; 37:4, 31–32; chs. 40–55: 43:8; 46:3–4; 49:1–6; chs. 56–66: 59:20; 60:21–22; 65:8–16).

Conclusion

D. Carr and A. Tomasino discuss similarities between Isaiah 1 and 65–66 and Isaiah 1 and 63:7—66:24 respectively, reaching different conclusions. Carr believes chs. 1 and 65–66 stand in contrast: ch. 1 predicts a division between righteous and wicked, calls the wicked to repentance, denies automatic security for Zion, and compares Zion with a prostitute; chs. 65–66 assume a division between righteous and wicked, assure the righteous of Yahweh's presence, emphasize the benefits of restored Zion, and compare Yahweh's care for Zion with a mother comforting her children. Carr argues

Sup 16; Sheffield: JSOT Press, 1981), 90–112; J. Blenkinsopp, *Isaiah 1–39* (AB 19; New York: Doubleday, 2000), 108.

[35] See Rendtorff, "The Composition of the Book of Isaiah," 155–59.

that the final editors/authors were more interested in the cohesiveness of small units to be read to an audience at one hearing than that of the whole book. Modern readers may choose to read the entire book as a literary coherence, but this was not the concern of ancient authors and hearers.[36]

Tomasino contends that Isa 1:2—2:4 and 63:7—66:24 treat the same themes in the same order with essentially the same vocabulary, which he summarizes in a diagram. He reasons that the editors/authors of Isa 63:7—66:24 knew Isaiah 1 and used its structural pattern in composing their own work. An earlier redaction of the book did not contain chs. 65 and 66:22–24, but the final redaction did.[37]

The present essay argues that the structure, themes, and recurrence of words and expressions in Isaiah 1–5 suggest these chapters are the first unit in the book. Its purpose is to summarize the major teachings throughout this prophetic work. Isaiah 1–5 and 63:7—66:24 may well form an inclusio around the book. The final editors/authors composed the work to impact a relatively small mixed or diverse Jewish audience in and around Jerusalem in the latter half of the fifth century BCE: on the one hand, assuring the faithful of Yahweh's presence and care; on the other hand, denouncing the rebellious for various social and religious sins and calling them to repentance.

---

[36] D. Carr, "Reaching for Unity in Isaiah," *JSOT* 57 (1993): 61–80 (esp. 71–75); idem, "Reading Isaiah from Beginning (Isaiah 1) to End (Isaiah 65–66): Multiple Modern Possibilities," in *New Visions of Isaiah* (ed. R. F. Melugin and M. A. Sweeney; JSOTSup 214; Sheffield: Sheffield Academic, 1996), 188–218 (esp. 214–18).

[37] A. J. Tomasino, "Isaiah 1.1–2.4 and 63–66, and the Composition of the Isaianic Corpus," *JSOT* 57 (1993): 81–98 [chart on 93].

11

Seeing the Faith as Paul Sees It

Wendell Willis

Although the famous hymn in Phil 2:5–11 has received much scholarly attention, such has not been the case with the rest of the book (although recently this gap has partially closed). In his new book on pastoral instruction in Paul, James Thompson has given helpful attention to Philippians by emphasizing Paul's purpose of community formation in the letter.[1] This essay seeks to offer a small support for his assessment of the letter, which I consider fundamentally correct. Beginning with a key word in the letter, we will expand to a representative passage in Philippians and then to some general observations on how Paul conceives ethics as acting in agreement with a Christian outlook.

I proceed by (1) examining some special uses of the word φρονέω in nonbiblical Greek, (2) looking at the use of this word in Philippians, and (3) proposing how this terminology points to a fundamental understanding of a Christian outlook in Paul.

The Significance of φρονέω

When reading the Philippian letter it is striking to notice the frequent appearance of the word φρονέω and its cognates. Of 22 times Paul uses the verb (not including once in Colossians), ten are in Philippians and nine in Romans. He uses the noun forms of φρήν 4 times and φρόνημα 3 times, and compound verb forms 8 times. Several commentators have remarked

---

[1] James Thompson, *Pastoral Ministry according to Paul* (Grand Rapids: Baker Academic, 2006).

that this word for thinking has a connotation of something much more than cogitation. In exploring Paul's use of this language in Philippians (and with a closing glance at other letters), I argue that this word highlights one understanding essentially related to some fundamental concerns of his theology, and stands at an intersection of his ecclesiology, christology, and ethics. It refers to how Paul envisions—and wants the Philippians to follow him in envisioning—the proper way followers of Christ look at their life in the general society.

There are a wide variety of connotations for the verb φρονέω (and its cognates). Danker says that it means "to have an opinion with regard to something . . . to give careful consideration to something . . . to develop an attitude based on careful thought."[2] Liddell, Scott, and Jones, noting that it occurs early and broadly in Greek literature, make a similar observation: "have understanding, be wise, prudent, to think rightly, to think, feel by experience, and be in possession of one's senses."[3] (They give as one submeaning "make common cause," which accords well with conclusions the present study). Paulsen in *EDNT* says this word group "usually refers to a person's insight or inner reflection as opposed to indistinct emotions."[4] Thus there is broad agreement that the basic meaning is to understand, to think, or to have an opinion with regard to something. But there are some particular connotations found in non-biblical Greek associated with special situations, which are especially pertinent to the Philippians usage.

There are uses that focus upon how one regards someone or some group (or is regarded). Of particular importance are those times when φρονέω expresses political or social factions or allegiances.[5] This usage occurs already in Herodotus who says that "the faction (τωυτὸ φρονήσαντες) of Megacles and Lycurgus made common cause to drive Pisistratus from Athens" (*Hist.* 1.60). Dionysius of Halicarnassus, in his *Roman History* (5.21), says that the Fabii family because of their birth and wealth "were regarded as like to the very best" (ὅμοια τοῖς ἀρίστοις φρονοῦντες). Dio (6.80.4) quotes Brutus who criticizes the Senate members who are unwilling to associate as fellow citizens with those regarded as of humble estate (ταπεινοτέρους φρονοῦντες). Dio makes similar comments when describing Pompey fleeing Rome with some senators as Julius Caesar approached, but other senators stayed behind "being at-

---

[2] *BDAG*, 1065–66.

[3] *LSJ*, 1955–56.

[4] Henning Paulsen, "φρονέω," in *EDNT* 3:438–39.

[5] In most cases the political and social groupings are inextricably interwoven.

tached to Caesar's cause" (οἱ μὲν τὰ τοῦ Καίσαρος φρονοῦντες, 41.7). Almost identical is the description of how factions gathered around Caesar vs. Bassus (οἱ τὰ τοῦ Καίσαρος φρονοῦντες, 47.3).[6]

Josephus too has descriptions of political factions around King David. He says for a time Abner was able to sustain allegiance by some in Israel to Ishbosheth (τὰ ἐκείνου φρονοῦντες),[7] until Abner himself cast his lot with David (*Ant.* 7.23). Shortly later, he describes Joab's defense of killing Amasa by having a supporter ask the upset onlookers if they were "for the king" (φρονεῖτε τὰ τοῦ Βασιλέως) and, if so, they should support Joab (*Ant.* 7.286). Another example from Josephus is about the partisans of Aristobulus who were preparing to resist Pompey (*Ant.* 14.58, οἱ δὲ τὰ Ἀριστοβούλου φρονοῦντες) and shortly later (*Ant.* 14.124) to describe the "partisans of Pompey" (οἱ τὰ Πομπηίου φρονοῦντες).

This sense of having a shared outlook in support of a political faction[8] explains why the word may connote harmony. This is expressed in the idiom τὸ αὐτὸ φρονοῦντα. Dio Chrysostom laments the factionalism which divides Tarsus, by saying one could not find two men in the city "who think alike" (τὸ αὐτὸ φρονοῦντες).[9] Appian describes a faction in a Roman civil war led by Cinna and "those who were minded of the same things" (οἳ τὰ αὐτὰ ἐφρόνουν).[10] A Roman prefect in Alexandria gives an edict in which he describes a case of two governors having already reached agreement on guilt and punishment (τὸ αὐτὸ πεφρονηκότες).[11]

---

[6] The explicit contrast of loyalties illustrates the common attitude of society that to be a friend to one person, necessarily caused one to be an enemy of another. See Stanley Stowers, "Friends and Enemies in the Politics of Heaven," in *Pauline Theology* (ed. Jouette Bassler; Minneapolis: Fortress, 1991), 113–14.

[7] The same phrase is used in *Ant.* 12.392 to describe certain Jews who supported the ruler of Syria, Demetrius, and were persecuted by Judas Maccabee. Josephus specifically describes a political faction with this phrase.

[8] Wettstein pointed to Suetonius, *Nero* 63.1 for a parallel meaning, although in Latin (*unum sentientibus*). Jacob Wettstein, *Novum Testamentum Graecum* (reprinted, Graz: Akademische Druck und Verlagsanstalt, 1962), 2:267.

[9] Abraham Malherbe (*Moral Exhortation, a Greco-Roman Sourcebook* [Philadelphia: Westminster, 1986], 144) comments that this is a topos of friendship. That label fits with the Philippian letter, and also with the suggested connotation of factional loyalty. See also the insightful discussion by L. Michael White, "Morality between Two Worlds: A Paradigm of Friendship in Philippians," in *Greeks, Romans and Christians* (ed. David Balch, Everett Ferguson, and Wayne Meeks; Philadelphia: Fortress, 1990), 201–15.

[10] Appian, *Civil Wars* 1.65.

[11] *OGIS*, 669, l. 8. See also Aelius Aristides, 3.242, 24.8. Cited by P. van der Horst, *Aelius Aristides and the New Testament* (Leiden: Brill, 1980), 49, 50 who concludes "From all these passages it is clear that τὸ αὐτὸ φρονεῖν (just like μία γνώμη) is a political term."

This brief lexical sketch suggests that Paul's frequent use of this term in Philippians has a basic political cast, in the sense of his encouraging loyalty to one leader (Paul himself) and a shared outlook—implying rejection of another group and its outlook.[12] However, Philippians is among the least polemical of Paul's letters despite attempts (unsuccessful, in my view) to show that Paul is writing against a definable opposition influencing the Philippian church. How can we make sense of this factional language, in the absence of clear indications of any factions among the Philippians? In seeking an explanation we turn to a specific passage, where the φρονέω words are used with frequency, Philippians 3:15–21.

Philippians 3:15–21

Paul's specific purpose in writing Philippians is very much debated. Some relate it to the receipt of financial help from the Philippian church, and some suggest that there is a problem of disunity in the church.[13] Others suggest a disagreement between Euodia and Syntyche as the real occasion for the letter (but if their relationship was the occasion of the letter, Paul addresses it extremely unclearly and briefly).[14] Still others have suggested that the purpose of the letter is to support the Philippians in the face of inroads by false teachers.[15] However, John Fitzgerald has successfully shown

---

[12] Peter T. O'Brien, *Commentary on Philippians* (NIGTC; Grand Rapids: Eerdmans, 1991), 437. Stowers ("Friends and Enemies," 114–16) notes how in antiquity the assumptions of friendship assumed a friend had enmity to those who were not friends.

[13] Strongly argued by Davorin Peterlin, *Paul's Letter to the Philippians in the Light of Disunity in the Church* (NovTSup 79; Leiden: Brill, 1995). I find this an example of excessive mirror reading, but recognize the extreme thoroughness of his argument. He is aware of the difficulty in such reconstructions (76–79). See also Moises Silva, *Philippians* (Grand Rapids: Baker Academic, 2005), 8, 9, 178–79. Paul Holloway, (*Consolation in Philippians* [Cambridge: University Press, 2001], 422–23) sees a disunity arising from a sense of discomfort in this congregation.

[14] A good, succinct argument is Nils Dahl, "Euodia and Syntyche and Paul's Letter to the Philippians," in *The Social World of the First Christians* (ed. L. Michael White and O. Larry Yarbrough; Philadelphia: Fortress, 1995), 1–15. Dahl appeals to the phrase τό αὐτό φρονεῖν in support of his analysis of the *Sitz im Leben* for the letter. However, the phrase has wide usage and thus cannot be decisive in the historical reconstruction. See the critique by Morna Hooker, "Philippians: Phantom Opponents and Real Sources of Conflict," in *Fair Play: Diversity and Conflicts in Early Christianity* (ed. Ismo Dunderberg, Christopher Tuckett, and Kari Syreeni; Leiden: Brill, 2002), 381.

[15] Robert Jewett, "Conflicting Movements in the Early Church as Reflected in Philippians," *NovT* 12 (1970): 362–90. O'Brien, *Philippians*, 27–35. On the dangers of "mirror reading" the letter, see Marshall, *Philippians*, 98. Stowers ("Friends and Enemies," 116) notes that one cannot appeal τό βλέπετε to urge imminent danger of false teachers. It can

that Philippians can be characterized as a "friendly letter" and much of the prominent terminology in the letter serves this function.[16]

Although there is limited discussion, there is real scholarly disagreement about Phil 3:15–16. This debate includes whether these verses serve as the conclusion of the preceding pericope[17] or begin a new one that continues into ch. 4 (with various concluding verses suggested).[18] One's answer to this question impacts what is regarded as the focus of the pericope, and indirectly the letter itself. Those who see the τοῦτο as looking backward to the discussion of Paul's race, and his not yet having attained perfection, by mirror reading, understand that some Philippians thought that they had and Paul is seeking to correct an overrealized eschatology.[19] If the τοῦτο is understood as forward looking, as I argue, then Paul's emphasis is upon the Philippians continuing to hold to the Christian outlook which he has both preached and embodied among them. Of course, as is often the case, the verses actually may have strong connections both directions. In addition, there is significant disagreement about some of the ideas contained in these verses.

I begin with an observation regarding the placement of the verses, specifically concerning the word τοῦτο (this), used twice in 3:15. The double use of the word is one evidence suggested by Peterlin that 3:15–16 concludes the passage 3:2–14, and points back to that discussion.[20] Fee, who strongly disagrees about 3:15–16 concluding the previous discussion, still agrees that it [τοῦτο] "unquestionably points backward; the differences of opinion lie with to what in vv. 4–14 the τοῦτο refers."[21]

---

mean only "consider" or "reflect upon." "The Philippians may well never have seen Judaizers, but in Paul's rhetoric of friendship/enmity and antithetical exhortation, the Philippians have indeed *heard* about them."

[16] John Fitzgerald, "Philippians in the Light of Some Ancient Discussions of Friendship," in *Friendship, Flattery and Frankness of Speech* (ed. John T. Fitzgerald; NovTSup 82; Leiden: Brill, 1996), 141–62; also see Loveday Alexander ("Hellenistic Letter-forms and the Structure of Philippians," *JSNT* 37 [1989]: 87–101) who makes the comparison with family letters. Rather than seeking to locate a specific "friendship letter" genre it may suffice to say that the vocabulary, the appeals, and the tone of the letter are "friendly."

[17] Peterlin, *Philippians*, 83, 86–87. O'Brien (*Philippians*, 417–20) identifies the pericope as 3:12–16. Marcus Bockmuehl (*The Epistle to the Philippians* [London: A. & C. Black, 1998], 223) calls the section 3:15—21: "Paul's Example Applied."

[18] Gordon Fee, *Paul's Letter to the Philippians* (NICNT; Grand Rapids: Eerdmans, 1995), 351–53; Stephen Fowl, *Philippians* (Grand Rapids: Eerdmans, 2005), 163–64.

[19] Carl Holladay, "Paul's Opponents in Philippians 3," *ResQ* 12 (1969): 83–90.

[20] Peterlin, *Philippians*, 87–88.

[21] Fee, *Philippians*, 356 n. 21.

However, the other place in Philippians where Paul writes τοῦτο φρονεῖτε (2:5) it seems clear that the τοῦτο points forward (to the Christ hymn of 2:6–11). A single parallel cannot decide anything, of course, but it does open up the possibility that in 3:15 also τοῦτο may look forward, not backward. If so, what is "this" which the Philippians are urged to consider? (The significance of this decision is that if τοῦτο points backward, the focus seems to be on Paul's denial of perfection attained—sometimes considered a claim of the Philippians themselves).[22]

The second point to be noticed in 3:15–16 is that it is quickly followed with a summons to follow one positive example, Paul (3:17), as well as an example not to follow (3:18), the "many" who are "enemies of the cross of Christ" and who have their minds focused upon "the things of the earth" (τὰ ἐπίγεια).[23] This pattern also occurs in chapter two, where in explicating "think the same thing" Paul gives three examples for believers to be "mindful" of: Christ (2:6–11), Paul (2:16–17), and Timothy (2:19)[24] as well as another reference to a bad example, namely those who "seek their own things, and not the things of Jesus Christ" (which things can be regarded as the self-sacrificing example of Christ just described in the hymn, and could be summarized as his "cross" as in 3:18,19). [25]

A third observation is that in 3:15, Paul turns from the use of the first person singular (his autobiography from pre-Christian life to the present), and begins using the first plural, to which he returns in 3: 20–21.[26] Thus

---

[22] Peterlin, *Philippians*, 84–85. He argues that Paul is not denying perfection, but that it has been achieved or attained. "If some Philippians buttressed their tendency to perfectionism with false eschatological notions, it is easy to see how those would lead 'to a spirit of haughtiness and pride which in turn was causing strife and faction'" (89, quoting Holladay, "Opponents," 90). (In this way, Peterlin sees several problems: false doctrine, eschatology, Philippian pride, and internal strife. This suggests a multiplicity of interwoven problems in Philippi).

[23] Fowl, *Philippians*, 170. "These two descriptions would seem to indicate that Paul is not talking so much about false teaching (as in Galatians) as a false pattern of thought and action." He is referring to Fee, *Philippians*, 367.

[24] While it is not said here, in I Cor 4:17 Paul describes Timothy as a person who will "explain my ways." That is, Timothy will present the τύπος of Paul (by modeling?). Cf. Stowers, "Friends and Enemies," 116.

[25] Well argued by Paul S. Minear, "Singing and Suffering in Philippi," in *The Conversation Continues* (ed. Robert T. Fortna and Beverly R. Gaventa; Nashville: Abingdon, 1990), 202–19.

[26] Gerald Hawthorne (*Philippians* [WBC 43; Waco, Tex.: Word, 1983], 155) says that the hortatory first plural is used as more delicate than an imperative. O'Brien (*Philippians*, 437) calls the use of the hortatory subjunctive, "tactful." True of course, but the plural includes the Philippians in Paul's "corner."

the section 3:15–21 has a chiastic structure: (A) 3:15–16 the hortatory appeal; (B) 3:17–19 the negative-exemplar; and (A') 3:20–21 another appeal (again using first person plural, as in 3:15, 16).

A fourth consideration is that in 3:21 Paul specifically points the reader to their (his and the Philippians, ἡμῶν) bodies of humiliation (ταπεινώσεως) being transformed by Christ to a resemblance of his own glory. This recalls his appeal in 2:3 that they be "humble minded" (ταπεινοφροσύνῃ) towards each other, and accords with the description of Christ's self-abnegation in the hymn (2:7–8).[27]

For these reasons, I would argue that the pericope should be defined as 3:15–21 (or through 4:1),[28] although I certainly recognize that it builds upon 3:2–14, and, as I have indicated, coheres with the structure of ch. 2 as well.

If this attempt at explaining the passage is acceptable, there may be other useful insights that follow. The letter urges the Philippians to continue to share in the Christian outlook that Paul has conveyed in his presentation of the gospel. This consists of ideas and of examples (but cannot be limited to either alone). Thus it is notable that Paul presents himself as a model of the Christian life, and precisely for the situation in which the church finds itself. He embodies the outlook he is urging. What does Paul say about his life in this letter?

The first thing is that he presents himself as a sufferer for the gospel. In 1:12–18, he expressly says that he is "kept for a defense of the gospel," that is, he not only suffers, but does so precisely for the gospel. He does not know how his situation will end, but whether it is life or death it is a gain (1:19–23; cf. 2:17). This is pertinent information for the Philippians who have been "graced not only to believe in Christ, but to suffer for his sake, *engaged in the same conflict* which you saw and now hear to be mine" (1:29). Paul's example of faithful, hopeful suffering for the gospel while still acting for the benefit of others (1:24–25), serves as an example to the Philippians in their own conflicts for their faith.[29]

The second way in which Paul describes himself in the letter is as one who has renounced any status and privileges that were his in his former life (3:2–11) for the sake of knowing Christ. His example is thus in contrast

---

[27] White, "Morality," 214.

[28] Bockmuehl (*Philippians*, 223–24) and O'Brien (*Philippians*, 345–46) also make this division in the text.

[29] There is insufficient information to determine in what ways or in what degree the Philippians may be suffering.

to others who are unwilling to renounce their status markers (3:2) to serve Christ and thus are indeed "enemies of the cross of Christ" (3:18).[30]

The third way Paul describes himself immediately precedes the passage under consideration. He confesses that he has not yet attained his goal (he has not arrived),[31] but he lives with the goal in view, "the upward call in Christ Jesus" (v.14). He urges the Philippians in v. 16, and in vv. 20–21 to join him in this focused hope. Thus Paul shows the Philippians the correct outlook on the past, present, and future, when seen through the cross.[32]

In summary, in these verses Paul is calling the church to personal loyalty and offering himself as an example (3:17) in contrast to other examples of those who are self-interested. This same point is made in the oft-discussed passage of 4:8,9. Apart from the background and even the specific meaning of the terms in this list of virtues,[33] Paul emphasizes these can be learned through attention to "what you have learned, received, heard and seen *in me*." (In Phil 4:10 where Paul expresses gratitude for their financial gift, he uses φρονέω, which suggests that their gift is a concrete expression of their loyalty to Paul and his presentation of the gospel).

Thus I am in agreement with Troels Engberg-Pedersen who has noted that 3:15–16 most resembles 2:1–5 in that Paul instructs the Philippians how to "think rightly."[34] If, as seems to be the case, 2:1–5 serves to introduce the Christ hymn of 2:6–11 whose purpose is to give the Philippians

---

[30] Minear ("Singing and Suffering," 209) notes that the enemies are not "enemies of Christ" (that is, nonbelievers), but enemies of the "cross of Christ" (that is they minimize the role of the cross in their christology, and especially in their ethical instruction. He aptly summarizes: "they denied the revolutionary force of the *dio* in 2:9. As a result they could share neither the courage nor the joy from the kind of obedience the hymn celebrated."

[31] I agree with Fee that this description is not about personal perfection, but eschatological salvation. But this does not negate that Paul expects Christians to grow into the likeness of Christ (among other places, 4:8–9). Similarly, O'Brien, *Philippians*, 441. Troels Engberg-Pedersen ("Stoicism in Philippians" in *Paul and His Hellenistic Context* [ed. Troels Engberg-Pedersen; Minneapolis: Fortress, 1995], 256–90) presents an interesting analysis claiming that Paul does describe "progress" in the Christian life, using Stoic terms and categories (with variations).

[32] Fowl, *Philippians*, 161; Hooker, "Philippians," 387.

[33] Among other discussion see, Paul Holloway, "*Bono Cogitare*: An Epicurean Consolation in Phil 4:8,9," *HTR* 91 (1998): 89–96.

[34] Engberg-Pedersen, "Stoicism," 276–77; Stephen Fowl, *Story of Christian Ethics in Paul* (JSNTSup 36; Sheffield: Sheffield Academic, 1990). Bockmuehl (*Philippians*, 63) speaks of a "Christian mind" being described. It certainly is that, but perhaps more as well—it is specifically the one taught by Paul.

a master image for the shaping of their lives, then that is also true of 3:15–21.[35]

Having the Christian Outlook

As we noted, among the more interesting features of the letter is its strong irenic tone (with the exception of 3:2–4). The "friendly" nature of this letter makes it difficult to know how to understand a partisan use of the φρον- terminology in the letter. Some have urged that the terminology is about a need for unity in the church, and find confirmation for that demand in 4:2's appeal for Euodia and Syntyche to "think the same thing" in the Lord. But there is no other indication of division within the church (1:15–18 is not referring to people in Philippi, but those around Paul who seek to injure him with their activity), and the very oblique reference to these two women is inadequate to establish the existence of a church quarrel.

Rather, I suggest that the φρον- language does not imply strife, but loyalty to a leader (factionalism perhaps is too strongly negative, but otherwise is accurate). Paul is urging the Philippians to continue to share his cross-shaped outlook (well illustrated by the hymn, but not only there), which is in contrast to other outlooks held by some. Paul is certainly urging unity (as all commentators note)[36] but it is a unity grounded in a *specific outlook* that both he and the Philippians share.[37] This is more than a collection of true beliefs and ideas. It is an outlook determined by the self-sacrificing work of Christ,[38] a gestalt based upon the cross, which is concerned about others, not one's own personal achievements (3:2–6). It is on this basis that they are urged to think the same thing (τὸ αὐτὸ φρονῆτε), which is explicated as "have the same love, be co-souled, and

[35] Fowl, *Philippians*, 163–64.

[36] Fee, *Philippians*, 177–78; Bockmuehl, *Philippians*, 33; Hawthorne, *Philippians*, xlvii; O'Brien, *Philippians*, 36–37.

[37] Thus I share the conclusion of Minear, "Singing and Suffering," 211: "The use of the verb φρονεο (repeated ten times) makes it clear that the selection of one of two opposing mind-sets constituted the central issue of the letter." (This understanding also agrees with the textual variant of v. 16, which is surely not original, adding κανονι to τὸ αὐτὸ φρονεῖν. This understands Paul to be formulating a ruling, and implies a Pauline "canon" of outlook.)

[38] While he does not discuss the political coloring of φρονέω suggested here, C. F. D. Moule's paraphrase of 2:4 is agreeable with my interpretation when he says "adopt towards one another, in your mutual relations, the same attitude as you adopt towards Christ Jesus." C. F. D. Moule, "Further Reflections on Philippians 2:5–11," in *Apostolic History and the Gospel* (ed. W. Ward Gasque and Ralph P. Martin; Grand Rapids: Eerdmans, 1970), 265.

thinking the one thing" (2:2). The summons to "think thus among yourselves according to what also is in Christ Jesus" then is explicated by the hymn. If Euodia and Syntyche will "think the same thing" (that is accept the outlook shaped by the selflessness manifested on the cross), they will be loyal to Paul. What Paul wants is for the Philippians to "regard" and follow the pattern that he has given them in his own person, a pattern that also embodies the values of Christ presented in the hymn. Thus he desires them to be loyal to Christ specifically as taught and modeled by Paul.[39]

In the passage under examination the most controverted (and difficult) clause is in 3:15b, εἴ τι ἑτέρως φρονεῖτε, καὶ τοῦτο ὁ Θεὸς ὑμῖν ἀποκαλύψει. There is a temptation to regard it as ironic (cf. Gal 4:21),[40] but that does not accord with the general friendly tenor of the letter.[41] Taking the passage as straightforward in meaning, Paul is saying if he and the Philippians τοῦτο φρονῶμεν, as described in 3:17–21, then where there are things in their Christian life not yet resolved, God will reveal (instruct) them in these matters as long as they are loyal to the Christian outlook he presents.[42] Everything will be in accord with this basic cross-shaped outlook (cf. Rom 14:6).[43]

It is unnecessary to look for a specific conflict at Phillipi to support a view that φρονέω has a political dimension.[44] By this time Paul certainly knew that there were other Christian factions who also confessed Christ, but who had a radically different outlook (the circumcision party, for example). Because of those experiences he is anxious about the Philippians

---

[39] Fowl, *Philippians*, 166. Fee, *Philippians*, 381.

[40] Hawthorne, *Philippians*, 156.

[41] Andrew T. Lincoln, *Paradise Now and Not Yet* (Grand Rapids: Baker, 1981), 93–94. Bockmuehl (*Philippians*, 226–27). does not suggest it is ironical, but does think Paul is criticizing those who may differ with him. Possibly so, but I doubt he is doing so here—he is optimistic about their following his teaching and example, and learning by doing so. O'Brien (*Philippians*, 435–36) presents a good critique of the suggestion of irony in this passage.

[42] Fee, *Philippians*, 355) "The basic *assumption* of the application . . . is *mutuality between him and them*, not fundamental differences of opinion on things that really matter." See also Hooker, "Philippians," 391.

[43] So Bockmuehl, *Philippians*, 226.

[44] Minear ("Singing and Suffering," 208) describes those Paul characterizes here as "enemies," who are apparently leaders within the Philippian church (possibly including the overseers and deacons mentioned in 1:1 and even Euodia and Syntyche). I am less confident that there is an existing opposition addressed. While that is possible, it is sufficient to say Paul critiques a view held by some Christians, but his emphasis is positive: "remain loyal to me and my gospel."

being swayed from their loyalty to him (more accurately, from his view of the Christian outlook modeled upon the cross). Paul is writing to his friends, encouraging their loyalty to him and his gospel. (The brief description of the "dogs" in 3:2 only alludes to such groups, really to serve as a foil for Paul's self-description that follows.)[45]

Broadening the Field of View

While it not necessary to show that the meaning of φρονέω here suggested for Philippians is used in other Pauline letters, it may be that a quick review of other letters may support the suggestions made here. So in conclusion, let us look at some other occurrences in Paul.

Although proportionally less impressive, the number of uses in Romans is only slightly less than in Philippians. With two exceptions, they occur in the concluding chapters and Paul's response to tensions within the Roman church (without taking time to explore to what degree this discussion is related to specific presenting problems vs. Paul's own agendas). In Rom 12:16 the church is urged to think the same thing τὸ αὐτὸ φρονοῦντες) which is defined as not "thinking high-mindedly" (μὴ τὰ ὑψηλὰ φρονοῦντες; cf. 11:20), rather to "associate with the humble."[46]

The uses in Romans 14 and 15 are specifically related to the concerns in the church, and the first (14:6) uses φρονέω in the broad meaning of "regard" or "hold an opinion" as Paul describes those who eat and do not eat. But even here, the one who "regards" a certain day is still grouped with those who "regard the lord" and both are loyal to Christ. The same association of appeal for mutual acceptance based upon a common loyalty to Christ is found in the summary wish/prayer that the "God of encouragement" would give them "to think the same thing among themselves, according to Christ Jesus" (15:5).

The idiomatic phrase τὸ αὐτὸ φρονεῖτε is also found in the conclusion of 2 Corinthians within a list of five mutual encouragement terms. But most relevant to the present argument is Gal 5:10, where Paul says that he is persuaded concerning them (in the Lord) that despite the pressures from the Judaizers, the Galatian believers will not think otherwise

---

[45] Bockmuehl, *Philippians*, 182–83.

[46] The combination of terms recalls the criticism by Dionysius of Halicarnassus of those unsociable refusing to share (ἀκοινώνητα) with those regarded as of "humbler estate" (ταπεινοτέρους φρονοῦτες) VI.80.4. The essential role of Paul's life for his preaching is well argued by Victor Furnish in "Paul the ΜΑΡΤΥΣ," in *Witness and Existence* (eds. Philip E. Devenish and George L. Goodwin; Chicago: University of Chicago Press, 1989), 71–79.

(οὐδὲν ἄλλο φρονήσετε) and that those who seek to change their loyalty to Christ (as Paul preached him) will bear divine judgment. That is, the Galatians will remain loyal to Paul and his gospel.

Conclusion

The Philippian church has been exceptionally close to Paul since the beginning of his mission work in Greece. To our knowledge, only they have financially aided him, and they have done so since the beginning of their association together. The letter he sent them was one of friendship, and as a friend he stresses their mutual loyalty (as the frequent occurrence of the κοινον- words shows) and their shared outlook about the Christian faith. They see Christ as Paul does, and both seem to embody that vision in life.

The frequent use of φρονέω (and cognates) in this letter draws upon a background of political loyalties based upon common purpose (or a common leader). These loyalties are most commonly set in opposition to other groups (factions). So the word both means what one "regards" as correct, and the support of others who have the same outlook. Paul alludes to their common history to demarcate the group, he quotes the Christ hymn and points to his life to focus their shared vision, and he contrasts their group with others who have a different regard, especially those that disregard the paradigmatic role of the cross for Christian living. Paul and the church have a unity based on a common outlook and common loyalty to Christ and his cross. Paul's outlook, his view of Christ's work, his apostleship, the church, and the proper life in Christ are all unified in this appeal.

Renewing Contexts

12

Hebrews and Philosophy
A Question of Intersection

Frederick D. Aquino

Does the mode of argumentation in Hebrews rely primarily on other biblical texts? Or does the author of this epistle follow the Alexandrian tradition and use philosophy to "ensure that the interpretation of Scripture" coheres with the insights of reason?[1] Should Hebrews be construed as an early form of Christian philosophy, thereby challenging the claim that such a phenomenon does not emerge until the second century? This epistle has certainly made biblical scholars scratch their heads and wonder about its line of argumentation and its philosophical backdrop. In fact, James Thompson has dedicated a good portion of his scholarship trying to answer such questions, thus delving into the complex world of Hebrews and unearthing its exegetical, theological, and philosophical insights. I applaud his willingness to pursue the intersection of biblical and philosophical ways of thinking in the text of Hebrews.

Recently, Thompson has unpacked the significance of terms such as the fitting, the necessary, and the impossible in Hebrews while tracing their philosophical antecedents.[2] The question here is to what extent the

---

[1] James W. Thompson, "The Appropriate, the Necessary, and the Impossible: Faith and Reason in Hebrews," in *The Early Church in Its Context: Essays in Honor of Everett Ferguson* (ed. Abraham J. Malherbe, Frederick W. Norris, and James Thompson; Leiden: Brill, 1998), 302.

[2] In an unpublished paper, Thompson has also recently explored the connection between the one and many in antecedent philosophical traditions and the world of Hebrews.

Alexandrian tradition has shaped the philosophical moves and arguments in Hebrews. With this is mind, I turn my attention to this piece, offer a brief commentary on Thompson's basic argument, and then make some constructive suggestions mainly along the lines of how one might reconceive the intersection of philosophy and biblical studies. Thompson has helped us both to identify some key philosophical insights in Hebrews and to rethink our assumptions, at least implicitly, about the relationship between biblical studies and philosophy. The time has come to move the discussion along a bit.

The Logic of Hebrews: A Question of Philosophical Antecedents

In "The Appropriate, the Necessary, and the Impossible: Faith and Reason in Hebrews," Thompson notes that an appeal to axiomatic principles undergirds the logic and overall argument of Hebrews. The use of self-evident principles as a basis for theological reflection in Hebrews, though noted by scholars, has not received sufficient attention. Along with Scripture, the author of Hebrews appeals to indisputable principles (Heb 7:7) to substantiate a Christian soteriology of divine descent into the human situation. This mode of argumentation is without obvious parallel in other biblical texts, and the author like other writers in the Alexandrian tradition tries to support "the Christian confession on rational grounds."[3] Furthermore, the numerous linguistic affinities with Philo and the significance of Hebrews in Alexandrian Christianity warrant such an inquiry. Accordingly, Thompson's aim is to decipher whether Hebrews fits within the larger context of the Alexandrian tradition, or more precisely is a concrete example of this tradition.

The fitting, the necessary, and the impossible serve as givens and to some extent function as rational grounds for sustaining Christian faith. I say "to some extent" because the author, as Thompson points out, never explains how providing salvation through suffering is necessary, in what sense this kind of activity is a befitting of God, and why salvation without the sacrifice of Christ is impossible. Alternatively, the epistemic glue that links the author and readers is the list of principles that they readily accept as self-evident from a Christian point of view, not from some more widespread notion of what is befitting of God and necessary for human flourishing. These starting points perhaps function analogously to what Aristotle calls first principles—non-demonstrative starting points upon

---

[3] Thompson, "The Appropriate," 303.

which subsequent reasoning and argumentation emerge. That is, the author begins with particular assumptions, framed within a Christian narrative, while seeking some point of contact with the broader philosophical world. Thus, the author tackles the question of the fitting, the necessary, and the impossible as realities self-evident to Christians.

Thompson, however, queries whether the author's use of these first principles would be intelligible to philosophical predecessors in the Alexandrian tradition. The appeal to these principles as a soteriological basis for divine activity "is a remarkable *tour de force* in the ancient context, where the association of God with human suffering would have been abhorrent."[4] Most would struggle to see how the author's soteriological conclusion stems from the premises enunciated in Hebrews. For example, the idea that the divine descends into the human situation and provides salvation through suffering would be absurd to someone like Philo. He would have difficulty in following the author's use of these three principles: (1) suffering is a fitting means through which God saves humanity; (2) salvation is impossible without the sacrifice of Christ; and (3) and the sacrificial death of Christ is necessary for ratifying the new covenant.

In what sense, then, are these categories of the fitting, the necessary, and the impossible axiomatic? Thompson contends that the common ground, for example, between the author of Hebrews and Philo is the employment of philosophy to explain and defend the faith on rational grounds, even if there are different understandings of what constitutes a fitting and necessary activity of God.[5] So, the philosophical link is methodological in that both writers see the importance of thinking through the philosophical implications of their inherited conceptions of God without sacrificing their theological perspectives. Material differences aside, they "share a tradition in which their faith commitment stands in tension with and commonly takes precedence over their philosophy."[6] The conclusion here does not fit the standard accounts of fideism and rationalism. In fact, it may be time to flesh out more robust accounts of faith and reason, thereby expanding the options for understanding the process of belief-formation. The overall aim would be to carve out broader and more refined accounts of rationality that reflect actual conditions under which Christians form and sustain beliefs.[7]

---

[4] Ibid., 305.
[5] Ibid., 303.
[6] Ibid., 317.
[7] See Randall Basinger, "Faith/Reason Typologies: A Constructive Proposal," *CSR* 36

Thompson's main concern is the appeal to rational grounds as a basis for developing a soteriology of Christian faith. In fact, no other biblical texts tie the impossible and the necessary to soteriology. The argument in Hebrews "represents such a remarkable departure from the common soteriological reflection in Scripture that one must ask who would have been persuaded by it."[8] I wonder what Thompson means by "common soteriological reflection in Scripture." The soteriological terrain is conceptually fluid and diverse both in Scripture and in subsequent doctrinal developments.[9] The common ground is the attempt to connect salvation to human experience in all its variety. Thompson's point here may be that Hebrew appeals more to principles that have linguistic affinity with the Alexandrian tradition than to the antecedent insights of Scripture alone.

Hebrews, then, may be an early example of a specific kind of Christian philosophy that draws from various resources (e.g., Scripture, reason, tradition, and moral philosophy).[10] Yet, incorporating insights from different fields of knowledge is not necessarily unique to Hebrews. For example, Paul's epistemology of exemplarism in Philippians echoes other philosophical traditions, and so in reinterpreting Hebrews we need to rethink our hermeneutical and epistemic conceptions. In other words, Hebrews does not follow the logic of *sola scriptura* but seems to fit the long-standing tradition of working through philosophical concepts and pursuing their theological implications. Perhaps, Hebrews shows multifaceted ways of shaping Christian identity. Thompson's retort might be that Paul's

---

(1997): 62–73; William J. Wainwright, *Reason and the Heart: A Prolegomenon to a Critique of Passional Reason* (Ithaca, N.Y.: Cornell University Press, 1995); Mikael Stenmark, *Rationality in Science, Religion, and Everyday Life: A Critical Evaluation of Four Models of Rationality* (Notre Dame, Ind.: University of Notre Dame Press, 1995); Frederick D. Aquino, *Communities of Informed Judgment* (Washington, D.C.: Catholic University of America Press, 2004); "Broadening Horizons: Constructing an Epistemology of Religious Belief," *LS* 30 (2005): 198–213; and John Cottingham, *The Spiritual Dimension: Religion, Philosophy and Human Value* (Cambridge: Cambridge University Press, 2005).

[8] Thompson, "The Appropriate," 305.

[9] See Paul Fiddes, *Past Event and Present Salvation: The Christian Idea of Atonement* (Louisville: Westminster John Knox, 1989).

[10] Thompson (*The Beginnings of Christian Philosophy: The Epistle to Hebrews* [Washington, D.C.: Catholic Biblical Association of America, 1982], 17) argues that the impact of Greek philosophy can be seen already in Hebrews 5:11–14. Here the author employs "language that is greatly indebted to the tradition of Hellenistic *paideia* which was commonplace among philosophers of the Hellenistic period." In fact, Thompson argues that the presence of the language of instruction (e.g., levels of instruction) in this text "raises the possibility that Hebrews represents an initial stage in the adoption of Hellenistic *paideia* and in the development of Christian theology as it was further expanded by Christian Platonists" (18).

appeal to the cross is "wisdom to the initiated but foolishness to the world (1 Corinthians 2:6)," whereas the author of Hebrews employs "rational argument to persuade his readers and to provide the basis for his exhortations."[11] From another angle, one could say that Paul and the author of Hebrews embody different modes of argumentation, but they nonetheless draw from philosophical traditions. Though Paul steeps some of his arguments in moral philosophical trajectories (e.g., the use of paraenesis in Philippians), they do not function as a philosophical basis for his theological reflection. Later, I argue that we need to rethink the intersection of philosophical and biblical insights more as a correlation between discourse and way of life than as an apologetic task.

Notwithstanding some of my questions and observations, Thompson astutely uncovers the complex relationship between Hebrews and the Alexandrian tradition, thereby challenging facile assumptions about the formation of early Christian philosophy. His scholarly work has shown the extent to which Hebrews joins the conversation about the rationality of Christian belief, and it implicitly questions claims that construe Christianity and philosophical influences as mutually exclusive traditions. As a result, this may be a good place to make some constructive suggestions about the relationship between philosophy and biblical studies. As I intend to argue, the relationship between Christianity and philosophical schools is more about transformation than about faith taking precedence over philosophical reflection. It is out of the philosophical commitments that antecedent assumptions are transformed into doctrinal formulations and materialized as a specific way of being in the world.

Constructive Link: Discourse and Way of Life

Hebrews fits, though from a different angle and perhaps in an incipient way, the ancient and patristic reflection on what is befitting of the divine. As Pierre Hadot has shown, the shape of early Christian thought occurred within the larger of context of the schools of philosophy, though the doctrinal formulations (e.g., the Trinity, the incarnation) were materially specific to Christian identity. The distinction between spirituality and philosophical reflection is more modern than ancient. Philosophizing in the ancient world involved choosing a school and living out its practices.[12] Hebrews makes perfect sense here; it follows the logic and mode of reflection in the

---

[11] Thompson, "The Appropriate," 305.
[12] Pierre Hadot, *Philosophy as a Way of Life: Spiritual Exercises from Socrates to Foucault* (Oxford: Blackwell, 1995), 60.

ancient world by combining philosophical reflection (discourse) and way of life (liturgical practices). The appeal to principles most likely operates from a particularist epistemology in which the author begins with first principles, from a Christian point of view, and then proceeds to work out a more comprehensive understanding of the human situation.[13] Hence, Hebrews does not deduce a comprehensive theory of salvation from general philosophical principles nor does it provide a systematic philosophy of what is necessary and fitting of the divine. It engages in an early form of philosophical exegesis, from a Christian point of view, highlighting issues that subsequent thinkers such as Clement of Alexandria, Origen, and Gregory Nyssa pick up and develop.[14]

In ancient philosophy, the intersection of discourse and way of life held for most of the schools. Discourse refers to philosophical reflection mediated through particular exercises such as attention, meditation, self-control, and so on. Way of life is the existential form embodied in the practices of a particular school. Yet, forming a way of life is not an add-on to the process of philosophical reflection. Rather, way of life and discourse form "a complex interrelation with critical reaction to other existential attitudes, with global vision of a certain way of living and of seeing the world."[15] Moreover, an exegetical component plays an important role in the task of philosophy, since the search for truth includes grappling with authoritative texts and exploring their existential meaningfulness. In other words, the ancients did not divorce philosophical queries from exegetical procedures; rather, they tackled issues that arose from and were expressed through pivotal texts.[16] Our contemporary philosophical context is obviously different than the ancient one, spurning the appeal to authority and divorcing the intellectual from spiritual practices. However, the ancient practice of philosophy called for a more holistic approach and envisioned the philosophical task as a unitary act that entailed living out the im-

---

[13] For further reflection on particularism, see Roderick M. Chisholm, *The Problem of the Criterion* (Milwaukee: Marquette University Press, 1973); William J. Abraham, *Crossing the Threshold of Divine Revelation* (Grand Rapids: Eerdmans, 2006); and Brad Hooker and Margaret Olivia Little, eds., *Moral Particularism* (Oxford: Oxford University Press, 2000).

[14] For a fascinating treatment of the theological expressions of *paideia* in early Christianity, see Werner Jaegar, *Early Christianity and Greek Paideia* (Cambridge: Harvard University Press, 1961). For the pedagogical implications of the question of what is befitting of God in our contemporary context, see Frederick D. Aquino and Mark W. Hamilton, "Theological Higher Education Befitting God: An Experiment," *CHE* 5 (2006): 21–36.

[15] Pierre Hadot, *What is Ancient Philosophy?* (Cambridge: Harvard University Press, 2002), 3.

[16] Hadot, *Philosophy as a Way of Life*, 73.

plications of one's logic, cosmology, and ethics. In this regard, a person embedded in one of the ancient schools no longer simply studied different subject matters; rather, the aim was "above all the choice of a form of life, to which philosophical discourse then [gave] justifications and theoretical foundations."[17]

Perhaps the time has come to relocate the enterprise of biblical interpretation from the epistemic gatekeeper, mediated through historical criticism, to a more robust connection between skills of interpretation and spiritual practices. This certainly does not mean an abandonment of critical skills of interpretation; rather, it calls for seeing how biblical interpretation and its concomitant practices correlate discourse and way of life. For example, concern for historical details may be reconceived as a spiritual discipline. Obviously, intellectual virtues may materialize in thick and thin shades of training, background, demeanor, and expertise, assuming that not everyone comes to the table from the same vantage point. The intersection of domain-specific fields of knowledge certainly calls for stretching one's disciplinary neck and glancing at different critical issues. Taking seriously the dialectic of discourse and way of life is not an escape from rigorous or critical thought but a redirection of priorities. It includes conversation with different disciplines (e.g., history, philosophy, and science) but also calls for the self to be formed by the knowledge acquired. The whole business of deciphering what is befitting of the divine seems to be precisely a spiritual exercise honed by philosophical exegesis.

The concern about reconstructing the biblical world and separating it from philosophical imposition is a modern crisis, reflecting a certain view of history, tradition, and biblical texts. It may be helpful as we rethink the relationship between disciplines to see the importance of connecting the life of the mind with spiritual and philosophical exercises. In this regard, Jeffrey Stout has shown how the modern flight from authority solidified the privatization of religious discourse and accelerated the quest for canonizing the right theological methodology. With the emergence of competing religious authorities in the Protestant Reformation, conventional means for resolving theological disputes were no longer sufficient.[18] The failure to agree on the locus of authority for judging theological ideas pre-

---

[17] Ibid., 281.
[18] Jeffrey Stout, *The Flight from Authority: Religion, Morality, and the Quest for Autonomy* (Notre Dame: University of Notre Dame Press, 1981), 41.

cipitated both the long search for new grounds of epistemic certainty and a better way of achieving agreement in the public arena.[19]

The crisis of authority, thus described, warrants an expansion of both our interpretive horizons and our philosophical practices, even the assumption that early Christian philosophical reflection was nothing more than a rational defense of the faith. As Jaroslav Pelikan, for example, points out in his Gifford Lectures, the Cappadocians "stood clearly in the tradition of Classical Greek culture, and each was at the same time intensely critical of that tradition."[20] They operated with a dialectic of doctrine and clear reasoning. Thus, pitting the Greek tradition of natural theology and Christian thought against one another is unwarranted. In other words, theological reflection was both appreciative and critical of classical Greek thought, and thus it could appropriate the riches of various fields of knowledge in the Greek world. Ethics is one illustration of how Christian notions of morality fit the broader dialectic of discourse and way of life. Moral philosophy was not simply theoretical reflection about life but also internalized epistemic virtues (e.g., humility, understanding, and wisdom) so as to enable people to embody a particular way of being in the world. In this sense, "moral philosophy was promissory, it dealt with what could be. For this reason ethics in antiquity was a matter less of what one ought to do according to universal notions of right and wrong than of what kind of person one can become by living a certain way."[21]

---

[19] Hadot (*Philosophy as a Way of Life*, 107, 269) argues that Christianity, from its inception, presented itself as a philosophical way of being in the world." However, with the beginning of medieval Scholasticism, we see "a clear distinction between *theologia* and *philosophia*. Theology became conscious of its autonomy *qua* supreme science, while philosophy was emptied of its spiritual exercises which, from now on, were relegated to Christian mysticism and ethics. Reduced to the rank of a 'handmaid of theology,' philosophy's role was henceforth to furnish theology with conceptual—and hence purely theoretical—material."

[20] Jaroslav Pelikan, *Christianity and Classical Culture: The Metamorphosis of Natural Theology in the Christian Encounter with Hellenism* (New Haven: Yale University Press, 1993), 9. Pelikan adds (38) that "in the classical systems, natural theology tended to present itself primarily as an alternative or even an antidote to cultic practices. However, natural theology underwent a fundamental *metamorphosis*. It became not only an apologetic but a presupposition for dogmatic theology." Natural theology and the formation of Christian doctrine "were not to be seen as antithetical but as complimentary and mutually supportive. The Cappadocians could evoke the natural processes of growth and development as a key metaphor for the gradual additions, advances, progressions of Christian history to the divine revelation of what the New Testament had described as that faith which God had entrusted to his people once for all" (229).

[21] Robert Wilken, *The Spirit of Early Christianity* (New Haven: Yale University Press, 2003), 273. Wilken adds that "without an understanding of the ancient moralists Aris-

Thus, an apt description of such an enterprise might be transformation rather than accommodation. Early Christian writers interacted with philosophical concepts, not from some alien posture, but as concrete thinkers saturated in and critical of the antecedent philosophical terrain. Hebrews seems to follow the same logic. The author links the Christian story with existing philosophical ideas—e.g., the fitting, the necessary, and the impossible—and yet envisions a new understanding of divine activity from a Christian soteriological framework. Consequently, it seems fundamentally mistaken "to spurn Classical learning in the name of Christian piety and orthodoxy."[22] If anything, the early Christian writers, including the writer of Hebrews, took this philosophical backdrop seriously and moreover tried to show how Christian doctrine was the logical culmination of *paideia*.

Perhaps I need to clarify my comments about *paideia*. Hebrews may be an incipient form of Christian *paideia*, drinking from the well of this ancient tradition while rethinking its locus of expression.[23] The common ground is the advancement of knowledge and learning. While the author of Hebrews does not show explicitly thorough indebtedness to the model of *paideia*, as one sees in Philo and in Clement of Alexandria, "he shares the conviction of his contemporaries that one advances from lower to higher realities through training."[24] In this sense, the author agrees with the tradition of *paideia* that the self engages in the lifetime task of cultivating the ideal of a fully developed human mind.[25] The subject matter of Hebrews is the logic of "higher studies" materialized, for example, in "the heavenly high priesthood of Christ."[26] Consequently, the paragon of human excellence is found in the incarnation of the divine pedagogue—Christ the pioneer of human salvation.

The author of Hebrews moves the readers to see the incomparable nature of the Son, encouraging them to endure hardship and to reaffirm their Christian identity. The logic here, at least implicitly, seems to fit

---

totle, Seneca, Cicero, and Epictetus, one cannot enter the world of early Christian ethics, yet as soon as one takes in hand the essays of Clement, Tertullian or Ambrose or reads the sermons of Gregory of Nyssa or Augustine, it is clear that something new is afoot" (275).

[22] Pelikan, *Christianity and Classical Culture*, 21.

[23] Thompson (*Beginnings,* 17–40) provides a fascinating comparison of Hebrews 5:11–14 and the Greek philosophies of *paideia*.

[24] Thompson, *Beginnings*, 39.

[25] H. I. Marrou, *A History of Education in Antiquity* (trans. George Lamb; Madison: University of Wisconsin Press, 1990), 98–99.

[26] Thompson, *Beginnings*, 39.

the tradition of Christian *paideia* in that philosophical knowledge of the Christian faith leads to human flourishing.[27] Hebrews does not quite fit the later phenomenon of Christian paideia, but its overall argument presupposes it. Perhaps, this explains why its philosophical methodology does not entirely make sense in terms of the Old Testament or does not cohere with other New Testament writings. Nevertheless, it seems to represent an early Christian form of philosophy in which the author articulates a philosophical way of life and exhorts the readers to continue in their journey of faith.

Unearthing Early Christian Philosophical Ways of Life

Hebrews does not engage the rich conceptual vocabulary of the Greek tradition simply as an apologetic schema, but rather as a theological and philosophical rationale for the Christian community. It is a Christian philosophy, not in the narrow or modern sense of the word, but in the broader and ancient sense of the word, as we have seen in Hadot's account. In this regard, Thompson has argued that Hebrews is "a transition to Christian philosophy." [28] I suppose what he means here is that Hebrews is an early version of later developments of Christian philosophy seen in figures such as Clement, Origen, and Gregory of Nyssa. In terms of Hadot's discussion, Hebrews articulates a particular way of understanding God, self, and world and fleshes out a certain way of being in the world. Perhaps, one constructive possibility is greater focus on the connection between early Christian biblical texts and existing understandings of what constitutes a philosophical way of life. This is not equivalent to tracing the antecedent philosophical influences embedded in biblical texts. As we have seen, Hebrews shapes a philosophical theology that enables the community of faith both to embody an authentic Christian identity and to flourish in a restless and difficult world. The paragon to be imitated is the Son, who has freed the community from fear of death and has empowered it to reconfigure a fuller version of what it means to be human.

---

[27] As Jaeger (*Early Christianity and Greek Paideia*, 12) points out, "in calling Christianity the paideia of Christ, the imitator stresses the intention of the apostle to make Christianity appear to be a continuation of the classical Greek paideia, which it would be logical for those who possessed the older one to accept. At the same time he implies that the classical paideia is being superseded by making Christ the center of the new culture. The ancient paideia thereby becomes its instrument."

[28] Thompson, *Beginnings*, 159.

The options for exploring the intersection of philosophy and biblical studies are neither accommodation to the prevailing philosophical perspectives nor one-sided appeals to an uncontaminated approach to theological reflection. Rather, what we need is a theological model that synthesizes insights from various fields of knowledge without sacrificing the integrity of domain-specific procedures of inquiry. Hebrews fits such a description; it resists our purist impositions, challenges our fears of alien epistemic schemes, and resists rigid compartmentalization of subject matters. The apparent absurdity of the divine entering the world of becoming certainly revises and critiques the antecedent assumption about divine exemption from human contingency. The implicit argument here is that divine intervention in the human situation, especially when it is down and out, is an entirely fitting act. In this sense, Hebrews invites the readers and perhaps us today to consider whether the humanity of God is befitting or praiseworthy. Both descriptive enterprises without normative inquiry, couched within a broader network of spiritual practices, and constructive proposals without proper analysis of the interpretive intricacies fall short of unearthing the epistemic hints in early Christian texts. The time has come for us to rethink the intersection of the varied disciplines, perhaps with the distinction between discourse and way of life in mind.

It is common for biblical scholars to follow the old trajectory of historicism while guarding against the importation of alien epistemic schemes onto the strange world of Scripture.[29] The key is to sweep away the rubbish of the ages, take the Hellenism out of the pure gospel or distinguish the biblical from the antecedent philosophical influences. The claim is that doctrines such as the trinity and the incarnation were subtle impositions or imports of Greek philosophy on the Christian faith. In this regard, Thompson's reflection on Hebrews and the antecedent philosophical in-

---

[29] Pelikan (*Christianity and Classical Culture*, 21) aptly summarizes the interpretive issue: "Especially since the Protestant Reformation, charges and countercharges of 'Hellenization,' together with the question of whether Hellenization represented 'apostasy' or 'progress,' have shaped theological controversy, philosophical speculation, and historical interpretation. For those like the Cambridge Platonists, who affirmed the validity of attempts at a synthesis of Hellenism and the gospel, the kind of natural theology epitomized by the Cappadocians was a foundation for even bolder attempts. In contrast, those like Albrecht Ritschl and Adolf von Harnack, who strove to purify the gospel of alien elements, saw in such a natural theology the channel for a distortion that was all the more insidious because it was invoked in support of orthodox dogma. Frequently overlooked in the polemics of these debates have been the specifics of this 'natural theology' and of its place not only in the speculative system of the Cappadocians but in the Greek-speaking Orthodox Christianity for which they were such influential interpreters."

fluences is nuanced, showing that the text of Hebrews falls within the long-standing reflection, though not persuasively to all representatives of the Alexandrian tradition, on what is befitting of God.

Obviously, the shift from the ancient world to ours is complex and warrants careful mining of epistemic hints. Yet, the resurgence of interest in the ancient connection between discourse and way of life makes such constructive moves intriguing and fruitful.[30] I understand the difference between the context of early Christian thought and our own, but the eclipse of spiritual formation from theological reflection heightens our awareness of the need for greater inquiry about the conditions under which beliefs are formed, including the cognitive as well as the emotional, the practical as well as the theoretical.[31] Furthermore, the ancient connection between ethics and epistemology needs to be fleshed out with greater clarity and relevance. The key here is to avoid the mistaken assumption that knowledge implies that only good people can know. Rather, the key is to see how a set of interpretive practices and a network of intellectual virtues help us to spell out a vibrant epistemology of Christian theology.

---

[30] E.g., Martha C. Nussbaum, *The Therapy of Desire: Theory and Practice in Hellenistic Ethics* (Princeton: Princeton University Press, 1994); idem, *Love's Knowledge: Essays on Philosophy and Literature* (Oxford: Oxford University Press, 1990).

[31] Cottingham, *The Spiritual Dimension*, x. See also Mark R. Wynn, *Emotional Experience and Religious Understanding: Integrating Perception, Conception and Feeling* (Cambridge: Cambridge University Press, 2005).

13

A Reluctant Bride
Finding A Life For Damaris of Athens (Acts 17:34)

J. W. Childers

THE Royal Collection of the Victoria & Albert Museum in London boasts a painting done in 1515–16 by the Italian Renaissance artist Raphael de Urbino: "Paul Preaching at Athens." Executed in preparation for one of a set of ten ornate tapestries commissioned by Pope Leo X to adorn the Sistine Chapel, the cartoon depicts the Apostle Paul engaged in passionate discourse at the Areopagus (Acts 17).[1] The composition exhibits those qualities that enabled Raphael's work to make a lasting impact on the conventions of narrative history painting in Europe. The Apostle's intensity and the riveted aspect of the crowd combine with the grand scale of the classical setting to evoke within the viewer the sense of having become a privileged witness to a pivotal moment in history. Apart from one or two anachronistic touches—such as the conventional presence of the rotund Pope Leo at Paul's side—the scene anticipates the eventual outcome of the encounter between nascent Christianity and learned paganism by portraying an audience raptly attentive to Paul's speech. Most prominent in the audience is a couple in the lower foreground; the man extends his arms receptively towards Paul, while the woman accompanies her husband up the steps, looking on and vaguely pensive. The presence of the solitary

---

[1] See *The Cartons of Raphael D'Urbino* (London: Vernor, Hood, and Sharpe, 1809), 120 *et passim*; Johann David Passant, *Raphael of Urbino and his Father Giovanni Santi* (London: Macmillan, 1872; repr. *Connoisseurship, Criticism, and Art History in the Nineteenth Century*; New York; Garland, 1978), 256, 260–62.

woman confirms the identity of the couple: Dionysius the Areopagite and the woman clearly intended to be seen as his spouse, Damaris of Athens.

The woman's slightly bemused expression is understandable. Although in Acts 17:34 she receives no less notice than Dionysius, his reputation in later tradition would strikingly overshadow hers. However, the assessment that "while Damaris makes no further appearance in history, the destiny of Dionysius would be far different,"[2] is only half right. The subsequent fame of Dionysius is undeniable; yet Damaris herself does not, in fact, vanish without account. Although only slight notice of her occurs in the biblical text, Christian tradition developed for her an intriguing identity connubially subjugated to that luminary man of legend, Dionysius the Areopagite. In more recent times, she has been the focus of feminist interpretations of the New Testament. As the preoccupation of "pious fantasy"[3] or a champion of "philosophically engaged women" in early Christianity,[4] Paul's female convert could scarcely have anticipated the lore that has evolved around her as a result of the solitary reference to her in Acts 17:34.

Meager Notice: Naming Damaris

The present exploration of the Damaris tradition begins with a citation of that original notice, occurring just after Paul's Areopagus speech:

> τινὲς δὲ ἄνδρες κολληθέντες αὐτῷ ἐπίστευσαν, ἐν οἷς καὶ Διονύσιος ὁ Ἀρεοπαγίτης καὶ γυνὴ ὀνόματι Δάμαρις καὶ ἕτεροι σὺν αὐτοῖς. (Acts 17:34)[5]

---

[2] Claudio Moreschini and Enrico Norelli, *Early Christian Greek and Latin Literature. A Literary History*, vol. 2: *From the Council of Nicaea to the Beginning of the Medieval Period* (trans. Matthew J. O'Connell; Peabody, Mass.: Hendrickson, 2005), 665; cf. J. Roloff's observation that the name of Dionysius has evoked much more interest and speculation than that of Damaris (*Die Apostelgeschichte* [NTD 5; repr. Göttingen: Vandenhoeck & Ruprecht, 1988], 267).

[3] Ernst Haenchen, *The Acts of the Apostles. A Commentary* (trans. Bernard Noble et al.; Philadelphia: Westminster, 1971), 527 n.5.

[4] Ivoni Richter Reimer, *Women in the Acts of the Apostles: A Feminist Liberation Perspective* (trans. Linda M. Maloney; Minneapolis, Minn.: Fortress, 1995), 247.

[5] The text is that of NA^{27}; Constantin Tischendorf, *Novum Testamentum graeca: editio octava critica maior* (Leipzig: Hinrichs, 1872); and Hermann Freiherr von Soden, *Die Schriften des Neuen Testaments in ihrer ältesten erreichbaren Textgestalt hergestellt auf Grund ihrer Textgeschichte*, vol. 2.1: *Text mit Apparat* (Göttingen: Vandenhoeck & Ruprecht, 1913). The significant variations will be discussed below.

> But certain men joined him and believed, among whom were Dionysius the Areopagite and a woman by the name of Damaris, and others with them.

The very name *Damaris* is problematic. Its rare attestation in Greek literature and inscriptions has lead some modern scholars since at least Grotius (†1645) to conclude that the name is a corrupt form of Δαμάλις ("heifer"),[6] a female name that is better attested[7] and even occurs in the fifth-century Old Latin Acts palimpsest Floriacensis (*h*).[8]

Concerns about the rarity of the name and the supposed impropriety of a decent Athenian woman's presence in the setting of Acts 17 have led to the conjecture that she may have been a foreigner residing in or visiting Athens. Furneaux suggested that she was a Jew named Tamar, whose name was Graecized as *Damaris*.[9] J. G. Griffiths argued that she may have been

---

[6] See the discussions in Josef Schmid, "Damaris," in *Lexikon für Theologie und Kirche* (eds. Josef Höfer and Karl Rahner; Freiburg: Herder, 1959), 3:131; Jacobus Wettstein, *Novum Testamentum graecum* (Amsterdam: Dommerian, 1752; repr. Graz: Akademischen Druck-u. Verlagsanstalt, 1962), 2:573; William M. Ramsay, *St. Paul the Traveller and the Roman Citizen* (London: Hodder and Stoughton, 1897; repr. Grand Rapids, Mich.: Kregel, 2001), 252; E. Jacquier, *Les Actes des Apôtres* (2d ed.; Paris: Victor Lecoffre, 1926), 540; Haenchen, *Acts*, 526–27; Wilhelm Schmid, "Die Rede des Apostels Paulus vor den Philosophen und Areopagiten in Athen," *Philologus* 95 (1942–43): 118–19; F. F. Bruce, *Commentary on the Book of Acts* (NICNT; Grand Rapids: Eerdmans, 1986), 364 n. 65; C. K. Barrett, *A Critical and Exegetical Commentary on the Acts of the Apostles* (ICC; Edinburgh: T. & T. Clark, 1998), 2:855; Ben Witherington, *The Acts of the Apostles: A Socio-Rhetorical Commentary* (Grand Rapids: Eerdmans, 1998), 432–33.

[7] The regular insinuation that Damalis is "a rather common name" (BAGD, 170; see Witherington, *Acts of the Apostles*, 432) should be qualified since most authors appear to cite other authors on the matter rather than actual attestations—"Names based on the stems 'Damal-' and 'Damar-' both occur, but both may fairly be considered rather rare" (Colin J. Hemer, *The Book of Acts in the Setting of Hellenistic History* [ed. Conrad H. Gempf; WUNT 49; Tübingen: Mohr Siebeck, 1989; repr. Winona Lake, Indiana: Eisenbrauns, 1990], 232).

[8] Byzantine lexicographers related the name to δάμαρ ("wife"), itself from δαμάζειν ("to be made subject [to a husband]"; LSJ 368)—e.g. Pseudo-Zonaras, who has, Δάμαρ. γυνή. γαμετή. παρὰ τὸν γάμον, γάμαρ καὶ δάμαρ λέγεται καὶ δάμαρις, ἔνθεν ἡ δάμαρτος γενική . . . (J. A. H. Tittmann, *Iohannis Zonarae lexicon ex tribus codicibus manuscriptis* [Leipzig: Crusius, 1808; repr. Amsterdam: Hakkert, 1967], 1:468). Cf. also *Etymologicum magnum*: Δάμαρ. Ἡ γαμετή. Παρὰ τὸ γάμον, γάμαρ καὶ δάμαρ. Ἡ παρὰ τὸ δαμάζεσθαι ἀνδρὶ γυνή. φίλη. (T. Gaisford, *Etymologicum magnum*. [Oxford: Oxford University Press, 1848; repr. Amsterdam: Hakkert, 1967], 246). Varinus (see n. 95 below) and the Byzantine lexica may be responsible for some modern expositors taking "Damaris" to mean "wife" or "woman."

[9] William M. Furneaux, *The Acts of the Apostles* (Oxford: Clarendon, 1912), 291.

an Egyptian instead, her name "deriving from *Tʾ–mr* or from *Tʾ–mrt*,"[10] on the basis of a dental exchange (D–T) that has allegedly left echoes in a portion of the Coptic ("*tamaris*") and the Armenian ("*tamarīs*") biblical versions. Griffith's phonetic comparisons are only partly accurate, however, since the Armenian version of Acts 17:34 actually has the form *damaris*.[11] The Sahidic Coptic and the Coptic witnesses generally also have ⲆⲀⲘⲀⲢⲒⲤ (*damaris*),[12] though two Bohairic manuscripts have ⲦⲀⲘⲀⲢⲒⲤ (*tamaris*), as Griffiths notes.[13] However, the exchange D–T is not uncommon within and between languages and requires no extraordinary accounting— certainly not Griffiths' "farfetched explanation"[14] of an Egyptian provenance for Damaris, for which he offers only speculation and no other evidence. Furneaux's conjecture is equally without support.

In fact, the name may not be the singular phenomenon that many have presumed. The often-repeated assertion that Δάμαρις occurs nowhere else outside Acts[15] is debatable. It is indeed a rare form, but not without a measure of epigraphic support.[16] As for *Damalis* ("heifer")—

[10] J. Gwyn Griffiths, "Was Damaris an Egyptian? (Acts 17,34)," *BZ* 8 (1964): 294; cf. Rudolf Pesch, *Die Apostelgeschichte*, vol. 2: *Apg. 13–28* (EKKNT; Neukirchen-Vluyn: Neukirchener, 1986).

[11] "A Certain Woman Named Damaris", in *Scriptures of the Old and New Testaments*, Hovhann Zohrabian, ed. (Venice, 1805; repr. Delmar, N.Y.: Caravan, 1984), 740 [Armenian]. Griffiths' understanding of the Armenian seems to be derived from the note in George Horner, *The Coptic Version of the New Testament in the Southern Dialect otherwise Called Sahidic and Thebaic*, vol. 6: *The Acts of the Apostles* (Oxford: Clarendon, 1922), *s.v.* Acts 17:34.

[12] Horner, *Coptic Version*, s.v. Acts 17:34; also, Herbert Thompson, *The Coptic Version of the Acts of the Apostles and the Pauline Epistles in the Sahidic Dialect* (Cambridge: Cambridge University Press, 1932), *s.v.* Acts 17:34.

[13] Horner's MSS F (13th century) and S (19th century); see Horner, *The Coptic Version of the New Testament in the Northern Dialect otherwise Called Memphitic and Bohairic*, vol. 4: *The Catholic Epistles and the Acts of the Apostles* (Oxford: Clarendon, 1905), *s.v.* Acts 17:34. For the sake of completeness, it ought to be noted that other biblical versions exhibit no such dental exchange—e.g. the Syriac versions have *d[ʾ]am[ʾ]aris*); the Latin has *Damaris* (cf. *Damalis* in the Old Latin *h*); the Georgian has *damaris*; the Ethiopic has *damārʿs* (see n. 50 below); the Old Slavonic has *damarŭ*.

[14] Joseph A. Fitzmyer, *The Acts of the Apostles* (AB 31; New York: Doubleday, 1997), 613.

[15] So many commentators; also see Friedrich Bechtel, *Die historischen Personnamen des griechischen bis zur Kaiserzeit* (Hildesheim: Georg Olms, 1964), lacking an entry for "Damaris."

[16] Schmid, "Rede des Apostels Paulus," 118–19 n. 123; Gottfried Schille, *Die Apostelgeschichte des Lukas* (THKNT 5; Berlin: Evangelische Verlagsanstalt, 1983), 360. See the inscriptions: SEG XI, 669ab (4th–3d BCE); SEG XI, 903 (2d CE; cf. IG V/1, 972). BDAG, 211 notices that some debate exists as to the precise restoration of SEG XI, 669ab. Respect-

although it is possible that the names *Damaris* and *Damalis* are related via the interchange of L–R, positing such a connection is not a necessary explanation for the form of the name as it occurs in Acts 17:34, particularly in light of the epigraphic evidence. Floriacensis' reading is undoubtedly the result of scribal alteration to the more usual *Damalis*. Still, it must be acknowledged that the precise origin of the name Damaris is unknown and its form has shed no revealing light on the identity of the woman in Acts.

Social Location: Discrepant Texts & Elusive Context

More vexing than the form of Damaris's name is the question of her identity and role. Acts 17:34 offers nothing directly, beyond the fact that she was γυνή;[17] yet various readers have inferred from the context different implications about her social location.

For instance, it has been noticed that unlike with the reports of female converts in Berea, Thessalonica, and Pisidian Antioch, the text does not grace Damaris's name with a qualification of special honor.[18] Reflecting on the traditional ancient strictures regarding the public roles of women in Athens has led some interpreters to conclude that, since respectable Athenian women would not have been welcome ἐν μέσῳ τοῦ Ἀρείου πάγου (17:22),[19] Damaris may have been a foreigner (see above)— or perhaps one of the *hetairai*, an intellectual and sexual companion for the sophisticated male elites of the city.[20]

---

ing the epigraphic evidence, Hans Conzelmann concludes, "the alteration to Δάμαλις is superfluous" (*Acts of the Apostles* [trans. James Limburg et al.; Philadelphia: Fortress, 1987], 149 n. 95). See also the discussion in Hemer, *Book of Acts*, 232 n. 34.
For the epigraphic texts, see G. Daux, G. Klaffenbach, and M. N. Tod, *Supplementum epigraphicum graecum* (Leiden: A. W. Sijthoff, 1950), 11.669, 903; P. M. Fraser and E. Matthews, *A Lexicon of Greek Personal Names*, vol. 3a: *The Peloponnese, Western Greece, Sicily, Magna Graecia* (Oxford: Clarendon, 1997), 106–7; ibid., vol. 1: *The Aegean Islands, Cyprus, Cyrenaica* (1987), 113.

[17] Regarding textual variants that offer more—or less—about her, see below.

[18] I.e. γυναῖκες τῶν πρώτων (17:4), αἱ Ἑλληνίδαι γυναῖκες αἱ εὐσχήμονες καὶ ἄνδρες (17:12), αἱ σεβόμεναι γυναῖκες αἱ εὐσχήμονες (13:50). Some witnesses do actually elevate Damaris's status by supplying an honorable epithet (see below).

[19] Jacquier, *Actes des Apôtres*, 540.

[20] Contemporary interpreters who see her as possibly an *hetaira* (e.g. Witherington, *Acts of the Apostles*, 432) follow Ramsay's observation that "it is not said that she was of good birth" and his suggestion that Damaris was of questionable social standing—"it was impossible for a woman of respectable position and family to have any opportunity of hearing

Other interpreters have been inclined to see Damaris as a respectable woman of some influence, perhaps aristocratic,[21] citing such evidence as her proximity in the text to the distinguished Dionysius and the tendency of Acts to supply the names of persons when those persons have some prominence.[22] Augustine (†430) describes her as "mulier quaedam nobilis" and Theodor Zahn (†1933) suggests that her presence in a public place may be accounted for on the basis that she was the wife or mother of one of the "philosophers."[23] Growing uncertainty as to whether female roles in ancient Athens would have been so tightly controlled and predictable as some have presumed further calls the *hetaira*-theory into question.[24] Indeed, the biblical text does not even require Damaris's presence at the Areopagus speech—only that she converted to Paul's message in Athens. For instance, she could have been one of the God-fearing women of an Athenian synagogue, similar to the women of Pisidian Antioch (13:50),[25] though that view is also speculative. The setting of Paul's Areopagus speech and the fact of Damaris's conversion do not supply much sure direction in the quest to determine her social location.

Ancient scribes appear also to have been troubled by the text's lack of specificity, so that the extant New Testament textual tradition exhibits some ambivalence as to Damaris's status. In particular, the famous bilingual 5th-century "Western" witness Codex Bezae omits any mention of her, whereas the "mixed"-type 6th-century "Western" and Byzantine bilingual Codex Laudianus enhances her dignity:[26]

Paul;" hence, she was "perhaps one of the class of educated *Hetairai*" (*St. Paul the Traveller*, 252).

[21] See "Damaris," *Encyclopaedia Biblica* (eds. T. K. Cheyne and J. Sutherland Black; London: Macmillan, 1899), 1:987; A. T. Robinson, *Word Pictures in the New Testament*, vol. 3: *Acts* (Nashville: Broadman, 1930), 293; Haenchen, *Acts*, 526 n. 5.

[22] José Comblin, *Atos dos Apostolos*, vol. 2: *13–28* (Comentario Bíblico; Petrópolis, Brazil: Imprensa Metodista, 1989), 85.

[23] Augustine, *Sermon 150* (PL 38.808; see *Works of Saint Augustine. A Translation for the 21st Century*, Part 3, *Sermons*, vol. 5: *Sermons 148–183* [trans. Edmund Hill; New Rochelle: New City Press, 1992], 31); Theodor Zahn, *Die Apostelgeschichte des Lucas* (HKNT; Leipzig: Deichertsche, 1921), 2:608, 629, n. 5. Remarking on the usage of γυνή in 17:34, BDAG, 79, asks: "is Damaris the wife of one of the men?"

[24] See Reimer, *Women in the Acts of the Apostles*, 246–47.

[25] See Bruce, *Commentary on the Book of Acts*, 364; David J. Williams, *Acts* (NIBCNT; repr.; Peabody, Mass.: Hendrickson, 1990), 309.

[26] The Vulgate, Coptic, Armenian, Georgian, and Ethiopic versions do not support the variants in D/*d* nor E/*e*.

Codex Bezae[27] — D	d
ἐν οἷς καὶ Διονύσιός τις Ἀρεοπαγείτης	inquibus et Dionysius quis Areopagita
εὐσχήμων καὶ ἕτεροι σὺν αὐτοῖς	conplacens et alii cum eis

Codex Laudianus[28] — e	E
inquibus	ἐν οἷς
et Dionysius	καὶ Διονύσιος
Ariopagita	ὁ Ἀρεοπαγείτης
et mulier	καὶ γυνή
honesta	τίμια
nomine	ὀνόματι
Damaris	Δάμαρις
et alii	καὶ ἕτεροι
cum eis	σὺν αὐτοῖς

The esteem that E/e shows for Damaris in describing her as τίμια/honesta ("honorable") strongly contrasts with the notorious reading of Bezae, from which Damaris is totally absent yet in which Dionysius is εὐσχήμων/conplacens ("dignified"/"very pleasing"[29]).

It is possible that D and E represent two separate attempts to reduce some perceived awkwardness at the mention of Damaris in such a seting—one that ennobled her (E) and another that removed her from the

---

[27] The text of the bilingual D/d is based on inspection of the manuscript in microfilm format; see also the photographic facsimile in *Codex Bezae Cantabrigiensis. Quattuor Evangelia et Actus Apostolorum complectens graece et latine. Sumptibus academiae phototypice repraesentatus* (Cambridge: Cambridge University Press), 1899.

[28] The text of the bilingual E/e is based on inspection of the manuscript in microfilm format (f. 153); see also the edition of Tischendorf, *Codex Laudianus, sive Actus Apostolorum graeces et latine* (Monumenta sacra inedita, nova collectio 9; Leipzig, 1870).

[29] The Latin translation of *e* well represents the Greek of E, but the connection between the Greek and Latin in D/d is less obvious: "it looks as though the Latin translator in d thought that εὐσχήμων meant 'friendly'" (Kirsopp Lake and Henry J. Cadbury, *The Beginnings of Christianity*, Part 1, *The Acts of the Apostles*, vol. 4: *English Translation and Commentary* [London: Macmillan, 1931], 220).

scene altogether (D).³⁰ Yet the occurrence of similar honorifics in both manuscripts suggests a common origin. Perhaps a gloss (εὐσχήμων?) developed within the tradition, one that was originally applied to Damaris and influenced both texts.³¹ A scribe or translator seeking to elevate her above suspicion could have introduced a noble epithet into the passage.³² Or perhaps the addition/s occurred in response to a less deliberate, hagiographical impulse on the part of a scribe conditioned to describe Paul's female converts in lofty terms, under the influence of other passages in Acts—especially 17:12, in which εὐσχήμων is applied to the honorable women of Berea.³³

If the readings of both D and E are the results of a single complimentary gloss, why then is Damaris absent from D? Bezae's ancestor probably mentioned Damaris, qualifying her as εὐσχήμων. The pattern of usage for εὐσχήμων in Acts suggests that scribes might more naturally use it to modify Damaris rather than the male Dionysius, whose dignity was already underscored anyway by the title, Ἀρεοπαγίτης.³⁴ Yet at some point the reference to her dropped out—or was deliberately omitted. The latter explanation is favored amongst those who see in Codex Bezae an antifeminist scribal tendency. Observing that at 17:12 a substantial variant in Codex Bezae applies εὐσχήμων more to the male rather than the female converts, Ramsay (relying on J. Armitage Robinson) asserts, "The reason

---

³⁰ Tarcisia Stramore, "Damaride," in *Bibliotheca Sanctorum* (eds. Filippo Caraffa and Giuseppe Morelli; Rome: Pontificia Università Lateranense, 1964), 4:1964.

³¹ F. J. Foakes Jackson and Kirsopp Lake, eds. *The Beginnings of Christianity*, Part 1, *The Acts of the Apostles*, vol. 3: *The Text of Acts* (ed. James Hardy Ropes; London: Macmillan, 1926), 170.

³² Albert C. Clark, *The Acts of the Apostles. A Critical Edition with an Introduction and Notes on Selected Passages* (Oxford: Clarendon, 1933), xxxii–iii, 252.

³³ See Ramsay, *The Church in the Roman Empire before A.D. 170* (5th ed.; London: Hodder and Stoughton, 1897), 161; Bruce, *Commentary on the Book of Acts*, 66; James Hastings, "Notes of Recent Exposition," *ExpTim* 4 (1893): 436; M.-É. Boismard and A. Lamouille, *Le texte occidental des Actes des Apôtres. Reconstitution et rehabilitation*, ("Synthèse" 17; Paris: Éditions Recherche sur les Civilisations, 1984): 2:125; Richard Pervo, "Social and Religious Aspects of the Western Text," in *The Living Text: Essays in Honor of Ernest W. Saunders* (eds. Dennis E. Groh and Robert Jewett; Lanham, Md.: University Press of America, 1985), 238.

³⁴ Jacquier, *Actes des Apôtres*, 541, cites Blass in support of this observation; see also Clark, *Acts of the Apostles*, 367; Zahn, *Apostelgeschichte*, 629, n. 5; Haenchen, *Acts*, 526–27; Bruce, *Commentary on the Book of Acts*, 363, nn. 61, 66. Pervo's contention that D's retention of αὐτοῖς indicates that its text presumes the original mention of more than one name ("Social and Religious Aspects," 238) is unjustified, since αὐτοῖς is balanced by the occurrence of the plural ἐν οἷς at the beginning of the clause.

for both changes is the same: they are due to the dislike to the prominence assigned to women in the accepted text." In his view, ascending Catholic influences were responsible for downplaying the reports of the elevated status that women enjoyed in some primitive Christian circles. The omission in D was therefore "deliberate and intentional," leaving εὐσχήμων as "the last remaining trace of the vanished Damaris."[35] Ramsay's accusation of scribal anti-feminism has often been repeated and is of particular interest to late 20th-century interpreters.[36]

Ben Witherington has been the most outspoken recent proponent of D's alleged anti-feminist tendency.[37] Witherington's reading of Luke-Acts detects a desire "to present women in a new light, as an oppressed group 'set free' . . . ;"[38] consequently, he is predisposed to see a number of Bezae's adjustments as anti-feminist. He not only contends that the omission in 17:34 was deliberate and tendentious, but offers the explanation that the same scribe or editor added εὐσχήμων to Ἀρεοπαγίτης in order to apply a word normally used in Acts for women to men as well—a further Bezan slap at female dignity in primitive Christianity. Most exegetes, however, are struck by the redundancy of D's Διονύσιος τις Ἀρεοπαγείτης εὐσχήμων and concur with those who follow Robinson and Ramsay that εὐσχήμων is most likely a vestigial clue that Bezae's "Western" *Vorlage* once included Damaris. Witherington's protestation that if εὐσχήμων had been an early reading applied to Damaris we should expect to encounter other evidence for it, outside D,[39] is indefensible, since D represents a notoriously idiosyncratic textual tradition and boasts numerous singular readings.[40] Furthermore, E's parallel reading (τίμια) constitutes just such

---

[35] Ramsay, *Church in the Roman Empire*, 161; Ropes, *Text of Acts*, 170;

[36] E.g. Elisabeth Schüssler Fiorenza, *In Memory of Her. A Feminist Theological Reconstruction of Christian Origins* (New York: Crossroad, 1984), 52. See the discussion below.

[37] Witherington, "The Anti-Feminist Tendencies of the 'Western' text in Acts," *JBL* 103 (1984): 82–84; idem, *Acts of the Apostles: A Socio-Rhetorical Commentary*, 432–33. Cf. the derivative comments of J. Phillip Schaelling, "The Western Text of the Book of Acts: A Mirror of the Doctrinal Struggles in the Early Christian Church," in *Apocryphal Writings and the Latter-Day Saints* (ed. C. Wilfrid Griggs; Religious Studies Monograph Series 13; Provo, Utah: Brigham Young University Press, 1986), 155–72.

[38] Witherington, *Women and the Genesis of Christianity* (Cambridge: Cambridge University Press, 1990), 221; see also idem, *Women in the Ministry of Jesus* (Cambridge: Cambridge University Press, 1984), 129–30; idem, *Women in the Earliest Churches* (SNTSMS 59; Cambridge: Cambridge University Press, 1988), 143–56. Luke's interest in women's roles is well known (see Barrett, *Commentary on the Acts*, 2:855).

[39] Idem, "Anti-Feminist Tendencies," 83 n. 5.

[40] This is not to say that D is merely a deviant witness, nor that it is not part of a coher-

evidence, although the difference in terminology between the two manuscripts (εὐσχήμων /τίμια) is puzzling—as are many phenomena within the enigmatic "Western" textual tradition. Nevertheless, the evidence best fits the judgment that εὐσχήμων was introduced originally to magnify Damaris.

Whether Bezae's overall textual character can rightly be described as antifeminist is debatable.[41] In the absence of sufficient unequivocal evidence for a genuinely antifeminist scribal tendency in Bezae's ancestry, other motives for D's omission of Damaris could also be imagined. For instance, apart from the purported awkwardness of a woman's presence in that setting, some have proposed that the awkwardness of naming a woman among τινὲς ἄνδρες could have motivated a scribe to delete Damaris from the text in an effort to refine the style and content of the passage.[42] However, it is equally possible that the omission is entirely accidental. As Clark points out, "It is . . . not a word, but a line which has disappeared" from D.[43] Bezae's εὐσχήμων begins a sense-line in the bilingual's column of text; the absent phrase καὶ γυνὴ ὀνόματι Δάμαρις would, by length, fit snugly into the context as a line of its own, easily dropped. If indeed the line fell out by accident,[44] it would probably have done so prior to the Greek's coordination with the Latin of *d*, in which there is no trace of the missing line.

Ramsay, Witherington, and others have demonstrated the plausibility of the hypothesis that Damaris fell victim to an early misogynist editor of the "Western" text who deliberately expunged her distinguished name from the story of Paul's meager success in Athens. However, she may sim-

---

ent tradition (see D. C. Parker, *Codex Bezae: An Early Christian Manuscript and its Text* [Cambridge: Cambridge University Press, 1992], 95–96), but Witherington's *argumentum ex silencio* regarding the absence of εὐσχήμων elsewhere is especially weak in respect of D's status as the only surviving major, extensive witness to its distinctive tradition.

[41] See Parker, *Codex Bezae*, 191–92; also J. W. Childers and L. Curt Niccum, "Anti-feminist Tendency in the 'Western' Text of Acts?" in *Essays on Women in Earliest Christianity* (ed. Carroll D. Osburn; Joplin, Missouri: College Press, 1993), 1:469–92; cf. B. M. Metzger and Bart D. Ehrman, *The Text of the New Testament. Its Transmission, Corruption, and Restoration* (4th ed.; New York: Oxford, 2005), 290.

[42] See Haenchen, *Acts*, 506 n. 3; Boismard and Lamouille, *Le texte occidental*, 125; Pervo, "Social and Religious Aspects," 238.

[43] Clark, *Acts of the Apostles*, 367.

[44] So Clark; Zahn, *Die Apostelgeschichte*, 629, n. 5; Haenchen, *Acts*, 526–7, n. 5; Bruce M. Metzger, *A Textual Commentary on the Greek New Testament* (3d ed.; London: United Bible Societies, 1971), 459; Barrett, *Commentary on the Acts*, 2:855. For a thorough study of Bezae's sense-lines, see Parker, *Codex Bezae*, 73–96.

ply have been the casualty of a careless scribal error, instead. Either way, the variants of D/*d* and E/*e*—alongside which must be considered Augustine's "mulier quaedam nobilis" in a sermon preached in 413–14[45]—disclose that Damaris had become a subject of special distinction (εὐσχήμων τίμια) no later than the fifth century. The textual variants may owe their origins to the promptings of prior exegetical reflection upon Damaris, since by the time scribes were copying Bezae and Laudianus Damaris had already been attracting the attention of interpreters whose expositions focused and expanded the scant tradition about her.

Focusing the Ancient Tradition: Damaris Marries

The Georgian version of Acts attests to the patristic development of the Damaris tradition. Readers of Acts 17 in ancient Georgian churches received a clear sense of Damaris's identity. Speaking of Paul's converts in Athens, the ancient Georgian texts reads, ". . . among whom were Dionysius the Areopagite, and *his wife*, by name Damaris, and others with them." The phrase *da coli misi, saxelit damaris* unambiguously makes Damaris the wife (*coli*) of Dionysius. It occurs in the earliest extant recensions of the Georgian Acts[46] but was altered under the hand of Giorgi Mtacmideli in the mid-eleventh century. Giorgi systematically revised the Georgian text with reference to the prevalent Byzantine Greek standard to produce the Georgian *textus receptus*,[47] which here reads, "and a woman (*dedakaci*), by name Damaris . . ."[48] The vocabulary change and omission

---

[45] Hill, *Works of Saint Augustine*, 31; Hill concludes that "Augustine got his wires crossed with [Acts] 17:4, which tells us that among those who believed were 'noble ladies not a few'" (38, n. 5), but it seems more likely that Augustine was influenced by Damaris's growing distinction in the tradition, especially since that distinction occupies a special place in the "Western" and Old Latin tradition.

[46] The earliest extant recensions are preserved in two Sinai manuscripts, some manuscripts housed in Georgia, and an Athos manuscript—see Gérard Garitte, *L'ancienne version géorgienne des Actes des Apôtres* (Bibliothèque du Muséon 38; Louvain: University Press, 1955), 117; Ilia Abuladze, *The Acts of the Apostles according to the Old Manuscripts* (in Georgian; Monuments of the Old Georgian Language 7; Tbilisi: Mecniereba, 1950), 134. See J. Neville Birdsall, "The Georgian Versions of the Acts of the Apostles," in *Text and Testimony: Essays on New Testament and Apocryphal Literature in Honour of A. F. J. Klijn* (eds. T. Baarda et al.; Kampen: Kok, 1988), 45; J. W. Childers, "The Old Georgian Acts of the Apostles: A Progress Report," *NTS* 42 (1996): 67.

[47] P. Michael Tarchnishvili, *Geschichte der kirchlichen Georgischen Literatur* (Studi e Testi 185; Vatican City: Biblioteca Apostolica Vaticana, 1955), 36, 126–31, 154–62.

[48] See Abuladze, *Acts of the Apostles*, 135.

of the possessive pronoun effectively dissolve the marital bond found in the early Georgian recensions.

It is impossible to date precisely the origins of the Georgian version of Acts, but it probably came into existence not long after the conversion of the Georgians to Christianity, i.e. by the mid- to late-fifth century.[49] Although the reading, "his wife" is very rare among the biblical versions,[50] it must have occurred due to the influence of exegetical and homiletical traditions that were emerging elsewhere no later than the fourth century.

For instance, in his dialogue with Basil, *On the Priesthood* (ca.386[51]), John Chrysostom makes the point that the Apostle Paul was not such an inept speaker as some have supposed, asking,

ὁ δὲ Ἀρεοπαγίτης ἐκεῖνος, ὁ τῆς δεισιδαιμονεστάτης πόλεως ἐκείνης, οὐκ ἀπὸ δημηγορίας μόνης ἠκολούθησεν αὐτῷ μετὰ τῆς γυναικός; (*De sacerdotio* 4.7.15–17)[52]

---

[49] See Metzger, *The Early Versions of the New Testament: Their Origin, Transmission and Limitations* (Oxford: Clarendon, 1977), 184.

[50] So far as I know, it occurs only in the Georgian and the Ethiopic versions, though its appearance in the Ethiopic is anomalous. The A-text recension of the Ethiopic, whose text-form is the most primitive extant but still only concretely traceable to the fourteenth century, has "and a woman whose name [was] Damaris"), basically in agreement with the majority of witnesses. However, two B-text witnesses, one from the sixteenth century and another copied in 1736 (Bibliothèque Nationale, Antoine d'Abbadie Ms. Aeth. 41 and EMML 1119, respectively), and one mixed witness from the eighteenth century (British Museum, Orient. 532) have "his wife". Given the proportionally very slight and irregular evidence for the readings and the tendency of the Ethiopic to add pronominal suffixes, they probably "represent anomalies rather than an established textual trajectory or exegetical tradition" (L. Curt Niccum, from personal correspondence dated 21 April 2006). It is unlikely that the aberrant Ethiopic readings derive from the patristic tradition, though they produce the same sense. I am indebted to Niccum for information regarding the Ethiopic tradition (see idem, "The Book of Acts in Ethiopic [with Critical Text and Apparatus] and its Relation to the Greek Textual Tradition" [Ph.D. diss., University of Notre Dame, 2000], 177, 6, 83–87). According to Niccum, the Arabic version underlying the B-text revision and the text's gloss presume "no familiar relationship between Dionysius and Damaris." The article "Damaris," in *Encyclopaedia Biblica* (1899) 1:987, insists that the Latin of Codex E has *cum uxore sua*, allegedly on the authority of Wettstein. However, inspections of the manuscript itself and of Wettstein, *Novum Testamentum graecum*, 2:573 reveal that neither E nor Wettstein have any such thing. The origin of the note in *Encyclopaedia Biblica* is a mystery, but it may derive from one of the numerous Latin discussions of Damaris in the western exegetical tradition—perhaps one influenced by Ambrose (see below).

[51] Date based on information provided by Socrates, *Hist. eccl.* 6.3, though the precise date of this important text is uncertain. It was read by Jerome in 392 (see Quasten, 3:459–63); the editor, A.-M. Malingrey, *Jean Chrysostome. Sur le sacerdoce* (SC 272; Paris: Éditions du Cerf, 1980), 13, dates it at 390.

[52] Ibid., 272; see also PG 48:669.

> And that Areopagite, who belonged to that most superstitious city—was it not from (Paul's) public oratory alone that he came to follow him, along with (his) wife?

The occurrence of γυνή with the definite article in the context with Dionysius leaves no doubt that γυνή means "his wife" here.[53]

Not long after, in an allusion less frequently cited by modern scholars, Ambrose reveals awareness of the same tradition in the West. In 396, the Bishop of Milan sought to encourage and counsel the shepherdless flock of the church of Vercellae as they anticipated episcopal election. Reflecting on the Apostle Paul's slight but significant impact on the Athenian crowd, in a letter Ambrose explains,

> Ex hoc tamen numero non immunis gratiae abiit Apostolus. Siquidem etiam Dionysius Areopagites cum Damari uxore sua, aliisque multis credidit. (*Ep.* 63.23)[54]
>
> Yet not even from this number did the Apostle depart without profit, since Dionysius the Areopagite believed, along with Damaris his wife and many others.

Here the sense of *uxore sua* ("his wife") is unmistakable.[55]

Although these are the earliest extant identifications of Damaris as Dionysius's wife,[56] the casual nature of the references and the geographical distance between them indicates that a convention had emerged regarding Damaris's identity by the late fourth century.

Chrysostom's reference may provide a clue as to why some early exegetes paired Damaris with Dionysius as his spouse. In the text of Acts

---

[53] "Sa femme," in Malingrey's translation (ibid., 273); See LSJ 363b; compare Matt 18:25; 1 Cor 7:3–4; Col 3:18.

[54] PL 16:1196a. The editor notes that some manuscripts read *Damali* or *Damale* instead of *Damari* (see 209–11 above). Also, a small part of the tradition has *muliere sua* ("his woman"), instead of *uxore sua* ("his wife"). The sense is the same.

[55] The Latin versions of Acts do not have this reading—see n. 50 above.

[56] Unfortunately, Chrysostom's exegetical *Homiliae in Acta Apostolorum* 39.1 names Damaris only in its prefatory citation of the biblical passage, after which the interpreter comments, ἔπεισε τὸν Διονύσιον τὸν Ἀρεοπαγίτην καὶ ἑτέρους τινάς (PG 60:276). The text-critical problems associated with *Hom. act.* are notorious and their reliability suspect (see E. R. Smothers, "Toward a Critical Text of the Homilies on Acts of St. John Chrysostom," in *StPatr* 1.1 [ed. F. L. Cross; TU 63; Berlin: Akademie, 1957], 53–57; F. T. Gignac, "The Text of Acts in Chrysostom's Homilies," *Traditio* 26 [1970], 308–15). Neither does the text in Cramer's *Catenae* discuss Damaris (J. A. Cramer, *Catenae graecorum patrum in Novum Testamentum*, vol. 3: *Catenae in Acta SS. Apostolorum* [Oxford: Oxford University Press, 1838; repr. Hildesheim: Olms, 1967], 300).

17:34 γυνή could be taken in the sense "wife,"[57] as is clearly meant in Chrysostom—although the syntax of the phrase in Acts (καὶ γυνὴ ὀνόματι Δάμαρις) strongly favors reading γυνή as qualified by ὀνόματι Δάμαρις rather than by any affiliation with Dionysius. Taking γυνή as "wife" is not the most natural way to read the word in the Acts context. Nevertheless, it is just possible to do so, perhaps especially if one were impressed by the perceived greater prestige of Dionysius or if one felt the need to explain the woman's presence in such a place.

Whatever the origin of the tradition, from no later than the late-fourth century the understanding that Damaris was Dionysius's bride enjoyed significantly widespread currency,[58] though it must be acknowledged that most ancient and early medieval interpreters make no mention of her.[59]

In eastern tradition her status as Dionysius's wife remained secure. Although many interpreters offer no positive evidence for the identification,[60] echoes of it reverberate down through the hagiographical tradition. For instance, the Georgian version of Dionysius's "autobiography"[61]

---

[57] BDAG, 79, suggests that the occurrence of γυνή amongst τινὲς δὲ ἄνδρες could signify that she is the wife of one of the men.

[58] Augustine's reference, "mulier quaedam nobilis," could indicate that he was unaware of or even disagreed with the traditional identification of Damaris as Dionysius's wife (see nn. 23, 45 above).

[59] Jerome's oft-replicated explication of the meanings and etymologies of biblical names (ca. 390) mentions Damaris, along with the odd definition, "silens caput" ("still/silent head;" in *De nominibus hebraicum*, or *Liber nominum*), but says nothing about a connection to Dionysius (see PL 23:847). Acts has not received as much attention in the interpretive tradition as other biblical books. A survey of other commentaries and homilies on Acts has yielded nothing significant—e.g. Ephrem the Syrian, Ishoʿdad of Merv, Dionysius bar Ṣalibi, Bede, Theophylact of Acrida, and fragments of Didymus the Blind, Hesychius of Jerusalem, and Oecumenius in catenae. Searches of the *TLG Canon* and the online *Patrologia latina* show that Damaris (or the "wife of Dionysius") occurs infrequently, usually only in direct citations of Acts 17:34: other pertinent references I discuss here.

[60] E.g. the Byzantine poet Theodore Prodromus (†ca.1166) comments on Acts 17:34; he mentions Dionysius and Damaris but not does not connect the two by marriage: καὶ Διονύσιος καὶ Δάμαρις καὶ ἄλλοι ἐπίστευσαν/ καὶ λάβε Διονύσιον . . . / καὶ Δάμαριν ζώγρησε . . . ("Dionysius and Damaris and others believed/ and he took Dionysius . . . / and he caught Damaris . . . "); *Epigrammata in Vetus et Novum Testamentum, Act. Ap.* 288, ll.2, 9. Text in G. Papagiannis, ed., *Theodoros Prodromos—Jambische und hexametrische Tetrasticha auf die Haupterzaehlungen des Alten und Neuen Testaments*, vol. 2: *Text and Indices* (Meletemata: Beiträge zur Byzantinistik und neugriechischen Philologie 7.2; Wiesbaden: Beerenverlag, 1997).

[61] BHO 255 (*Bibliotheca hagiographica orientalis* [Société des Bollandistes, eds.; Subsidia hagiographica 10; Brussels: Société des Bollandistes, 1910], 59–60).

reports, "On that day [Paul] baptized me and my wife and many of the people of Athens, men and women; and from that time my wife Damaris followed the blessed Apostle."[62] The Armenian version, which Peeters argued derives from the Georgian (itself translated from Arabic) mentions the name Damaris twice in this passage.[63]

Medieval Meditations on the Wife of Dionysius

Commenting on Acts 17:34, the immensely popular *Glossa ordinaria* explains that Dionysius of Athens left behind "multa volumina,"[64] perpetuating the tradition that had already become a canonical reality—that the assortment of sixth-century mystical-theological texts now identified as the Pseudo-Dionysian corpus[65] were in fact composed by the Areopagite.[66]

---

[62] *Autobiography of St. Dionysius* 14; P. Peeters, "La version ibéro-arménienne de l'autobiographie de Denys l'Aréopagite," *AnBoll* 39 (1921): 311–12. The earliest Georgian manuscripts of the text date from the late tenth or early eleventh century (idem, "La version géorgienne de l'autobiographie de Denys l'Aréopagite," *AnBoll* 31 [1912]: 5–10). Although Peeters argues extensively for the lineage Greek—Arabic—Georgian—Armenian, here some Armenian witnesses preserve what must be the better text: "*I and* my wife Damaris . . . followed . . . Paul/the blessed Apostle"—though a branch of the Armenian testimony names her, "my wife Mary"; text edited by Nerses Akinian in *Handes Amsorya* 29 (1914): 217–18 (in Armenian); see also Peeters, "La version ibéro-arménienne," 279–86, 312; also the discussion in, idem, "La vision de Denys l'Aréopagite a Héliopolis," *AnBoll* 29 (1910): 301–8; see also idem., *Orient et Byzance: Le tréfonds oriental de l'hagiographie byzantine* (Subsidia Hagiographica 26; Brussels: Société des Bollandistes, 1950), 140 n. 5, 212.

[63] A Syriac version survives in two recensions, the earliest of which was translated in the late 6th or early 7th century. Neither recension mentions Damaris (M. A. Kugener, "Une autobiographie syriaque de Denys l'Aréopagite," *OrChr* 7 [1907]: 292–93, 310–13, 336–39).

[64] PL 114:461b. Though the German Walafrid Strabo (†849) is credited with compiling the *Glossa ordinaria*, portions date from the eleventh–twelfth centuries and were prepared by Anselm of Laon (†1117) and others. Here the wording of the *Glossa ordinaria* relies on Bede, who identifies the Areopagite as "the Dionysius who was afterwards ordained bishop and gloriously governed the church of the Corinthians" (see below); *The Venerable Bede: Commentary on the Acts of the Apostles* (trans. Lawrence T. Martin; Cistercian Studies Series 117; Kalamazoo, Mich.: Cistercian, 1989), 145.

[65] CPG 6600–35.

[66] The Greek text of the corpus is in PG 3. Modern scholarship on it has been sustained and complex—see Moreschini and Norelli, *Early Christian Greek and Latin Literature*, 665–73; Paul Rorem, *Pseudo-Dionysius: A Commentary on the Texts and an Introduction to their Influence* (New York: Oxford University Press, 1993), 3–17; Colm Luibheid et al., *Pseudo-Dionysius. The Complete Works* (CWS; New York: Paulist, 1987), 11–46; Paul

The *Glossa ordinaria* does not mention Damaris, yet the increased attention devoted to Dionysius as a result of the 9th-century translation of the Greek corpus into Latin brought her once again into the spotlight—or at least into the shade of the spotlight aimed at Dionysius. In particular, the literary manipulations of Hilduin (†840) helped fix Damaris's status as Dionysius's wife in the minds of medieval western scholars.

Hilduin was abbot of the monastery of San Denys in France. The ambitious monastic reformer attracted the attention of Louis the Pious, who was engaged in a campaign to consolidate royal power during a period of instability.[67] In 834 Louis commissioned Hilduin to write a biography of the Emperor's patron, Bishop Dionysius of Paris. Apparently some of the Pseudo-Dionysian works, in Greek, had come into the library of Pepin the Short around 758 as a gift from Pope Paul, though they made no measurable impact.[68] Yet the presentation of another Greek manuscript of the mystical works from the Byzantine Emperor Michael the Stammerer to Louis at Compiègne in 827 resulted in its being brought to San Denys later that year.[69] Between ca. 830–35 Hilduin composed a *Vita* and probably began translating the Pseudo-Dionysian corpus into Latin—certainly a crude and idiosyncratic Latin version existed by ca.838, for which Hilduin is normally credited.[70] P. G. Théry claims, "L'année 827 est une

---

Rorem and John C. Lamoreaux, *John of Scythopolis and the Dionysian Corpus: Annotating the Areopagite* (Oxford: University Press, 1998), 9–22.

[67] Marianne M. Delaporte, "Saint Denis, Hilduin's Headless Holy Man" (Ph.D. diss., Princeton Theological Seminary, 2004), 36–67. For studies of the San Denys legends, see Sumner McKnight Crosby, *The Royal Abbey of Saint-Denis from Its Beginnings to the Death of Suger, 475–1151* (New Haven.: Yale University Press, 1987); Raymond J. Loenertz, "La légende parisienne de S. Denys L'Aréopagite; Sa genèse et son premier témoin," *AnBoll* 69 (1951): 217–37.

[68] Delaporte, "Saint Denis," 24–26; P. G. Théry, *Études Dionysiennes*, vol. 1: *Hilduin, Traducteur de Denys* (Études de philosophie médiévale 16; Paris: Librairie philosophique J. Vrin, 1932), 3. See also the earlier study by R. Foss, *Über den Abt Hilduin von St. Denis und Dionysius Areopagita* (Wissenschaftliche Beilage zum Programm des Luisenstädtischen Realgymnasium; Berlin: Gaertners, 1886), 1–9.

[69] Delaporte, "Saint Denis," 28–29; Théry, *Hilduin*, 5–6.

[70] Hilduin's version, of which only fragments survive, turned out to be basically unusable due to its poor quality, but Scotus' thoroughly revised translation and commentary, commissioned by Charles the Bald ca. 860 and finished in 862, ensured that Pseudo-Dionysius would have a deep impact on western medieval thought (ibid., 6–7, 13–22); see B. R. Suchla, "Dionysius the Areopagite," in *Dictionary of Early Christian Literature* (1998): 178-179; Jean Leclerq, "Influence and Noninfluence of Dionysius in the Western Middle Ages," in Luibheid, *Pseudo-Dionysius*, 26. For a thorough survey of the influence of Pseudo-Dionysius see R. Roques et al., "Denys l'Aréopagite (Le Pseudo)," in *Dictionriaire de Spiritualité* 3 (1957): 244–429.

date capitale pour l'histoire de la pensée médiévale; elle marque le point de départ de l'influence dionysienne sur la philosophie et la théologie occidentales."[71] It turned out to be a significant moment for the Damaris tradition as well.

Hilduin's history of Saint Dionysius was the most influential *Vita Dionysii* in the west until the thirteenth century,[72] popularizing for western medieval scholarship the view that Dionysius of Paris and Dionysius the Areopagite were one and the same person.[73] The recurrence of the name in different times and places, exacerbated by the creative energy generated by prolonged engagement with the Pseudo-Dionysian corpus, had produced a complex web of fictive associations.[74] In the fourth century, Eusebius had followed a tradition handed down by Dionysius of Corinth (ca.170) that the Areopagite was the first bishop of Athens.[75] After the Dionysian corpus of mystical-theological writings appeared in the 6th century, John of Scythopolis commented on them between 537 and 543,[76] identifying the author with the Dionysius of Acts 17 and the first bishop of Athens.[77] The literary attribution came to be almost universally accepted, despite the fervently argued objections of certain late antique scholars (e.g., Hypatius of Ephesus). Also during the sixth century, a third-century martyr named Dionysius, much celebrated in Gaul and famous for his trick of walking about while decapitated, was identified as the first bishop of Paris.[78] A passion composed before Hilduin's time (*Post beatam et gloriosam*)[79] associated

---

[71] Théry, *Hilduin*, 12.

[72] In the mid-thirteenth century it came to be replaced by the compilation, *Vita et actus beati Dionysii* (Delaporte, "Saint Denis," 9).

[73] See Rorem, *Pseudo-Dionysius*, 15–16; also, the entries *BHL* 2171–203.

[74] See Suchla, "Dionysius the Areopagite," 78–79; David Luscombe, "Denis the Pseudo-Areopagite in the Middle Ages from Hilduin to Lorenzo Valla," in *Fälschungen im Mittelalter*, vol. 1: *Kongressdaten und Festvorträge; Literatur und Fälschung* (Schriften der Monumenta Germaniae Historica 33; Hannover: Hahnsche, 1988), 133–52.

[75] *Hist. eccl.* 3.4.10; 4.23.3. The late foutth-century *Apos. Con.* 7.46.11 follow this tradition (Marcel Metzger, *Les constitutions apostoliques, Tome 3, Livres VII et VIII* [SC 336; Paris: Éditions du Cerf, 1987], 110).

[76] Rorem and Lamoreaux, *John of Scythopolis and the Dionysian Corpus*, 39, 144–45.

[77] The pseudonymous texts themselves make the claim of having been written by the Areopagite (see *de Divinis Nominibus* 2.11; *Epistula* 7.3 [*ad Polycarpum*]); see Suchla, "Dionysius the Areopagite," 178–79.

[78] See L. Duchesne, *Fastes Épiscopaux de l'Ancienne Gaul*, vol. 2: *L'Aquitaine et les Lyonnaises* (Paris: A. Fontemoing, 1910), 464–65; Walter Goffard, *The Le Mans Forgeries* (Harvard Historical Studies 76; Cambridge: Harvard University Press, 1966), 195, 201.

[79] *BHL* 2178–79. Also known as *Acta fabulosa*. See Léon Levillain, "Études sur l'Abbaye

the Parisian with the Athenian, thereby blending traditions regarding eastern and western figures. In composing *Post beatam ac salutiferam (PBS)*,[80] Abbot Hilduin expounded on the tradition, taking pains to connect the author of the corpus—obviously the Areopagite—with the Parisian saint. Pointing to the occurrence of miracles upon receiving the aforementioned manuscript gift from Emperor Michael, Hilduin contended that the eponymous saint was buried in the abbey, having arrived at that spot at the end of his cephalaphorous perambulations. Hilduin did not invent the expanding tradition, but for political reasons was "champion to the cause" and has been credited with "du bon usage des légendes" due to the masterful way he established and applied his inheritance.[81] In time, Dionysius was confirmed as France's patron, his name becoming the most prominent feature of the traditional war cry of French kings.

Hilduin draws on a number of sources in his composition of Dionysius's life and passion—including the aforementioned patristic passages.[82] Although he does not devote much space to Damaris, his few references reflect the patristic tradition. Hilduin's rescript to Louis (834),[83] *Exultavit cor meum*, recounts Dionysius's conversion, ordination, and preaching. In it he explains,

> Quia vero cum *omni domo et Damari uxore sua* crediderit, lectio Actuum apostolorum docet, et evidentius dialogus Basilii et Joannis, capitulo 5 libri quarti, demonstrat. Sed et beatus Ambrosius in epistola ad Vercellenses, *eamdem uxorem eius ex nomine designans*, perspicue manifestat. Beatus denique Pater Augustinus in sermone . . .[84]

> For indeed that he believed, along with (his) whole house and Damaris his wife, a passage in the Acts of the Apostles shows and the Dialogue of Basil and John, Chapter 5, Book 4 clearly demonstrates. The blessed Ambrose, in Epistola ad Vercellenses,

---

de Saint-Denis à l'époque mérovingienne," *Bibliothèque de l'École des chartes* 82 (1921): 6–28; text in *Acta Sanctorum*, Oct. IV, 792b–855d; Delaporte, "Saint Denis," 6–8. The brief *Vita* known as *Gloriosae* also predates Hilduin (BHL 2171; *Acta Sanctorum*, Oct. IV, 925d–930a), but has little in the way of narrative detail.

[80] BHL 2175–76. Also known as *Passio sanctissimi Dionysii* and *Historia sancti Dionysii*. See Levillain, "Études sur l'Abbaye de Saint-Denis," 28–51; text in PL 106:23d–50c.

[81] Delaporte, "Saint Denis," 34; Édouard Jeauneau, "L'Abbaye de Saint Denis: Introductrice de Denys en Occident," in *Denys L'Aréopagite et sa Posterité en Orient et en Occident* (ed. Ysabel de Andia; Paris: Institut d'Études Augustinienne, 1997), 365.

[82] Théry, *Hilduin*, 18.

[83] Ibid., 15–17.

[84] BHL 2174; text in PL 106:16a (emphasis mine).

also makes it very plain, *designating her his wife by name*. Finally, blessed Augustine, in a sermon . . . .

Hilduin reads the biblical and patristic witnesses to affirm that "with (his) whole house and Damaris his wife [Dionysius] believed," pointing out that the Blessed Ambrose even designates "his wife by name."[85] In *PBS* 8 Hilduin even offers an explanation for their marriage when he reports that Dionysius responded to Paul "cum omni domo et Damari uxore sua quam ut sumeret more terranae nobilitatis, propter amorem suscipiendae charae sobolis, eum sui coegere parentes" ("with his whole house and Damaris his wife, whom her parents had urged to take him up in the fashion of earth's nobility, on account of their love of bringing up beloved offspring").[86] In this account, Damaris finds herself the vehicle of fulfilling her parents' ambitions for solid aristocratic ties and a suitably rewarding grandparenting experience.

The publication of Hilduin's text renewed scholarly and hagiographical interest in the legend of Dionysius, confirming his identity as bishop of Athens and of Paris, author of the Dionysian corpus, abbot and resident saint of the monastery of San Denys—and the husband of Damaris, although it should be noticed that in the hagiographical tradition, Dionysius leaves his wife and children for the sake of the Lord's service as bishop.

Although growing medieval interest in Dionysius brought some attention to Damaris, she found herself unable to step out of the Areopagite's shadow. The splendid illuminated *Vie de St. Denis* manuscript (ca.1317) illustrates her predicament.[87] The scene depicting Dionysius's conversion

---

[85] Given the identification of Damaris as Dionysius's spouse, a natural correlation is that "alii plures," also converted by Paul in Athens, include the couple's household ("omni domo"), a recurrent interpretation of the biblical reference (see below). In the Preface to his scholia on Pseudo-Dionysius, John of Scythopolis remarks, ἐπιβάλλω δὲ μᾶλλον, ὅτι. . . μνημονευθῆναι μετὰ τῆς οἰκίας αὐτοῦ—"and moreover I add that... [Dionysius] is mentioned with his house;" (text in Balthasar Corderio, S. J., ed., *Opera S. Dionysii Areopagitae cum scholiis S. Maxami et paraphrasi Pachymerae* [Antwerp: 1634], 1:xxxiii–iv; repr. PG 4:16). Although John does not explicitly identify Damaris as Dionysius's spouse, he obviously concludes that she is. Incidentally, the text here is that of John, not Maximus as earlier believed (see Rorem and Lamoreaux, *John of Scythopolis and the Dionysian Corpus*, 144, n. 1, 36–37).

[86] *BHL* 2175; text in PL 106:28d. Hilduin also cites Augustine's more vague description, "mulier quaedam nobilis, nomine Damaris" (PL 106.16b); see nn. 23, 45 above.

[87] Bibliothèque Nationale de France, Richelieu Manuscrits Français 2090–92. Cited 4 January 2006. Plates viewable online: http://gallica.bnf.fr/ Catalogue/noticesInd/ MAN01121.htm. See Henry Martin, *Légende de Saint Denis: Reproduction des miniatures du manuscrit original presenté en 1317 au Roi Philippe le Long* (Paris: Champion, 1908); Charlotte Lacaze, *The 'Vie de St. Denis' Manuscript (Paris, Bibliothèque Nationale, Ms. Fr.*

(folio 48v) shows Damaris just behind her husband. In another picture, she cowitnesses Paul's miracle alongside Dionyius (folio 52v). In the scene of his baptism (folio 54v), she stands alongside him in resplendent scarlet, as one of the three most prominent figures in the scene. Yet by the time Dionysius is ordained by Paul as bishop of Athens (folio 78v), Damaris must be content with a viewing position several rows distant from the action, behind interposing layers of male clergy.

Throughout the Middle Ages, Damaris seems to have attracted interest only as the wife of the renowned Areopagite. In his infamous *Epistola 11, Ad Adam abbatem de Dionysio Areopagita* (ca.1122) Peter Abelard debunks the Dionysian legend, guiding Abbot Adam and the monks of San Denys through the ancient literary evidence in an effort to disentangle the three Dionysii conflated by Hilduin, thereby undermining the abbey's self-understanding and prestige. He does not challenge the traditional views of the authorship of the corpus, yet his irreverent scholastic critique of the Dionysius legends gave him opportunity to reiterate conventional notions about Damaris:

> Constat quippe Dionysium Areopagitam qui praedicatione Pauli conversus est, tempore Christi et apostolorum exstitisse, ac iam virum adultum adeo fuisse, ut uxorem Damarim iam tunc eum constet habuisse, de qua pariter cum eo in Actibus apostolorum fit commemoratio.[88]
>
> It is certain that Dionysius the Areopagite, who was converted by Paul's preaching, lived in the time of Christ and the Apostles and was already an adult, so that it could be said that he already had his wife Damaris then, of whom mention is equally made with him in the Acts of the Apostles.

Around 1136, the Norman historian Orderic Vitalis (†ca.1142) composed the second book of his *Historia ecclesiastica*, drawing on the New Testament and many current popular *Vitae* and *Passiones Sanctorum* to recount the founding of the church and the exploits of the apostles.[89] In describing their mission he narrates, "tunc Dionysius Areopagita, et mulier eius Damaris, aliique cum eis adhaerentes, apostolo crediderunt . . ."

2090–2092) (New York: Garland, 1979).

[88] Edme R. Smits, ed., *Peter Abelard: Letters IX–XIV: An Edition with an Introduction* (Groningen: Bouma, 1983), 249–55. See also PL 178:342b.

[89] Marjorie Chibnall, *The Ecclesiastical History of Orderic Vitalis*, vol. 1: *General Introduction, Books I and II* (Oxford Medieval Texts; Oxford: Clarendon, 1980), 29–39, 45, 467; on the legend of Dionysius of Paris, see idem, vol. 3: *Books V and VI* (1972), 37, n. 5.

("then Dionysius the Areopagite, and his wife Damaris, along with others adhering to them, believed the apostle . . .").[90] Later he relates, "Dionysius Areopagita, cum Damari uxore sua, credens baptizatus est . . ." ("Dionysius the Areopagite, along with Damaris his wife, believing was baptized . . .").[91] The medieval bestseller *Legenda aurea*, a Latin collection of hagiographical cycles compiled by Jacobus de Voragine in the thirteenth century, follows the tradition consolidated by Hilduin: "Dionysius and his wife Damaris and their whole household were baptized forthwith. Having received the faith, Dionysius was instructed by Paul for three years and then ordained bishop of Athens."[92] Caxton brought the same tradition to English readers in 1483, in one of the earliest English printed books: "Denis was baptized and Damaris his wife and all his meiny . . ."[93] Nicholas of Lyra (†1349) concurs that she was his wife.[94] In the early sixteenth century, the Italian Benedictine lexicographer Varinus Favorinus provides the following gloss on her name: Δάμαρ, γυνή, γαμετή. λέγεται καὶ Δάμαρις.[95] Though little appreciated, Damaris was never forgotten during the Middle Ages—so long as her alleged husband was in view.

Objecting to the Marriage: Early Modern and Modern Assessments of the Tradition

The late medieval humanist scholar Lorenzo Valla raised critical doubts about the authenticity of the Dionysian corpus in 1457.[96] He was followed by John Colet, Erasmus and most Protestant reformers, who typi-

---

[90] *Hist. eccl.* 2.4 (PL 188.117b).

[91] *Hist. eccl.* 2.6 (PL 188.124d).

[92] Jacobus de Voragine, *The Golden Legend. Readings on the Saints* (trans. William Granger Ryan; Princeton: Princeton University Press, 1993), 2:239; for information regarding de Voragine's sources, see J.-B. M. Roze's preface in *La légende dorée* (Paris: Rouveyre, 1902), 1:xiv–xvii.

[93] *Meiny* = household; text in *The Golden Legend, or Lives of the Saints: Compiled by Jacobus de Voragine* (trans. William Caxton; repr. ed. Frederick S. Ellis; Temple Classics; London: Dent & Sons, 1900), 5:117.

[94] See discussion in John Lorinus, S. J., *In Acta Apostolorum commentaria* (Lyon: 1605), 742.

[95] See n. 8 above. According to Wettstein's report, *Novum Testamentum graecum*, 2:573. Varinus draws on earlier Byzantine lexicographers who relate the name to δάμαρ ("wife"), from δαμάζειν ("to be made subject [to a husband]"; LSJ 368b)—see n. 8 above.

[96] Some pre-modern scholars had occasionally (and ineffectually) questioned the authenticity of the corpus, e.g., as reported by Photius in the ninth century (Rorem, *Pseudo-Dionysius*, 41, n. 12).

cally found the Platonism distasteful and were wary of being taken in by what they understood to be a major piece of the fraudulent Roman Catholic tradition.[97] For instance, Calvin rejected the connection between the Ps.-Dionysian corpus and the Areopagite. Commenting on Acts, he sticks close to the details of the biblical text, insisting only that, "Luke maketh mention of Dionysius above the rest, because he was in no small authority among his citizens. Therefore, it is likely that Damaris was also a woman of some renown. . . ."[98] Calvin's reluctance to embellish the biblical text with traditional elements is balanced by his impulse to enhance Damaris's honor by receiving her as a prominent person due to the context of her mention in Acts 17.

Debates about the authenticity and worth of Pseudo-Dionysius continued through the sixteenth century and into the seventeenth. Damaris came to function as a lesser pawn in the mighty battles between conservative traditionalists and those enamored of early modern critical sensibilities. On the one hand, the humanist John Baptist Spagnuolo of Mantua (†1516), in commenting on the conversion, life, and passion of Dionysius, had described Damaris as his "consors thori" ("spouse").[99] Paolo Emilio Santoro (†1635), in his *Vitae beatorum apostolorum Petri & Pauli* 3.30,[100] similarly explains, "credidit etiam eodem die Damaris, non ignobilis femina, ipsius uxor Dionysii" ("On the same day Damaris believed, a woman not undistinguished, herself the wife of Dionysius").[101] Yet John Lorinus (†1634) discusses the Damaris tradition, casting critical doubt on the testimony of revered authorities by pointing out that if the author of Acts had wanted readers to see Damaris as Dionysius's wife, he could simply have used the obvious phrase, γυνὴ αὐτοῦ.[102]

---

[97] Karlfried Froehlich, "Pseudo-Dionysius and the Reformation of the Sixteenth Century," in Luibheid, *Pseudo-Dionysius*, 33–46. Even after the abandonment of Hilduin's legend and the traditional views on authorship and an early date, "the corpus could still find interest as a patristic source, or at least as a target for polemics" (idem, 43).

[98] *Commentary upon the Actes of the Apostles by John Calvin. Edited from the Original English translation of Christopher Fetherstone* [1585] *by Henry Beveridge* (Edinburgh: Calvin Translation Society, 1844; repr. Grand Rapids: Baker, 2005), 2:178.

[99] I. Baptistae Mantuani, *Opera omnia* (ed. Laurentius Cuperus; Antwerp: Bellerus, 1576), 2:1.166.

[100] *Vitae beatorum apostolorum Petri & Pauli* (Rome: Zannetti, 1597).

[101] Cited in *Acta Sanctorum, Jun. VII*, 22c.

[102] Lorinus, *In Acta Apostolorum*, 742. Jean de Launoy (†1678) of the Sorbonne vehemently rejected many aspects of the Dionysian tradition on historical and literary critical grounds—see his *Varia de duobus Dionysiis Atheniensi et Parisiensi opuscula* (Paris: Martin, 1660).

In response to the growing assault on the venerable tradition, the Platonist Jesuit Pierre Halloix (†1656) mounted one of the most extensive defenses of the entire Dionysian heritage, including the place of Damaris as spouse.[103] He advances four principal reasons for affirming her conjugal connection to the Areopagite: (1) the wording of Acts 17:34 implies it. He takes the text to be designating Dionysius's wife and household, in accord with traditional authorities. Although, he admits, Luke could have been clearer, the wording in Chrysostom's reference and other biblical passages show that γυνή alone can designate "wife," without the addition of αὐτοῦ. (2) If Luke had wanted to indicate some other woman, with no connection to Dionysius, he would have qualified Damaris as such by means of the impersonal τις. Halloix dismisses Syriac attestation for just such a qualification as secondary and irrelevant. (3) and (4) the patristic evidence and the bulk of the evidence from traditional *Vitae* confirm that she is his wife. For Halloix, Damaris's marital status is significant because of the need to affirm the received tradition generally—and the authoritative quality of the beloved Dionysian corpus in particular.

In the eighteenth century Jesuit Bollandists sought to apply some measure of modern critical methods to the hagiographical tradition in their contributions to the ongoing mammoth Bollandist project. The critically minded Bollandist Cornelius de Bye discussed Halloix's arguments in the *Oct. IV* volume of the *Acta Sanctorum* in 1780.[104] Following Abelard and Launoy, de Bye chastened the tradition, disentangling the various conflated Dionysii. He exposes the weaknesses in Halloix's arguments regarding Damaris, concluding that Dionysius and Damaris are not to be joined in matrimony.[105]

Outside the debates regarding tradition and authority thrust upon Roman Catholicism by the incursion of critical methodologies, modern Protestant interpreters easily dismissed the traditions regarding Dionysius and Damaris. John Wesley's remarks represent the view that came to be normative among Protestant scholars when he mentions "Dionysius the Areopagite . . . on whom some spurious writings have been fathered in later ages, by those who are fond of high sounding nonsense."[106] Few discuss Damaris. Yet where she appears, commentators are quick to discredit the

---

[103] See especially the text in PG 4:707–19.

[104] *Acta Sanctorum, Oct. IV*, 771d–774a.

[105] "Dionysium cum Damari matrimonio non fuisse conjunctum, verosimilius appareat" (ibid., 773e).

[106] John Wesley, *Explanatory Notes upon the New Testament* (repr. London: Epworth, 1952), 467.

Catholic tradition about her—yet as in Calvin's commentary their handling of her tends to display hagiographical sensibilities nonetheless. This is illustrated by the following examples from a range of popular modern Protestant expositors:

> *The woman named Damaris* was, as some think, the wife of Dionysius; but, rather, some other person of quality . . . (Matthew Henry, ca.1710)[107]

> . . . some of the ancients, and also some modern writers, take this woman to be the wife of Dionysius; but had she been his wife, she would have been doubtless called so; however, by the particular mention of her name, she seems to have been a person of some note and figure . . . (John Gill, 1747).[108]

> In some of the popish writers we find a vast deal of groundless conjecture concerning Dionysius . . . ; that Damaris was his wife, &c., &c., concerning which the judicious Calmet says, "Tout cela est de peu d'autorité" (Adam Clarke, 1817).[109]

> Damaris was not his wife, as some imagine. Being named with others of less fame, we must regard her as a lady of some distinction in Athens (Alexander Campbell, 1848).[110]

Critical nineteenth- and twentieth-century exegetes have continued to dismiss the medieval traditions (e.g. Ramsay, Brown, Jacquier, Blass, Clark, Zahn, Pesch, Haenchen, Conzelmann, Bruce, Barrett, and Witherington), though some also continue to infer from the passage that we are to receive Damaris as a person worthy of some reverence:

> Not the wife of Dionysius as some have thought, but an aristocratic woman, not necessarily an educated courtezan as Furneaux holds. (A. T. Robertson, 1930)[111]

---

[107] *Matthew Henry's Commentary on the Whole Bible* (repr. London: Revell, 1935), 231.

[108] John Gill, *An Exposition of the New Testament*, vol. 2 (London: Ward, 1747), s.v. Acts 17:34. Cited 24 March 2006. Online: http://bible.crosswalk.com/Commentaries/GillsExpositionoftheBible/gil.cgi?book=ac&chapter=017&verse=034&next=&prev=033.

[109] Adam Clarke, *The New Testament of our Lord and Saviour Jesus Christ*, vol. 5: *Matthew–Acts* (repr. Nashville: Abingdon, 1832), 829.

[110] I.e. since she is named while ἕτεροι σὺν αὐτοῖς are not; Alexander Campbell, in *Millenial Harbinger* (1848): 144; see Lee Snyder, *The Book of Acts according to Alexander Campbell: An Historical and Rhetorical Commentary* (Studies in American Religion 75; Lewiston, N.Y.: Mellen, 2002), 3:1087.

[111] A. T. Robertson, *Word Pictures*, 3:293.

> Também Damaris devia ser uma senhora importante de cidade, já que Lucas somente dá os nomes das pessoas de alta condição ou pelo menos de certa importância social (José Comblin, 1989).[112]

Comblin's understanding of patterns of name usage in Acts is reminiscent of the remarks made by Dionysius bar Ṣalibi (†1171) in his comment on the passage: "There were many who believed, but he mentioned the name[s] of these because they were distinguished."[113] Overall, the quotes remind us that modern critical interpreters struggle to find for Damaris a suitable social location, as discussed above.

Raphael's depiction of Damaris inspired Thomas Holloway (†1827) to eulogize: "Her discreet distance, her modest deportment, her pious and diffident eye, discovering a degree of awe, the decorum and arrangement of her train, all interest the mind in her favour"[114]—a picture that is at great variance with some of the most intriguing recent attempts to read into the taciturn biblical account an identity for Damaris. These also center on her gender and are inspired partly by the alleged antifeminist strain in the textual tradition. In particular, some contemporary scholars seek to liberate Damaris from her subjugation to Dionysius and to read her notice as a signal of the esteem accorded women leaders in primitive Christianity. For example, Witherington has taken up and amplified the earlier suggestion that Acts deliberately focuses on the prominent role of women in the early Christian movement, including the mention of Damaris as an instance of this editorial agenda.[115] In a reversal of the ancient trend to see the reference to "others with them" as an indication of their familial household, he suggests that the phrase could point to the conversion of the separate households of Dionysius and Damaris, along with their clients.[116] Paul W. Walaskay infers from the context that both Dionysius and Damaris were philosophers and that their mention follows the "Lukan pattern of identifying a believer of each gender."[117]

---

[112] Comblin, *Atos dos Apostolos*, 2:85.

[113] I. Sedlacek, ed., *Dionysius bar Ṣalibi in Apocalypsim, Actus et Epistolas Catholicas* (CSCO, Scriptores syri 2/101; Paris: Typographeo reipublicae, 1909), 100.

[114] Cited by Clarke, *New Testament*, 5:831.

[115] Witherington, *Women and the Genesis of Christianity*, 210–11, 220–22; idem, *Women in the Earliest Churches*, 143–44, 156; Ramsay, *Church in the Roman Empire*, 161; Hastings, "Notes," 434–36.

[116] Witherington, *Acts of the Apostles*, 433.

[117] Paul W. Walaskay, *Acts* (Westminster Bible Companion; Louisville: Westminster John Knox, 1998), 167.

A more concentrated feminist perspective is offered by Ivoni Reimer who, after observing that female philosophers did exist in the ancient world, like Walaskay presents her conviction that Damaris must have been one, due to the context in which she is mentioned:

> It was possible for philosophically engaged women to join early Christianity, in whatever form, for, because of her independence and her association with the Areopagus, Damaris should be regarded as a philosopher. It is marvelous that we can conclude from this that such women were also able to devote themselves to the service of God's righteousness . . . in the Christian community of equals.[118]

Reimer does not significantly engage the complicated scholarly discussions regarding Damaris's social location and her reception of Damaris as a champion of primitive Christian feminism goes well beyond the evidence[119]—though the creativity manifested in her theory is reminiscent of the inventive identities previously crafted for Damaris.

Schüssler Fiorenza exemplifies a more measured feminist approach. She cites the text of Codex Bezae as evidence that "the early Christian traditioning and redactional processes followed certain androcentric interests and perspectives . . ." and that "the androcentric selection and transmission of early Christian traditions have manufactured the historical marginality of women."[120] Indicating her belief that even the "best" text of Acts betrays such androcentric impulses, she points to the brief mention of Damaris as proof that "Acts probably reflects historical experience in stressing that women were involved in the Christian missionary movement at every stage of its expansion."[121] For Schüssler Fiorenza, Damaris's significance is as an echo of the prominence and formative impact of female participants in the early Christian movement and as a clue to the special interests of the various preservers and redactors of the Acts tradition.

James M. Arlandson acknowledges that "[Damaris's] social location is unknowable."[122] Yet he insists that a study of the literary patterns in

---

[118] Reimer, *Women in the Acts of the Apostles*, 247–48.

[119] E.g. Reimer presumes that Damaris must have been present at the Areopagus during Paul's speech; "it is therefore necessary to read the whole story in light of the last verse" (ibid., 246), with the consequence that Damaris becomes for Reimer the lens through which to read the entire Athenian episode.

[120] Schüssler Fiorenza, *In Memory of Her*, 52.

[121] Ibid., 167.

[122] James M. Arlandson, *Women, Class, and Society in Early Christianity: Models from Luke-*

Luke-Acts reveal that in the text she is to be understood as a person of significance (socially, of a "retainer or religionist" class, or perhaps even an aristocratic landowner), due to her having been mentioned by name and in parallel to the eminent Areopagite. Since neither she nor her co-convert suffer social demotion or hardship as a result of their conversion, Arlandson concludes that she is meant to communicate to readers that the status and welfare of upper class women will not be damaged by their association with God's kingdom.[123] Her equal and unqualified mention alongside Dionysius and τινὲς ἄνδρες fits into a larger agenda: "In contrast to his own culture Luke was conveying the value that in the kingdom of God women can be made equal to men or even rise above them."[124]

In a curiously similar vein, Damaris now also finds herself in the midst of heated debate regarding gender-inclusive Bible translations. Wayne Grudem argues against the appropriateness of gender-inclusivity, partly on the grounds that translators ought not to take ἀνήρ generically, as if it were at times equivalent to ἄνθρωπος.[125] Although the mention of Damaris in Acts 17:34 begins with the remark that τινὲς ἄνδρες responded to Paul, Grudem insists that the reference is "ambiguous at best," and that τινὲς ἄνδρες is better understood as a group distinct from Damaris: "It just means some men . . . believed, and some others like Dionysius and Damaris were added to them." Paul's speech is addressed to ἄνδρες Ἀθηναῖοι (17:22), but since women were not allowed at the Areopagus, Damaris could not even have been in the audience—therefore, she is no ἀνήρ. Ann Nyland directly engages Grudem, citing ancient evidence to the effect that women (including *hetairai*) might well have been present. She argues lexically and grammatically[126] that the passage favors understanding Damaris to be among τινὲς ἄνδρες, in agreement with most commentators.[127] Neither Grudem or Nyland is particularly interested in Damaris, but only in whether her presence allows reading ἀνήρ generically.

Acts (Peabody, Mass.: Hendrickson, 1997), 136.

[123] Ibid., 127, 136.

[124] Ibid., 191.

[125] Wayne Grudem, "Can Greek *Aner* ('Man') Sometimes Mean 'Person?' No." Cited 5 January 2006. Online: http://www.cbmw.org/tniv/aner.php.

[126] For the judgment of BDAG, see n. 57 above.

[127] Ann Nyland, "Against Grudem: *Aner* and Masculinist Misprisions of New Testament Meaning," *Seachanges* 3 (December 2003). Cited 28 August 2005. Online: http://www.wsrt.com.au/seachanges/volume3/pdf/nyland.pdf

Contemporary Christian feminist interest in Damaris extends to the mission of the Damaris Project, based in Dallas, Texas, the stated purpose of which is to "provide women with resources to begin a conversation in their communities about women's lives, culture and the teachings of Jesus." The Project's principal implementation takes the form of an event known as the Damaris Salon.[128] Of broader mission is the Damaris Trust, or Damaris International, an organization that exists to help people in "relating Christian faith and contemporary culture."[129] Damaris International fosters community through promoting Christian conversation about expressions of contemporary culture, such as popular films and music. Both namesakes reveal an interest in receiving Damaris within her Athenian context as an inspiration for distinctively Christian intellectual inquiry—in the case of the Damaris Project, especially for women. The one constructs Damaris as the patron of thoughtful Christian engagement of culture and the other as the exemplar of an intellectually robust female presence within the church.

Conclusion: Nothing More to be Discovered?

Undoubtedly more of the Damaris tradition remains to be unearthed, in ancient sources, medieval reflections, and modern expositions. This survey has roughly marked out the contours of her multifaceted story as it has been received, elucidated, and handed down through the centuries. The traditioning process has bequeathed a complicated portrait of this first-century woman from Athens. Many Orthodox and Roman Catholic adherents continue to honor the hagiographical traditions regarding her.[130] The phrase Διονύσιος . . . καὶ γυνή can still plausibly be read, "Dionysius . . . and wife."

---

[128] Cited 18 February 2006. Online: www.damaris.org.

[129] Cited 18 February 2006. Online: www.damaris.org.

[130] E.g., see the popular devotional compendium on the saints compiled by the Serbian Nikolai Velimirovich (†1956), *The Prologue from Ochrid*, vol. 4: *October, November, December* (trans. Mother Maria; Birmingham, England: Lazarica, 1986).

Damaris does not enjoy the concentrated hagiographical attention that her pseudo-husband, Dionysius receives. She has no entry in *BHG* or *BHL*, though Dionysius's entries are fairly extensive. See *BHG* 554–58; also, François Halkin, *Novum auctarum Bibliothecae hagiographicae graecae* (Subsidia Hagiographica 65; Brussels: Société des Bollandistes, 1984), 63–64; *BHL* 2171–2203; idem, *Bibliotheca hagiographica latina antiquae et mediae aetatis. Supplementi* (eds. Société des Bollandistes; Subsidia Hagiographica 12; Brussels: Société des Bollandistes, 1911), 92–93.

In the eastern calendar her feast (2 October) precedes Dionysius's by one day. In the western calendar his date has been shifted from 3 October to the 9th due to the conflation

Faced with the accumulation of Damaris lore modern critical scholarship has understandably sought to penetrate the haze of "pious fantasy" in order to clarify a historically pristine likeness of Paul's female convert. Yet even the main object of such researches—the biblical witness itself—speaks in multiple voices, impeding any attempt at the simple determination of her significance, and the results of critical historical inquiries have been uncertain. The polyvalent and fluctuating image of who Damaris appears to be has not clearly illuminated the fact of who she was. Yet in each age it is inevitably the constructed image to which interpreters cling.

Engaging the larger Damaris tradition has disclosed to us that it is a living phenomenon and that, for all the chastening of accrued fictions and the application of modern critical acumen to historical sources, both the popular reception and scholarly interpretations of Damaris tend to participate in the same creative dynamic that has accompanied her all along. The biblical narrative offers only meager and vague information and it is into the mysterious silence surrounding her that Damaris's devotees have read their understandings of her identity—as faithful spouse subordinate to a famous husband, one of the disreputable *hetairai*, a distinguished lady, the trophy wife of an ambitious aristocrat, an early believer in need of liberation from a hopelessly patriarchal ecclesial tradition, or an independent female intellectual leader. In 1605 Lorinus pronounced the following judgment: "Nihil autem amplius de Damari potui reperire ("Nevertheless, nothing more can be discovered about Damaris").[131] As readers continue to search the scriptures in the hope of finding voices and models relevant for the day, Lorinus' skeptical modern judgment is liable to be shown both true and false where Acts 17:34 is concerned.

---

of Dionysian traditions but she enjoys no comparable prominence. Still, Roman Catholics have not completely forgotten her, as evidenced, for example, by the convent dedicated to Saint Damaris in Bridgeport, Connecticut.

[131] Lorinus, *In Acta Apostolurum*, 742 (1605).

14

Looking through the Fish-Eye Lens
Panoramic Exegesis for Preaching

Thomas G. Long

Not long ago I had a revealing conversation with an educational researcher, a man who had just finished a project analyzing the effectiveness of professional education. He and his team had set out to determine how various professionals (lawyers, physicians, and ministers) learn their crafts. The research group covered the obvious ground, the formal curricula of law schools, medical schools, and seminaries. They also poked between the seams and around the edges to discover how professionals are actually shaped in the standards, norms, and rituals of their vocations. In other words, the team sought to know not only how professionals are "schooled," but also how they are formed and traditioned.

"Every professional education," he said, "has a signature discipline, one course in the curriculum where everything comes together, one place where everything the professional is supposed to be able to know and do gets synthesized."

That aroused my curiosity. "What is the signature discipline for seminary?" I asked.

"Preaching," he replied without hesitation. "In my opinion, it's definitely preaching." He went on to describe how the act of preaching, seemingly simple and effortless to the naïve observer, actually involves an intricate blend of hermeneutics, rhetoric, pastoral discernment, and a score of other skills and layers of knowledge. "Listen to a good preacher preaching a sermon," he said. "It's amazing how many different skills and knowledge bases are involved."

Astute Christian pastors will immediately recognize the truth in this. They remember that preaching class was often the place where the rest of the theological curriculum —the biblical, theological, and historical courses—coalesced. They recognize that everything they know about God, faith, life, and ministry operates together in the act of preaching. They also know that good preaching is not merely "sharing from the heart" or providing religious inspiration; it is rather a high wire trapeze act, a complex, multifaceted performance of bringing aspects of the contemporary situation into the force field of a biblical text and then finding apt language and structure for allowing that interaction to come to expression in a sermon that teaches, delights, and moves Christian hearers.

Few have grasped the complex, multifaceted character of the preaching act as fully as James W. Thompson. His book *Preaching Like Paul*, just to cite one example, offers a remarkable description of how able preachers move, like nimble spiders across the strands of a web, from text to memory to theological reflection to cultural analysis and back again.[1]

It is to one small aspect of this nimble movement that I want to turn in this essay, an aspect so enmeshed in others that able preachers perform it almost without noticing. Specifically, I want to explore what I call "panoramic exegesis," namely the need for preachers to be able to correlate a biblical text to its literary context in biblical interpretation. Effective exegesis involves looking at texts through a fish-eye lens, that is, developing the essential skill of being fully attentive to a particular biblical text while at the same time viewing and understanding that text as a part of some larger whole. I have chosen this topic in part as a sign of my gratitude and appreciation for the contributions to homiletics of James Thompson, whose training both as a biblical scholar and a preacher has made him an effective advocate for careful and creative exegesis in preaching.

Panoramic Exegesis

The canons of biblical exegesis are widely known and ably taught in theological schools. Well-prepared preachers know how to "do" exegesis, namely the linguistic, literary, theological, and sociological steps and strategies they need to take in order to access textual power and meaning in a sermon. Much of what preachers consider responsible biblical exegesis for

---

[1] James W. Thompson, *Preaching Like Paul: Homiletical Wisdom for Today* (Louisville: Westminster John Knox, 2001).

preaching, however, could be called "microexegesis" in that it quite rightly turns the microscope upon the specific details and features of the text at hand: the grammar, the structure, the theological terms and themes, and the historical background of the passage in question. Billy Graham may be able to get away with a broad "the Bible says . . ." as a rhetorical flourish, but well-trained preachers know that the right phrase is "the text says." A good sermon should be based not on some generic notion of the biblical message but rather upon what this one text has to say that other texts do not say.

What can get lost, however, in microexegesis is the impact on textual meaning generated by the larger literary context in which a particular text occurs. "I am preaching next Sunday on the Parable of the Prodigal Son," a preacher may say, and we know that this preacher is trying to wrest some word for today from that familiar story. But the Prodigal Son does not stand in isolation from its context. It is a part of a complex of parables in Luke 15; it is an intrinsic piece of what scholars call Luke's "travel narrative" (roughly Luke 9:51–19:28); and it is a part of the overall flow of Luke's Gospel. We may by custom and convenience preach on a textual unit like the Prodigal Son story, but these textual units are, after all, artificial creations, wrenched from their contexts by a kind of literary violence. We tear a swatch from the biblical wallpaper for next Sunday's sermon, but the overall pattern can be left behind and out of sight.

Panoramic exegesis is a balancing act. It calls for a preacher to focus on a single text, a discrete pericope, but never to lose sight of the larger literary and theological pattern from which the pericope came. But that immediately raises a question: what constitutes a suitable and manageable literary context? How wide-angled should the fish-eye lens be? How far should we pull back from a single text to see the overall pattern?

Lately some biblical scholars have been arguing, in a fully critically informed way, for the recovery of an ancient and precritical principle of biblical interpretation, namely that particular texts should be read and understood in the widest literary frame possible: the context of the whole Bible, both Old and New Testaments, seen as a coherent narrative. "While the Bible does not have the kind of unity and coherence a single human author might give a literary work," writes Richard Bauckham, "there is nevertheless a remarkable extent to which the biblical texts themselves recognize and assert, in a necessary cumulative manner, the unity of the story they tell."² And again, "Any part of Scripture contributes to or illuminates in some way this one story, which is the story of God's purpose for the world."³

Following this interpretive rule, a particular text, say the story of Jesus' cleansing of the Temple, would not appear simply as a moment in the life of Jesus or only as a theological and political critique of first-century Temple practices, but instead as a piece of a larger pattern of prophetic action instigated by a God whose grand purpose is to judge and redeem all of creation.

While acknowledging the value of viewing a text as one small moment in the great arc of the biblical narrative taken as a whole, panoramic exegesis also operates in a kind of middle range as well. In particular, the preacher should see a single biblical text as a working literary unit in the specific document in which it appears. In the same way that this very paragraph is a part of the larger flow of this chapter and has been placed at this point because, in my authorial judgment, this is what needs to be said at this very moment in the argument, just so, a particular biblical text has an organic and strategic relationship to the document in which it appears. The parable of the Prodigal Son can be seen as a freestanding story, of course, but it can and should also be seen as a gear in the overall machinery of Luke. The fact that it appears in Luke, and not Mark or John, as well as the fact that it appears in chapter 15 of Luke, and not earlier or later, are hermeneutically significant facts.

A Test Case: The Gospel of Mark

Suppose, as a test case of how this middle-range panoramic exegesis might work, that a preacher is preparing a sermon on Mark 10:46–52, the healing of a blind man named Bartimaeus. Panoramic exegesis demands that this preacher not only explore every nook and crevice of the chosen passage but also stand back and see the text in light of the structure, flow, and theological purposes of Mark's Gospel as a whole. This poses a problem, of course, since no one is quite sure about the structure, flow, and purposes of Mark, or at least these matters are the subjects of considerable debate.

However, uncertainties about any aspect of biblical exegesis are paralyzing problems for interpretation only if we see our homiletical task as one of capturing the fixed, absolute, and immutable meanings of texts and

---

² Richard Bauckham, "Reading Scripture as a Coherent Story," in *The Art of Reading Scripture* (ed. Ellen F. Davis and Richard B. Hays; Grand Rapids: Eerdmans, 2003), 40.
³ Ibid., 38.

dropping those meanings intact on congregations in sermons. In truth, however, preachers do not go to texts seeking to pull from them fixed meanings, lifting unchanging truths from texts like a pathologist might lift a kidney from a dead body at an autopsy. If this were what biblical interpretation were all about, we could go through the Bible passage by passage, prying loose the stable meaning from each and every text, and then, once we had determined the ensemble of textual truths, we could throw the Bible away and just work with the extracted meanings. The Bible, however, is a living witness, and preachers go to texts not to find biblical principles but to hear the voice of the living God speaking today to our new situation.

This means that good exegesis is both prayerful and playful, academic and artful, systematic and unpredictably creative. Differing opinions about texts have to be weighed and evaluated, of course. Not every idea that springs from the head of some biblical scholar is worthy, but even when the garden of interpretation has been weeded, many differing ideas will still remain in full flower. For the nimble preacher, varied ideas about texts can become heuristic devices, windows through which the preacher can look to see how the text appears from this or that angle.

We can see how this works in practical terms by exploring various proposals about the overall structure of the Gospel of Mark. If our preacher, wrestling with the story of blind Bartimaeus, wishes to do panoramic exegesis, that is to view that text in the light of Mark's larger structure, then he or she must make some determinations about what that overall structure might be. Unfortunately, the author of Mark has not provided for us a handy outline, so we have to puzzle that out for ourselves, and, to put it mildly, scholars are not in agreement about how to solve that puzzle. As Markan scholar Joel Marcus has observed, "Of the making of many Markan outlines there is, seemingly, no end . . . ."[4] But the nimble exegete recognizes that multiple views of the structure of Mark are not necessarily a product of confusion, but more likely a result of the fact that Mark itself is a complex literary creation with multiple design strategies. As Joanna Dewey has argued,

> [T]he Gospel of Mark does not have a single structure made up of discrete sequential units but rather is an interwoven tapestry or fugue made up of multiple overlapping structures and sequences, forecasts of what is to come and echoes of what has already been

---

[4] Joel Marcus, *Mark 1–8: A New Translation with Introduction and Commentary* (AB27; New York: Doubleday, 2000), 62

said. . . . [S]uch a nonlinear recursive compositional style is characteristic of aural narrative . . . .[5]

In other words, the Gospel of Mark, like almost every complex form of communication, has more than one structure. Therefore, panoramic exegesis of a text in Mark, which involves moving back and forth between a text and its larger literary context, must proceed by a kind of experimentation. When the preacher doing exegetical research discovers several reasonable proposals for the overall structure of Mark, the preacher can look at the text from the perspective of each of these proposals, determining what is revealed and what is obscured by each of them. Much like an optometrist who slides first one lens and then another in front of the patient's eyes, asking each time, "Can you see better with this, or with that?" the preacher evaluates what can be seen through each structural lens.

As a way of showing how this might operate, let us examine the story of blind Bartimaeus from the perspective of three different proposals for the overall literary structure of Mark. Obviously, we can make only some brief and illustrative observations about the interaction of text and context. A full exegesis of this passage would involve much more detail and many more steps.

Lens One: Reading Backward from the Passion

It has been over a century since Martin Kähler described the Gospels as "passion narratives with extended introductions."[6] Following Kähler's lead, Joel Marcus reads the structure of Mark backward, from the end to the beginning, and he perceives three large divisions in the Gospel (plus a prologue [1:1–15] and an epilogue [16:1–8]).[7] The third and governing section, the passion narrative (14:1—15:47), describes Jesus' traveling of the "way" of suffering into the dominion of God. Mark tells the passion story in ways that express his core theology, namely that "the explosive power of God…is visible only to the eyes of faith, since it is not manifested in a way that eliminates weaknesses, suffering, and death from the lives of community members, any more than it shielded the life of Jesus himself . . . ."[8] Mark is trying to get the message across to his readers that

---

[5] Joanna Dewey, "Mark as Interwoven Tapestry: Forecasts and Echoes for a Listening Audience," *CBQ* 53 (1991): 224.

[6] Martin Kähler, *The So-Called Historical Jesus and the Historic Biblical Christ,* trans. Carl E. Braaten (1892; Philadelphia: Fortress, 1964), 80 n. 11.

[7] Marcus, *Mark 1–8,* 63–64.

[8] Ibid., 78.

the Christian "way," the Christian life, is just as Paul described it: "When I am weak, then I am strong" (2 Cor 12:10).[9]

The first section of Mark (1:16—8:21) features three stories in which Jesus calls his disciples to participate in his life and mission (1:16–20; 3:13–19; and 6:7–13), but succeeding each of these commissioning stories is an account of how Jesus is misunderstood and opposed, first by the Pharisees (3:1–6), then by the townspeople of Nazareth (6:1–6a), and finally by the disciples themselves (8:14–21).

If, therefore, the third section of Mark describes the suffering-filled "way" of God and the first section describes Jesus' calling people to that "way," only to have his call met by blindness and hostility, the middle section (8:22—10:52) portrays the disciples (and the readers) being enlightened about the "way." This section includes three predictions of the passion, two instructions about servanthood, Jesus' teaching about picking up a cross and following him, and a number of references to the "way." Intriguingly, this middle section of Mark begins and ends with stories of people being healed of blindness, the second of which is our Bartimaeus text. According to Marcus, this framing device accentuates the central theme of the section, namely "the 'illumination' of the disciples as to the meaning of the Christian life—Jesus' teaching about what it means to suffer with him, to follow him 'in the way,' and so to enter into the dominion of God."[10]

Now when we let our exegetical vision move back and forth between the Bartimaeus story and this larger, passion-driven understanding of Markan structure, the accent clearly falls on the last line of the text: "Immediately he regained his sight and followed him on the way" (10:52). Framed this way, this is not so much a story about Jesus' power as a healer of physical blindness as it is a story about a disciple who finally "gets it," who finally "sees" that what it means to be human, faithful, and obedient is to follow Jesus in the way of the cross. That this story immediately precedes the entry into Jerusalem and into the passion is not insignificant.

Lens Two: Breaking the Myth of Plato

In his splendid work of liturgical theology, *Holy Ground*, Gordon W. Lathrop begins by comparing the Gospel of Mark to an influential essay of Plato, *Timaeus*.[11] Plato's essay concerns cosmology and the ability of philo-

---

[9] Ibid.

[10] Ibid., 63.

[11] Gordon W. Lathrop, *Holy Ground: A Liturgical Cosmology* (Minneapolis: Fortress,

sophical insight to perceive the design of the creator in the universe. Aside from Homer, *Timaeus* was the most widely read work among educated people in the Hellenistic world and the most deeply influential description of the accepted view of the cosmos.[12]

Timaeus consists of two main parts, punctuated by a hymnic interlude. In the first part, Plato describes "the great perfect pattern of all things" (the Platonic ideal), which served as the master plan by which the demiurge formed the created order. All of the heavenly bodies, fashioned from the four essential elements (earth, air, fire, and water) are arranged in perfect symmetry. Human bodies were created by "lesser gods" and thus lack perfection, but the human head, the organ of thought and the best part of the human body, is according to Plato, "the most divine part of us and lord of all that is in us."

The second part of *Timaeus* contains a more general philosophical and ethical reflection on the cosmos. In this section, we find Plato's astounding speculation that animals are recycled failed human beings. Fish are reincarnated stupid people, those whose souls are so dull that they are not even worthy of having lungs to breathe. Horses and donkeys are made out of people who lack philosophical ability, birds are fashioned out of flighty and insignificant people, and women are recycled cowardly males.

Between these two sections appears an interlude, a hymn to philosophy. According to Plato, only the philosopher (and thus only educated males of a particular social rank) could engage in philosophy, "than which no greater good ever was or will be given by the gods to mortal man." In this hymn, a dismissive line appears about the "ordinary man." If an "ordinary man" is blind, Plato asserts, he would foolishly lament his loss of sight out of the ignorant assumption that, were it restored, he could see. But of course, not being a philosopher, he can never really see. The key statement, in Lathrop's translation is,

> But those [gifts of sight] which are lesser, why should we hymn them here? Those very gifts, even if they are lamented with wailing by the blind person who is not a philosopher are certainly lamented in vain![13]

Mark, according to Lathrop, is constructed as a direct counterpunch to Plato's *Timaeus*. Like Plato's essay, Mark is also constructed in two parts, the Galilean part (chapters 1–10) and the Jerusalem/Passion part (chap-

2003), 25–38.
[12] Ibid., 25.
[13] Ibid., 29.

ters 11–16). The first part gets going when Jesus is baptized in the Jordan River. As Jesus comes up from the baptismal waters, the heavens are "torn apart." For one steeped in Plato, the meaning is clear: the God of Jesus has ripped to shreds the ideal Platonic universe with all of the heavenly bodies arrayed in perfect symmetry and pointed at the man in the muddy waters of the Jordan, saying, "This is what pleases me." Then Jesus comes up from the river and proceeds to focus his ministry on human beings Plato considered lesser throwaways: fishermen, lepers, women, paralytics, and demoniacs.

The second part of Mark counters Plato's philosophical way of wisdom with Jesus' way of the cross. Following this man on the way of suffering and servanthood leads on to, Mark claims, the true ethics, the true way of wisdom. In Plato's essay, as we have seen, the segue between the two main sections is a hymn to philosophy praising those with the elite gift of philosophical insight and sneering at the "ordinary man." Mark also includes an interlude, but of a very different sort. At the end of the Galilean section of the Gospel, two of Jesus' disciples engage Jesus in a dialogue closely modeled on the Socratic dialogues between a philosopher and his students. They ask Jesus, "Grant us to sit, one at your right hand and one at your left, in your glory" (Mark 10:37), but Jesus tells them they do not know what they are asking. This leads to a teaching, addressed to all of the disciples, about servanthood in which Jesus states, "You know that among the Gentiles [i.e., like those who follow the teachings of Plato] those whom they recognize as their rulers lord it over them and their great ones are tyrants over them. But it is not so among you; but whoever wishes to be great among you must be your servant" (Mark 10:43).

Having announced that servanthood is the way to greatness, Jesus now turns toward Jerusalem and proceeds to achieve greatness through costly service on the cross. But before Jesus enters the city, he has one more encounter. As Jesus and his group pass through Jericho on the way to Jerusalem, they meet a blind beggar sitting literally (and metaphorically) "beside the way." His name is Bartimaeus, the son of Timaeus. It is an important name; Bartimaeus is the only recipient of a miracle in Mark who is named, and Mark stresses his name by giving it twice, once in Aramaic and once in Greek. It is also an unusual name, one that many commentators have noted is virtually unheard of in ancient Jewish contexts.[14]

In Lathrop's view, Jesus has encountered here the very son of Timaeus, thus the son of Plato, wearing a philosopher's cloak. Ironically, however,

---

[14] Ibid., 30–31.

he is a blind beggar, and he is lamenting his blindness, the very picture of the "ordinary man" dismissed in *Timaeus*. When Jesus, over the protests of those around him, calls to Bartimaeus, he flings off his (philosopher's) cloak and comes to Jesus. Jesus asks what he wants, and Bartimaeus responds like a student, calling Jesus "my teacher." Then begs, "Let me see again."

Viewed through Lathrop's literary frame, we see something different in our Bartimaeus text. Mark is doing nothing less than taking on the reigning Platonic view of cosmological reality. Mark believes Plato's elitist, male-dominated, head-oriented, philosophy, which was widely accepted as true sight, actually to be a kind of blindness. God tears this cosmology to shreds and points to the way of his Son as true sight. In our story, the son of Plato meets the son of David, and finds wisdom and life.

Lens Three: The Dawn of the New Creation

In the eighth chapter of Mark, a most odd and perplexing exchange takes place between Jesus and the disciples. The disciples are in the middle of one of their characteristic failures to understand Jesus, and Jesus responds by interrogating them about the two times that he fed the multitudes. "When I broke the five loaves for the five thousand, how many baskets full of broken pieces did you collect?" Jesus asks.

"Twelve," the disciples respond, correctly.

"And the seven for the four thousand," Jesus continues, "how many baskets full of broken pieces did you collect?"

"Seven," the disciples say, again correctly.

"Do you not yet understand?" Jesus says.

No, as a matter of fact they do not yet understand, and neither do most contemporary commentators. This business of the number of baskets collected after the feedings is obviously a major issue for Mark, but it is not readily apparent why. In fact, the mystery gets compounded when we look at Mark's story of Jesus walking on the sea and calming the wind (6:45–52). That story ends with the statement that the disciples "were utterly astounded" (6:51), but why were they astounded? Because Jesus walked on water? Because Jesus stilled the wind? No, not exactly. As Mark puts it, they were astounded because "they did not understand about the loaves."

What does an understanding about the loaves have to do with the disciples' astonishment over Jesus' walking on the sea, and more broadly what is going on for Mark about these loaves? What seems to concern

Jesus in his interrogation of the disciples is the actual number of baskets full left over, twelve in the first feeding event and seven in the second. Joel Marcus is surely on the right track when he says that Mark intended Jesus' statements about the twelve and seven baskets, so puzzling to later readers, to be revealing and obvious, not obfuscatory.[15] Mark's readers would have no doubt recognized the numbers twelve and seven (and their multiples) as indications of completion, perfection, and eschatological fullness, and reinforcing this, as Marcus goes on to point out, is the fact that these numbers are associated in Mark with two Greek words derived from the *plēr* root (*plerēis*, meaning "full of," and *plērōmata*, meaning "fullnesses"). Throughout Mark, *plēr*- root words always connote eschatological fulfillment (see 1:15, 2:21, 4:28, 6:43, and 14:49).[16] Thus, the result of Jesus' feedings in Mark is not simply twelve and seven baskets full of fragments, but rather twelve and seven baskets of eschatological *fullness*.

As for the number twelve, some Jews expected that in the fullness of time the twelve tribes of Israel would be restored (see Ezek 37:15–23), and in the Book of Revelation, the number of the redeemed is composed of twelve thousand from each of the twelve tribes (Rev. 7:1–8). In Mark, Jesus, not arbitrarily, chooses twelve disciples, and two of his miracles involve the number twelve: the healing of a woman with a flow of blood for twelve years (5:25–34) and the raising from the dead of a twelve-year-old girl (5:21–24, 35–43). "Do you not yet understand?" Jesus asked the disciples, and what they were supposed to see is that Jesus' ministry inaugurates the long awaited eschatological restoration.

As for the number seven, the root image is the seven days of creation described in Genesis 1:1—2:3, the seventh day being the day of completion, the day of God's resting, the true Sabbath, the eschatological sign of completion, and it is here that we begin to discern yet another overall structure for the Gospel of Mark. Mark begins with the Greek word *archē* ("beginning") which is precisely the same term found in Genesis 1:1 in the Septuagint, the scriptures of Mark's community. The use of the word "beginning" in the opening verse of Mark may be just a literary device ("this is the beginning of this document"), or it may be a theological introduction ("this document describes the beginning of the gospel"), more likely it may also be an overt allusion to Genesis ("this is the new genesis, the account of the new creation").

---

[15] Marcus, *Mark 1–8*, 513.
[16] Ibid., 514.

Adding force to the latter suggestion is the echo in Mark of the refrain of Genesis 1 that marks each of the six days of creation: "and there was evening and there was morning." There are six such references in Genesis 1, and there are six in Mark. The Markan evening and morning references are as follows:

> End of Day 1—evening (1:32) and morning (1:35)
>
> End of Day 2—evening (4:35) and morning (missing)
>
> End of Day 3—evening (6:47) and morning (6:48)
>
> End of Day 4—evening (11:19) and morning (11:20)
>
> End of Day 5—evening (14:17) and morning (15:1)
>
> End of Day 6—evening (15:42) and morning (16:2)

So what happens to our understanding of the Bartimaeus story if we place it in the framework of the Gospel of Mark as the new Genesis, as a recounting of the six days of the new creation? It becomes one of several descriptions of the new humanity, human beings restored to the status God intended in creation. Perhaps the most dramatic of these is the "young man" (16:5) outside the tomb on Easter morning (on the seventh day, the day of completion). He wears a white (baptismal?) robe, seated on the right side (the position of authority and power), and proclaiming the resurrection. But he is not the only one. There is also the Gerasene demoniac, who is also seated, clothed, in his "right mind," and ready to tell of the mighty acts of God and "how much Jesus had done for him" (5:15–20). Bartimaeus also appears in a seated position, and from that position he can proclaim that Jesus is the son of David and a source of mercy. When called, he throws off his old clothing (ready for the new garment of baptism?) and follows Jesus on the way. Bartimaeus is a part of the new and restored creation, a sign of what human beings are intended to be and can become in the power of Jesus.

Conclusion

Reading backward from the Passion, seeing Mark as a counter to Plato, understanding Mark's Gospel as the new Genesis—these are three possible ways of viewing the larger literary and theological shape of Mark, and each of them leads to a different insight about the Bartimaeus text. When employed as a part of panoramic exegesis, each one provides a fresh, interesting, and productive perspective for the preacher, and for the sermon. Which is the best angle of vision on the text? That cannot be determined at a distance. Working at some remove from the place and time of preaching, biblical commentators, no matter how wise, cannot name in advance what will happen when a text is placed in the midst of a congregation's life. Only the preacher, with one foot firmly planted in the biblical text and the other in the life of a particular congregation in its own cultural moment can discern whether "there is a word from the Lord" for today.

15

Language and the Reshaping of Life
Speech-Act Theory and the
Use of the Bible as Scripture

Roy F. Melugin

The Bible and the Limits of a Historical-Critical Paradigm

Most modern biblical scholars have been taught to focus primarily on the explanation of past meanings in their interpretation of texts. Our discipline's rootage in the Enlightenment has encouraged us to equate reliable interpretation with what texts originally meant. Yet we know that redactors of biblical books were by no means preoccupied with original meaning; they readily reinterpreted earlier meanings to give new significance to texts that originally had a somewhat different meaning. Rabbis and New Testament writers also behaved in analogous ways in their interpretation of the Israelite Scriptures. One might indeed doubt whether those early interpreters would have passed our modern exegesis courses.

If indeed biblical redactors, rabbinic interpreters, and New Testament writers regularly felt free to depart in significant ways from original meanings in order to use earlier traditions to address communities of faith in new situations in which they found themselves, why has the modern community of biblical scholars so often felt compelled to focus primarily on original meanings? Why should modern biblical scholars who are interested in the use of the Bible as Scripture not regard present-day reinterpretation of biblical texts for use as Scripture in our own time as an important aspect of their scholarly task? Could it not be seen as remarkably strange for scholars who believe in using the Bible as Scripture to cling so single-mindedly to a historical-critical paradigm, when it is obvious that producers of ancient biblical texts operated with paradigms markedly different from the dominant paradigm used in the modern guild of biblical scholars?

It is not difficult to understand why modern biblical scholars tend to believe that their primary task is the reproduction of original meaning. In the philosophical heritage that has influenced our ways of thinking in Western civilization there has long been an assumption that the most important function of language is its ability to represent an object or an idea. Responsible use of language, according to the philosophical tradition originating with Socrates, involves the use of language to describe reality as accurately as possible.[1] What biblical scholarship learned in the Enlightenment represents a modification of the tradition that began with Socrates. The task of biblical scholars, according to conventional Enlightenment-rooted biblical hermeneutics, is not to represent reality in a metaphysical sense but rather to describe as accurately as possible the contexts in which texts arose as well as to explain the meanings that the producers of biblical texts espoused as they spoke or wrote in their particular settings.

Why is this kind of hermeneutic not fully adequate for interpreting the text for its use as Scripture? In the first place, as I already indicated, it seems to be at variance with the uses of language in the ancient communities that produced and first used these texts. But it is also the case that twentieth-century studies in the philosophy of language—in what can be called speech-act theory—have shown that use of language is by no means limited to the representation of reality (see, e.g., Ludwig Wittgenstein, J. L. Austin, John Searle).[2] For example, the utterance, "I pronounce you husband and wife," is not fundamentally a description of reality. Its function is not to explain or describe a marriage but rather to do something; its function is primarily performative or transformational rather than representational or descriptive. Indeed, this pronouncement of marriage is neither true nor false in a referential sense. Its significance has to do

---

[1] J. H. Ware, Jr., *Not With Words of Wisdom: Performative Language and Liturgy* (Lanham, Md.: University Press of America, 1981), 9.

[2] See especially Ludwig Wittgenstein, Philosophical Investigations (trans. G. E. M. Anscombe; Oxford: Blackwell, 1953); J. L. Austin, *How to Do Things with Words* (New York: Oxford University Press, 1962); J. R. Searle, *Speech Acts: An Essay in the Philosophy of Language* (Cambridge: Cambridge University Press, 1970).

instead with what it performs, i.e., its force in transforming the lives of the woman and the man by conferring upon them a new status of being married. Analogously, Independence Day pageants in the United States are often more performative in character than they are descriptive of reality. Although they might seem to describe events in the past, their primary function is to create something, i.e., to shape the identity of their audience so that they will be transformed into "good Americans." Obviously the pageants purport to represent reality in some sense or other. But because the primary purpose of the pageant is usually transformational, namely to shape lives, the accuracy of historical representation might not be of great importance in the formation of the narrative.

The Bible and Performative Language Theory

Biblical traditions were (and are) in large measure employed primarily for transformational purposes. The commandment "You must love YHWH your God with all your heart and with all your soul and with all your strength" (Deut 6:5) is not primarily representational. Its purpose is not to describe or explain. Its main function is instead to direct and shape the behavior of its audience. Proverbs likewise are typically designed to affect behavior. Psalms, too, are characteristically performative in character: hymns are designed to praise God; thanksgiving psalms are performatives which give thanks; complaint psalms lament and petition God to act.

Narratives also may be more primarily performative than informational in character. To be sure, narratives do depict persons and events, whether what they depict is historical or fictional. Nevertheless, a narrative's portrayal of persons and events may be primarily performative in function. Let me illustrate from Exodus 1–2.[3] There, we are told, Israel was in Egypt, and "the Israelites were fruitful and increased greatly and they multiplied and grew exceedingly strong, so that the land was filled with them." Now a new king arose in Egypt who did not know Joseph. And, because he feared the rapidly growing Israelite population, he forced them into slave labor gangs to build the cities of Pithom and Rameses. "But the more they were oppressed the more they multiplied." So Pharaoh tried out a new plan. He commanded the Hebrew midwives that, when they came to assist in childbirth, they kill the baby boys and let only baby

---

[3] See, for example, B. S. Childs, *The Book of Exodus* (OTL; Philadelphia: Westminster, 1974), 4–26; T. E. Fretheim, *Exodus* (Louisville: John Knox, 1991), 23–31; J. S. Ackerman, "The Literary Context of the Moses Birth Story," in *Literary Interpretations of Biblical Narratives* (ed. K. R. R. Gros Louis et al.; Nashville: Abingdon, 1974), 74–119.

girls live. "But the midwives feared God and did not do as the king of Egypt commanded." And they let the baby boys live. "Why did you do this and let the baby boys live?" Pharaoh reprimanded them. "Because the Hebrew women are not like the Egyptian women; for they are vigorous and give birth before the midwife comes to them."

So Pharaoh tried still another plan. He commanded that every baby boy born to the Hebrews be thrown into the Nile. So the infant boy Moses had to be hidden for three months. And when his mother could hide him no longer, she put him in a basket—a *tebah*.[4] And she took bitumen and pitch—somewhat like Noah—and daubed the little "ark" with it, put the baby Moses in the basket, and placed it among the reeds at river's edge. Now Pharaoh's daughter, having come to the river to bathe, saw the basket among the reeds and sent one of her maids to fetch it. And, lo and behold, there was an innocent Hebrew boy upon whom she took pity. Moses' sister, standing by, asked if she could get a nurse from among the Hebrew women. And Pharaoh's daughter said "Go!" And so she brought Moses' mother to nurse him. And Moses grew up right in the house of Pharaoh.

In this story I find the irony of power. Powerful Pharaoh forces Israel into slave labor gangs to reduce the population. Yet powerless Israelites, quietly copulating in their humble homes, grow great in numbers despite the might of Pharaoh. And two lowly midwives, armed with nothing more than the power of their wits, undo mighty Pharaoh's plan. In their mock-servility—the pretense of obeying orders—these two nobodies undermine Pharaoh with their tongue-in-cheek report which (as I paraphrase) only *seems* serious: "Why, sir, we did our best, but they delivered those suckers so fast we couldn't get there till it was all over."[5] And, finally, a tiny babe, protected only by a flimsy "ark" and three women—*mere* women, according to ancient stereotype, two of whom were only Hebrews—finally escapes the power of Pharaoh.[6] And powerless Moses, one day to show more power than Pharaoh, ironically grows up unharmed right under Pharaoh's nose. God uses that which is weak in the world to shame the strong. God chooses what is low and despised in the world, even things that are not, to bring to nothing things that are.

I have just made use of performative language hermeneutics. Although I followed rather closely the language of the text in Exodus 1–2,

---

[4] Ackerman, "Moses Birth Story," 91.

[5] See Ackerman's discussion of deception stories in biblical literature ("Moses Birth Story," 87–88).

[6] Ibid., 95.

also I combined it with language from the Apostle Paul about God's using what is weak in the world to shame the strong.[7] Obviously Exodus 1–2 and the New Testament passage that I juxtaposed share a common theme, namely the triumph of what is weak in the world over worldly powers. But it is also the case that my use of this New Testament passage in connection with Exodus 1–2 does in some ways reconstrue the significance of Exodus 1–2.[8] The purpose of my juxtaposition of texts here is performative, namely for shaping the identity of a particular community of faith, i.e., a Christian faith community.[9]

Referential Meaning and Significance

Obviously I could have chosen to stick much more closely to the language of the text itself, i.e., to what we might call the referential meaning of the text. An interpretation by James Ackerman, lively though it is, confines itself largely to the text's own referential meaning as an ancient Israelite narrative. Ackerman has skillfully shown us a way to read the text as an ancient Israelite text by connecting the Exodus story with its literary context in the book of Genesis. Indeed, he makes use of a five-verb blessing that reminds us of Genesis 1:28 and Genesis 9:1–2:

---

[7] The Pauline text is 1 Cor 1:27–29. Although I originally made the connection between Exodus 1–2 and 1 Corinthians 1:27–29 on my own, later I saw that Terence Fretheim had come to the same understanding. See Fretheim, *Exodus*, 37.

[8] My connection of the Israelites in slave labor gangs, the midwives, and the infant Moses in Exodus 1–2 with what Paul says about God's use of what is weak in the world in 1 Cor 1:27–29 extends the significance of the Exodus text. In connecting the specific events narrated in Exod 1–2 with a broad theological statement regarding God's purposeful use of whatever is weak in the world (1 Cor 1), Exod 1–2 is given a significance more far-reaching than the Exodus text had before it was joined with 1 Cor 1:27–29. Indeed, we can see how using texts together in a larger canonical context can profitably serve to reconfigure the symbolic world of a faith community in its use of Scripture.

[9] If a text's referential meaning were to be considered the only kind of meaning a text could have, my reconstrual of meaning in the connection of meaning between Exod 1–2 and 1 Cor 1:27–29 would be problematical. Indeed, it would be nothing more than supplementing an exegetical insight (my exegesis of Exod 1–2) with an out-of-place "eisegetical" interpretation of a Pauline text that would have legitimate exegetical meaning only in its context in 1 Corinthians. But because an important function of the canonical use of the Bible as Scripture involves the shaping and reshaping of human life in a larger context of interpretation, reinterpretation of texts for creation of a larger significance is theologically both legitimate and important. Furthermore, the fact that using the Bible in its entirety as Scripture for the sake of the performative reshaping of life in relationship with God can be a part of its legitimate function means that the connection I have made between Exod 1–2 and 1 Cor 1:27–29 is quite appropriate.

And the Israelites *were fruitful*, and they *teemed*, and they *multiplied*, and they *became vast* in exceeding abundance, so that the land *was filled* with them.[10]

Moreover, Ackerman shows us other ways in which Exodus 1–2 connects with the Genesis narrative: There are connections with the Tower of Babel narrative through the repetition of *haba . . . pen . . .* ("come now, let us make bricks . . . lest . . ." [Gen 11:3–4] "come now, let us deal shrewdly . . . lest . . ." [Exod 1:10]).[11] And, as I have already mentioned, the little basket in which Moses is put (Exod 2:3) is called an "ark" (*tebah*), which is the same term used for the boat that, in Genesis, Noah built.

I did not, however, limit myself narrowly to this text's own referential meaning. I commented also on its potential significance for usage in a Christian community.[12] Indeed, in using language performatively, I combined language from the Exodus story with that of the Apostle Paul. Moreover, in order to speak performatively to a twenty-first century audience, I made use of American colloquial language: "Why, sir, we did our best, but they delivered those suckers so fast we couldn't get there till it was all over." Yet I would insist that I was not indulging in cheap relevance in my interpretation of the text. Instead, I chose quite carefully the language I employed with the intent of being responsible in the effective use of performative language hermeneutics in a present-day North American cultural context.

Perhaps some readers may worry that I may be running the danger of using Scripture capriciously and irresponsibly. But what counts as responsible or irresponsible usage in employing texts as Scripture? Despite historical criticism's claim to provide objectivity regarding textual meaning, such a claim simply presumes that what a text originally meant is its primary meaning. But why is this necessarily so? Attractive as the objectivity it seems to provide might be, we must recognize that never in the biblical period did "original meaning" have such exalted status. The primacy of "original meaning" is a modern creation—an invention of the

---

[10] Ackerman, "Moses Birth Story," 76.

[11] Ibid., 81.

[12] I am indebted to my former Austin College colleague, James H. Ware, for the distinction between "referential meaning" and "significance." "Referential meaning" is that to which the language of a text points to or describes, i.e., that to which the language of the text refers. "Significance" has to do with the importance or value that a text has come to have for an individual or community. For example, Lincoln's Gettysburg address, as Ware pointed out to me, was a speech to dedicate a battlefield in its referential meaning, while the address later came to have a much broader significance in American culture.

Enlightenment that has been made into almost an orthodox practice. Yet reinterpretation of texts for performative or transformational purposes is indeed more consistent with how biblical redactors, ancient rabbis, and New Testament writers dealt with issues of textual meaning.

Furthermore, as Hayden White has argued, reconstruction of past historical reality is not as objective as has sometimes been believed.[13] White argues that, because there is generally too much in the total "historical" record, the historian must make choices as to what in the totality of the historian's sources is relevant for a particular task of historical reconstruction. At the same time, White contends, there is also too little in the historian's record; that is, the historian must decide how to connect the various relevant parts of the record into a credible story of the past. It is indeed the historian who must create links between various elements in the record and thereby emplot the story that is to be told by the historian as history.[14] Moreover, the historian will inevitably inject his or her worldview into the activity of construing what supposedly did or did not happen in the past. History writing, therefore, is not nearly as objective as we sometimes make it out to be.

My purpose is not to reject historical method. It continues to be immensely valuable, even in the use of biblical texts as Scripture. If one were to argue, for example, that God has been involved with various communities in the many periods and cultural situations in which biblical texts arose, historical questions will surely often continue to be of relevance.[15] Or if reinterpretation of earlier texts is said to be of great importance in the performative use of texts as Scripture, historical analysis can be useful in gaining a clearer understanding of how earlier texts are reconfigured.[16] Yet historical reconstruction is not an end in itself in using biblical texts as Scripture. Indeed, use of historical method in the activity of interpreting the Bible as Scripture is but one thing an interpreter might find useful to do. But using historical analysis as only one aspect of a larger hermeneutic that is concerned primarily with employing the language of Scripture for the purpose of existential transformation of life in relationship with God

---

[13] Hayden White, *Tropics of Discourse: Essays in Cultural Criticism* (Baltimore: Johns Hopkins University Press, 1978).

[14] Ibid., 51, 61–75.

[15] Theology that confesses God as having been active throughout all of Israelite and Christian history could profit from the way the divine activity was understood in various historical contexts.

[16] Depiction of "original" meanings could aid in understanding more sharply the nature and purpose of particular reconfigurations of meaning.

might significantly alter, for some biblical scholars at least, the hermeneutical choices they make.[17]

The Role of Analogy in Referential Meaning and Significance

It is the thesis of this essay that language is so often geared toward performative (i.e., transformational) uses rather than primarily for explanatory purposes that we must reconsider many of the assumptions about language that we have inherited from the Enlightenment. This thesis has particular relevance for biblical scholars because most of the texts in the Bible do not appear to have been heavily influenced by the dialectical methods of philosophical schools of antiquity and their commitment to metaphysical arguments for explaining the nature of reality.[18] Instead, I would argue, language in most biblical texts is likely to exhibit many of the characteristics of performative speech. That is why much of the language in biblical texts, though amenable to analysis regarding referential meaning, is also often used with concern for the larger significance certain texts are seen to reflect, especially as given texts are used and reused in the larger context of the Bible as a whole and in the ongoing life of faith communities.

Many in our scholarly guild have been taught to define the interpretation of referential meaning as "exegesis." And many also might be inclined to label what seem to be somewhat looser linguistic and thought relationships between texts as "eisegetical," especially if the particular significance that someone finds there appears to reinterpret textual meaning in ways remarkably different from texts' referential meaning.

For example, my use of 1 Cor 1:27–29 in interpreting the narrative in Exodus 1–2 is clearly not a part of the referential meaning of the Exodus narrative. The language of the Exodus text itself does not expressly indicate or even strongly hint at the generalization that God uses what is

---

[17] Despite the tendency in much modern biblical scholarship to focus primarily on "original meaning" for the purpose of bringing control to the study of meaning, such a scientific understanding of meaning fails to recognize that in the biblical period itself texts were regularly reinterpreted, so that the life and behavior of communities of faith could be shaped and reshaped in various contexts of textual usage throughout history. In my judgment, a performative hermeneutic is more expressive of the ways in which biblical texts were typically used than is the more "scientific" model of historical reconstruction that has become the dominant model for the guild.

[18] Although many texts, especially in the New Testament, exhibit Hellenistic language and thought, the technicalities of metaphysical argumentation are not widely evident in biblical texts.

weak in the world to shame the strong. But the Pauline assertion in 1 Cor 1:27–29 does appear capable of supporting a theological understanding that meaningfully extends the significance of the Exodus text. Although the differences between referential meaning in the two texts might possibly suggest to some scholars that my use of this text from 1 Corinthians 1 is an example of eisegesis, I would argue instead that my reinterpretation derived from Paul is more closely related to the Exodus text than the term "eisegesis" would seem to imply. My use of the Pauline text in this way appears to create an *analogy* between the Exodus text's referential depiction of the Pharaoh (i.e., as someone who is strong), the Israelites, their midwives, and the infant Moses (i.e., depicted as those who are weak) on the one hand and the Pauline statement about the weak and the strong on the other. While I would not claim that Paul saw the connection I made between Exodus 1–2 and 1 Corinthians 1:27–29, I would contend that the analogy I have drawn between them does have theological merit and can thus be said to make a connection that has significance. Indeed, there is a meaningful canonical interrelationship between the two texts, even if it is seen only by a biblical interpreter rather than by a biblical writer.

It is indeed quite common in the usage of biblical texts to find analogies between the referential meanings of a biblical text and the significance that the text displays in subsequent usage. Isaiah 53 offers an obvious illustration. Surely Isaiah 53, whose admittedly ambiguous referential language was undoubtedly formulated and used in Israel before explicit traditions concerning Jesus of Nazareth came into existence, was a textual entity that continued to be used in Israel—and in all likelihood was sometimes used performatively in the enterprise of shaping Israelite understanding of the purposes of YHWH. Indeed, David J. A. Clines suggests that Isaiah 53 often functioned as a "language event" that in different contexts could acquire different meanings.[19] How many different understandings may have actually taken shape regarding the significance of Isaiah 53 we cannot know, but we do know that relatively early in the life of the Christian community Isaiah 53 functioned performatively in shaping specifically Christian self-understandings. According to Acts 8:26–40, for example, Philip tells an Ethiopian eunuch of the significance of this text with regard to Jesus; indeed, Isaiah 53 functions in Acts 8 in a performative way in that the eunuch's life was existentially transformed, as his decision to be baptized makes evident.

---

[19] See Clines in *I, He, We, and They* (JSOTSup 1; Sheffield: JSOT Press, 1983), 59–61. See also pp. 61–65 for further relevant discussion.

Brevard Childs's understanding of interpretations connecting Isaiah 53 with Jesus Christ is also relevant for my discussion here.[20] Though Childs sees the importance of "hear(ing) Israel's own voice in the plain sense of the text,"[21] he contends that Isaiah 53 itself, functioning authoritatively as Scripture in the Christian church, "exercised pressure on the early church in its struggle to understand the suffering and death of Jesus Christ."[22] The church saw in Isaiah 53 a connection between Isaiah and Jesus, yet not by means of the theological category of promise and fulfillment; instead, Childs argues, "an analogy was drawn between the activity of the Isaianic servant and the passion and death of Jesus Christ,"[23] an analogy that is "substantive" or "ontological" rather than an expression of Jesus' suffering and death as as fulfillment of a *promise* made in Isaiah 53. Indeed, it seems to me that the way in which I have connected "referential meaning" with "significance" in this essay often times manifests an analogical relationship between the two—a relationship that can sometimes fit the "ontological" connection that Childs sees between Isaiah 53 as "text" regarding the servant's suffering on the one hand and later Christian "ontological" affirmations associating Isaiah 53 with Jesus' passion and death on the other. I am less certain, however, whether Childs would share my conviction about the potential connections between the performative force of Isaiah 53's own language regarding the servant's suffering and the transformational power of some later Christian claims about the suffering and death of Jesus, especially those that are expressed in language with a certain liturgical bent.

Additional Hermeneutical Observations

There is not sufficient space here to demonstrate the sheer magnitude of the number of biblical texts that could instantiate my arguments about the performative use of the Bible as Scripture. I must instead rest content with a few additional observations about hermeneutics regarding the use of the Bible as Scripture.

---

[20] Childs, *Isaiah* (Louisville: Westminster John Knox, 2001), 422–23.
[21] Ibid., 420.
[22] Ibid., 423.
[23] Ibid., 423.

Speech-Act Theory and Its Importance

First, and of fundamental importance, my proposals concerning speech-act theory should not be understood as a hermeneutical stance that takes precedence over all other hermeneutical approaches. Instead, I am offering a valuable but limited hermeneutical outlook that can usefully be applied in the enterprise of interpreting the Bible as Scripture. Indeed, I have no interest here in speech-act theory as an end in itself. Instead, in my view, speech-act theory's attention to the performative character of many linguistic utterances helps us see more clearly the transformational function of much of the language of the Bible on those occasions when the faith community uses it as Scripture.

Second, my readers should recognize that, although I stand ready to challenge the widespread tendency in the modern-day community of professionally trained interpreters of the Bible to regard historical-critical reconstruction of referential meaning as almost the only legitimate interpretive game in town, I do not question the importance of continued attention to referential meaning. Nor do I doubt that study of historical setting, including the reconstruction of layers of redaction that presumably constitute many biblical texts, can sometimes be valuable in the enterprise of scholarly attention to referential meaning.[24] Yet historically-reconstructed interpretation of referential meaning by no means gets at the only useful kind of referential meaning. Many interpretations of referential meaning that derive from careful synchronic readings of texts. Indeed, because biblical texts in their canonical forms most often do not expressly indicate to the interpreter that primary attention needs to be given to reconstructing layers of redaction in texts or to other aspects of the history of texts' usage, we may draw the conclusion that synchronic readings can often be sufficient.[25]

Thirdly, those who employ biblical texts as Scripture must themselves inevitably play a significant role in determining how the relevant biblical texts are to be interpreted and used. Using texts as Scripture in communities of faith involves not only attention to language of the text but also to the role of the interpreter and/or the interpretive community that employs the text as Scripture. Indeed, as Brevard Childs observed many years ago,

---

[24] Many attempts to reconstruct historical setting, however, are much too speculative to be successfully undertaken.

[25] James Ackerman's interpretation of Exodus 1–2 is synchronic in character. No references to literary sources (e.g., J, E, P) or earlier oral tradition seem needed in order for the reader to have an adequate understanding of the text.

employment of biblical text as Scripture means that they are subject to usage in every epoch of the community's history,[26] from the times of their origin to the present.

Using texts again and again throughout the entirety of a faith community's history inevitably means that the significance that is seen in a text may well undergo change as the faith community's history of usage of the text undergoes change. What the story of deliverance in the book of Exodus might have signified in its earliest usage is clearly not completely identical with the significance that was seen in the Exodus story as it was employed in Isaiah 40–55. Nor was the Exodus narrative's significance to African-American slaves or to Latin-American liberation theologians precisely the same as in other usages of that narrative. Indeed, the response of each act of reading seems to have led to a number of unique understandings of the Exodus narrative's significance.

Interpretation of *referential meaning* is also substantially influenced by what readers bring to the activity of interpretation. Yet referential meaning at its best is tied more tightly to the specificity of what the text *says* than is reflection about texts' significance more broadly understood. Even though referential meaning may often be expressed poetically and thereby may appear to be ambiguous or multivalent in indicating that to which the text's language refers, its interpretation nevertheless needs to be undertaken with the greatest care.

Despite the obligation of interpreting referential meaning with careful attention to what the text itself says, however, a good reader's prejudgments regarding the activity of interpretation will nonetheless color what the text is interpreted to mean. For example, S. R. Driver's interpretation of the Exodus narrative consistently chooses to pay attention to the Wellhausenian literary sources reflected in the text.[27] By contrast, Brevard Childs has consciously chosen to emphasize the final canonical form of the Exodus narrative, together with the use of Exodus passages in the New Testament.[28] Yet Childs also argues that it is of importance for the church's theological interpreters of Scripture to be significantly concerned with prescriptural matters, e.g., Wellhausenian literary sources or oral usages

---

[26] Childs, *Introduction to the Old Testament as Scripture* (Philadelphia: Fortress, 1979), 326–27.

[27] See S. R. Driver, *The Book of Exodus* (Cambridge: Cambridge University Press, 1911), 1–12.

[28] See Childs, *Exodus*.

of prescriptural forms of the Exodus traditions contained within the book of Exodus.[29]

Terence Fretheim has chosen a still different approach. His interpretation of the Exodus narrative is largely dedicated to reading and interpreting the Exodus narrative in synchronic fashion.[30] Fretheim's stated intention of focusing primarily on the text's "last major redactional stage"[31] seems to be grounded, in part at least, in his theological commitments.[32] Yet at many points his choices about interpretive method appear to be more literary than theological. Sometimes Fretheim seems to emphasize a synchronic approach because it fits with "new literary method" rather than because it represents the canonical form of the church's biblical text.[33] Moreover, his special interest in irony[34] appears also to suggest a strong commitment to recent literary method. In sum, each of these three scholars has consciously chosen approaches to the interpretation of the Exodus text, and the meaning they find in that text results in no small measure from their hermeneutical prejudgments.

It seems probable to me that the differences in approach that I have discussed in the previous paragraph are but three examples of what we will generally find in biblical scholarship, namely, that there are widespread hermeneutical differences among biblical interpreters and that, typically, these different hermeneutical prejudgments measurably affect each scholar's interpretation of the text. If this is so, it would seem likely that what a good interpreter brings to the interpretive task generally plays an important role in that scholar's construal of textual meaning. A recognition of this fact would materially affect what could credibly be said about the degree of subjectivity and objectivity that may be found even in careful and detailed interpretation of most texts—even of texts' referential meanings. As I have argued elsewhere, a good case can often be made for more than one interpretation of referential meaning with regard to the same text.[35] At the same time, a good interpreter should be able to show why a particular

---

[29] Ibid., xiii.

[30] Fretheim, *Exodus*, 23–49.

[31] Ibid., 6.

[32] Ibid., 1–4, 9–12.

[33] Ibid, 6.

[34] Ibid., 7.

[35] Roy F. Melugin, "The Book of Isaiah and the Construction of Meaning," in *Writing and Reading the Scroll of Isaiah: Studies of an Interpretive Tradition* (ed. C. C. Broyles and C. A. Evans; Leiden: Brill, 1997), 1: 39–55.

interpretation does or does not fit the text—even if it can be shown that other interpretations also fit the text equally well.[36]

If textual meaning at both the levels of referential meaning and significance is normally shaped to some extent in distinctive ways by each of the text's interpreters, we must recognize the difficulty, if not the virtual impossibility, of recovering anything approximating what could be considered to be the single accurate meaning of a given biblical text. At the same time, however, we should not run pell-mell to the opposite claim that interpretations of textual meaning are necessarily completely relative and arbitrary.

Further, if the reliability of important biblical texts seemed to be typically dependent primarily on the recovery of propositional truths, conflicting interpretations of texts' referential meaning might raise serious doubt about the ability of the Bible to guide us. But if, on the other hand, important scriptural traditions seem to be performative and thus largely concerned with the shaping and reshaping of human life in the presence of God, the appropriateness of the ongoing fresh construal of biblical texts' meaning and function in an ever-changing world could be seen as a positive hermeneutical insight. Indeed, a somewhat limited range of differences available in the understanding of referential meaning,[37] combined with greater room for reinterpreting the significance of the canonical witness, can provide us with a relative degree of constancy of understanding on the one hand and the possibility of even greater freedom in reinterpreting texts' significance on the other.

To conclude, then, the purpose of this essay has been to propose hermeneutical options that would nourish interpreting the Bible as Scripture more adequately than a diet consisting of little more than historical criticism. Because the language of the Bible is in large measure performative in character, historical criticism, as a result of its confinement almost entirely to the task of explanation of past meanings, needs to be complemented by interpretive approaches that are more in accordance with use-theory's

---

[36] Ibid., 48, 50.

[37] By "a somewhat limited range of differences in the available understanding of referential meaning," I am referring to my earlier-mentioned essay, "The Book of Isaiah and the Construction of Meaning" (see fns. 35–36 above), in which I argued that, even at the level of referential meaning, there might well be multiple meanings that could "fit" the language of a text. The phrase, "a somewhat limited range of differences," implies that multiple meanings are possible but that the possibilities are somewhat limited because interpretation of referential meaning requires careful analysis that is concerned with how well a particular interpretation fits the specifics of what is the text articulates.

understanding of language as transformational or performative. I hope the arguments articulated above will be helpful in that regard.

It is a distinct pleasure to present these arguments in honor of my friend James Thompson—a scholar who is greatly interested in the interpretation of the Bible as Scripture. He and I have been involved over many years in theologically-oriented studies of the Bible, especially in the Southwest Biblical Studies Seminar. His many contributions to that Seminar—both as presenter of papers and in his discussion of papers presented by others—have fed both my intellect and my soul. The friendship I have enjoyed with him and with Carolyn his wife has indeed enriched me greatly.

16

The Reformation and Believer's Baptism

Erasmus and the Anabaptists on the Great Commission

Darren T. Williamson

Introduction

THE sixteenth-century Reformation was the greatest reconsideration of doctrine in the history of the Christian Church. What began with Luther's critique of indulgences soon exploded into a full-blown rebellion against much of the medieval Christian system. Beyond the central issue of salvation by faith alone, reformers of various stripes reevaluated long accepted practices in light of the principle of *sola scriptura*. Reformers intensely debated the sacraments and pared the medieval seven down to two: the Lord's Supper and baptism. The disagreement between Luther and Zwingli over the former seriously limited the unity of the early reform movement, but theologians also wrestled over the latter, particularly regarding the doctrine of infant baptism. Mainline reformers revisited baptism in light of Scripture and added new theological insights, but most accepted the scriptural validity of infant baptism.[1] The Anabaptists, how-

---

[1] For an overview see Alister E. McGrath, *Reformation Thought* (3d ed.; Oxford: Blackwell, 1999), 169–96, esp. 186–89, 193; for particular Reformers see, Paul H. Zeitlow, "Martin Luther's Arguments for Infant Baptism," *Concordia Journal* 20 (1994): 147–71; and Timo-

ever, insisted upon the baptism of believers and rejected infant baptism because it lacked biblical support and ran counter to important baptismal passages, foremost the Great Commission of Matthew 28:19–20.[2] The Anabaptist position, epitomized by Balthasar Hubmaier, alienated them from other reformers, but their interpretation of the Great Commission was consistent with that of Erasmus of Rotterdam, the classic representative of Renaissance Christian humanism. Although his view of the *consensus fidelium* and concern for unity led him to accept the validity of infant baptism, his exegesis of the Great Commission and his innovative proposal for a baptismal reaffirmation ceremony indicate he considered believer's baptism the scriptural ideal. This essay explores Erasmus's and Hubmaier's interpretations of Matt 28:19–20 and reflects on the factors that may have led them to a common appreciation of believer's baptism.

Erasmus and the Great Commission

Biblical scholars have long honored Erasmus for his work on the Greek New Testament and *Annotations*, but recently, Reformation historians have called increasing attention to the importance of the *Paraphrases on the New Testament*, where he brought his grammatical and theological insights to bear on the exposition of Scripture.[3] The *Paraphrase on Matthew* (1522) contains a lengthy explanation of the Great Commission. The first section is based on the phrase "go therefore and teach all the nations" and addresses the manner of the disciples' proselytizing and the content of the preaching, indicating that his disciples were to evangelize not through military conquest, but through holy teaching, gospel-shaped life, kindness, and longsuffering.[4]

---

thy George, "The Presuppositions of Zwingli's Baptismal Theology," in *Prophet, Pastor, Protestant: The Work of Huldrych Zwingli after Five Hundred Years* (ed. E. J. Furcha and H. W. Pipkin; Allison Park, Pa.: Pickwick, 1984), 71–87.

[2] See Roland Armour, *Anabaptist Baptism: A Representative Study* (Scottdale, Pa.: Herald, 1966); for a more concise and accessible overview, see William R. Estep, *The Anabaptist Story: An Introduction to Sixteenth-Century Anabaptism* (3rd ed.; Grand Rapids: Eerdmans, 1996), 201–35. For the importance of the Great Commission, see Franklin H. Littell, "The Anabaptist Theology of Missions," *Mennonite Quarterly Review* 21 (1949): 12; Abraham Friesen, *Erasmus, the Anabaptists, and the Great Commission* (Grand Rapids: Eerdmans, 1998), 54–57.

[3] See the essays in Hilmar M. Pabel and Mark Vessey, eds., *Holy Scripture Speaks: The Production and Reception of Erasmus' Paraphrases* on the New Testament (Toronto: University of Toronto Press, 2002).

[4] *Des. Erasmi Roterodami opera omnia* (ed. J. Leclerc; Leiden, 1703–6; reprint: London: Gregg, 1962), 7: 145B. Abbreviated as LB.

Erasmus utilizes the distinctions between the persons of the Godhead to organize his description of the apostolic message. Potential converts must recognize the Father's omnipotence, eternal wisdom, and benevolence. They must learn about the Son's divine mission, virgin birth, atoning death, resurrection and ascension, his heavenly philosophy, and the juridical and punitive nature of his second coming. The disciples were to remember that the Holy Spirit comforts, teaches, strengthens, and unites believers until Christ's return. In distinctively Erasmian tones, the Jesus of the paraphrase stresses the unifying role of the Holy Spirit, who "binds together" (*conglutinare*) those who had publicly declared a heartfelt faith. Rejecting the Holy Spirit's unifying work is dangerous, since forgiveness of sins is only available for those who do not "separate themselves from the alliance and companionship of the saints." Finally, Erasmus's Jesus instructs his disciples to assure potential converts that following him would not produce material gain or the easy life, but would result in their own resurrection and glorification when he returns to his loyal servants.[5]

The second section takes its cue from the phrase "baptizing them into the name of the Father, the Son, and the Holy Spirit" and is critical for Erasmus's attitude toward faith and baptism. Erasmus's Jesus tells the disciples what to do with those who accept the message:

> When you have taught them these things, if they believe what you have taught, if they have repented of their prior lives, and if they are prepared to embrace the doctrine of the Gospel, then immerse them in water, in the name of the Father, and the Son and the Holy Spirit, so that by this holy symbol they may be confident they are freed from the filth of all their sins by the gracious benefit of my death, and are now admitted into the number of the children of God.[6]

In Erasmus's paraphrase of the verse, Jesus explicitly identifies the proper candidates for baptism through the use of three conditional clauses leading up to the command to baptize. Essentially, baptism was the culmination of a conversion process involving teaching and the volitional response of baptismal candidates. The first clause requires belief in the

---

[5] LB 7: 145C–146A.

[6] LB 7: 146A–B: "Haec ubi illos docueritis, si crediderint quae docuistis, si poenituerit vitae prioris, si parati fuerint amplecti doctrinam Evangelicam, tum tingite illos aqua, in nomine Patris, & Filii, & Spiritus Sancti, ut hoc sacro symbolo confidant sese liberatos ab omnium peccatorum suorum sordibus gratuito beneficio mortis meae, iamque cooptatos in numerum filiorum Dei."

doctrines contained in the Apostles' Creed (*si crediderint quae docuistis*); the second clause emphasizes a consciousness of sin and repentance (*si poenituerit vitae prioris*); the third part refers to the determination to embrace gospel teaching (*si parati fuerint amplecti doctrinam Evangelicam*). Then (*tum*) the converts are baptized into the name of the three divine persons and receive confidence of salvation. Erasmus concludes the section by assuring the newly baptized that their baptism was sufficient for salvation and there was no need to be "burdened by Mosaic or human ceremonies," which can add nothing to the simple and easily obtainable washing of baptism.[7]

The final section of the paraphrase expounds the phrase "teaching them to obey all that I have commanded you" and addresses the need for postbaptismal teaching. Erasmus's Jesus corrects those who suppose that salvation had been obtained simply through baptism and profession of faith. After baptism, converts must again be instructed (*rursus docendi sunt*), not in the basics of the Apostles' Creed, but in material that promotes piety, spiritual growth, and endurance.[8]

In this sense, baptism functions as a hinge between rudimentary teaching and mature instruction, both of which were necessary but differed in purpose, content, and chronological relationship to baptism. Erasmus is probably alluding to the same kind of education that forms the central themes of the *Enchiridion* (1503), one of his most popular treatises on spiritual growth. In that work he advocates attention to *pietas*, "a life lived wholly in the love of Christ," and constant spiritual advancement from an emphasis upon visible things, to a concentration on the invisible—spiritual—things.[9]

To summarize, Erasmus's interpretation of the Great Commission depends on the fundamental exegetical conclusion that Jesus' final instructions to his apostles involved three distinct commands: (1) to teach (make disciples of) the nations; (2) to baptize those who believe and repent of sin; (3) and to continue instructing the new converts. For Erasmus the passage presented a model of primary and secondary education that blended nicely with his commitment to the revival of Christianity through continued instruction in, and prolonged exposure to, the "philosophy of Christ."[10]

---

[7] LB 7: 146B.

[8] LB 7: 146B–C. "Again there must be teaching, by which means they will be able to preserve innocence and by which methods they may be able to go forward to the perfection of Gospel piety."

[9] James McConica, *Erasmus* (Oxford: Oxford University Press, 1991), 49–62, 51.

[10] See McConica (*Erasmus*, 45–62) for a concise explanation of the concept in Erasmus's

The appearance of two words for "teach" in the Great Commission afforded Erasmus the opportunity to underscore the need for Christians to be thoroughly instructed in their faith and increasing in Christlike piety, things that in his view characterized the early Church. According to John Payne, Erasmus found in Matt 28:19–20 the biblical basis for catechesis,[11] the thorough prebaptismal instruction of converts. As early as the second century, formal periods of catechesis were required of those seeking entrance into the Church, and the great influx of new converts in the fourth century led to the composition of important catechetical works. Due to the dominance of infant baptism, however, prebaptismal catechesis had largely died out as a regular characteristic of Church life by the sixth century.[12] Erasmus's stress upon prebaptismal catechesis is striking, for it was practically irrelevant in the world of sixteenth-century Christendom, where infant baptism was dictated by law and custom, and adult converts were extremely rare. Erasmus's interpretation of the Great Commission suggests that he hoped that somehow catechesis could be revived in the modern church as one front in the reformation of Christianity.

Erasmus's *Preface*[13] to the *Paraphrase on Matthew* makes this point explicit. In it he envisions a renewal of something akin to ancient catechesis as an antidote to moral and spiritual degeneracy of the Church. Throughout, Erasmus complains about the ignorance of Christians concerning the fundamental tenets of the faith, and as a cure he recommends a program that would adequately navigate the tension between infant baptism and Scriptural injunctions for prebaptismal catechesis. He proposes that during adolescence children would undergo instruction on the meaning and significance of their baptism and be queried as to their personal acceptance of it. Assuming a positive response, Erasmus urges a public service to commemorate the fact: "If they respond with an affirmation, let that profession be renewed publicly, while gathered together with their

---

thought, particularly in his *Paraclesis*, *Enchiridion*, and *Ratio*.

[11] John B. Payne, *Erasmus: His Theology of the Sacraments* (Richmond: John Knox, 1970), 171.

[12] See Robert M. Grant, "Development of the Christian Catechumenate," in *Made, Not Born: New Perspectives on Christian Initiation and the Catechumenate* (Notre Dame: University of Notre Dame Press, 1976), 32–49.

[13] *Des. Erasmus Roterodamus pio lectori* (14 January 1522), LB 7:**. The preface may be found in the nonpaginated section marked with **; see *Praise of Folly and other Writings*, trans. Robert Adams (New York: Norton, 1989), 127–41, esp. 135–37. The treatise is misidentified in *Praise of Folly and Other Writings* as "another Introduction to the New Testament."

peers, and that in solemn ceremonies—appropriate, chaste, serious, and splendid—whatever suits that profession which nothing can surpass in holiness."[14] He goes on to point out that similar ceremonies are held to honor the admission of novices into monastic orders of human origin. Why not hold such a ceremony to commemorate an individual's entrance into an order of divine source? If this is done, he envisions a joyous scene:

> But how truly magnificent this spectacle would be: to hear the voices of so many young people dedicating themselves to Jesus Christ, so many new recruits swearing their loyalty to him, renouncing this world, which is completely saturated in wickedness, and renouncing and hissing at Satan with all his pomps, pleasures, and worldly works; to see new Christs, wearing on their brows the sign of their commander; to see a flock of candidates advancing from the sacred bath; to hear the sound of the awaiting crowd applauding and wishing well the young soldiers of Christ.[15]

Erasmus placed much hope in what this catechetical program could accomplish, supposing that if the ceremony "is carried out as it ought to be, either I am mistaken, or we will have somewhat more genuine Christians than we do now."[16] Erasmus expected and addressed the potential complaint that the ceremony constituted a "rebaptism" and would undoubtedly produce a two-tiered system of Christians, since some youths would fail to affirm their faith, thereby disrupting the unity of Christendom. He addressed the former briefly by stressing that the adolescents would be carefully instructed that the ceremony did not repeat their baptisms, but only ratified them. As to the latter criticism, Erasmus recommended that youths refusing to affirm their baptismal pledge simply were to be exposed to good preaching and books on the philosophy of Christ; in the meantime, they should not be punished, but only denied the sacraments until they could agree with the faith of the Church.[17] Despite his attempt at defusing the criticisms, Catholic opponents censored Erasmus's

---

[14] LB 7:**3b.

[15] LB 7:**3b: "Quam vero magnificum esset hoc spectaculum, audire vocem tot juvenum sese Jesu Christo dedicantium, tot tironum in illius verba jurantium, abrenuntiantium huic mundo, qui totus in malitia positus est: abjurantium & exsibilantium Satanam cum omnibus pompis, voluptatibus & operibus ipsius? Videre Christos novos, Imperatoris sui signum gestantes in frontibus? Videre gregem candidatorum prodeuntem a sacro lavacro? Audire vocem reliquae multitudinis acclamantis beneque ominantis Christi tironibus?"

[16] LB 7:**3b: "Hac si fierent, quemadmodum oportet, aut ego fallor, aut haberemus aliquanto sinceriores Christianos, quam habemus."

[17] LB 7:**3b.

proposal as arrogant, divisive, and defaming of the sacrament of baptism. He was forced to defend it more than five times between 1526 and 1532 against various critics, particularly Noël Béda, the syndic of the Faculty of Theology at the University of Paris.[18] Erasmus insisted that in his proposal he had desired only to recapture the spirit of ancient prebaptismal catechism, not to repeat the baptism itself, and he defended his pedagogical approach to recalcitrant youths as more in keeping with Christ than the coercive tactics of the Inquisition.[19]

The proposal of the preface, with its catechetical emphasis and vision of a voluntary Church, reveals the salient features of Erasmus's interpretation of the Great Commission, as well as his attempt to navigate a tension in his theology of baptism. Payne suggests the preface brings to light two of Erasmus's central concerns for Church reform:

> Erasmus thus wishes to have a voluntary church without the Anabaptist consequences of a denial of the validity of the first baptism and of a divided Christendom. He is saved from the former by the belief that baptism is indeed valid for youths until they reach maturity but requires in adults supplementation by the inward appropriation in faith and life of the grace of the sacrament.[20]

Erasmus's program for reinvigorating Christendom without dividing the Church soon became irrelevant, since his proposal was rejected by Catholics, and the Reformation tore apart the unity of the West. Yet he continued to expresses his concern for catechesis and believer's baptism in later references to Matt 28:19–20. One instance appears on his *Paraphrase on Acts* 2 (1524), and was highlighted by Abraham Friesen who attempted to prove that Erasmus had placed nearly every instance of baptism in Acts into the context of the Great Commission.[21] The evidence from the *Paraphrase on Acts*, however, does not support this aspect of Friesen's argument.[22] But Friesen is right to direct scholars to Erasmus's use of the Great

---

[18] Erika Rummel, *Erasmus and His Catholic Critics* (2 vols.; Nieuwkoop: De Graaf, 1989), 2:33–43, esp. 40–41; for Erasmus's various responses, see LB 9: 445C–F, 459, 484B–C, 557–563B, 1062A–C, 820A–822E.

[19] Payne, *Erasmus: His Theology of the Sacraments*, 174.

[20] Ibid., 173.

[21] Friesen, *Erasmus, the Anabaptists, and the Great Commission*, 51.

[22] *The Collected Works of Erasmus*, vol. 50: *Paraphrase on Acts* (Toronto: University of Toronto Press, 1974–). Volumes from the *Collected Works of Erasmus* are abbreviated as CWE. Erasmus makes no explicit reference to the Great Commission in his version of the baptismal accounts of the Samaritans (Acts 8:4–25), Paul (Acts 9:18; 22:16), Lydia (Acts 16:15), the Philippian jailer (Acts 16:33), or Crispus (Acts 18:8). See CWE 50: 57–59, 65,

Commission in his paraphrase of Acts 2 and its importance to the question of believer's baptism. Alluding to Peter's Pentecost sermon, Erasmus comments:

> What is thus far handed down is the milk of teaching; one must progress to solid food. Evangelical pastors ought to have both kinds of food prepared, for the Lord has given them this commission: *Go, teach all nations, baptizing them, teaching them to keep whatever I have commanded you.* Teach those who are to be baptized the rudiments of the gospel philosophy; unless one believes these he will in vain be baptized with water. Teach those who have been baptized to live according to my teaching and always to progress to more perfect things.[23]

The distinction between pre- and postbaptismal catechesis is evident in this passage. Prebaptismal teaching is milk (*lac*) and rudiments (*rudimenta*), while postbaptismal instruction is the solid food (*solidum cibum*) and more perfect things (*perfectiora*). As noted above, in the *Paraphrase on Matthew*, the three conditional clauses preceding the command to baptize imply that the efficacy of baptism depends upon the faith, repentance, and conscious will of the convert.[24] In the *Paraphrase on Acts*, however, implication gives way to the explicit declaration that without belief, "he will in vain be baptized in water" (*frustra tingitur aqua*). This statement confirms the emphasis in the *Paraphrase on Matthew* and highlights the importance of personal appropriation of faith for Erasmus. Taken at face value, some readers reasonably could have viewed the phrase as a tacit denial of infant baptism.

Erasmus did, to be sure, accept the validity of infant baptism, but only on the basis of the Church's authority, a concept that modern scholarship has linked to his complex view of the *consensus fidelium*. According to this theory, Christ ensured the truthfulness of the Church's teachings by bringing about consensus among Christians on various practices and be-

---

102, 131. For other problems with Friesen's book see Thomas Scheck, review of Abraham Friesen, *Erasmus, the Anabaptists, and the Great Commission, Erasmus of Rotterdam Society Yearbook* 20 (2000): 82–87.

[23] LB 7:674A: "Quod hactenus traditum est doctrinae lac est, proficiendum est ad solidum cibum. Utrunque cibum debent habere paratum Evangelici Pastores. Sic enim mandat illis Dominus: Ite docete omnes gentes, baptizantes eos, docentes eos servare quaecunque praecepi vobis. Docete baptizandos Evangelicae Philosophiae rudimenta, quibus nisi quis crediderit, frustra tingitur aqua. Docete baptizatos, ut iuxta doctrinam meam viventes, semper ad perfectiora proficient" [translation from CWE 50:24].

[24] LB 7:146B.

liefs, even if those beliefs have no explicit scriptural basis.[25] This principle emerges in Erasmus's comments on baptism in the *Exposition on Psalm 85* (1528), another place he pressed Matt 28:19–20 into support for his views on catechesis. Erasmus's Psalm commentaries, which usually took the form of homiletical expositions, represent his sole foray into Old Testament exegesis and were published between 1515 and 1533.[26]

Erasmus's citation of the Great Commission stems from his meditation on Psalm 85:11: "Lead me, O Lord, in your way, and I shall walk in your truth," which sparked his comment on the several steps or stages of salvation. Erasmus insists there are two distinct kinds of teaching in the second step: The first precedes baptism and is meant for catechumens since it is more elementary (*simplicior*) and involves "certain mysteries of Christian philosophy," and the second follows baptism and is more complete (*perfectior*), particularly because it concerns instruction in the Christian "way of living" (*vivendi ratio*).[27]

Erasmus clarifies that the twofold schema for teaching derived from the Great Commission:

> It might be a dream of my own imagination, except that the Gospel of Matthew openly declares this: "Therefore, go, teach all nations, baptizing them in the name of the Father, the Son, and the Holy Spirit, teaching them to obey all the things that I have commanded you." Did you not hear the twofold teaching, one before baptism, another after baptism, which he mentions on the subject of keeping his commandments?[28]

In the *Paraphrases*, Erasmus does not qualify his interpretation of the Great Commission, insisting that candidates must learn and embrace the rudiments of the faith prior to baptism. By 1528, however, when he wrote the *Exposition on Psalm 85* he was fully aware of Anabaptism, and this may have led him to add a comment that removed any doubts about his view of infant baptism and Matt 28:19–20. He observes:

---

[25] The seminal essay is James McConica, "Erasmus and the Grammar of Consent," in *Scrinium Erasmianum* (2 vols., ed. J. Coppens; Leiden: Brill, 1969), 2:77–99.

[26] Dominic Baker-Smith, introduction to *Exposition on the Psalms*, CWE 63: xiii, xvii. Erasmus was using the Vulgate and consequently his Psalm 85 corresponds to Psalm 86 in English versions.

[27] *Opera omnia Des. Erasmi Roterodami* (Amsterdam: North-Holland, 1969-), V–3:389, abbreviated as ASD.

[28] ASD V–3: 389 (=CWE 64: 77).

> There is no doubt that the Gospel here speaks about adults. But now, since on the ancient authority of the Church infants are baptized—who are able to be baptized, yet not able to be taught—at least after baptism they should learn those things which it is an outrage for a Christian person not to know.[29]

Erasmus demonstrates his exegetical convictions about the passage's original intent as well as his view of the Church's authority. Although the passage assumes believer's baptism, his theological commitment to consensus led him to accept infant baptism. But this is clearly a concession, and Erasmus insists that if the church has left behind the original practice of prebaptismal catechesis, it must at least develop a teaching program that mitigates the negative effects of infant baptism. To do otherwise, and leave "Christian" people ignorant of the basic truths of the faith, is not just wrong, but an outrage (*nefas*).

In sum, Erasmus consistently based his interpretation of Matt 28:19–20 on the conviction that the literal word order (*docete . . . baptizantes . . . docentes*) was theologically significant and was the divinely ordained basis for catechesis. His passing nod to it lends support to John Payne's suggestion that infant baptism was "an embarrassing fragment of his baptismal theology which is not easily reconciled with the other elements and which he integrated not intrinsically but rather primarily on the basis of the authority of the church."[30] Erasmus's view of the Great Commission simply did not fit well within a context of infant baptism, and his proposal for a baptismal reaffirmation ceremony represented his attempt at integrating the "embarrassing fragment" into a sacramental theology that valued believer's baptism.

Anabaptists and the Great Commission

Balthasar Hubmaier (d. 1528), doctor of theology, popular pilgrimage preacher, and reforming pastor, wrote several treatises that represent the Anabaptist approach to baptism. Although marginalized in much of the Anabaptist historiography, this fascinating reformer was the most educated and prolific of the early Anabaptist leadership, and his theological impact

---

[29] ASD V-3: 389 (=CWE 64:77) "Ne dubium est quin de adultis loquatur Evangelium. Nunc vero quoniam ex prisca ecclesiae autoritate baptizantur infantes, qui tingi possunt, doceri nondum possunt, utinam saltem post baptismum ea discant quae nefas est hominem christianum nescire."

[30] Ibid., 177–78.

was felt for generations after his death.³¹ The Great Commission was extremely important to Hubmaier, and in a private letter to Oecolampadius dated months before his conversion to Anabaptism, he stated that his opposition to infant baptism stemmed from those very words of Jesus.³² In three of his foremost baptismal writings, Hubmaier cites the passage and the Marcan parallel (Mark 16:16) more than thirty times. Often he assumes the meaning is obvious, providing "clear" or "plain" or "explicit" evidence that the Church should baptize only those who respond to the gospel in faith.³³ Hubmaier indicates twice that he viewed the Great Commission as an impregnable argument against infant baptism: "His Word, Matt 28 and Mark 16, stands firm as a Greek marble wall."³⁴ For Hubmaier, the Great Commission was the Achilles heel of the doctrine of infant baptism.

Hubmaier highly valued Matt 28:19–20 because he believed it to be the place where Christian baptism, as opposed to John's baptism, had been initiated. Moreover, the fact that Christ had instituted baptism shortly after claiming all authority and in reference to the powerful Trinitarian formula meant that the issue of baptism did not belong to the category of things over which the reformers could amicably disagree. On the contrary, it was essential to the true reformation of Christianity.³⁵ Hubmaier also

---

³¹ For a concise biography, see Christof Windhorst, "Balthasar Hubmaier: Professor, Preacher, Politician," in *Profiles of Radical Reformers* (ed. Hans-Jürgen Goertz; Kitchener, Ont.: Herald, 1982), 144–57; for Hubmaier's importance to early Anabaptism see C. Arnold Snyder, *Anabaptist History and Theology: An Introduction* (Kitchener, Ont.: Pandora, 1995), 63–64, n. 13.

³² Hubmaier's writings are found in *Balthasar Hubmaier Schriften* (ed. G. Westin and T. Bergsten (Gütersloh: Gerd Mohn, 1962), abbreviated as HS; *Balthasar Hubmaier: Theologian of Anabaptism* (ed., and trans. H.W. Pipkin and John Howard Yoder; Scottdale, Pa.: Herald, 1989); abbreviated as PY. For the reference to the Great Commission see, *Letter to Oecolampadius* (PY 69–70); see Yoder ("Balthasar Hubmaier and the Beginnings of Swiss Anabaptism," *Mennonite Quarterly Review* 33 [1959]: 8) for a discussion of the importance of Matthew 28:19–20 to Hubmaier, and Oecolampadius's immediate response to the letter.

³³ *On the Christian Baptism of Believers* (PY 104, 114–115, 120, 121, 122, 125, 129, 130, 142); *Dialogue with Zwingli's Baptism Book* (PY 179, 188, 189, 191, 198–202, 205, 207, 211, 222, 223, 224, 225, 228); *Old and New Teachers On Believer's Baptism* (PY 247, 249, 250, 253, 255, 261).

³⁴ *On the Christian Baptism of Believers* (PY 129; HS 146); *Dialogue with Zwingli's Baptism Book* (PY 198; HS 189).

³⁵ David Steinmetz, "The Baptism of John and the baptism of Jesus in Huldrych Zwingli, Balthasar Hubmaier and Late Medieval Theology," in *Continuity and Discontinuity in Christian History: Essays Presented to George H. Williams on the occasion of his 65th Birthday* (ed. F. F. Church and Timothy George; Leiden: Brill, 1979), 169–81. For Hubmaier's

believed that the Great Commission presented a pattern of conversion that precluded baptizing babies largely because he relies upon the same exegetical conclusions as Erasmus: the literal word order is significant to the proper interpretation of the passage. Hubmaier organized his argument in *On the Christian Baptism of Believers* around the fundamental point that the New Testament presented a discernible pattern of conversion involving preaching, faith, baptism, and good works. He summarized the schema at the beginning of the chapter on "The Baptism of Christ," where he calls the reader's attention to the order of conversion in the earliest church:

> Here once again I would like to ask you, dear reader, in the following passages on the baptism of Christ to observe the following order, both in regard to the words and the meaning: (1) word, (2) hearing, (3) faith, (4) baptism, (5) work. From this sequence you can certainly fathom whether one should baptize infants.[36]

Wayne Pipkin pointed out that the order of conversion was important to Hubmaier for two basic reasons. Obviously, preaching had to precede baptism so as to teach people the doctrines of the Christian faith, but it also had to produce repentance. For Hubmaier, biblical faith was not merely intellectual acquiescence to Christian doctrines, but belief combined with a sincere desire to turn away from sin, i.e., repentance. By emphasizing the importance of faith and repentance as prerequisites for baptism, Hubmaier strengthened his argument against his opponents because, although some thought infants were capable of a kind of incipient faith, no one suggested they were capable of repentance.[37] Hubmaier succinctly stated his entire view of baptism and his exegetical approach to the Great Commission in *A Christian Catechism* (1526), where he notes the inadequacies of infant baptism and the urgency of rebaptism, that is, true baptism:

---

references to Christ's institution of Christian baptism at the Great Commission see *On the Christian Baptism of Believers* (PY 97–98; HS 119–20). Numerous other references use similar language, see [PY 118 (HS 137), 119 (HS 138), 121–22 (HS 140), 125 (HS 143), 129 (HS 146), 145 (HS 160]; they are repeated in the *Dialogue with Zwingli's Baptism book* (PY 198–213; HS 188–99).

[36] *On the Christian Baptism of Believers* (PY 129; HS 146). See also *On the Christian Baptism of Believers* (PY 114–18; HS 134–137) where Hubmaier cites the Great Commission concerning the sequence of the Apostles' preaching: "From these words one understands clearly and certainly that this sending of the apostles consists of three points or commands: First, preaching; second, faith; and third, outward baptism."

[37] Pipkin, "The Baptismal Theology of Balthasar Hubmaier," 39–40.

> *Leonhart*: If only believers are to be baptized who publicly confess with their mouth, as Christ instituted water baptism for believers alone, Matt. 28; Mark 16, must we submit to rebaptism? What seems right to you?
>
> *Hans*: Our approving, supposing, and thinking are of no importance; we must ask advice of the mouth of the Lord who said: Go therefore and teach all nations and baptize them; he who believes and is baptized will be saved. Since Christ commanded his disciples to preach and baptize, that very command orders us to hear the preaching and to be baptized. For whoever then loosens one of the least of these commandments shall be called least in the kingdom of heaven, Matt. 5:19; James 2. But now water baptism is a very earnest command; it has been proclaimed to be performed in the name of the Father, the Son, and the Holy Spirit. If we accept this baptism, even though we were one hundred years old, it would still not be a rebaptism, because infant baptism is no baptism and is unworthy of being called baptism. For the infant knows neither good nor evil and cannot consent or vow either to the church or to God.[38]

Hubmaier viewed baptism as a personal pledge of discipleship to God and the Church, an enrolling in the Christian community. By including repentance and a volitional response into his definition of faith, he removed the sacrament far beyond the capabilities of children. Infants simply could not meet the requirements for baptism: personal belief in the truths of the faith, an awareness of good and evil and sin, and public commitment to the Christian community.[39]

Unlike most Anabaptists, Hubmaier demonstrates some concern that his baptismal views be supported by Christian tradition. Hubmaier wrote *Old and New Teachers on Believer's Baptism* (1526) to demonstrate that believer's baptism was not only within the bounds of orthodoxy, but that it represented the practice of the early Church, and that authorities and some of his own contemporaries held views that logically precluded infant baptism.[40]

---

[38] *A Christian Catechism* (PY 350; HS 314).

[39] *A Christian Catechism* (PY 350; HS 314).

[40] Armour, *Anabaptist Baptism*, 49–52; Christof Windhorst, *Täuferisches Taufverständnis. Balthasar Hubmaiers Lehre zwischen traditioneller und reformatorischer Theologie* (Leiden: Brill, 1979), 108–12; Pipkin, "The Baptismal Theology of Balthasar Hubmaier," 48–50.

Hubmaier begins the discussion of contemporary authorities by appealing to Erasmus's *Paraphrase on Matthew* at the Great Commission.[41] Hubmaier was particularly interested in a phrase from Erasmus's *Paraphrase on Acts* that highlighted the subjective element of the sacrament and tied its efficacy to faith. As noted above, Erasmus had indicated that baptism apart from faith was a vain act,[42] and Hubmaier seized upon this phrase in a marginal note, a technique he used to highlight important phrases and guide readers through the argument of the treatise. The only nontextual marginal note for the quote of Erasmus corresponds with *frustra tingitur aqua* and reads, "ineffectual water" (*Ein vergeblich Wasser*).[43] The inefficacy of infant baptism was a crucial theological point for Hubmaier because it sheltered him from the charge of rebaptism since infant baptism was "unworthy of being called baptism."[44] For Hubmaier, baptism, as seen in the Great Commission, was originally intended exclusively for believers, and the efficacy of the sacrament was linked to the faith of the baptismal candidate. Apart from it, as with infants, baptism was a useless rite bearing no resemblance to Christ's original intentions.

The parallels between Erasmus and the Anabaptists on the Great Commission are striking, especially when compared with the interpretations offered by other major reformers such as Zwingli and Luther. Zwingli knew the Anabaptists well and faulted their interpretation of the Great Commission,[45] precisely for assigning theological significance to the word order. According to him, in the passage Christ "was not laying any conscious stress upon the order."[46] Zwingli's interpretation coincides roughly with the conclusions of many modern New Testament scholars who emphasize in the passage one primary command (to make disciples) carried by two related means (baptism and teaching),[47] and bears little

---

[41] *Old and New Teachers on Believer's Baptism* (PY 255; HS 233).

[42] *Paraphrase on Acts* LB 7: 674A. "quibus nisi crediderit, frustra tingitur aqua."

[43] *Old and New Teachers on Believers Baptism* (HS 233; PY 256).

[44] *A Christian Catechism* (PY 350; HS 314). See also *On the Christian Baptism of Believers* (PY 121; HS 140) where Hubmaier explicitly asserts that "infant baptism is no baptism."

[45] Bergsten, *Balthasar Hubmaier*, 263–65; Yoder, "Balthasar Hubmaier and the Beginnings of Swiss Anabaptism," 149.

[46] *Of Baptism* in *Zwingli and Bullinger* (trans. G. W. Bromiley; Philadelphia: Westminster, 1953), 141–42.

[47] For example, see Leon Morris, *The Gospel According to Matthew* (Grand Rapids: Eerdmans, 1992), 748–49; Craig S. Keener, *A Commentary on the Gospel of Matthew* (Grand Rapids: Eerdmans, 1999), 718–19; Donald A. Hagner, *Matthew 14–28* (WBC 33B; Dallas: Word, 1995), 886–87.

resemblance to that of Erasmus or Hubmaier. The same can be said of Luther. Outside his specific treatment of Matt 28:19–20 in the context of Anabaptism, Luther cites the text in support of the doctrine of the Trinity, the international nature of Christianity, the office of preaching, and the power of the sacrament.[48] In *Concerning Rebaptism* (1528) he specifically rejected the argument from word order, less for exegetical imprecision than for theological naivete. He mocks a view of baptism that made it contingent upon personal faith, for in that situation the sacrament becomes a work and the fickleness of personal faith would provide no assurance of salvation. Faith itself was the gracious gift of God and its chronological relationship to baptism was ultimately inconsequential.[49] Further on, Luther finds a literal understanding of πάντα τὰ ἔθνη to be crucial since infants are included in "all the nations" and therefore are candidates for baptism.[50] Unlike Erasmus, who accepted infant baptism because of its antiquity, Luther believed that the Great Commission sanctioned it.[51]

Conclusion

The Anabaptists are usually viewed as the radicals, or left wing of the Reformation, who went further than anyone else in uprooting questionable components of the medieval Church, whereas Erasmus is considered the moderate humanist reformer, who was unwilling to the leave the Catholic Church, despite his deep criticisms of it. How is it that Erasmus and the Anabaptists occupy common ground in their emphasis upon believer's baptism in the Great Commission? Is it coincidental, or is there something more significant at work in the convergence of these seemingly opposite theological perspectives?

---

[48] *Luther's Works* (ed. Jaroslav Pelikan and Helmut T. Lehman; 55 vols.; Philadelphia: Fortress, 1955–86); abbreviated as *LW*. On the Trinity, see *Psalm 45* (*LW* 12: 288); universality of Christianity, *Psalm 45* (*LW* 13: 271–2), *Zechariah* (*LW* 20: 338), *Galatians* (*LW* 26: 101), *I Timothy* (*LW* 28: 263); on the preaching office, *Psalm 82* (*LW* 13: 49), Marburg Colloquy (*LW* 38: 213); on the efficacy of baptism, Marburg Colloquy (*LW* 38: 27,57,198–99), *Genesis* (*LW* 6: 128), *Against Hans Wurst* (*LW* 41: 196), *Avoiding Doctrines of Men* (*LW* 35: 148), *Defense of Infant Baptism* (*LW* 54: 74).

[49] *Concerning Rebaptism* (*LW* 40: 239–41). On this point, see also McGrath, *Reformation Thought*, 97–101.

[50] *Concerning Rebaptism* (*LW* 40: 245, 252); see also his defense of infant baptism in the Table Talk where he asserts that children were encompassed in the Great Commission (*LW* 38:113).

[51] Zeitlow, "Martin Luther's Arguments for Infant Baptism," 147–71.

One approach is to assert Erasmian influence. The study of the relationship between humanism and the Reformation has a long history and one component has been the question of Erasmus's influence upon Anabaptism. Recently, scholars have noted interesting parallels between the thought of Erasmus and Anabaptism on issues such as pacifism, free will, asceticism, and the sacraments.[52] The period of Hubmaier's conversion to the Reformation and Anabaptism witnessed his explicit approval of humanist theological method, association with humanists of south Germany, and a personal meeting with Erasmus.[53] In connection with the Great Commission, the point would simply be that Hubmaier learned his interpretation directly from Erasmus's *Paraphrase on Matthew* and adopted it as his own. Hubmaier took Erasmus's exegetical conclusions and transplanted them into a theological context emphasizing a radical version of *sola scriptura* which demanded believer's baptism.[54]

Another approach is to point to the common theological emphases between Erasmus and the Anabaptists that naturally led to a convergence on the issue of believer's baptism. A few examples should suffice. A cornerstone of Renaissance humanism was its emphasis upon free will and the correlative belief in the dignity of the human being. Erasmus was the great champion of free will in the early sixteenth century, and his refutation of Luther's view in 1524 permanently alienated him from many reformers. Yet, the Anabaptists all agreed with Erasmus, Hubmaier penning his own treatise on the topic. Both believed that fallen man could reach out to God prior to conversion, and after regeneration was able to carry out the commands of Christ, making moral reform an absolute imperative. The

---

[52] For example, see Hans Hillerbrand, "The Origin of Sixteenth-Century Anabaptism: Another Look," *Archiv für Reformationsgeschichte* 53 (1962): 152–80, esp. 154–58; Kenneth R. Davis, "Erasmus as Progenitor of Anabaptist Theology and Piety," *Mennonite Quarterly Review* 47 (1973): 163–78; Edward K. Burger, "Erasmus and the Anabaptists" (Ph.D. diss. University of California, Santa Barbara, 1977); Dale Schrag, "Erasmian and Grebelian Pacifism: Consistency or Contradiction?" *Mennonite Quarterly Review* 62 (1988): 431–54; and Abraham Friesen, *Erasmus, the Anabaptists, and the Great Commission* (Grand Rapids: Eerdmans, 1998). For the most recent overview of the topic, see Marc Lienhard, "Die Radikalen des 16. Jahrhunderts und Erasmus," in *Erasmianism: Idea and Reality* (ed. M. E. H. N. Mout, H. Smolinsky, and J. Trapman; Amsterdam: North Holland, 1997), 91–104.

[53] See Torsten Bergsten, *Balthasar Hubmaier: Anabaptist Theologian and Martyr* (trans. Irwin Barnes and William R. Estep, ed., William R. Estep; Valley Forge, Pa.: Judson, 1978), 70–78. More research is needed on the quality of Hubmaier's personal contact with Erasmus.

[54] See Darren T. Williamson, "Erasmus of Rotterdam's Influence upon Anabaptism: The Case of Balthasar Hubmaier" (Ph.D. diss., Simon Fraser University, 2005), 64–112.

Great Commission's requirement of prebaptismal teaching meant that in some small way, salvation was contingent upon the volitional response of individuals exercising their free will.

Discipleship was another key component of Erasmus's view of reforming Christianity, and the last thirty years of his life were dedicated to biblical scholarship and devotional literature, designed to help produce serious Christians. The *Handbook of the Christian Soldier* (1503) makes this clear, and much of his paraphrasing of the New Testament continued that project by illuminating Scripture for the educated laity. Again, his innovative proposal for catechesis culminating in a baptismal reaffirmation ceremony directly related to his concern for discipleship. It is not far-fetched to suppose that this idea was directly related to his interpretation of the Great Commission. Anabaptists were well known for their focus on discipleship which began with the baptismal pledge of believers.

Erasmus was one of the foremost proponents of moral and ethical reform of the Church. He longed for a visible body of believers who were saints in reality, not theory. For him, continual scriptural teaching and preaching would help Christians advance in piety and holiness. The two references to teaching in the Great Commission gave him an opportunity to expound further on the importance of teaching. As noted, the Anabaptists emphasized teaching as imperative to creating the visible church, and Hubmaier produced a catechism designed for the instruction of baptismal candidates. But he also related the Great Commission to the uniquely Anabaptist practice of the ban. How could a congregation hold a Christian accountable for breaking the pledge of discipleship when the practice of infant baptism had robbed him of the opportunity to make the decision in the first place? According to Hubmaier, "where the water of baptism of Christ has not been restored according to the order of Christ, then it is impossible to know who is in the Church or who is outside, whom we have authority to admonish or not, who are brothers or sisters."[55] The Great Commission's "order of conversion" had great ramifications for maintaining the purity of the visible Church.

Erasmus appears to have sympathized with the Anabaptists for their emphasis upon discipleship and pious lives.[56] His overarching commitment to the Church's unity and the *consensus fidelium*, however, kept him from advocating believer's baptism, even if that was the logical extension

---

[55] *On the Christian Ban* (PY 420; HS 374).

[56] See Irvin B. Horst, *Erasmus, the Anabaptists and the Problem of Religious Unity* (Haarlem: H.D. Tjeenk Willink en Zoon, 1967), 1–32.

of his exegesis of the Great Commission and consistent with his theology of baptism. Hubmaier and the Anabaptists did not share Erasmus's degree of commitment to either of these principles, and implemented reforms that sought to create a visible Church of saints with believer's baptism as a cornerstone of the movement.

The Anabaptists tenaciously held to their view of baptism, and many lost their lives for it, including Balthasar Hubmaier. They maintained this conviction out of obedience to a biblical order of conversion revealed in the Great Commission, and also because they saw in it important principles related to the nature of discipleship and the purity of the visible Church. For the most part Christian humanists like Erasmus shared these fundamental convictions but were not willing to incorporate them into their program of reform at the expense of practices confirmed by the Church's consensus. Advocates of believer's baptism might attribute such reticence to cowardice or relativism. One should, instead, remember that in every Christian thinker, competing convictions wrestle for dominance, often producing tensions. For Erasmus, erring on the side of concord and enduring the problems accompanying infant baptism was more pious than advocating believer's baptism and destroying the unity of the Church.

Publications of James W. Thompson

Books

Pastoral Ministry according to Paul: A Biblical Vision. Grand Rapids: Baker Academic, 2006.

God's Holy Fire. With Ken Cukrowski and Mark W. Hamilton. Abilene, Tex.: Abilene Christian University Press, 2002.

Preaching Like Paul: Homiletical Wisdom for Today. Louisville: Westminster John Knox, 2000.

The Early Church in Its Context: Essays in Honor of Everett Ferguson. Edited with Abraham Malherbe and Frederick Norris. NovTSup 90. Leiden: Brill, 1998.

Equipped for Change. Abilene, Tex.: Abilene Christian University Press, 1997.

Translator of Horst Balz and Gerhard Schneider, editors. *Exegetical Dictionary of the New Testament.* Vols. 1–2. Grand Rapids: Eerdmans, 1990–92.

The Church in Exile: God's Counter Culture in a Non-Christian World. Abilene, Tex.: Abilene Christian University, 1990.

The Mark of a Christian. Tulsa: Christian Communications, 1983.

The Beginnings of Christian Philosophy: The Epistle to the Hebrews. CBQMS 13. Washington, D.C.: Catholic Biblical Association, 1982.

Strategy for Survival: A Plan for Church Renewal from Hebrews. Austin: Sweet, 1980.

Our Life Together. Journey Books. Austin: Sweet, 1977.

The Letter to the Hebrews. Living Word Commentary 15. Austin: Sweet, 1972.

The Second Letter of Paul to the Corinthians. Living Word Commentary 9. Austin: Sweet, 1970. French translation, 1992.

Major Articles in Journals and Chapters in Books

"The Epistle to the Hebrews in Clement of Alexandria." In *Transmission and Reception: New Testament Text-Critical and Exegetical Studies,* edited by J. W. Childers and D. C. Parker, 239–54. Texts and Studies 3d ser., 4. Piscataway, N.J.: Gorgias, 2006.

"The Epistle to the Hebrews and the Pauline Legacy." *ResQ* 47 (2005): 197–206.

"Reflections on the Last Fifty Years." *ResQ* 46 (2004): 131–38.

"Preaching the Letters as Narrative." In *Narrative Reading, Narrative Preaching: Reuniting New Testament Interpretation and Proclamation,* edited by Joel B. Green and Michael Pasquarello III, 81–105. Grand Rapids: Baker Academic, 2003.

"The Formation of an Academic Tradition in Biblical Studies at Abilene Christian University." *ResQ* 45 (2003): 15–28.

"Creation, Shame, and Nature in 1 Cor 11:2–16: The Background and Coherence of Paul's Argument." In *Early Christianity and Classical Culture: Comparative Studies in Honor of Abraham J. Malherbe,* edited by John Fitzgerald, Thomas Olbricht, and L. Michael White, 237–57. NovTSup 110. Leiden: Brill, 2003.

"Did Anything Happen?" In *Preaching Hebrews,* edited by David Fleer and Dave Bland, 141–48. Rochester College Lectures on Preaching 4. Abilene, Tex.: Abilene Christian University Press, 2003.

"Narrative Preaching from Romans." In *Preaching Romans,* edited by Dave Bland and David Fleer, 53–72. Rochester College Lectures on Preaching 3. Abilene, Tex.: Abilene Christian University Press, 2002.

"Paul's Argument from *Pathos* in 2 Corinthians." In *Paul and Pathos,* edited by Thomas H. Olbricht and Jerry Sumney, 127–45. SBLSymS 16. Atlanta: SBL, 2001.

"Reading Romans Today." *Leaven* 8/4 (2000): 197–200.

"The Holy Spirit in the Churches of Christ." *Leaven* 8/3 (2000): 129–34.

"The Background and Function of the Beatitudes in Matthew and Luke." *ResQ* 41 (1999): 109–16.

"The Appropriate, the Necessary, and the Impossible: Faith and Reason in Hebrews." In *The Early Church in its Context: Essays in Honor of Everett Ferguson,* edited by Abraham J. Malherbe, Frederick Norris, and James Thompson, 302–17. NovTSup 90. Leiden: Brill, 1998.

"The Hermeneutics of the Epistle to the Hebrews." *ResQ* 38 (1996): 229–37.

"The Rhetoric of 1 Peter." *ResQ* 36 (1994): 237–50.

"What Every Christian Should Know: Tradition in the Early Church." *Christian Studies* 11 (Spring 1991): 5–14.

"Hermeneutics Then and Now." *Christian Studies* 11 (Fall 1990): 5–17.

"What Happened to Evangelism?" *Christian Studies* 10 (Fall 1989): 5–14.

"Community, Ethics, and the Christian Faith on Campus." *Institute for Christian Studies Faculty Bulletin* 9 (Fall 1988): 36–49.

"Ministry in the New Testament." *ResQ* 27 (1984): 143–56.

"New Testament Studies and the Restoration Movement." *ResQ* 25 (1982): 223–32.

"Hebrews 9 and Hellenistic Concepts of Sacrifice." *JBL* 98 (1979): 567–78.

"Outside the Camp: A Study of Heb 13:9–14." *CBQ* 40 (1978): 53–63.

"The Conceptual Background and Purpose of the Midrash in Hebrews VII." *NovT* 19 (1977): 209–23.

"The Structure and Purpose of the Catena in Heb 1:5–13." *CBQ* 38 (1976): 352–63.

"Authentic Discipleship: An Introduction to II Corinthians." *ResQ* 19 (1976): 1–6.

"That Which Cannot be Shaken: Some Metaphysical Assumptions in Heb 12:27." *JBL* 94 (1975): 580–87.

"The Underlying Unity of Hebrews." *ResQ* 18 (1975): 129–36.

"On Whose Terms: The Offense of the Gospel." *Mission* 9/7 (1976): 15–16.

"The Gentile Mission as an Eschatological Necessity." *ResQ* 14 (1971): 18–27.

"Recent Studies on the Basileia." *ResQ* 12 (1969): 211–16.

"Be Submissive to your Masters: An Exegesis of 1 Peter 2:18–25." *ResQ* 9 (1966): 66–78.

Indices

Scripture

Genesis

1:1–2:3	246–47
1:1	18 n. 36, 246
1:27	159–60
1:28	253
9:1–2	253
11	6, 17 n. 31, 18
11:1	8, 11, 16, 17, 19, 20, 22, 27
11:3–4	254
15:3	35
16:6	35
16:8	35
16:11	35
17:1	151
22:2	142, 142 n. 30
22:4	142
25:13–14	113 n. 25
29:29–35	34
30:16–20	34
31	33
31:14–16	34 n. 25
31:24	34
31:26–30	34 n. 25
31:26	35 n. 31
31:50	34–35, 35 n. 29
31:53	34
31:54	34
32:29	152
34:2	35
34:31	35 n. 31
35:3	109 n. 16

Exodus

chs. 1–2	251–54, 253 n.7, 253 n.8, 253 n.9, 256–57, 259
1:10	254
1:11–12	35
2:3	254
3:14	150–54
12	135–36, 138–39
12:6	142
12:14	136
12:15	136
12:21	136 n. 12
12:43–50	141
13:21	94
15	18
20:7	34 n. 28
24:3	8
25:8 (9 MT)	160 n. 101
25:40	160 n. 101
26:30	160, 160 n. 101
27:8	160 n. 101

Leviticus

23:5	142

Numbers

chs. 13–14	93
13:1–2	99
20	99

Deuteronomy

1–3	97
1	84 n. 3
1:19–46	84, 92–102
6:5	251
12:25	52 n. 20
12:28	52 n. 20
13:19	52 n. 20
16	139
16:2	136 n. 12
16:5–6	136 n. 12
16:15	136
21:9	52 n. 20
21:15–17	34
26:6	35
31:6	94
31:8	94

Judges

20:5	35

2 Samuel

13:12	35
13:14	35
13:32	35

1 Kings

18:26	109 n. 16

2 Chronicles

3:1	142, 142 n. 30
18:12	4

Ezra

5:9	29 n. 9
6:24	29 n. 9

Nehemiah

9:36–37	143

Job

chs. 1–2	142
6:25	110 n. 19, 112 n.21
26:2–3	110 n. 19, 112 n.21

Psalms

6	108 n. 12
15:1	113 n. 26
18:7–20	112
40	114 n. 30
50:15	109 n. 16
55:18–19	107 n. 11
57:5b	112 n. 22
64:4	112 n. 22
65:5	113 n. 26
78:55, 60	113 n. 26
78:60	113 n. 26
81:8	109 n. 16
86:7	109 n. 16
86 (85):11	272, 272 n. 26
94:17	113 n. 27
101	90, 90 n. 18
102:3	109 n. 16
105:18	35
106:10, 41	113 n. 28
107 (106):6–7	18 n. 36
107 (106):13	18 n. 36
110	128–29
120	104–115
121	108 n. 14
123:4	113 n. 27
133:1	110 n. 19

Proverbs

1:7	156
6:24	110 n. 17
25:18	112 n. 22
26:18–19	112 n. 22

Ecclesiastes

12:11	6

Song of Solomon

8:13	12
8:14	12

Isaiah

chs. 1–39	163–68
chs. 1–35	168
chs. 1–34	168
chs. 1–12	168–70
chs. 1–5	172–80
1	168
chs. 2–66	168
2:6—4:1	164
2:6	164
6:1—9:6 (7)	166
6:1	167
6:3	13 n. 23
6:9–10	164
6:11	167
8:6–20	166
8:6	164
8:7–8	166
8:12	164
8:17	124
9:1–2	72 n. 15
10:24–27	166
11:12–16	164
12:1	165
chs. 13–14	167
13:1—14:23	164
13:4	17 n. 31
19:2	29 n. 9
19:23	164
21:17	113 n. 25
27:12–13	164
28:11	8 n. 13
28:14	164
29:13	164
29:18	164
30:8	166
30:9	164
32:3	164
35	164
35:5	164
chs. 36–39	166–68
37:16	167

Isaiah (*continued*)

37:21–29	166
37:26	166
39	164
39:5–7	166
chs. 40–66	163–68
chs. 40–55	163–68, 260
40:1	165
40:21	166
41:8–16	166
41:22–23	166
42:16	164
42:18–20	164
43:1–4	166
43:5–7	166
43:8	164
43:9	166
44:1–5	166
44:7–8	166
44:18	164
44:26	167
45:21	167
46:10	166
48:3	167
48:5	167
49:19	167
51:12	165
52:13	167
53	257–58
53:10	168
chs. 56–66	163–68
56:1–8	69 n. 8
56:7	66, 69–70
57:15	167
62:6–12	164
chs. 65–66	179–80
66:13	165
66:24	167

Jeremiah

2:33	110 n. 19, 112 n. 21
2:36	110 n. 19, 112 n.21
7:11	69–70
9:7	112 n. 22
31:31	139

Ezekiel

37:15–23	246

Jonah

2	114 n. 30

Micah

7:1–7	28 n. 7
7:6	28

Zechariah

14:21	69, 69 n. 6

Matthew

4:12–25	72 n. 15
5:3–12	174
10:5–10	73 n. 16
10:5–6	73 n. 16
10:37–38	27
13:1–3	72 n. 15
15:20–31	75 n. 19
15:22	75 n. 19
15:29–30	72 n. 15
17:22–23	72 n. 15
18:25	219 n. 53
19:1–2	72 n. 15
21:12	69
21:13	66, 69
22:34–40	71
26:57—27:26	174
26:61	76 n. 23
28:10	77
28:16–20	77
28:19–20	265, 268, 270, 272, 273, 274, 278
28:19	16

Mark

1:1–15	241
1:14–15	73
1:14	72
1:15	246
1:16—8:21	242
1:16–20	73, 242
1:21–28	73
1:21	69 n. 7
1:32	247
1:35	247
1:38–39	72
1:45	72
2:13	69 n. 7
2:13–14	73
2:21	246
3:1–6	242
3:6	67 n. 2
3:7–19	73
3:13–19	242
3:14	72
3:21	28 n. 6
3:22	72, 73
3:31–35	28 n. 6, 73
4:2	69 n. 7
4:11–12	73
4:28	246
4:33–41	73
4:35	247
5:1–20	73
5:2	72
5:15–20	247
5:20	73
5:21–24	246
5:21	74
5:25–34	246
5:35–43	246
6:1–6	72 n. 14, 73, 242
6:7–30	73
6:7–13	242
6:12	72
6:14–24	74
6:30—8:22	74, 75
6:30–44	74
6:31–44	74
6:43	246
6:45–52	245
6:45	74 n. 17
6:47	247
6:48	247

Mark (*continued*)
6:51	245
6:52	74, 75
6:53–56	75
6:53	74
7:1–23	74
7:1	72
7:19	75
7:24–30	75
7:26	75 n. 19
7:27	73 n. 16, 75 n. 19
7:31–37	75 n. 19
7:36	72
8:1–10	74
8:14–21	74, 242
8:15	74
8:17	74
8:19–21	245
8:19	74
8:20	74
8:21	74
8:22—10:52	75, 242
8:22	74 n. 17
8:31–38	75 n. 20
8:31	77
9:12	72
9:30–37	75 n. 20
9:30–31	77
9:31	69 n. 7
10:1	69 n. 7, 72
10:32–45	75 n. 20
10:32–34	77
10:37	244
10:43	244
10:46–52	239
10:52	242
11:1—14:11	68
11:1—14:9	68
11:11–25	68
11:12–14	68
11:15–19	68, 69
11:15–18	76
11:15–17	76
11:15	69
11:16	69
11:17	66, 69, 70

Mark (*continued*)
11:18	67 n. 2
11:19	247
11:20–26	68
11:20	247
11:22–26	70
11:24–25	70
11:26	68, 68 n. 3
11:27–33	68
12:1–12	68
12:5	70
12:9	70
12:12	67 n. 2, 68
12:13–34	68
12:28–34	71
12:29–31	71
12:32–34	71
12:32–33	71
12:33	71
12:35–37	68
12:37—14:11	68
12:38–44	68
12:38–40	70
13:2	68, 76
13:3–37	68
13:5–23	68, 71
13:9–13	71
13:10	71, 76, 79
13:13	71
13:24–27	71
13:27	72
13:28–31	71
13:32–37	71
14:1–9	67 n. 2, 68
14:1—15:47	241
14:3–9	75
14:3	75
14:8	75
14:9	76
14:12—16:8	75
14:12–26	138, 139 n. 21
14:17	139, 247
14:25	139
14:26	77
14:28	77, 77 n. 25
14:49	246
14:53—15:20	174

Mark (continued)

14:53–72	76
14:55–59	76
14:55	76
14:58	70, 76, 77
15:1	247
15:26	75
15:29	77
15:39	77
15:42	247
16:1–8	241
16:2	247
16:5	247
16:7	77, 77 n. 25
16:8	77
16:16	274
16:20	75

Luke

10:25–28	71
10:39–40	71
12:51–53	28
14:26–27	27
18:31—19:46	174
19:45	69
19:46	66, 69
20:16	70
23:43	19

John

2:15	69 n. 6
2:19	76 n. 23
6:38	118

Acts

2:6	18
4:11	71
8:4–25	270 n. 22
8:26–40	257
9:18	270 n. 22
10:24	25
10:44–48	25
11:14	25
16:15	25, 270 n. 22
16:31–34	25

Acts (continued)

16:33	270 n. 22
17:24	19
17:34	207–35
18:8	270 n. 22
19:34	8
22:16	270 n. 22
24:21	8

Romans

1:16	75 n. 19
3:2–3	121
3:3	120
3:21–31	121
3:21–26	117
3:22	117, 119, 120, 121, 122
3:26	117, 119, 120
3:29–30	78
5	127
5:18–19	122
6:6	136
8:15	141
8:32	142
11:20	191
12:16	191
14:6	190, 191
15:5	191
15:6	7
15:15	143 n. 31

1 Corinthians

1	253 n. 8
1:2–3	144
1:7–10	144
1:7–8	144
1:13	137
1:16	26
1:17–18	137
1:18	140
1:22–23	140
1:23	26, 141 n. 26
1:24–25	140
1:27–29	253 n. 7, 253 n.8, 253 n. 9, 256–57

294

Scripture

1 Corinthians (*continued*)
2:2	137
2:6	199
2:8	137
3:10–11	140
4:17	186 n. 24
5:6–8	137
5:7–8	133, 135
5:7	134, 135, 136, 136 n. 12, 138, 141
5:8	136
7:3–4	219 n. 53
8:6	144
10:1–13	139
10:14–22	141
10:1	144
11:1	120
11:7–12	50
11:23–26	138, 139 n. 21
11:23–25	141 n. 27
11:26	139
12:2	140
12:3	144
14:16	141
14:21	8 n. 13
14:33–36	50
14:33	7
15:3–5	137
15:3–4	137, 140
15:3	143 n. 31
15:23–28	144
15:54–57	127
16:8	141
16:15	26
16:17	26
16:22	141

2 Corinthians
12:10	242
13:11	191

Galatians
1:14–16	143 n. 33
2:11–14	141 n. 27
2:16	118

Galatians (*continued*)
2:20	118, 119
3:13	143 n. 31
3:22	118
4:6	141
4:21	190
4:26	144
5:5–6	122
5:10	192
5:23	64

Ephesians
2:8	118
3:12	118
6:9	43

Philippians
1:12–18	187
1:15–18	189
1:19–23	187
1:24–25	187
1:29	187
2:1–5	188
2:3	187
2:4	189 n. 38
2:5–11	181
2:5	186
2:6–11	186
2:7–8	187
2:8	122
2:16–17	186
2:17	187
2:19	186
3:2–14	185–86
3:2–6	189
3:2–4	189
3:2	188, 191
3:9	118
3:4–14	186
3:4–11	143 n. 35
3:14	188
3:15–21	184–91
3:20–21	144
3:20	134 n. 6
4:1	187
4:2	189

Philippians (continued)

4:8–9	188
4:10	188

Colossians

3:18	219
4:1	43

1 Timothy

1:10	34 n. 28
2	56
2:1—3:13	47
2:1–7	46
2:1–2	48
2:2–4	48
2:2	49, 50 n. 13, 52
2:3–4	48
2:5–7	52
2:8–15	46
2:8	46, 46 n. 8, 48
2:9–15	45–53, 64–65
2:9	60
3:2	64
4:6	52 n. 18
4:13	52 n. 18
5:4	52 n. 20
6:3	52 n. 18
6:20	52 n. 18

2 Timothy

1:4	52 n. 18
2:2	52 n. 18
3:10	52 n. 18
4:2	52 n. 18
4:3	52 n. 18

Titus

1:8	64
2:2–10	48–49
2:2–6	64
2:11–15	49
2:11–14	52
3:3–7	52

Hebrews

1:8–9	127
1:9	125
2:5–18	125–27
2:10	131
2:13	124
2:17	130
3:2	125, 130
3:5	125
3:6	125, 128, 130
4:11	125
4:14—5:10	129
4:16	125
5:3	128
5:5–10	127–29
5:5	126
5:11–14	198 n. 10
6:11	125
6:12	124
7:7	196
7:26–28	129
9:12	124 n. 34
10:14	127
10:19	125
10:23	124
10:35–39	123
10:35	125
11	116, 124, 130
11:2–3	130
11:6	124
11:11	124, 125
11:23	124
11:26	124
11:27	124
11:35–38	130
12:1–4	130
12:1–3	130
12:2	116, 125
13:7	125
13:12–13	131–132
13:13	130

James

2	276

1 Peter

chs. 2–3	44
2:4–10	70 n. 10
2:7	71
2:13–17	31
2:15	31
2:18—3:6	30
2:18–20	30
2:18	43
2:20	30, 37
2:21–25	30
2:21–24	44
3:1–6	30–31
3:3–4	60
3:3	50
3:5	50
3:6	30
3:14	30
4:13	44

1 John

4:18	42

Revelation

7:1–8	246
9:13	9

Other Ancient Literature

Greco-Roman

Aelius Aristides
Speeches
3.242, 24.8 — 183 n. 11

Aeschylus
Suppliants
724–25 — 60 n. 57

Apollodorus [Ps.]
Library 3.5.8 — 10

Appian
Civil Wars
1.65 — 183 n. 10

Aristophanes
Knights
670 — 5
Lysistrata
519–20 — 32 n. 18

Aristotle
Interpretation
11 (20b) — 9
Nicomachean Ethics
5.1 (1129b26–1130a10) — 155 n. 68
Politics
2.2 — 26

Aristotle (*continued*)
Problems
10.38 (895a) — 9
19.16 (918b) — 9
Rhetoric
1.10 — 95 n. 34

Aristotle [Ps.]
On Virtues and Vices
1250b12–13 — 55
1250b20–24 — 155 n. 70

Athenaeus
Learned Banquet
1.6.87 — 11
2.1 — 11

Cassius Dio
Roman History
5.21 — 182
44.36.2 — 11
47.3 — 183
54.23 — 36 n. 35

Chariton
Chaereas and Callirhoe
1.4.5 — 44 n. 53
8.1 — 11

Cicero

On Duties

1.15	54 n. 27, 57 n. 39
1.41	42 n. 50
1.54	26
1.93	57 n. 41
1.93–94	57 n. 42
1.94–95	58 n. 47
1.98–99	59 n. 48
142.142	57 n. 36
1.144	57 n. 44
2.5	158 n. 92
2.24	42 n. 50

On Ends

1.14	58 n. 43
1.93	58 n. 43
4.18	57–58, 58 n.43

On the Nature of the Gods — 149 n. 29

Tusculan Disputations

3.16–17	53–54

Crates [Ps.]

Epistles

9	61 n. 61

Demosthenes

Oration 22 (Androtion)

55	31

Dio Chrysostom

Orations

32.15–16	59 n. 49
32.95	57 n. 38
39.3	10

Diodore of Sicily

Library

11.19.3	9
11.26.6	9
11.92.4	9
16.10.3	9
16.79.3	9
17.33.4	9
19.81.2	9 n. 15

Diogenes Laertius

Lives of Eminent Philosophers

7.125	55 n. 30
7.125–26	57 n. 37
7.175	149 n. 26
10.27	149 n. 25

Dionysius of Halicarnassus

Roman Antiquities

4.67.2	9
6.80.4	182
6.87.1	10

Epictetus

Discourses

1.28.19–23	58 n. 43
2.10.15	60 n. 52

Encheiridion

40	60 n. 52

Euripides

Children of Heracles

476–77	60

Galen

On the Passions and Errors of the Soul

1.2	39
1.4	38
1.4–5	41–42
8.8	40

Greek Anthology

14.64.1	10 n. 16

Herodotus
Histories
1.60   182

Hierocles
On Duties   63 n. 68

Hippocrates [Ps.]
Epistles
13   60 n. 53

Libanius
Letters 1350.3   11

Lucian of Samosata
Nigrinus
14   11
On Dance
76   11

Melissa [Ps.]
Letter to Clearata
(ed. Städele)
160–62   62 n. 64

Musonius Rufus
Fragments
3   59–60, 59 n. 51
4   56 n. 34, 57 n. 42, 60 n. 55
8   55–56, 58 n. 45, 60 n. 54
11   58 n. 46
12   63 n. 69
13A   63 n. 68
13B   63 n. 68
14   63 n. 68
15   63 n. 68
16   58 n. 46

Musonius Rufus (*continued*)
18B   56 n. 33, 58 n. 46

Phintys
On a Woman's Sophrosyne
(ed. Thesleff)
152, 3–4   62
152, 9–10   62
152, 10–22   62
152, 11   62
152, 17–18   62
152, 20–21   62
152, 21–
153, 12–28   62
152, 25   62
153, 1–2   62

Plato
Charmides
159B–161B   52 n. 20
160C   52 n. 20
Euthyprho
12E   155 n. 67
Laws
634E   5, 9
777C   9
Philebus
17B   9
Republic
364A   5
430E   57 n. 41
617B   9
Timaeus   242–45

Plotinus
Enneads
6.4.14   11

Plutarch
Advice to Bride and Groom
138A   51
138C   51 n. 17
141D   60

Plutarch (*continued*)
141e	61
145Df	60
148Bc	51 n. 17

Calumny
frag. 153	36

Dialogue on Love
767E	62 n. 63

On Stoic Self-Contradictions
1046E	55 n. 30
1051E–F	149 n. 28
1052B	149 n. 27

On Talkativeness
502D	10
507B	60

On the Control of Anger
455C	30 n. 12
455F	30 n. 12
457A	30 n. 12
457B	40, 43 n. 53
459D	29 n. 11
459F–460A	29 n. 11, 40
460C	29 n. 11
460F	30 n. 12
461A	30 n. 12
461C	30 n. 12, 40
461B	37 n. 38
461E	40
462A	30 n. 12, 36
462E	29 n. 11
463A–B	37
464A	30 n. 12

On the Obsolescence of Oracles
414C	10

Table-Talk
615B	10, 15

Aratus
10.2	10

Cato the Younger
71.1	10

Demetrius
18.7	10

Galba
14.5	10
26.3	10

Pompey
72.2	10

Plutarch (*continued*)
Timoleon
38.3	10

Plutarch [Ps.]

On Education
7D–F	59 n. 49

Seneca

Epistles
47.1	42
47.2	42
47.5	39, 41
47.11	41, 42
47.13	42
47.16	42
18.18	42
18.19	43
89.5	158 n. 92

On Anger
2.25.1	40
3.5.4	36
40.40	36 n. 35

On Benefits
3.18–28	42
3.22–27	42

Sextus Empiricus

Against the Professors [M.]
9.13	158 n. 92

Sophocles

Ajax
586	60

Soranus

Gynecology
1.40	63 n. 68

Stobaeus

Anthology
2.594–60,2	54 n. 28

Stobaeus (continued)

3.3,42	155 n. 69
4.22,54	60 n. 53
4.23,3	60 n. 58
4.509,9	63 n. 66
4.510,3–5	63 n. 66
4.588,17–593,11	61 n. 62

Suetonius

Claudius

25.3	26
Nero 63.1	183 n. 8

Tacitus

Annals

15.44	26, 27
16.5	26

Theophrastus

Characters

12	37

Xenocrates

Fragments

15	154 n. 64

Xenophon

Oeconomicus

3.4	37 n. 40
13.6–8	39
9.9	39

Jewish

Song of the Three Youths

(Additions to Daniel)

	7, 22
v. 28	4–5
(Dan 3:51 LXX)	

4 Maccabees

8:29	8

Sirach

51:5–6	112 n. 22

Tobit

3:9	40

1 Enoch

47:2	11–12
56:7	29 n. 9
61:6, 9, 11	12
100:1–2	29 n. 9

4 Ezra

5:9	29 n. 9
6:24	29 n. 9

Jubilees

chs. 17–18	142
17:15	142
17:16	142

Josephus

Against Apion

1.225	149 n. 30

Jewish Antiquities

1.17	159 n. 99
2.313	143
2.317	136 n. 13, 143
3.248	143
7.23	183
7.286	183
11.8.5, 332	11
12.302–303	143
12.392	183 n. 7
14.58	183
14.124	183
17.213	143

Jewish War

Josephus (continued)	
4.402	143
5.99	143
5.98–105	143
6.420–434	143

Philo of Alexandria

De Abrahamo
60	155 n. 76
80	150 n. 42
114	155 n. 79, 156 n. 85
120	145 n. 2
121	150 n. 37, 153 n. 59
135	145 n. 6
270	150 n. 40

De aeternitate mundi
59	145 n. 6

De agricultura
171	150 n. 40

De cherubim
97	145 n. 1, 152 n. 52

De confusione linguarum
1.1	11
5.15	11
65	150 n. 40
95	150 n. 40
97	150 n. 40
138	145 n. 1, 152 n. 52

De vita contemplativa
1	159 n. 98
2	150 n. 40
59	145 n. 6

De congressu eruditionis gratia
1–70	157 n. 88
2–3	157 n. 89
8	150 n. 40
11–12	158 n. 91
11–14	157 n. 90
12–13	157 n. 89
51	150 n. 41
79	146 n. 7, 158 n. 93

Philo of Alexandria (continued)
130	156 n. 80
160	156 n. 81

De decalogo
52	156 n. 85
119	145 n. 5, 155 n. 73
132	145 n. 6

De deo
41	145 n. 2, 150 n. 40
11	150 n. 41
33	150 n. 40
52	150 n. 40, 155 n. 78
55	150 n. 40
69	150 n. 40
81	150 n. 40

Quod deterius potiori insidari soleat
89	145 n. 1, 152 n. 52
92	150 n. 37
139	150 n. 38
153–54	150 n. 40
159	150 n. 37
160	150 n. 35, 150–151, 151 n. 43
161	150 n. 41

De ebrietate
43	150 n. 40
47	145 n. 6
83	150 n. 41
86	150 n. 40
108	150 n. 40
117	150 n. 40

In Flaccum
17.144	11

De fuga et inventione
61	156 n. 82
78	150 n. 40
89	150 n. 40
141	152 n. 51

De gigantibus
52	150 n. 40

Philo of Alexandria (*continued*)
Quis rerum divinarum heres sit
170	145 n. 1, 150 n. 40, 152 n. 49
229	150 n. 40, 152 n. 54

De Iosepho
31	145 n. 6

De vita Mosis
1.75	150 n. 35, 153 n. 58
1.146	155 n. 77
7.7	145 n. 6
2.48	145 n. 6
2.67	150 n. 42
2.74, 76	160 n. 102
2.82	145 n. 6
2.161	150 n. 40
2.245	145 n. 6

De mutatione nominum
7	150 n. 40
8	150 n. 40
9	150 n. 40
10	145 n. 1, 150 n. 40, 152 n. 52
11	150 nn. 35, 39; 151, 151 n. 44
11–14	145 n. 2
12–13	151 n. 46
14–15	145 n. 1, 152 n. 49
14	150 n. 40
15	152 n. 47
17	150 n. 40
27–28	145 n. 2
57	150 n. 37
82	150 n. 37
87	150 n. 40
182	150 n. 40

De opificio mundi
5	159 n. 97
8	158 n. 95
13	145 n. 6

Philo of Alexandria (*continued*)
15	145 n. 3
15–35	154 n. 60
16	145 n. 4
17–18	154 n. 62
19	154 n. 63
24–25	160 n. 100
71	146 n. 8
129–30	154 n. 61
154	155 n. 79
171	145 n. 6
172	156 n. 86

De plantatione
21	150 n. 40
22	150 n. 40
26	150 n. 37
72	150 n. 40
86	150 n. 40
132	145 n. 6

De posteritate Caini
9	150 n. 40
9	150 n. 40
10	145 n. 1
11	150 n. 40, 152 n. 52
21	150 n. 40
28	150 n. 40
168	145 n. 2, 150 n. 40
175	150 n. 40
185	145 n. 6

De praemiis et poenis
27	150 n. 40
42	145 n. 6
53	155 n. 74
56	150 n. 40
108	145 n. 6

Quod omnis probus liber sit
43	150 n. 40

De providentia
2.23	145 n. 6

Quaestiones . . . in Genesin
2.38	155 n. 73

Quaestiones . . . in Exodum
2.19	145 n. 6
2.52	160 n. 102
2.82	160 n. 102

Philo of Alexandria (continued)

2.90	160 n. 102

De sacrificiis Abelis et Caini

10	150 n. 37
59	152 n. 53
101	145 n. 2

De somniis

1.35	150 n. 40
67.67	145 n. 1; 152 nn. 49, 50, 52
1.157	150 n. 40
1.182	150 n. 40
1.184	150 n. 40
1.218	150 n. 40
229.229	145 n. 2
229.230	150 nn. 35, 40
1.230–32	153 n. 57
1.234	150 n. 37
174.174	145 n. 6
227.227	150 n. 37
237.237	150 nn. 37, 40
2.292	150 n. 37

De specialibus legibus

47.47	145 n. 1, 152 n. 52
1.81	150 n. 37
1.155	145 n. 6
1.202	145 n. 6
1.209	150 n. 40
1.306	145 n. 6
1.307	150 n. 40
3.32	145 n. 6
3.112	145 n. 6
3.169–171	63 n. 66
4.97	155 n. 75
4.135	145 n. 5, 155 n. 73
4.147	145 n. 5, 155 n. 73
4.205	145 n. 6

De virtutibus

65	158 n. 96
95	145 n. 5, 155 n. 73

Philo of Alexandria (continued)

185	150 n. 40
215	150 n. 40

Babylonian Talmud

Yoma

77b	35 n. 30

Midrash Rabbah on Song of Solomon

8.13.2	12
8.14.1	12

Christian

1 Clement

34.7	5, 13 n. 23

Acts of Peter

36[7]	14

Acts of Thomas

83	39 n. 43

Apocalypse of Peter

19	13

Apostolic Constitutions

7.56.1	6

Ascension of Isaiah

7.15	12
8.18	12
9.28	12, 13

Gospel of the Egyptians

	15

Gospel of Thomas

16:1–4	28
49	28 n. 8
55:1–2	27
75	28 n. 8
101:1–3	27
101:3	28 n. 6

Martyrdom of Perpetua and Felicitas

12	13 n. 23

Ambrose

Epistles

63.23	219

Explanation of the Psalms

1.9	21–22

Athanasius

Apology to Constantius

10	16
16	17

Augustine

City of God

7.28	154 n. 65

Confessions

19.19.19	33 n. 23
19.19.20	40 n. 46

Basil the Great

Against Eunomius

	17 n. 32
	17 n. 34

Against Sabellius and Arius

	17 n. 32

Commentary on Psalms

1.2	17

Hexaemeron

4.7	21 n. 45
9.4.32	17

Basil the Great (*continued*)

Homily on Envy

	17 n. 32

Homily on "I pull down my barns"

	17 n. 32

Homily on Pentecost

3	17

Homily on the Assumption of the Lord

	17 n. 32

Homily on the Festival

	17 n. 32

Letters

74.3	17 n. 33
96.1	17
207.3	6
237.2	17 n. 32
243.2	17

On the Faith

prol. 8	17 n. 32

Basil [Ps.]

Commentary on Isaiah

1.31	17 n. 30
13.259	17 n. 30

Clement of Alexandria

Exhortation

9.88	15

Instructor

2.4.44.3	15

Miscellanies

1.1.14.4	15
7.6.31.8	15

Cyprian

On the Lord's Prayer

8	5 n. 7

"Cyprian of Antioch"

Confessions

17	19

Epiphanius

Ancoratus
10.3	13 n. 23
26.3–4	13 n. 23

Eusebius of Caesarea

Church History
6.11.2	16

Commentary on Psalms
70:222–24	16 n. 29
91:2–3	16 n. 29

Ecclesiastical Theology
2.9.12	16 n. 28

Life of Constantine
1.41.2	16

Preparation for the Gospel
11.6	149 n. 31
12.1.2	5 n. 9
14.3	16

Proof of the Gospel
3.6	16
5 intr. 25	16
132a	16

Theophany
frag. 1.6	16 n. 28

Gregory of Nazianzus

Letters
46.4	18

Orations
4.12	18
4.15	18
23	6
31.17	18 n. 35
41.15	18
43.68	18

Gregory of Nyssa

Against Eunomius
1.203	18
1.210	18 n. 37
3.5.18	18 n. 37

Beatitudes
7	18 n. 36

Gregory of Nyssa (*continued*)
The Forty Martyrs
1b	19

Inscriptions of the Psalms
1.8.82	18 n. 36
1.8.87	18 n. 36
2.13.202	18 n. 36
2.12.171	19 n. 31

On Canticles
hom. 7	19
hom. 10	18 n. 37

On the Deity of the Son and Holy Spirit
	18 n. 37

Refutation of the Confession of Eunomius
79	18 n. 37
169	18 n. 36

Usury
9	18

Gregory of Nyssa [Ps.]

On the Creation of Humanity
	18 n. 36

Gregory Thaumaturgus

Paraphrase of Ecclesiastes
12:11	6

Ignatius of Antioch

To the Ephesians
4.1–2	13

Irenaeus

Against Heresies
1.10.2	5
1.14.1	14
2.28.3	14

John Chrysostom

De studio praesentium
5.1	20–21

John Chrysostom (*continued*)
Encomium on John the Evangelist
      19 n. 41
Homilies on Genesis
30   20 n. 43
Homilies on Matthew
68[69].3   7
68[69].4   7
Homilies on Acts
39.1   219 n. 56
38   19
50   8 n. 14, 19 n. 41
Homilies on Romans
7   20
Homilies on 1 Corinthians
24   20 n. 43
36.9   7
Homilies on Ephesians
15   40–41, 42
On Psalms
145.2   21
On Stephen
      19 n. 41
On the Ascension
hom. 4   20
On the Beheading of John
      19 n. 41
On the Change of Names
      19 n. 41
On the Devil
1.2   20 n. 43
1.4   20 n. 43
On the Four Days of Lazarus
      20 n. 42
On the Obscurity of the Prophets
      20, 20 n. 43
On the Priesthood
4.7.15–17   219
On Vainglory and Education of the Young
4   20
12   20 n. 44
To the People of Antioch
15.3   20

John Chrysostom [Ps.]
On Forgiveness
      19 n. 41
On John the Theologian
      19 n. 41
On One Born Blind
      19 n. 41
On the Dance of Herodias
      20 n. 42
On the Cross and the Thief
6.3   20 n. 42

Jerome
De nominibus hebraicum
      220 n. 59

Justin [Ps.]
Hortatory Address to the Greeks
8   5–6

Martin of Braga
On Anger
7   40 n. 45

Niceta of Remesiana
On the Utility of Hymn Singing
13   22

Origen
Against Celsus
8.37   16
Commentary on Matthew
14.1   16
Commentary on Romans
10.7.6   4 n. 4
Selections in Genesis
      16

Paulinus of Nola
Songs
21.275   7

Other Ancient Literature

Socrates
Church History
6.3   218 n. 51

Theodore of Mopsuestia
On Eucharist and Liturgy
6   6 n. 11

Modern Authors

A

Abraham, William J., 200
Abuladze, Ilia, 217
Ackerman, James, 251–54, 259
Ackroyd, Peter R., 165, 168–69
Adams, Robert, 268
Adna, Jostein, 69
Akinian, Nerses, 221
Albright, William Foxwell, 113
Alexander, Loveday, 37, 185
Algra, K., 148
Allen, Leslie, 108
Alonso-Schökel, Luis, 105
Anderson, Gary, 95
Aquino, Federick D., xiv, 195, 198, 200
Arlandson, James M., 233
Armour, Roland, 265
Attridge, Harold W., 126–28
Aune, David E., 35
Austin, J. L., 251

B

Baer, D., 152
Baker-Smith, Dominic, 272
Balch, David L., 62–63, 183
Banks, Robert, 128
Barnes, J., 148
Barré, M. L., 95
Barrett, C. K. 50, 209, 215–16, 231
Bartchy, S. Scott, 31, 36
Bartelt, A. H., 168–70
Barth, Karl, 118, 120
Basinger, Randall, 197
Bassler, Jouette, 180
Bateson, Frederick W., 105, 115
Bauckham, Richard, 78, 141–42, 238–39
Beal, T. K., 165
Bechtel, Friedrich, 210
Berger, Peter, 136
Bergsten, Torsten, 274, 277, 279
Berkey, R. F., 218
Berlin, Adele, 105–6
Berthrong, John, 136
Beuken, W. A. M., 168
Beveridge, Henry, 228
Billerbeck, Margarethe, 58
Birdsall, J. Neville, 217
Bitzer, Lloyd F., 171
Black, C. Clifton, 67
Black, J. Sutherland, 212
Blenkinsopp, Joseph, 168, 171, 179
Blundell, Sue, 32
Bockmuehl, Marcus, 185, 187–91
Boismard, M.-E., 214, 216
Bokser, Baruch M., 141
Boobyer, G. H., 74
Borgen, Peder, 149, 157
Bousset, W., 147–48
Braaten, Carl E., 241
Bradley, Keith, 39
Braulik, Georg, 94
Brekelmans, F. S., 93
Brettler, Marc, 93
Briggs, Charles A., 107, 110, 112–13
Bromiley, G. W., 277
Brown, Raymond E., 76, 78, 231
Brox, Norbet, 47, 50
Broyles, C. C., 165–66, 168, 261
Bruce, F. F., 142, 209, 212–14, 216, 231
Brueggemann, Walter, 165

Bryan, Christopher, 140
Bryant, Donald C., 171
Bultmann, Rudolf, 118, 120, 122
Burger, Edward K., 279
Buttenwieser, Moses, 112

C

Cadbury, Henry J., 214
Campbell, Alexander, 142, 230
Campbell, Antony, 92
Campbell, Douglas A., 142
Carabine, D., 152
Carr, D., 179–80
Casey, Maurice, 136–39
Casson, Lionel, 33
Ceresko, Anthony, 108
Chevallier, Raymond, 33
Cheyne, T. K., 212
Chibnall, Majorie, 227
Childers, J. W., xiv, 207, 216–17
Childs, Brevard S., 163–64, 251, 258–60
Chisholm, Roderick M., 200
Choi, Hung-Sik, 177, 121–22
Church, F. F., 274
Clark, Albert C., 214, 216
Clarke, Adam, 230–31
Clements, R. E., 164
Clifford, Richard, 114
Clines, David J. A., 173, 257
Cogan, Michael, 35
Cogan, Mordechai, 96
Colautti, Frederico M., 143
Collins, Raymond F., 45, 50–51, 53
Comblin, José, 212, 231
Combrink, H. J. Bernard, 170
Conrad, E. W., 166
Conzelmann, Hans, 47, 50, 210, 231
Cope, Lamar, 67
Corderio, Balthasar, 225
Cottingham, John, 198, 206
Cramer, J. A., 219
Crosby, Sumner McKnight, 222
Cross, F. L., 219
Croy, N. Clayton, 130–31
Crüsemann, Frank, 107–8, 113
Culley, Robert, 93

D

D'Urbino, Raphael, 207
Dahl, Nils Alstrup, 140, 142, 184
Dahood, Mitchell, 107, 109–10, 112–13
Dance, Douglas, 93
Daniélou, Jean, 147–48, 152
Danker, Frederick W., 182
Daux, G., 210
Davidson, R., 108
Davies, E. W., 178
Davies, P. R., 173
Davis, Ellen, 239
Davis, Kenneth R., 279
de Voragine, Jacobus, 227
Delaporte, Marianne M., 222, 224–25
Deming, Will, 63
DeSilva, David A., 126
Devenish, Philip E., 191
DeWette, Wilhelm M. L., 107
Dewey, Joanna, 240–41
Dibelius, Martin, 47, 50
Diggle, J., 37
Dillon, John, 155, 161
Dodd, C. H., 133
Dodds, E. R., 123
Donahue, John, 67, 78
Donelson, L. R., 45
Driver, S. R., 260
Drury, John, 143
Duchesne, Louis, 224
Duhm, Bernhard., 163
Dunderberg, Ismo, 184
Dungan, David, 78
Dunn, James D. G., 117
Dyck, Andrew R., 54–55, 57

E

Eaton, John, 115
Eemeren, Frans H. van, 84, 103
Ego, Beate, 69
Ehrman, Bart D., 138, 216
Eichhorn, J. G., 163
Eichler, B. L., 35
Elliott, Neil, 140
Ellis, Frederick S., 227

Engberg-Pedersen, Troels, 46, 188
Eph'al, Israel, 97
Eriksson, Anders, 84, 103, 125
Esler, Philip F., 117, 119–20
Estep, William R., 265, 279
Evans, C. A., 33, 142, 165–66, 168, 261
Evans, C. F., 77–78

F

Farmer, William R., 72, 78
Fee, Gordon D., 185
Feldman, Louis H., 143
Ferguson, Everett, xiii, 3, 195
Ferguson, John, 53
Fiddes, Paul, 198
Finkelstein, Israel, 97
Finley, Harvey E., 109
Fisher, Loren R., 110
Fisher, Walter R., 171
Fitzgerald, John T., xiii, 24, 30, 33–37, 53, 184–85
Fitzmyer, Joseph A., 210
Foakes-Jackson, F. J., 214
Fohrer, Georg, 177
Foley, Edward, 3
Fortenbaugh, William W., 155
Fortna, Robert T., 186
Foss, R., 222
Foster, Benjamin R., 90
Fowl, Stephen, 185, 188
Frankel, David, 93
Fraser, P. M., 279
Fredrickson, Paula, 136–37
Fretheim, Terrence E., 251, 253, 261
Friesen, Abraham, 265, 270–71, 279
Froehlich, Karlfried, 228
Fuglseth, P., 149
Fuhs, Hans F., 112
Furcha, E. J., 265
Furneaux, William H., 209–10, 231
Furnish, Victor P., 191

G

Gaca, Kathy, 63
Gaisford, T., 209

Garitte, Gérard, 217
Garnsey Peter, 39
Gasque, W. Ward, 189
Gaventa, Beverly R., 186
Geddeit, Timothy J., 68
Gempf, Conrad H., 209
George, Timothy, 274
Gerstenberger, Erhard S., 35, 174
Gesenius, Wilhelm, 163
Gignac, F. T., 219
Gill, John, 230
Gitay, Yehoshua, 170–71
Goertz, Hans-Jürgen, 274
Goessler, Lisette, 53
Goffard, Walter, 224
Goodwin, George L., 191
Goulder, Michael D., 143
Goulet, R., 146
Gowan, D. W., 178
Graham, William, 92
Grant, Robert M., 26, 41, 268
Gray, Mark, 83
Grayson, A. K., 88
Griffiths, J. Gwyn, 209–10
Griggs, C. Wilfird, 215
Groh, Dennis, 214
Grossberg, Daniel, 210–11, 213
Grottanelli, David, 97
Grözinger, Karl Erick, 13
Gruber, Mayer, 97
Grudem, Wayne, 233–34
Gunkel, Hermann, 107, 111–13
Guthrie, Kenneth Sylan, 61

H

Hadot, Pierre, 199–200, 202, 204
Haenchen, Ernst, 208–09, 212, 214, 216, 231
Hagner, Donald A., 277
Halkin, François, 235
Hamilton, Mark W., xiv, 83, 200
Hammarskjöld, D., xv
Hanson, A.T., 45
Harkins, Paul W., 37
Harnack, Adolf von, 205
Harper, Vicki Lynn, 61
Harrill, J. Albert, 30

Harvey, W. W., 14
Hastings, James, 33, 214, 231
Hauser, Alan, 83
Hawthorne, Gerald, 187, 189–90
Hay, David M., 117 , 119
Haynes, S. R., 170
Hays, Richard B., 117, 119–20, 239
Hebert, A. G., 117
Heidel, Alexander, 84
Heinemann, I., 147
Heinrichs, H., 158
Hemer, Colin J., 209–10
Hengel, Martin, 50
Henry, Matthew, 230
Herzer, Jens, 46
Herzog, Ze'ev, 97
Hijmaus, B. L., 58
Hillerbrand, Hans, 279
Hock, Ronald F., 61
Holladay, Carl R., 45, 116, 185–86
Holloway, Paul, 184, 188
Holtzmann, Heinrich Julius, 50
Hooker, Brad, 188, 190, 200
Hooker, Morna, 184
Horner, George, 210
Horsley, Richard A., 134, 140–41, 147
Horst, Irvin B., 280
Houtman, Cees, 93
Hubbard, Thomas K., 32
Hubmaier, Balthasar, 265, 273–81
Hunter, Virginia J., 37
Hurtado, Larry W., 135

J

Jacobsen, Thorkild, 90
Jacquier, E., 209, 211, 214, 231
Jaegar, Werner, 200, 204
Jarick, John, 6
Jeaneau, Edouard, 224
Jervis, L. Ann, 134
Jewett, Robert, 184
Johnson, E. Elizabeth, 117
Johnson, Luke Timothy, 45, 117, 122
Johnson, Marshall D., 78
Joyce, Paul, 143
Judge, E. A., 62
Juel, Donald, 70, 76

K

Kähler, Martin, 241
Kato, Zenji, 72
Kaufmann-Büchler, 156
Keener, Craig S., 277
Keet, Cuthbert C., 107, 112
Kelber, Werner, 74
Kelhoffer, James A, 67.
Kennedy, George A., 171
Kittel, Rudolf, 107
Kitts, Margo, 35
Klaffenback, G., 210
Klijn, A. F. J., 217
Knuuttila, Simo, 95
Koester, Craig R., 124–25, 129
Koester, Helmut, 138, 147
Köstenberger, Andreas J., 72
Kraus, Hans-Joachim, 107, 110–11
Kruger, Paul, 95
Kselman, J. S., 95
Kugel, James, 105
Kugener, M. A., 221
Kyrtatas, Dimitris, 43

L

Lacaze, Charlotte, 226
Läger, K., 45
Lake, Kirsopp, 214
Lamb, W. R., 53, 54
Lambert, W. G., 90
Lamouille, A., 214, 216
Lampe, Peter, 78
Lange, Armin, 69
Lathrop, Gordon W., 242–45
Lattimore, Richmond, 59
Lau, A. Y., 45
Lawson, Beryl, 64
Leclerq, Jean, 223, 265
Lehman, Helmut T., 278
Levenson, Jon D., 139, 142
Levillain, Léon, 224
Levinson, Bernard, 93
Lewy, H., 147
Lienhard, Marc, 286
Linafelt, T., 165
Lincoln, Andrew T., 190

Lindars, Barnabas, 119, 127
Littell, Franklin H., 265
Little, Margaret Olivia, 200
Liwak, R., 164
Loenertz, Raymond J., 222
Lohfink, Norbert, 92–94, 97
Long, A. A., 54
Long, Burke O., 93
Long, Thomas G., xiv, 236
Longenecker, Richard N., 117, 128, 134
Loretz, Oswald, 107
Lorinus, John, 227, 229, 235
Louis, K. R. R. Gros, 251
Lovering, Eugene H., 165
Luck, Ulrich, 53
Luibheid, Colm, 222–23, 228
Luscombe, David, 223
Lust, J., 93

M

Malherbe, Abraham J., xiii, 26, 33, 36, 45–46, 49, 52–53, 57, 61–63, 183, 195
Malingrey, A.-M., 219
Maloney, F. J., 67
Mansfeld, J., 148
Markus, Joel, 67, 240–41, 246
Marrou, Henri I., 203
Marrs, Rick R., xiv, 104
Marshall, I. Howard, 46, 49, 51–53
Marshall, R. J., 168–69, 184
Martin, Henry, 226
Martin, Lawrence T., 221
Martin, Ralph P., 189
Marxsen, Willi, 77
Matthews, E., 211
McArthur, H. K., 118
McConica, James, 267, 272
McGrath, Alister E., 264, 278
McKenzie, Steven L., 170
McKinlay, D. B., 174
McKinnon, James, 22
McNicol, Allan J., xiii, 66–67, 71
Meeks, Wayne, 34, 183
Meier, John P., 78
Mellink, Machteld, 113

Melugin, Roy F., xiv, 165, 168, 178, 180, 249, 261
Metzger, Bruce M., 216, 218
Metzger, Marcel, 223
Meynet, Roland, 173–74
Miller, James D., 46
Miller, Patrick D., 89, 99
Minear, Paul S., 186, 188–90
Mitchell, Margaret M., 134–35, 137
Mittmann, Siegfried, 93
Mobley, Gregory, 84, 100
Möller, Karl, 170–71
Montes-Peral, L. A., 150, 153
Moreschini, Claudio, 208, 222
Morgan, Robert, 118
Morris, Leon L., 128, 277
Morrow, Glenn R., 37
Moule, C. F. D., 189
Mout, M. E. H. N., 278
Mowinckel, Sigmund, 110–11, 113
Muilenburg, James, 83, 170
Münster, Hans-Peter, 84

N

Nelson, Richard, 92, 94, 97, 99, 100
Neusner, Jacob, 147
Neville, Robert C., 136
Niccum, L. Curt, 216, 218
Nikiprowetzky, V., 157
Noak, C., 152
Norelli, Enrico, 208, 222
Norris, Frederick W., 195
North, Helen, 53–56, 58, 64, 94
Noth, Martin, 92
Nussbaum, Martha C., 206
Nyland, Ann, 233–34

O

O'Brien, Mark, 92
O'Brien, Peter T., 72, 184–85, 187–90
Oberlinner, Lorenz, 49
Oded, Bustanay, 96
Olbrechts-Tyteca, Lucie, 85, 89, 95, 98, 101
Olbricht, Thomas H., xiv, 36, 53, 84, 95, 103, 116, 125, 170

Ollenburger, Ben C., 166
Olmstead, Albert T., 113
Olyan, Saul, 93
Orton, David E., 143
Osburn, Carroll D., 216
Osiek, Carolyn, 63
Otto, Eckart, 93

P

Pabel, Hilmar M., 265
Paradize, L., 35
Parente, Fausto, 143
Parker, D. C., 216
Passant, Johann David, 207
Patrick, Dale, 171
Patterson, Cynthia, 51
Paulsen, Henning, 182
Payne, John B., 268, 270, 273
Peabody, David B., 67, 69
Peeters, P., 221
Pelikan, Jaroslav, 202–03, 205, 278
Perelman, Chaim, 84–85, 89, 95, 98, 101
Perlitt, Lothar, 92, 97
Pervo, Richard, 214, 216
Pesch, Rudolf, 209, 231
Peterlin, Davorin, 184–86
Peterson, David L., 129
Peterson, Jeffrey, xiv, 133, 138, 143
Pilhofer, Peter,, 69
Pipkin, H. W., 267, 274–76
Pomeroy, Sarah B., 51, 53, 61
Pongratz-Leisten, Beate, 88–89
Porter, Stanley E., 33, 125, 143, 170

Q

Quasten, Johannes, 3, 19, 23, 218
Quinn, Jerome, 47

R

Rad, Gerhard von, 34–35, 93
Radice, P., 147
Ramsay, William M., 33, 209, 211, 213–15, 217, 231
Reimer, Ivoni Richter, 208, 232

Rendtorff, Rolf, 165, 179
Renz, T., 171
Rice, Ann, 162
Richards, Kent, 105
Richardson, Peter, 134
Ridley, Ronald T., 87
Riggi, Calogero, 22
Ritschl, Albrecht, 205
Robinson, A. T., 212
Robinson, J. Armitage, 215
Robinson, James M., 15
Roetzel, Calvin,133
Roloff, Jürgen, 45–47, 51–52, 208
Roques, R., 223
Rorem, Paul, 222–23, 225, 228
Royse, J. R., 151
Roze, J.-B. M., 227
Rummel, Erika, 270
Runia, David T., 147–48, 151, 153, 161
Russell, Donald, 61

S

Saggs, Henry W. F., 113
Saldarini, Anthony J., 71
Sanders, E. P., 76
Saunders, Ernest W., 214
Schaelling, J. Phillip, 215
Scheck, Thomas P., 4
Scheidle, Kurt, 54–55
Schille, Gottfried, 210
Schmid, Josef, 209
Schmid, Wilhelm, 209–10
Schmidt, Ludwig, 93
Schmitt, Rüdiger, 97
Schneemelcher, Wilhelm, 12, 14
Schofield, M., 148
Schrag, Dale, 279
Schüssler Fiorenza, Elisabeth, 215, 232–35
Scult, Allen, 171
Searle, J. R., 250
Sedlacek, I., 231
Sedley, D. L., 54
Seitz, Christopher R., 166–67, 171
Senior, Donald, 72
Seybold, Klaus, 108

Shaw, C. S., 171
Sievers, Joseph, 143
Sihvola, Juha, 95
Silva, Moses, 184
Skarsten, R. , 149
Skeris, Robert A., 3
Smith, Mark, 95
Smith, Morton, 143
Smits, Edme R., 226
Smolinsky, H., 279
Smothers, E. R., 219
Snaith, Norman H., 34
Snyder, C. Arnold, 274
Snyder, Lee, 230
Soden, Hermann Frieherr von, 208
Soldt, W. H. van, 84
Spicq, Ceslas, 50, 57
Städele, Alfons, 52, 62
Stankiewicz, Edward, 105–06, 115
Stansell, G., 28, 178
Starr, James, 46
Steck, O. H., 166
Steinmetz, David, 274
Stendahl, Krister, 134
Stenmark, Mikael, 198
Sterling, Gregory E., xiv, 145, 161
Stout, Jeffrey, 201
Stowers, Stanley K., 134, 183–84, 186
Strabo, Walafrid, 221
Stramore, Tarcisia, 214
Streck, Maximillian, 113
Stuhlmueller, Carroll, 72
Suchla, B. R., 223
Sumney, Jerry L., 95
Sweeney, M. A., 28, 167–68, 178, 180
Synodinou, Katerina, 29
Syreeni, Kari, 184

T

Talbert, Charles H., 127–28, 131–32
Tarchnishvili, P. Michael, 218
Théry, P. G., 222–24
Thesleff, Holger, 61
Thiselson, Anthony C., 137, 141
Thom, Johan C., 62
Thompson, Carolyn, xv, 263
Thompson, Herbert, 210

Thompson, James W., xiv, 24, 79, 116, 122–24, 126, 128, 133–34, 144, 162, 181, 195–99, 203–05, 237, 263
Thompson, Michael B., 141
Tigay, Jeffrey H., 35, 92, 96–7, 99
Tischendorf, Constantin, 208, 213
Tittmann, J. A. H., 209
Tobin, Thomas H., 117, 120, 146, 161
Tod, M. N., 210
Tomasino, A. J., 179–80
Toorn, Karel van der, 84
Toulmin, Stephen, 84, 94
Trapman, J., 279
Treggiari, Susan, 32
Trible, Phyllis, 83, 170
Tucker, Gene M., 164
Tuckett, Christopher, 184
Übelacker, Walter, 84, 103, 125
Ussishkin, David, 97

V

Van der Watt, Jan G., 46
Van Geytenbeek, A. C., 55
Van Neste, Ray, 46
Van Rensburg, F. J., 30
Van Rooy, H. F., 30
Vatin, Claude, 33
Veijola, Timo, 92
Velimirovich, Nikolai, 235
Verillac, Anne–Marie 33, 59
Vermeylen, J., 166
Vervenne, M, 93
Vessey, Mark, 265
Viál, Claude, 33

W

Wacker, William C., 47
Wagner, S., 164
Wainwright, William J., 198
Waithe, Mary Ellen, 61
Walaskay, Paul W., 232
Walker, Donald Dale, 43
Walters, John R., 126, 131
Ware, J. H., Jr., 250, 254
Warren, Austin, 105

Watson, Duane F., 83
Watson, Wilfred G. E., 105
Wegner, Paul, 35
Weinfeld, Moshe, 92
Weiser, Artur 107, 111–112
Weiss, Johannes, 135–37, 141
Weissbach, J. F., 113
Welch, J. W., 174
Wellek, Rene, 105
Wesley, John, 230
Westermann, Claus, 34
Westin, G., 274
Wettstein, Jacobus, 183, 209, 218, 227
White, Hayden, 255
White, L. Michael, 34–35, 53, 183–84, 187
Wiklander, B., 171
Wilken, Robert, 202
Williams, David J., 212
Williams, George H., 274
Williams, Sam K., 117, 120
Williamson, Darren, xiv, 264, 279
Williamson, H. G. M., 167
Willis, John T., xiv, 163
Willis, Wendell, xiv, 181
Wilson, R. R., 164
Windhorst, Christof, 274, 276
Winston, David, 147, 161
Winter, Bruce W., 60
Witherington, Ben, 209, 211, 215–17, 231–32
Wittgenstein, Luwig, 250
Wolff, Hans Walter, 28
Wolfson, Harry A., 146, 152, 156
Wright, N. T., 121
Wynn, Mark R., 206
Wyrwa, D., 150

Y

Yarbrough, O. Larry, 34, 63, 184
Yoder, John Howard, 274, 279
Young, Francis, 45

Z

Zahn, Theodor, 212, 214, 216, 231
Zeitlow, Paul H., 264, 278
Zohrabian, Hovhann, 210

www.ingramcontent.com/pod-product-compliance
Lightning Source LLC
Chambersburg PA
CBHW070230230426
43664CB00014B/2260